To *Assure* **Pride** *and*
Confidence
in the **Electoral**
Process

National Commission on Federal Election Reform

organized by
Miller Center of Public Affairs, University of Virginia
The Century Foundation

supported by
The David and Lucile Packard Foundation
The William and Flora Hewlett Foundation
The John S. and James L. Knight Foundation

THE COMMISSION

Honorary Co-Chairs
President Gerald R. Ford
President Jimmy Carter

Co-Chairs
Robert H. Michel
Lloyd N. Cutler

Vice-Chairs
Slade Gorton
Kathleen M. Sullivan

Commissioners
Griffin Bell
Rudy Boschwitz
John C. Danforth
Christopher F. Edley, Jr.
Hanna Holborn Gray
Colleen C. McAndrews
Daniel Patrick Moynihan
Leon Panetta
Deval L. Patrick
Diane Ravitch
Bill Richardson
John Seigenthaler
Michael Steele

Executive Director
Philip Zelikow

PUBLIC HEARINGS

March 26, 2001

Citizen Participation
The Carter Center
Atlanta, Georgia

April 12, 2001

Election Administration
The Ronald Reagan Presidential
  Library
Simi Valley, California

May 24, 2001

What Does the Law Require?
Lyndon B. Johnson Library and
  Museum
Austin, Texas

June 5, 2001

The American and International
  Experience
Gerald R. Ford Library
Ann Arbor, Michigan

To Assure Pride and Confidence

Confidence

in the Electoral

Process

Report of the
National Commission on
Federal Election Reform

Jimmy Carter
Gerald R. Ford
Lloyd N. Cutler
Robert H. Michel
Co-Chairs

Philip Zelikow
Executive Director

BROOKINGS INSTITUTION PRESS
Washington, D.C.

Copyright © 2002

THE MILLER CENTER FOUNDATION

All rights reserved. No part of this publication may be reproduced or transmitted in any form or by any means without permission in writing from the Brookings Institution Press.

To Assure Pride and Confidence in the Electoral Process may be ordered from the Brookings Institution Press, 1775 Massachusetts Avenue, N.W., Washington, D.C. 20036. Telephone: 1-800/275-1447 or 202/797-6258 Fax: 202/797-6004

Library of Congress Cataloging-in-Publication data

National Commission on Federal Election Reform.
    To assure pride and confidence in the electoral process / report of the National Commission on Federal Election Reform ; Gerald R. Ford . . . [et al.], co-chairs.
      p. cm.
    ISBN 0-8157-0631-6 (paper ; alk. paper)
      1. Elections—United States. 2. Election law—United States. I. Ford, Gerald R., 1913–
II. Title.

JK1965 .N38 2002
324.6'5'0973—dc21   2002020054

1 3 5 7 9 8 6 4 2

The paper used in this publication meets minimum requirements of the American National Standard for Information Sciences—-Permanence of Paper for Printed Library Materials: ANSI Z39.48-1992.

Typeset in Sabon

Text design and composition by Circle Graphics
Columbia, Maryland

Printed by R. R. Donnelley and Sons
Harrisonburg, Virginia

Contents

v

Letter to the American People

In 2000 the American electoral system was tested by a political ordeal unlike any in living memory. From November 7 until December 12 the outcome of the presidential election was fought out in bitter political and legal struggles that ranged throughout the state of Florida and ultimately extended to the Supreme Court of the United States. The American political system proved its resilience. But we must think about the future.

The ordinary institutions of election administration in the United States, and specifically Florida, just could not readily cope with an extremely close election. Many aspects of the election process were put under a microscope and viewed by an anxious nation. With dismay and growing anger we saw controversial ballot design; antiquated and error-prone voting machines; subjective and capricious processes for counting votes; voter rolls that let unqualified voters vote in some counties and turned away qualified voters in others; confusion in the treatment of overseas military ballots; and a political process subjected to protracted litigation.

Stepping back from Florida, the picture is no more encouraging. The chief election official of Georgia, Cathy Cox, testified to our Commission that: "As the presidential election drama unfolded in Florida last November, one thought was foremost in my mind: there but for the grace of God go I. Because the truth is, if the presidential margin had been razor thin in Georgia and if our election systems had undergone the same microscopic scrutiny that Florida endured, we would have fared no better. In many respects, we might have fared even worse." Across America, we have heard from official after official who feels the same way.

1

There is good news, though. In the last few years, and now spurred by the events last year, election reform has returned to the legislative agenda in many states. In much of the country cadres of able and dedicated election administrators are in place who can show what is possible and carry reforms into practice. In a world of problems that often defy any solution, the weaknesses in election administration are, to a very great degree, problems that government actually can solve.

In this report we and our colleagues offer very specific recommendations on what should be done. In other words, Americans can and should expect their electoral system to be a source of national pride and a model to all the world.

Gerald R. Ford

Jimmy Carter

Robert H. Michel

Lloyd N. Cutler

Co-Chairs of the National Commission on Federal Election Reform

Preface to the Report

The report begins with a summary of the principal policy recommendations. To understand why those recommendations were chosen, and why some others were not, readers should take the time to study the entire report before passing judgment.

To share some of the wealth of background material that informed our work, please read the Background Papers prepared by the Commission's task forces on the Federal Election System and on Legal and Constitutional Issues. Those Background Papers are published at the back of this volume. They, like the transcripts of our Commission's public hearings around the country, are also available on the Commission's website—www.reform elections.org. The task force coordinators who performed such formidable labors are John Mark Hansen of the University of Chicago, David King of Harvard University, and Daniel Ortiz of the University of Virginia.

Richard Leone, president of The Century Foundation, was critical at every stage of the Commission's creation, development, and work. As much as anyone, he was the person who turned this Commission from an idea into reality. Robert Pastor of Emory University was a senior adviser to the Commission and offered especially valuable counsel. Leonard Shambon, of the law firm Wilmer, Cutler & Pickering, added his outstanding energy and professional judgment to our work.

This project would not have been successful without the work of the joint professional staff of the University of Virginia's Miller Center and The Century Foundation. Among our professional staff, day-in and day-out Ryan Coonerty's contribution was central. Margaret Edwards, Thad Hall, Mary McKinley, Wistar Morris, and Lisa-Joy Zgorski rounded out the core of our team, with frequent aid from Margaret Bell, Hillary Bracken, Anne Chesnut, Ryann Collins, Tina Doody, Kimberly Girard, Rick Gunning, Christy Hicks, Rachael Kelly, Shirley Kohut, Robin Kuzen, Cynthia Maertz, Carol Starmack, Tova Wang, and Garth Wermter.

The Carter Center, Ronald Reagan Presidential Library, Lyndon Johnson Presidential Library, and Gerald Ford Presidential Library all offered their facilities and staff to help with the Commission's public hearings in a gracious, hospitable spirit.

Finally, everything the Commission may accomplish is the result of the public-spirited generosity of Paul Brest, representing the William and Flora Hewlett Foundation; Richard T. Schlosberg, representing the David and Lucile Packard Foundation; and Hodding Carter III, representing the John S. and James L. Knight Foundation.

Philip Zelikow

Philip Zelikow
Executive Director

Summary of
Principal Recommendations

THE GOALS OF FEDERAL ELECTION REFORM

When they choose the president, the vice president, and members of Congress, the American people should expect all levels of government to provide a democratic process that:

- Maintains an accurate list of citizens who are qualified to vote;
- Encourages every eligible voter to participate effectively;
- Uses equipment that reliably clarifies and registers the voter's choices;
- Handles close elections in a foreseeable and fair way;
- Operates with equal effectiveness for every citizen and every community; and
- Reflects limited but responsible federal participation.

For Americans, democracy is a precious birthright. But each generation must nourish and improve the processes of democracy for its successors. In the near-term, the next three to five years for instance, we envision a country where each state maintains accurate, computerized lists of who can vote, networked with local administrators. Using that system, qualified voters in our mobile society would be able to vote throughout their state without being turned away because of the vagaries of local administration. Using the system we recommend here, millions of military and other overseas voters would find it easier to get and return their ballots. Election Day would be held on a national holiday, freeing up more people to serve as poll workers and making polling places more accessible. Voting machines would meet a common standard of excellent performance. Each state would have its uniform, objective definitions of what constitutes a vote.

5

News organizations would exert necessary restraint in predicting election outcomes. Every jurisdiction and every official would obey the Voting Rights Act and other statutes that secure the franchise and prohibit discrimination. In all of this there would be a delicate balance of shared responsibilities between levels of government, and between officials and the voters they serve.

This report sets forth our recommendations for the next, immediate steps on the road to attainment of these goals.

POLICY RECOMMENDATION   1

Every state should adopt a system of statewide voter registration.

1. The statewide computerized voter file should be networked with and accessible to every election jurisdiction in the state so that any level can initiate registrations and updates with prompt notification to the others. It should include provisions for sharing data with other states.
2. When a citizen either applies for a driver's license or registers to vote, each state should obtain residential address and other information, such as a digitized signature, in a form that is equally usable for both the motor vehicle and voter databases. The address information can then be linked to a statewide street index.
3. Each state's driver's license and voter registration applications should require applicants to provide at least the last four digits of their Social Security number. States should also ask applicants if they are registered in another state, so that that state can be notified of the new registration.
4. Each state's voter registration applications should require a separate and specific affirmation that the applicant is a U.S. citizen.

POLICY RECOMMENDATION   2

Every state should permit provisional voting by any voter who claims to be qualified to vote in that state.

1. Provisional voting authorizes any person whose name does not appear on the list of registered voters, but who wishes to vote, to be issued a ballot. The ballot shall be counted only upon verification by election officials that the provisional voter is eligible and qualified to vote within the state and only for the offices for which the voter is qualified to vote.

2. Another option, for states with statewide computerized voting lists, would be to let a voter who is not on the list submit proof of identification and swear to or affirm an appropriate affidavit of eligibility to vote in that jurisdiction. This information could then be used as an application for voter registration and the voter list would be amended accordingly. If qualified, the voter could either be issued a regular ballot or, if the state preferred, be allowed to vote provisionally pending confirmation of the voter's eligibility.

POLICY RECOMMENDATION 3

Congress should enact legislation to hold presidential and congressional elections on a national holiday.

1. Holding national elections on a national holiday will increase availability of poll workers and suitable polling places and might make voting easier for some workers.
2. One approach, which this Commission favors, would be to specify that in even-numbered years the Veterans Day national holiday be held on the Tuesday next after the first Monday in November and serve also as our Election Day.

POLICY RECOMMENDATION 4

Congress should adopt legislation that simplifies and facilitates absentee voting by uniformed and overseas citizens.

1. Each state should designate a responsible official for absentee voting by uniformed and overseas citizens who are residents of that state. That official should become the single point of contact for the citizens of that state who are served by the Federal Voting Assistance Program, which helps such uniformed and overseas citizens.
2. In 1986 Congress passed the Uniformed and Overseas Citizens Absentee Voting Act (UOCAVA) to help eligible members of the armed services and their families, and other citizens overseas, to vote. Utilizing standardized forms for voter registration and absentee ballot requests, all UOCAVA-covered residents from a home state should be authorized to mail these applications to the designated official for their state. If that state uses a statewide voter registration system networked to local jurisdictions, as we have recommended, the state official should

be authorized to act directly on these applications or to forward them for action by the appropriate local jurisdiction. States should accept one absentee ballot application as a valid application for all subsequent elections being held by that state in that year.

3. The designated state official should be authorized to accept either a voted ballot being returned for any jurisdiction of that state or a standardized Federal Write-In Absentee Ballot that is an option for a UOCAVA-covered citizen. States should be obliged to accept and tally a Federal Write-In Absentee Ballot for those contests in which they determine the voter was eligible to vote.

4. Properly filed absentee ballots should be accepted if they have been received by the time the polls of that state have closed on Election Day. States and the Federal Voting Assistance Program should develop common standards for validation of ballots that have been voted and mailed on or before Election Day, even if they are received after that date.

POLICY RECOMMENDATION   5

Each state should allow for restoration of voting rights to otherwise eligible citizens who have been convicted of a felony once they have fully served their sentence, including any term of probation or parole.

POLICY RECOMMENDATION   6

The state and federal governments should take additional steps to assure the voting rights of all citizens and to enforce the principle of one person, one vote.

1. Federal and state governments should intensify efforts to enforce compliance with the several statutes guaranteeing the right to vote and prohibiting various forms of discrimination in voting and registration.

2. The methods for funding and administering elections—from investments in equipment through voter education to procedures at the polling place—should seek to ensure that every qualified citizen has an equal opportunity to vote and that every individual's vote is equally effective. No individual, group, or community should be left with a justified belief that the electoral process works less well for some than for others.

3. Federal and state governments should consider uses of technology, for example when developing voting equipment system standards, that will make it feasible to provide greater assistance to language minorities.

POLICY RECOMMENDATION 7

Each state should set a benchmark for voting system performance, uniform in each local jurisdiction that conducts elections. The benchmark should be expressed as a percentage of residual vote (the combination of overvotes, spoiled votes, and undervotes) in the contest at the top of the ballot and should take account of deliberate decisions of voters not to make a choice.

1. Benchmarks should consider the results obtained by best practices within that state, taking local circumstances into account. In general, we suggest that the benchmarks in the next election cycle should be set no higher than 2%, with the goal of further reductions in succeeding cycles.
2. Each state should require its election jurisdictions to issue a public report on the number of residual votes after every statewide election, including the probable causes of error, if any.
3. Each state should determine for itself how to hold its election jurisdictions accountable for achieving the benchmarks.

POLICY RECOMMENDATION 8

The federal government should develop a comprehensive set of voting equipment system standards for the benefit of state and local election administration.

1. Congress should grant statutory authority to an appropriate federal agency to develop such standards in consultation with state and local election officials.
2. The scope of the voting system standards should include security (including a documentary audit for non-ballot systems), procedures for decertification as well as certification of both software and hardware, assessment of human usability, and operational guidelines for proper use and maintenance of the equipment. The agency should maintain a clearinghouse of information about experience in practice.

3. Voters should have the opportunity to correct errors at the precinct or other polling place, either within the voting equipment itself or in the operational guidelines to administrators for using the equipment.
4. Each voting tally system certified for use should include, as part of the certification, a proposed statement of what constitutes a proper vote in the design and operation of the system.
5. New voting equipment systems certified either by the federal government or by any state should provide a practical and effective means for voters with physical disabilities to cast a secret ballot.
6. In addition to developing the voting system standards, the federal agency should provide its own certification and decertification of hardware and software, including components in voter registration systems. These federal certifications and decertifications, like the remainder of the standards, will be recommendations to states which they can adopt or not.
7. This federal service should include selection and oversight of a federally supervised set of independent testing authorities who will apply the standards in assessing equipment. After the federal agency develops and approves the relevant voluntary voting system standards in consultation with state and local administrators, this further, technical task should be delegated to the highly regarded and relatively independent National Institute of Standards and Technology (NIST) of the Department of Commerce.

POLICY RECOMMENDATION   9

Each state should adopt uniform statewide standards for defining what will constitute a vote on each category of voting equipment certified for use in that state. Statewide recount, election certification, and contest procedures should take account of the timelines for selection of presidential electors.

1. Statewide standards for defining a vote in advance of an election should be uniform and as objective as possible.
2. Each state should reevaluate its election code to consider adopting a predictable sequence of: a) vote tabulation and retabulation; b) machine or manual recounts to encompass the entire jurisdiction of the office being recounted, triggered by whatever threshold the state may

choose; c) certification of a final count; followed then by d) contests of the certification limited to allegations of fraud or other misconduct.

3. In such a sequence, each state should allow at least 21 days before requiring certification of the final count. But we recommend retention of a federal deadline under which the "safe harbor" for conclusive state determination of presidential electors will expire.

4. Each state should also develop a uniform design for the federal portion of the state ballot, for use in each of that state's certified voting equipment systems.

POLICY RECOMMENDATION   10

News organizations should not project any presidential election results in any state so long as polls remain open elsewhere in the 48 contiguous states. If necessary, Congress and the states should consider legislation, within First Amendment limits, to protect the integrity of the electoral process.

1. In practice, this would mean that news organizations would voluntarily refrain from projecting the outcomes of the presidential elections in any state until 11:00 p.m. Eastern Standard Time (8:00 p.m. Pacific Standard Time). Voluntary restraint is preferable to government action.

2. If news organizations refuse to exercise voluntary restraint, Congress and the states should consider prohibiting any public disclosure by government entities of official tallies in the race for president and vice president at the precinct level and above until 11:00 p.m. EST (8:00 p.m. PST), where such regulations are consistent with existing provisions for public observation of the vote tabulation process.

3. If news organizations refuse to exercise voluntary restraint and other measures cannot protect the integrity of the electoral process, Congress should impose a plan for uniform poll closing hours in the continental United States for presidential elections.

4. National television broadcasters should provide, during the last thirty days of the presidential campaign, at least five minutes each night of free prime television time to each presidential candidate who has qualified for federal matching funds. They or their local affiliates should further make free time available for state and local election officials to provide necessary voter education.

POLICY RECOMMENDATION   11

The federal government, on a matching basis with the governments of the 50 states, should provide funds that will add another $300–400 million to the level of annual spending on election administration in the United States. The federal share will require a federal contribution totaling $1–2 billion spread out over two or three years to help capitalize state revolving funds that will provide long-term assistance.

1. These responsibilities should be apportioned about 50–50 between the federal government and the states, so that the federal contribution has the effect of raising the annual federal and state level of spending on election administration by an added $150–200 million. This is a modest sum, lower than some other current estimates about what is needed.
2. The federal expenditures should be made in the form of matching grants to the states, and the states should directly administer the disbursement of funds for administration at the state, county, and local level.
3. Instead of planning on permanent expenditures of federal funds, Congress should instead consider leveraging temporary funding over a two- or three-year period in an amount, totaling perhaps $1–2 billion, that will be sufficient to capitalize the federal share of state revolving funds. These funds can leverage the initial federal contribution, after it has been matched by the states, to create a long-term source of federal and state support to election administration. The capitalization should be sufficient to sustain our proposed federal increment of $150–200 million of continued additional spending on election administration that, when matched by state contributions to the funds, will reach the $300–400 million annual nationwide target.
4. Such state revolving funds would be used to carry out flexible state programs, allowing the states to support a variety of election administration activities undertaken by state, county, and local governments and do so with a variety of financing options that can include grants, loans at or below market rates, loan guarantees, and other arrangements. States would assess relative needs among their election jurisdictions and be accountable for maintaining the fund.
5. Federal funds should be allocated among the states in proportion to the electoral votes that each state will cast in the presidential election of 2004. This reflects a slight per capita weighting toward rural states.

Such a modest weighting is appropriate, given the greater average per capita cost of election administration in rural counties.

POLICY RECOMMENDATION 12

The federal responsibilities envisioned in this report should be assigned to a new agency, an Election Administration Commission (EAC).

1. The number of governing commissioners in this agency should be small; the members should be distinguished citizens with a reputation for integrity.
2. The commission should: a) develop federal voting system standards in consultation with state and local election administrators; b) oversee the implementation of these standards in conjunction with the National Institute of Standards and Technology; c) maintain a national clearinghouse of information on best practices in election administration; and d) administer the limited federal assistance program to the states.
3. Enforcement of other federal election laws should remain a separate function, centered in the Civil Rights and Criminal Divisions of the Department of Justice.
4. States that do not have them should also consider establishing nonpartisan election commissions.

POLICY RECOMMENDATION 13

Congress should enact legislation that includes federal assistance for election administration, setting forth policy objectives for the states while leaving the choice of strategies to the discretion of the states.

The Commission as a whole takes no position on whether Congress should use the powerful incentive of conditional grants or instead establish requirements or mandates wholly independent of funding. A majority of the Commission members suggests the approach described below. However, a minority suggests a more direct federal role as detailed in an additional statement of views appended to this report.

1. Congress should enact legislation to create a new federal election administration agency, to facilitate military and overseas citizen voting, to address a national election holiday, to constrain—if necessary—

premature official disclosure of presidential election results, and to appropriate federal assistance in election administration.

2. To be eligible for federal assistance, states shall:
   a. match the federal assistance with an added contribution of their own in the proportion fixed by Congress;
   b. adopt legislation that will establish a statewide voter registration system networked to every local jurisdiction in that state, with provisions for sharing data with other states;
   c. permit on-site provisional voting by every voter who claims to be qualified to vote in that state, or adopt an alternative that achieves the same objective;
   d. set a uniform statewide benchmark for voting system performance in each local jurisdiction administering elections expressed as a percentage of residual vote in the contest at the top of the ballot, and require local jurisdictions to report data relevant to this benchmark;
   e. either agree to comply with the federal voting system standards and certification processes or develop their own state voting system standards and processes that, at a minimum:
      i. give voters the opportunity to correct errors, either within the voting equipment itself or in the operational guidelines to administrators for using the equipment at a precinct or other polling place and
      ii. require that new voting systems should provide a practical and effective means for voters with physical disabilities to cast a secret ballot; and
   f. adopt uniform statewide standards that define what will constitute a vote on each category of voting equipment certified for use in that state;
   g. certify that they are in compliance with existing federal voting rights statutes.
3. Specific choices on how to comply with these conditions should be left to the discretion of the states.
4. States that qualify for federal assistance should have broad discretion in how they disburse this money, so long as the money is expended on: a) establishing and maintaining accurate lists of eligible voters; b) encouraging eligible voters to vote; c) improving verification of voter identification at the polling place; d) improving equipment and methods for casting and counting votes; e) recruiting and training election officials and poll workers; f) improving the quantity and quality of available polling places; and g) educating voters about their rights and responsibilities.

THE COMMISSIONERS

Gerald R. Ford
Honorary Co-Chair

Jimmy Carter
Honorary Co-Chair

Robert H. Michel
Co-Chair

Lloyd N. Cutler
Co-Chair

Slade Gorton
Vice-Chair

Kathleen M. Sullivan
Vice-Chair

Griffin Bell

Rudy Boschwitz

John C. Danforth

Christopher F. Edley, Jr.

Hanna Holborn Gray

Colleen C. McAndrews

Daniel Patrick Moynihan

Leon Panetta

Deval L. Patrick

Diane Ravitch

Bill Richardson

John Seigenthaler

Michael Steele

I

The Goals of
Federal Election Reform

In 2000 the American electoral system was tested by a political ordeal unlike any in living memory. From November 7 until December 12 the outcome of the presidential election was fought out in bitter political and legal struggles that ranged throughout the state of Florida and ultimately extended to the Supreme Court of the United States. Not since 1876–77 has the outcome of a national election remained so unsettled, for so long. That nineteenth century political crisis brought the United States close to a renewal of civil war. Fortunately no danger of armed conflict shadowed the country in this more recent crisis. The American political system proved its resilience.

Nonetheless, last year's election shook American faith in the legitimacy of the democratic process. The effect is measurable. In 1996, three-quarters of the population thought the election had been at least somewhat fair. After 2000 that proportion fell to about one-half. About three-quarters of Democrats doubted the fairness of the process.

But this is not simply a story of happy Republicans and unhappy Democrats. In 1996 just 12% of Republicans thought the election was unfair. But that proportion doubled after 2000. Beliefs about fairness are influenced by whose candidate won, but people also become uneasy when the process begins to seem arbitrary. Among those who called themselves Independents, only 11% labeled the 1996 election as unfair, but in 2000 that number rose to more than 40%.[1]

This is not the first time the United States has undergone an election crisis. But the great electoral crises of the nineteenth century arose from serious structural problems. The 1800 crisis led to prompt passage in 1804

17

of a constitutional amendment, the Twelfth. The 1824 crisis transformed the American political system, forging the Democratic Party and leading to near-universal adoption of direct popular election for presidential electors. In 1824 only 27% of eligible voters went to the polls. Four years later 56% of the electorate cast ballots for president. The 1876 crisis arose from the special circumstances of the post-Civil War reconstruction of the South.

In the electoral crisis of 2000, by contrast, the ordinary institutions of election administration in the United States, and specifically Florida, simply could not readily cope with an extremely close election. Every aspect of the election process was put under a microscope and viewed by an anxious nation that saw controversial ballot design; antiquated and error-prone voting machines; subjective and capricious processes for counting votes; rolls that let unqualified voters vote in some counties and turned away qualified voters in others; confusion in the treatment of overseas military ballots; and a political process subjected to protracted litigation.

Stepping back from Florida, the picture is no more encouraging. The chief election official of Georgia, Cathy Cox, testified to this Commission that: "As the presidential election drama unfolded in Florida last November, one thought was foremost in my mind: there but for the grace of God go I. Because the truth is, if the presidential margin had been razor thin in Georgia and if our election systems had undergone the same microscopic scrutiny that Florida endured, we would have fared no better. In many respects, we might have fared even worse." Across America, we have heard the same from other election officials.

"There is probably no other phase of public administration in the United States which is so badly managed as the conduct of elections. Every investigation or election contest brings to light glaring irregularities, errors, misconduct on the part of precinct officers, disregard of election laws and instructions, slipshod practices, and downright frauds. . . . The truth of the matter is that the whole administration—organization, laws, methods and procedures, and records—are, for most states, quite obsolete. The whole system, including the election laws, requires a thorough revision and improvement." That judgment, by election expert Joseph Harris, was published in 1934.[2] In the previous decade voter turnout had sunk to a low never again equaled before or since. So the problem is hardly new.

But the character of the problem has evolved. In the second half of the century the federal government and federal courts established national voting rights, nationally defined. Permanent voter registration replaced the old pattern of requiring voters to re-register again and again. Election administration became more professionalized and non-partisan. Voting machines were introduced to gain greater efficiency and reduce the opportunities for the election fraud that had so frequently accompanied human vote counts. Yet, in much of the country, too many counts of that 1934 indictment remain valid.

But in a world of problems that often defy any solution, the weaknesses in election administration are, to a very great degree, problems that government actually can solve. In the last few years, and now spurred by the events last year, election reform has returned to the legislative agenda in many states. In much of the country cadres of able and dedicated election administrators are in place who can show what is possible and carry reforms into practice. To support these efforts already under way and to encourage immediate and significant state and federal action, we make the following recommendations.

When they choose the president, the vice president, and members of Congress, the American people should expect all levels of government to provide a democratic process that:

- Maintains an accurate list of citizens who are qualified to vote;
- Encourages every eligible voter to participate effectively;
- Uses equipment that reliably clarifies and registers the voter's choices;
- Handles close elections in a foreseeable and fair way;
- Operates with equal effectiveness for every citizen and every community; and
- Reflects limited but responsible federal participation.

For Americans, democracy is a precious birthright. But each generation must nourish and improve the processes of democracy for its successors. In the near-term, the next three to five years for instance, we envision a country where each state maintains accurate, computerized lists of who can vote, networked with local administrators. Using that system, qualified voters in our mobile society would be able to vote throughout their state without being turned away because of the vagaries of local administration. Using the system we recommend here, millions of military and other overseas voters would find it easier to get and return their ballots. Election Day would be held on a national holiday, freeing up more people to serve as poll workers and making polling places more accessible. Voting machines would meet a common standard of excellent performance. Each state would have its own uniform, objective definitions of what constitutes a vote. News organizations would exert necessary restraint in predicting election outcomes. Every jurisdiction and every official would obey the Voting Rights Act and other statutes that secure the franchise and prohibit discrimination. In all of this there would be a delicate balance of shared responsibilities between levels of government, and between officials and the voters they serve.

This report sets forth our recommendations for the next, immediate steps on the road to attainment of these goals.

II

The Federal Government and the Federal Election System

THE CONSTITUTION'S ALLOCATION OF AUTHORITY

The conduct of federal elections is a federal function—as the Supreme Court reiterated just this year, states have no inherent or reserved powers over federal elections because federal elections only came into being when the United States Constitution was ratified.[3] Nonetheless, the framers of the Constitution foresaw a federal-state partnership in the administration of federal elections, and delegated to the states a substantial role in the conduct of those elections. Article 1, Section 4, of the U.S. Constitution states that: "The Times, Places and Manner of Holding Elections for Senators and Representatives, shall be prescribed in each State by the Legislature thereof; but the Congress may at any time by Law make or alter such Regulations, except as to the Places of choosing Senators." And Article II, in conjunction with the Twelfth Amendment, provides that the states shall choose electors for the President and Vice President, but that "the Congress may determine the Time of choosing the Electors and the Day on which they shall give their Votes," and specifies rules by which the Congress might settle contested presidential elections.

As Alexander Hamilton explained in Federalist No. 59, the Constitutional Convention deliberately chose to submit "the regulation of elections for the federal government" to local governments that, ordinarily, "may be both more convenient and more satisfactory." But the Constitution "reserved to the national authority a right to interpose, whenever extraordinary circumstances might render that interposition necessary to its

21

safety." After all, Hamilton wrote, the national government should not subject its existence "to the pleasure of state governments."[4]

The federal courts have therefore long ruled that Congress has broad authority to regulate elections where candidates for Congress are on the ballot, either in a primary or a general election.[5] State power to set neutral rules for federal elections is limited to time, place, and manner, and the federal government may pass laws to supersede any of these rules.[6] Thus the National Voter Registration Act of 1993 was upheld by the courts even though it effectively told states exactly how they had to register voters in federal elections, right down to the layout of the registration form.[7] Though in theory, and occasionally even in practice, states have tried to mitigate such federal edicts by setting up separate systems for federal and state elections, none has found such bifurcated systems sustainable.

The federal power created by the Elections Clause is reinforced by the constitutional authority granted Congress to enforce the Equal Protection Clause of the Fourteenth Amendment and by other constitutional amendments prohibiting discrimination in voting. Because the Supreme Court's decision in *Bush* v. *Gore* found that differing definitions of a vote within Florida during the recount violated the Equal Protection Clause, Congress may well have authority under the Fourteenth Amendment to legislate to ensure greater uniformity within each state's voting procedures.[8]

Presidential Elections and the Electoral College

The Constitution confided the choice of how to select presidential electors to the judgment of "[e]ach state." For a generation, most electors were chosen by the state legislatures without any popular vote. But by the 1820s almost every state had decided to move to direct election of presidential electors by popular vote. By the Civil War, the practice had become universal. The Constitution was not, however, amended to reflect this new custom.

From the outset this Commission decided that it would not make recommendations about whether or how the Constitution should be amended in order to do away with or refashion the choice of presidential electors, the institution generally called the Electoral College. We are aware of the critique that the Electoral College is an anachronism that can award an election to a candidate who did not win the majority of the popular vote and that it gives somewhat more proportional weight to the populations of small states.[9] The supposed disproportionate influence of small states may be counterbalanced by the "unit rule" adopted by 48 of the 50 states that allows the popular vote winner, whatever the margin, to claim all the state's electors.[10]

Yet the compromises embodied in the Electoral College are central to the organization of our republic. The basic political units of the country were the states; yet the president and vice president were to be elected by the entire nation. The Electoral College was a delicate compromise that solved one of the most difficult problems of the Constitutional Convention and did so in a way that satisfied even most anti-Federalist critics of the new document.[11] James Madison put it well:

> The executive power will be derived from a very compound source. The immediate election of the President is to be made by the states in their political characters. The votes allotted to them are in a compound ratio, which considers them partly as distinct and coequal societies, partly as unequal members of the same society. . . . From this aspect of the government it appears to be of a mixed character, presenting at least as many federal as national features.[12]

Within the Commission there are different views about how to strike the balance of state and national "features," and we are reluctant to suggest refashioning such a fundamental balance unless our search for constructive answers compels us to do so. Fortunately, a strong and effective set of ideas for federal election reform is available that can satisfactorily address most of the problems that came into national view last year without reaching out to rewrite the Constitution.

THE PRIMARY ROLE OF STATE GOVERNMENTS

Even though the federal government has broad constitutional authority to mandate how the states conduct federal elections, we believe that state governments should have a primary role in the conduct of such elections for a simple reason: federal elections are, as a practical matter, conducted in conjunction with a vast array of state and local elections across widely varying conditions. The last presidential election involved more than 100 million voters casting ballots at more than 190,000 polling places, staffed by more than 1.4 million regular or temporary administrators and poll workers. The original constitutional premise, that state governments should oversee the conduct of elections, subject only to limited and necessary federal intervention, remains sound.

But we recommend that state governments should do far more to accept their lead responsibility for improving the conduct of elections, especially federal elections. Most congressional elections involve multiple local jurisdictions, and often more than one county. All presidential and senatorial elections are statewide contests in their states. State governments should ensure uniformity of procedures and standards within the state and provide the essential guidance for the consistent and constitutional conduct of these elections.

Thus the states are vital partners to the federal government in any plan for nationwide reform. They are also a necessary bridge between federal policy and local administration.

III

A Democratic Process That Maintains an Accurate List of Citizens Who Are Qualified to Vote

One of the most serious problems in America's elections is also one of the most basic—identifying who can vote. For some this is a problem of disfranchisement. For others this is a problem of the integrity of the voting system. The controversial effort to clean up voter rolls in Florida was itself a reaction to prior scandals, especially the 1997 election for mayor of Miami, an election invalidated by the courts due to widespread vote fraud.

The issue of voter lists now has well-drawn battle lines. Some argue that the "purging" of voter lists has been used to push minority voters off the rolls. Others maintain that "list maintenance" is essential to preventing fraud. A major development in this political struggle was the passage of the National Voter Registration Act of 1993, the "motor voter" law often referred to by its acronym, NVRA. This act strictly regulated the procedures that had to be followed before voters could be removed from lists and made such removals more difficult.

THE PROBLEM OF ACCURATE VOTER LISTS

State and local election administrators have testified to the Commission that they are generally comfortable with the NVRA and the Commission does not advocate making any changes to it. But, as a result of the law, administrators agree that their voter lists are now swollen with larger numbers of named voters who have moved, or died, or are no longer eligible to vote in the local jurisdiction where they are registered. Duplicate registration is also common. In Oklahoma, which gathers statewide data in its unitary election system, the number of inactive voters had averaged about

15% of the list.[13] After NVRA that percentage grew to 25%. As might be expected, a number of jurisdictions have compared their voter lists to census numbers and observed that they have thousands, sometimes tens of thousands, more registered voters than people.

Some contend that swollen voter rolls are harmless, since the individuals have moved or died and therefore do not vote, and since poll worker scrutiny and signature verification can prevent fraud. We disagree:

- Significantly inaccurate voter lists add millions of dollars in unnecessary costs to already underfunded election administrators and undermine public confidence in the integrity of the election system and the quality of public administration.
- Significantly inaccurate voter lists invite schemes that use 'empty' names on voter lists for ballot box stuffing, ghost voting, or to solicit "repeaters" to use such available names. For generations these practices have been among the oldest and most frequently practiced forms of vote fraud. One of our Commissioners (President Jimmy Carter) has written a book mentioning his encounter with such practices early in his political career. The opportunities to commit such frauds are actually growing because of the trend toward more permissive absentee voting.[14]
- Significantly inaccurate voter lists often penalize poor or ill-educated voters. Among the most mobile citizens in the country, these voters find that even modest residential changes, within a state or county, will keep them from appearing on the list of eligible voters at their new residence.

Although we recognize the problem of accurately establishing who is eligible to vote, we do not simply endorse more aggressive measures to prune voter lists within the existing system. Rather than take a side in the ongoing partisan arguments, we think the problem needs to be recast in terms that can break away from the old controversies over "purging." Instead we should look toward the more positive objective of accurately registering every eligible voter on lists that people can trust. To do that we need to step back for a moment and take a broader perspective of what has happened to voter registration in America.

VOTER REGISTRATION, PAST AND PRESENT

The U.S. Constitution does not provide a right to vote. It provides that state governments shall determine who is eligible to vote in either state or federal elections, though subsequent amendments offer guards against discrimination in the grant or denial of the franchise.[15] In the first half of the nineteenth century state governments established that they, not municipal governments, were the final arbiters of who could vote in the state.[16]

The registration of voters before Election Day was a more modern innovation, adopted in most states as a good government reform, especially for the growing cities, in the years after the Civil War. With most voter registration systems tied to local residence and set up for locally run elections, practically all these systems relied on local administration. Further, new registrations of voters were usually conducted every two or four years, requiring every voter to register anew at least that often—and more often if they had changed their address. What followed was a new decentralization of power to determine the eligibility of voters, devolving from state governments down to the local and county governments that managed this process and maintained the rolls. Those governments, in turn, often delegated the work directly to precinct officers. The results were various but, too often, dismally predictable. By the 1920s, voter turnout in the United States had reached an all-time low.[17]

The next wave of reform in voter registration concentrated on replacing periodic registration with permanent registration, to reduce costs and the opportunity for fraud. In subsequent decades almost every state adopted permanent registration. Meanwhile, voting rights laws and litigation of the 1960s reduced residency requirements and did away with some of the other more elaborate devices that were used by local officials to thwart registration and were used, in particular, against black Americans. The NVRA effectively forced every state to offer voter registration in combination with the single civic act performed almost universally by American adults—obtaining a driver's license.

Thus we have created a system where voter registration is relatively easy and permanent but is still usually recorded and maintained in the separate files of the nearly 13,000 local election jurisdictions of the United States. There is no authoritative list of American citizens maintained by the federal government. Passport records cover only a fraction of the citizen population. Federal tax and social security records, whatever their value, are also insulated by law against inquiries from, or data sharing with, state and local election officials.

At the same time Americans have become a remarkably mobile society. About one-sixth of the population moves every year. The more local the database of permanently registered voters, the more likely it is that the voter will have moved into or out of it.[18]

A BETTER WAY:
STATEWIDE VOTER REGISTRATION SYSTEMS

Our preference for permanent voter registration and our observation of constant voter mobility prompt this conclusion:

POLICY RECOMMENDATION

Every state should adopt a system of statewide voter registration.

1. The statewide computerized voter file should be networked with and accessible to every election jurisdiction in the state so that any level can initiate registrations and updates with prompt notification to the others. It should include provisions for sharing data with other states.
2. When a citizen either applies for a driver's license or registers to vote, each state should obtain residential address and other information, such as a digitized signature, in a form that is equally usable for both the motor vehicle and voter databases. The address information can then be linked to a statewide street index.
3. Each state's driver's license and voter registration applications should require applicants to provide at least the last four digits of their Social Security number. States should also ask applicants if they are registered in another state so that that state can be notified of the new registration.
4. Each state's voter registration applications should require a separate and specific affirmation that the applicant is a U.S. citizen.

Eleven states and the District of Columbia have already implemented statewide registration systems that cover all their jurisdictions. Seven more states have adopted them and are in the process of implementing them; three more are close to adoption. A statewide registration system was part of the reform program adopted earlier this year in Florida. These 21 states and D.C. include 39.2% of the voting-age population in the United States. In its June 2001 report to Congress, the bipartisan Federal Election Commission, after consulting with state and local election officials, recommended that states "1) develop and implement a statewide computerized voter registration database; 2) insure that all local registration offices are computerized; and 3) link their statewide computerized system, where feasible, with the computerized systems of the collateral public agencies relevant to the NVRA (motor vehicle offices, public assistance offices, etc.)"[19]

With a sense of how voter registration has evolved over the past century, we believe four factors weigh heavily in favor of placing the core responsibilities for voter registration in the hands of state governments.

The constitutional allocation of responsibilities. Under the U.S. Constitution, voter qualifications are defined primarily by state governments. So it makes sense to center registration responsibility at this same level of government. Local issues and ballots may vary, but a resident of a given state, voting in a state or presidential election, will find the same voter eligibility rules and the same candidates at the top of the ballot anywhere within the state.

The nature of the data. The most important source of applications for new voter registration has become the application for a driver's license. This is already a statewide database, and it is estimated that 92% of all registered voters also have a driver's license. The most effective systems have made DMV (Department of Motor Vehicles) information congruent, and thus interoperable, with the voter information called for by the state's election code. When people move within a state, they are still in the database even if they are slow to get a new license. When they move from one state to another, one of the first—and perhaps the only—civic act they must accomplish is to get a driver's license valid for that state. DMV change-of-address information is thus considered even more comprehensive and reliable than the useful National Change of Address database maintained by the U.S. Postal Service.[20]

Accuracy can mean access. People are mobile, but more than three-quarters of all moves are within the same state. An effective statewide database can therefore be quite useful, including its capacity to address such common issues as the registration of in-state college students and people with second homes within a state. But perhaps the most important beneficiaries of statewide registration systems will be members of lower-income groups, who are more likely to move than higher-income groups and, when they do move, are much more likely to move from one place to another within the same state. They are thus more likely to fall off local voter rolls and bear the burden of re-registration.

Accountability. A clear statewide registration system will be more transparent and accountable to outside scrutiny. Some advocates for disadvantaged groups are uneasy about statewide registration proposals, fearing that these will turn into still more powerful tools for "purging." Yet one of the clearest findings from the U.S. Civil Rights Commission's investigation in Florida is that, with purely local administration of list maintenance, local variations on statewide guidelines can be critical yet difficult to track.

Beyond the general recommendation in favor of statewide registration systems, several specific policy issues deserve mention. One is the question of whether to require voters to display some proof of identification at the polls.

All states hope that precinct officials and poll watchers will have at least some familiarity with the residents of their precincts. Seven states, all but one of them rural, do nothing more. In the rest, the most common practice now is to require voters to sign their names in an official registry or on a ballot application. About a third of the states require poll workers to check signatures against those provided at registration. Fourteen states insist that voters produce some form of identification.[21]

Most states that have histories of strong party rivalry or election fraud require signature verification or voter identification at the polls. Signature verification puts an extra burden upon administrators, and especially on often ill-trained poll workers practicing a very subjective, often impossible, task while voter lines lengthen. Also, many polling places lack the means to provide poll workers with accurate copies of the voter's actual signature (the one the voter used in order to register) and a signature may change over time.

One alternative, favored by several Commissioners, is to require those who are registering to vote and those who are casting their ballot to provide some form of official identification, such as a photo ID issued by a government agency (e.g., a driver's license). A photo ID is already required in many other transactions, such as check-cashing and using airline tickets. These Commissioners point out that those who register and vote should expect to identify themselves. If they do not have photo identification then they should be issued such cards from the government or have available alternative forms of official ID. They believe this burden is reasonable, that voters will understand it, and that most democratic nations recognize this act as a valid means of protecting the sanctity of the franchise.

A small percentage of adults, perhaps about 5 to 7%, do not possess a driver's license or other photo identification. They are disproportionately poor and urban (since they may use public transit rather than drive a car). Some Commissioners also object to requiring voters to produce a photo ID or some alternative form to verify their identity because some members of minority groups believe such a process can be used to intimidate voters or turn them away in a racially discriminatory fashion.

We believe that an assessment of how to strike the right balance between administrative burden and voter responsibility turns too much on the assessment of local conditions to be amenable to any categorical recommendation by this Commission. We do believe, however, that states should be able to verify a voter's identity.

In recommending the adoption of statewide voter registration systems, we looked at the experience of those states that have adopted them. The outstanding models appear to be Michigan and Kentucky. Michigan deserves particular scrutiny because it is the most populous state to have fully implemented such a system and it is also a state with a larger number of separate election jurisdictions, more than 1,600, than any other. The Michigan system is new, having been put in place just in the last few years, and it passed the test of the 2000 election with flying colors. The software solution developed in Michigan has been inexpensive and is not exclusive to a particular vendor. Any state can copy it. A more complete description of the Michigan voter registration system is attached in Appendix B to this report.[22]

Any state adopting a statewide voter registration system will confront the problem of uniquely identifying voters, figuring which Joseph Smith is the same as that Joe Smith. That is why, following the Michigan example, we recommend obtaining residential addresses, with the DMV and voter registration address required in identical form.

An added identifier is desirable, given the various spellings and the clerical errors that frustrate reliance only on a given name and address. For this purpose some numeric identifier can be useful. Given the danger from overuse of entire Social Security Numbers as an individual identifier we suggest that states obtain the last 4 digits of this number as an added identifier.[23] The Federal Election Commission has made the same recommendation.

Some states also seek added identifiers, such as information on the place of birth and prior residential address. We take no position on the value of having this added information, but we do believe that federal law and regulations should be amended over time where state experience provides evidence that a change is needed. Used cumulatively, this information could improve the accurate exchange of information affecting voter eligibility and help avoid mistaken voter removals like those that occurred in Florida.

Our policy recommendation need not require any immediate amendment of the NVRA. The NVRA specifies how voters can be registered. In general, those provisions will benefit from and work much more effectively with a statewide registration system. The NVRA also specifies how voter lists should be maintained. We believe those provisions do not take ade-

quate account of the kind of statewide voter registration system we recommend. But we see no need to amend the list of maintenance provisions
of the NVRA either to add more safeguards or pare them back until more
and wider experience with new systems can give us more evidence about
just what is needed.

All states require voters to declare, by their signature, that they are U.S.
citizens and meet other criteria for eligibility to vote. Twelve states require
applicants at least to check a box specifically affirming they are a citizen,
though most of these accept the national mail-in and NVRA forms that do
not have such a box. Inability to verify citizenship is a weakness in every
state's voter registration system. The problem is not hypothetical. Noncitizens do vote, albeit illegally.[24] We therefore recommend that a specific
enforceable affirmation of citizenship be included in all voter registration
applications. Combined with enforcement of the relevant state and federal
vote fraud laws, this should be sufficient to contain this potential problem.

IV

A Democratic Process That Encourages Every Eligible Voter to Participate Effectively

An especially infuriating barrier eligible voters can face is to show up on Election Day, believing (perhaps rightly) that they are qualified to vote, and then be turned away because the poll worker cannot find their name on the list of qualified voters. In every recent national election there are certainly hundreds of thousands, and possibly millions, of such frustrating encounters.

Sometimes it is the voter's fault. Americans change their residence often, and often they forget to re-register or do not know they need to do it. This mobility has the effect of taking much of the population back to the requirements of temporary, periodic registration that were so widespread early in the 20th century. A reform movement starting in the 1920s and 1930s eventually led to adoption of permanent voter registration in every state. That reform now needs to be adapted to our still more mobile society. A statewide voter registration system can capture most of this social mobility.

Sometimes voters are turned away because of administrative errors. Poll workers may overlook their names or not match them up with a different spelling. The poll workers usually still work from printed lists of voters produced for each precinct—a process that must begin weeks before Election Day. Staff in the offices that produce those lists can make clerical errors. Motor vehicle departments or social service agencies that receive registration applications may fail to get them, get them in the wrong form, or fail to forward them quickly enough.

The NVRA has also had the unanticipated effect of causing the disfranchisement of many thousands of the very people it sought to bring into the political process. Although the act does not require it, most states allow practically anyone to go out and register voters by taking and transmitting their mail-in applications. These people thus act in effect as deputy registrars. Election administrators we have encountered in every part of the country tell us of numerous cases where these unofficial registrars, often meaning well, mishandle or lose such applications.[25] The applicants, of course, rightly believe they have registered. Then they show up on Election Day and find out they are not on the list.[26]

PROVISIONAL VOTING

The NVRA tried to tackle the problem of frustrated voters who are not found on voter lists with a set of mandates on "fail-safe" voting. Though these provisions are complicated enough to confuse experts, our best summary of what the NVRA requires is this: let us suppose a voter does not show up on a voter list because the voter has moved, or perhaps the registrar erroneously thinks the voter had moved. The state must still let the voter cast some sort of ballot if the voter is registered in that jurisdiction and claims to have stayed in the same registrar's jurisdiction (usually a county). Such a fail-safe ballot must be made available whether or not the registrar has sent a mailing to confirm the voter's new address and whether or not the voter has replied to such a mailing, if the voter is willing to swear to or (in special circumstances) present evidence to verify the claim. States can decide whether the person should vote at their old or new polling place.[27]

State practice follows no set pattern. Some states have very broad provision for fail-safe voting. A provisional ballot was pioneered more than ten years ago by California and Washington state (where it is called a special ballot). Nineteen states use provisional ballots to comply with NVRA. Florida has just adopted the provisional ballot in its new election law. These states include a majority of the voting-age population of the United States. Other states have a wide variety of procedures to comply with NVRA. Several states do not appear to comply with the "fail-safe" provisions of the Act at all.[28]

The NVRA's fail-safe provisions are oriented to voter files held by counties and cities. We have recommended adoption of statewide voter registration systems that are networked to local election jurisdictions. Our vision of provisional balloting is connected to this different world in which there are more accurate state voter files. In both we are motivated by a consistent goal: No American qualified to vote anywhere in her or his state should be turned away from a polling place in that state.[29]

POLICY RECOMMENDATION

Every state should permit provisional voting by any voter who claims to be qualified to vote in that state.

1. Provisional voting authorizes any person whose name does not appear on the list of registered voters, but who wishes to vote, to be issued a ballot. The ballot shall be counted only upon verification by election officials that the provisional voter is eligible and qualified to vote within the state and only for the offices for which the voter is qualified to vote.

2. Another option, for states with statewide computerized voting lists, would be to let a voter who is not on the list submit proof of identification and swear to or affirm an appropriate affidavit of eligibility to vote in that jurisdiction. This information could then be used as an application for voter registration and the voter list would be amended accordingly. If qualified, the voter could either be issued a regular ballot or, if the state preferred, be allowed to vote provisionally pending confirmation of the voter's eligibility.

The model for this recommendation is the provisional voting system used in the state of Washington. A provisional ballot is offered to defer resolution of arguments about eligibility, whether because people have moved, or claim they have no criminal record, or claim not to have received their absentee ballot, or because of other disputes. Washington also issues a "special ballot" to voters who have moved into a new county or have moved from another state. After the election, officials research the eligibility issue. If the voter is eligible to vote in another jurisdiction within the state, they mail the ballot there to be tallied. We think such an effort to relay ballots may not be possible in every state. That is why, instead, we have suggested counting such ballots as limited ballots, valid only for those races in which the voter was qualified to vote. California applies a similar law, but does so only within the counties.

In Washington's King County (with the city of Seattle) about 17,000 such special ballots were cast, about 2% of the total, and 78% were eventually found valid and tallied. In California's Los Angeles County more than 100,000 provisional ballots were cast, about 4% of the total, of which 61% were ultimately tallied either fully or in part (depending on the contests in which the voter was entitled to vote).

Provisional voting has three key advantages:

- Eligible voters are no longer turned away at the polls.
- Election administration is easier and more efficient. Poll workers have an easier option to handle angry, frustrated voters. These often ill-trained and low-paid temporary workers do not have to research or resolve cases on the spot, while other voters impatiently wait in line. Nor are more senior election officials tied down in resolving such questions during Election Day.
- Voter registration becomes more accurate. The process becomes another way to amend registrations for people who evidently wish to vote. Officials can catch and correct mistakes and the research process, by helping senior administrators notice which problems are causing the mistakes, thus can help many other current and potential voters.

Some caveats about this policy recommendation are in order, however. We certainly support county-wide provisional voting procedures. Our more ambitious recommendation of statewide provisional voting is linked to establishment of a statewide computerized voter file, networked to local jurisdictions, as we have also recommended. That networking can help local officials check voter eligibility and note whether and where the voter has voted.

Our recommendation also would penalize voter error. If a voter turns up in the wrong jurisdiction within the state, states should not have to require local jurisdictions to somehow provide a ballot tailored for the voter's proper home jurisdiction. In such cases the voter would, in effect, be receiving a limited ballot, in that officials would only count the choices the voter can mark and is eligible to make on the ballot that is offered in the place he or she has chosen to vote.[30]

Post-election research does take time and money, similar to the staff resources required for processing absentee ballots. Handling the 17,000 "special ballots" in Washington's King County occupied 15 staff for nine days. Commission staff directly observed how the process worked in the counting rooms of Los Angeles County, which included individual verification of signatures. There the easy ballots took 5–10 minutes, the hard ones up to an hour to reconcile, so that administrators estimate it takes 30 staff two weeks to count 12,000 provisional ballots.

Since provisional ballots can mean additional work, like absentee and overseas military ballots, some officials are reluctant to count them. In at least some local jurisdictions, such ballots are not even counted in a national election if they are not numerous enough to make any predictable difference in the outcome of the presidential race, or whatever race is at the top of the ballot. This little noticed practice is disturbing, partly because every vote should count and partly because those ballots might still make a difference in some of the less publicized 'down-ballot' contests. This is one reason why the Commission recommends that any provisional voting plan should require that all provisional ballots be counted and included in the certified results.

Like the growing use of absentee ballots, use of provisional ballots slows official election counts. Although jurisdictions that receive many such ballots have not yet encountered major problems, growing use of provisional ballots may oblige some states to extend their current deadlines for certification of elections.

"SAME DAY" REGISTRATION?

Election day, or "same day" voter registration has been proposed as a way of making it easier for citizens to register and vote (or as a way to get an exemption from the strictures of the NVRA). As a result of court rulings and legislation, no state has either a registration deadline or a residency requirement that extends more than 30 days before an election. But "same day" voter registration, already the law in six smaller states, is being considered by others—even California.

We make no recommendation on the appropriate deadline for voter registration. There is some evidence that "same day" voter registration might have a modest (5–8%) effect in improving voter turnout. But that evidence was largely gathered in elections before voter registration was simplified around the country by adoption of NVRA. In 1996, the next presidential election after passage of NVRA, voter registration was up but voter turnout was down.[31] Nor is there much evidence on how durable such an added effect may be.

Even if there is a slight turnout benefit in allowing "same day" registration, that benefit must be substantial enough to outweigh the added administrative burden election officials would have to shoulder in states, especially large states, that strongly prefer to register voters in advance of Election Day so that they will not have to confront a deluge of new registrants at thousands of polling places. Another disadvantage of "same day" registration is the lost opportunity for voter education. Voters registered weeks before Election Day are often mailed information such as sample ballots, the location of their polling place, and a voter manual.

As a practical matter, large jurisdictions need a few weeks before Election Day in order to prepare and distribute the lists of voters to all the polling places. If registration deadlines are set shortly before an election, many voters will not be included in the printed lists. Their omission will thus dramatically increase the number of provisional votes to be counted on and after Election Day which, as we mentioned, takes time. This is one reason why veteran administrators believe that citizens can have "same day" voter registration in large states, or they can have "same day"election results, but they are unlikely to be able to have both.

Although we have not adopted a recommendation for "same day" registration, we do agree that states requiring advance registration need to make some allowance for citizens who have just moved to their new home. We have already noted repeatedly how mobile our population is, and a large number of these moves occurs in the month or two before a November election. No person should be denied the right to vote in a federal election just because that person has changed his or her residence shortly before an election.

This goal can be recognized within the allowance for provisional voting that we have recommended above. If a voter does not show up on the voter lists because the voter has moved to the jurisdiction shortly before Election Day, we recommend that states allow such voters to cast a provisional ballot, especially if the voter is prepared to offer some type of proof that they have established such a new residence. In such cases, as in Michigan, the provisional or affidavit ballot can then also become a tool for registering a new voter and amending the statewide voter list accordingly.

IMPROVING VOTER PARTICIPATION

If we want to encourage eligible voters to turn out, a good place to start is to ask those citizens who did not vote, "Why?" After the 2000 election the Census Bureau posed this question to thousands of non-voters. Here are the top ten reasons that non-voters gave for not voting:

1. Too busy, conflicting work or school schedule	22.6%
2. Illness or disability	16.0%
3. Not interested, felt my vote wouldn't matter	13.2%
4. Out of town or away from home	11.0%
5. Didn't like candidates or campaign issues	8.3%
6. Registration problems	7.4%
7. Forgot	4.3%
8. Inconvenient polling place or hours or lines too long	2.8%
9. Transportation problems	2.6%
10. Bad weather conditions	0.7%

Registration problems are relatively low on the list, and concerns about convenient access to polling places or the hours they are open are lower still.

We are concerned about whether our system does enough to welcome eligible, disabled voters to the polls. Allowing absentee voting is not a sufficient solution. We believe Americans with disabilities should have the same right as their fellow citizens to be able to vote at the polls on Election Day. Poll workers should be trained to respect this right.

This concern is not new. In 1984 Congress enacted the Voting Accessibility for the Elderly and Handicapped Act. Broader protections were adopted in 1990 in the Americans with Disabilities Act of 1990 (ADA). Courts have held that Title II of that Act applies to all elections and requires election jurisdictions to make adequate numbers of polling places accessible to voters with physical disabilities.[32] The General Accounting Office is completing a substantial study of voting and the disabled, to be published later in 2001, that we expect will shed much more light on the extent of compliance and noncompliance with the ADA. That law does create a right of private action to enforce its provisions, so pressure on governments to provide the required physical access may grow.

As that pressure grows, state and local officials face a difficult trade-off. On the one hand they want to expand or maintain a large number of polling places. On the other hand, the only polling places they can often rely on to be accessible to Americans with disabilities are those in a relatively small number of public buildings, particularly in public schools. Rebuilding requirements should not be mandatorily imposed on private buildings, like churches, just as a cost of being able to borrow them from time to time as polling places. So this issue seems to require very particular state and local assessments of what can be done, especially as more and more private buildings around the country become ADA-compliant. But we think the laws on the books are sufficient to encourage continued progress.

ELECTION DAY HOLIDAY

One way of addressing the shortage of accessible polling places, low voter turnout, and the challenge of recruiting poll workers is to move or redefine Election Day. There are calls to establish a national holiday on Election Day. Others have suggested turning Election Day into an Election Weekend or opening the polls for much longer portions of the day. However, many local jurisdictions already have difficulty finding qualified poll workers to staff current polling hours. There is also little evidence that longer hours would have much effect on voter turnout.

The idea of a national holiday is better founded. It would help working people vote without having to hire poll workers to staff added or longer shifts. Skeptics counter that many Americans will find other things to do with a holiday than go to the polls. Some election administrators who have experience with local elections held on weekends observe no particular benefit in voter turnout. Putting aside those clashing speculations about turnout, a holiday has other advantages for election administration. More public buildings, especially schools, would be available for use as polling places.[33] More, and better trained, poll workers might be available to staff polling places. Several encouraging programs have been created around the nation to engage civic-minded high school and college students to work at the polls on Election Day and a holiday from classes may release more students into the pool of potential candidates. Notably, at our Ann Arbor hearing we heard testimony from Congressman Steny Hoyer about his proposed 'Help America Vote' (HAV). HAV will make money available to colleges and universities across the United States to recruit and train students to be poll workers, helping to solve the poll worker shortage and, at the same time, helping to spark young people's interest and participation in elections. Similarly the nonpartisan effort to create a Youth Voter Corps is a promising idea for how to encourage and train school and election administrators to recruit and energize high school students as poll workers and poll watchers.

True, national holidays are very expensive, mainly to employers.[34] But these employers have already assumed the cost of a national holiday every year during the second week of November—Veterans Day. That leads us to an idea with considerable civic virtue as well as practical merit.

POLICY RECOMMENDATION

Congress should enact legislation to hold presidential and congressional elections on a national holiday.

1. Holding national elections on a national holiday will increase availability of poll workers and suitable polling places and might make voting easier for some workers.
2. One approach, which this Commission favors, would be to specify that in even-numbered years the Veterans Day national holiday be held on the Tuesday next after the first Monday in November and serve also as our Election Day.

Veterans Day honors those who have served in the armed forces and those who died in the service of this country. It originated as Armistice Day, set aside to commemorate the end of the First World War on November 11, 1918. After World War II it became a day of tribute to the veterans and those who lost their lives in that conflict as well. In 1954, after the Korean War, the date was officially designated as Veterans Day to honor those who served in all the nation's wars.[35] After being moved into October for several years, Veterans Day was moved back to November 11, but is generally observed on the second Monday of November.

Could Congress establish a national holiday on which elections were held? The Constitution grants Congress the power to set the date of congressional elections and the time at which presidential electors are chosen. A federal statute now places Election Day on the "Tuesday next after the first Monday in November."[36] And it would be a reasonable corollary to this power for Congress to declare Election Day a national holiday.

Whenever this proposal is mentioned, politicians tell us, almost as a reflex, that veterans groups may not like it. Certainly veterans groups will have a decisive say in any adjustment in the Veterans Day national holiday, and well they should. But such an automatic assumption about their views may underestimate the people who lead these groups, and the men and women who belong to them. Starting with our chairmen, we understand the perspectives of veterans. Gerald Ford is a combat veteran who served with the Navy in the Pacific Theater in World War II. Jimmy Carter is a graduate of Annapolis who served as a naval officer from 1946 to 1953. Bob Michel is a decorated combat veteran who served with the Army in the European Theater in World War II. Lloyd Cutler served during that conflict as well. So we would not endorse any idea that would dilute the significance of Veterans Day, and what it represents.

For many Americans, Veterans Day is a day for ceremony and remembrance, ceremonies often held at the grave sites of soldiers, sailors, and airmen. That is fitting. We reflected on the notion of holding the supreme national exercise of our freedom on the day we honor those who preserved it. On reflection, we found something very fitting about that too. There is time enough to do both these things, once every two years. Perhaps some veterans organizations may even encourage some of their members to serve again, at the nation's polling places, as one way to start or finish this day. We certainly hope that the private sector will permit and even encourage their employees to volunteer in this way. Many businesses are already setting a good example.

MILITARY AND OVERSEAS VOTING

It is in this context that we turn to the problems encountered by servicemen and women when they try to cast their own votes. Understandably, voter turnout among members of the armed forces is very high. So too is the level of frustration when their votes cannot be counted through no fault of their own. The most serious problems are:

- The time needed to apply for an absentee ballot, receive one, and return it, especially when each of these three steps requires a mailing to and from someone stationed overseas. This is not a new problem. One of our co-chairs, Bob Michel, recalls applying for an absentee ballot while moving with his unit across France well before the election of 1944, but not receiving it until he was trying to fight into Germany well after the election was over. He mailed it in anyway, sure that he wanted to vote though he was not so sure that anyone would count it.
- Numerous and varying local requirements for ballot return, registration deadlines, and ballot format.

In 1986 Congress passed the Uniformed and Overseas Citizens Absentee Voting Act (UOCAVA) to help eligible members of the armed services and their families, and other citizens overseas, to vote. The GAO estimates that UOCAVA covers more than six million U.S. citizens, including 2.7 million active military personnel and their relatives.[37]

We have already recommended adoption of statewide voter registration systems and new procedures for provisional voting. Those innovations can yield a further payoff here, allowing a more streamlined process for getting and voting absentee ballots from citizens living overseas. Overseas and military ballots should also be counted according to uniform statewide rules. We emphasize later, in Chapter VI, the importance of having foreseeable, objective, statewide standards for defining what constitutes a vote. That applies to absentee ballots too.

POLICY RECOMMENDATION

Congress should adopt legislation that simplifies and facilitates absentee voting by uniformed and overseas citizens.

1. Each state should designate a responsible official for absentee voting by uniformed and overseas citizens who are residents of that state. That

official should become the single point of contact for the citizens of that state who are served by the Federal Voting Assistance Program, which helps such uniformed and overseas citizens.[38]

2. In 1986 Congress passed the Uniformed and Overseas Citizens Absentee Voting Act (UOCAVA) to help eligible members of the armed services and their families, and other citizens overseas, to vote. Utilizing standardized forms for voter registration and absentee ballot requests, all UOCAVA-covered residents from a home state should be authorized to mail these applications to the designated official for their state.[39] If that state uses a statewide voter registration system networked to local jurisdictions, as we have recommended, the state official should be authorized to act directly on these applications or to forward them for action by the appropriate local jurisdiction. States should accept one absentee ballot application as a valid application for all subsequent elections being held by that state in that year.

3. The designated state official should be authorized to accept either a voted ballot being returned for any jurisdiction of that state or a standardized Federal Write-In Absentee Ballot that is an option for a UOCAVA-covered citizen. States should be obliged to accept and tally a Federal Write-In Absentee Ballot for those contests in which they determine the voter was eligible to vote.[40]

4. Properly filed absentee ballots should be accepted if they have been received by the time the polls of that state have closed on Election Day. States and the Federal Voting Assistance Program should develop common standards for validation of ballots that have been voted and mailed on or before Election Day, even if they are received after that date.

EARLY, REMOTE, AND INTERNET VOTING

We wish to comment on one final trend to encourage eligible voters to participate. It is a trend that troubles us, however. This is the increasing adoption of procedures that encourage "no excuse" absentee voting, early voting, and voting-by-mail. Though this trend is justified as promoting voter turnout, the evidence for this effect is thin.[41] Analysts have even noted the possibility that voter turnout in such states may eventually decline, as the civic significance of Election Day loses its meaning.

This trend is adopted in the name of voter turnout, but often seems to be motivated at least as much by considerations of administrative convenience and saving money. More votes by mail mean less need for polling places and poll workers.

The benefits of the new remote and early voting schemes should be weighed against some important costs and dangers:

- Federal law states that presidential elections should be held on the same day throughout the nation.[42] Courts nonetheless have understandably been reluctant to invalidate state laws on this basis. But we believe the statutory plan offers wise guidance.
- Citizens should vote with a common base of information about candidates. If they vote over a period of weeks before Election Day, they vote based on the knowledge available on a scattering of different dates.
- Wherever possible, citizens should vote alone and in secret. The United States adopted the secret ballot a century ago in order to help voters resist pressure to disclose their choices, whether to relatives or to interested "friends." Permissive early voting threatens the hard-won right to a secret ballot.
- The institution of a national Election Day is one of the only remaining occasions in which Americans come together as a nation to perform a collective civic duty. We think rituals and ceremonies do have a part in forming a nation's traditions and habits. We think this one should not be discarded lightly.
- Growing use of absentee voting has turned this area of voting into the most likely opportunity for election fraud now encountered by law enforcement officials. These cases are especially difficult to prosecute, since the misuse of a voter's ballot or the pressure on voters occurs away from the polling place or any other outside scrutiny.[43] These opportunities for abuse should be contained, not enlarged.
- Absentee ballots are often counted last. As their numbers rise, timely reporting of election results is more difficult. After Election Day 2000 California alone had more than a million absentee ballots waiting to be tallied over the following weeks.

We know how difficult it will be for states that have already adopted such practices to roll them back. We do hope to do what we can to undermine the hitherto largely uncritical acceptance of this "convenient" trend and discourage states that have not yet traveled down this problematical path.

Our concerns about early and remote voting plans are even stronger as we contemplate the possibility of Internet voting. In addition to the more general objections, the Commission has heard persuasive testimony that Internet voting brings a fresh set of technical and security dangers all its own.[44] This is an idea whose time most certainly has not yet come.

CITIZENS WITH CRIMINAL RECORDS

We also considered the issue of felon disfranchisement. Almost all the states provide that citizens lose their right to vote, at least temporarily, if they are convicted of a felony. States vary in the crimes that trigger this disfranchisement. Also, in some states felons only lose the right to vote while they are in prison. In others they can petition for restoration of their voting rights. In others the loss of the franchise is permanent and irrevocable. In states that enact a permanent loss of the right to vote, this feature combined with the demographics of the criminal justice system produces a significant and disproportionate effect on black citizens, to the extent that as many as one-sixth of the black population is permanently disfranchised in some states.

The practice of denying the vote to individuals convicted of certain crimes is a very old one that existed under English law, in the colonies, and in the earliest suffrage laws of the states. But these laws have evolved. Over the last forty years the most significant trends in the treatment of felons and voting have been that states have narrowed the list of relevant crimes, and more than 15 states have eliminated lifetime disfranchisement, making the loss temporary or creating some procedure that could allow restoration.[45]

Except in the rare case where a felon disfranchisement law was provably passed with the intent of disfranchising black voters, the courts have held that such laws are constitutional. The U.S. Supreme Court has specifically ruled that these laws do not violate the Equal Protection Clause, as there is language in Section 2 of the Fourteenth Amendment that appears to carve out a specific exception allowing denial of the right to vote "for participation in rebellion, or other crime." Taken together with the Qualifications Clause's grant to state governments of responsibility for determining eligibility to vote, we doubt that Congress has the constitutional power to legislate a federal prescription on this subject.[46]

We believe the question of whether felons should lose the right to vote is one that requires a moral judgment by the citizens of each state. In this realm we have no special advantage of experience or wisdom that entitles us to instruct them. We can say, however, that we are equally modest about our ability to judge the individual circumstances of all the citizens convicted of felonies.

Therefore, since the judicial process attempts to tailor the punishment to the individual crime, we think a strong case can be made in favor of restoration of voting rights when an individual has completed the full sentence the process chose to impose, including any period of probation or parole. In those states that disagree with our recommendation and choose to disfranchise felons for life, we recommend that they at least include some provision that will grant some scope for reconsidering this edict in particular cases, just as the sovereign reserves some power of clemency even for those convicted of the most serious crimes.

POLICY RECOMMENDATION

Each state should allow for restoration of voting rights to otherwise eligible citizens who have been convicted of a felony once they have fully served their sentence, including any term of probation or parole.

ENSURING THE VOTING RIGHTS OF ALL CITIZENS

Voting rights in the United States have come a long way since the bloodshed and political strife of the 1960s. The Voting Rights Act and related legislation have outlawed and dramatically reduced most forms of voter discrimination and disfranchisement. There are still instances, however, where these laws are violated and not enforced. The Commission has heard testimony— as have Congress and others studying election reform—of instances where the election system did not work equally for all citizens or groups of citizens. In response to court decisions, Congress amended the Voting Rights Act to make clear that proof of racial animus or intent to discriminate is not necessary to find a violation of law. Practices that have a racially disparate impact can suffice if, based on the totality of circumstances, equal opportunity to participate in the political process has been abridged.

Moreover, it is critical that all Americans have confidence in our electoral system, and we should strive to eliminate any reasonable perception that the basic mechanisms of democratic participation favor some citizens over others. No voter should ever feel that the process of voting was intimidating or that there were improper barriers, either intentional or unintentional, that prevented the exercise of their right to vote.

A number of civil rights organizations have alleged that minority voters are discriminated against because of the greater use of inferior voting technologies in heavily minority and low-income districts, perhaps in combination with such other factors as inadequate numbers of well trained poll workers in those same districts. For example, several studies and news accounts in the last several months point to poor technologies and other factors as possible explanations for the very troubling observation that the proportions of uncounted ballots are often higher, sometimes dramatically so, in precincts and counties with heavily minority populations. Nor is this just an issue of race. Elsewhere in this report we address the difficulties, some of them illegal, faced by voters with disabilities.

Voters and election administrators also told us that the provisions of the NVRA are not being followed or enforced as Congress intended. For example, in our task force work we heard many stories of public agencies that are responsible for offering and processing voter registration but do not offer registration as required, or do not complete the paperwork accurately, or do not transmit the applications in a timely manner to election administrators. When such agencies make these mistakes, voters often show up at the polls to find they are not on the voting list, and hence are denied the ability to vote. Some have alleged that such failures by these public entities have had a discriminatory impact. (Our recommendations concerning provisional ballots and state-wide voter lists will only help with some of these problems.)

Finally, one other area that should be closely watched is the level of service provided to language minority voters. Data from the 2000 Census show that our nation's ethnic minority populations have grown dramatically over the past decade, and the growth can be expected to continue. Many of our new citizens are not yet fluent in English and need ballots written in their native language. Many of them also come from countries that do not have a democratic tradition of voting, and they are unfamiliar with our election processes. They may also be unaccustomed to questioning or challenging a poll worker who has the trappings of official authority. Election administrators must ensure that language minority voters receive the assistance at the polls that is legally required—and wherever feasible go beyond that to provide what the voter actually needs—such as translators, bilingual poll workers, translated voter education materials, and assistance in the voting booth. Interest groups that represent language minority voters should work with their local elections administrators to assist in recruiting translators and bilingual poll workers to assist in polling places. Voter education is especially important for these citizens. Los Angeles, for example, tries to prevent many problems at the polls by providing translated sample ballots to voters before every election.

POLICY RECOMMENDATION

The state and federal governments should take additional steps to assure the voting rights of all citizens and to enforce the principle of one person, one vote.

1. Federal and state governments should intensify efforts to enforce compliance with the several statutes guaranteeing the right to vote and prohibiting various forms of discrimination in voting and registration.
2. The methods for funding and administering elections—from investments in equipment through voter education to procedures at the polling place—should seek to ensure that every qualified citizen has an equal opportunity to vote and that every individual's vote is equally effective. No individual, group, or community should be left with a justified belief that the electoral process works less well for some than for others.
3. Federal and state governments should consider uses of technology, for example when developing voting equipment system standards, that will make it feasible to provide greater assistance to language minorities.

There are important opportunities to lower barriers by using emerging technologies, as we discuss in the next chapter. Specifically the newer, programmable ATM-like machines, can make translated ballots more readily available for a wider range of language minorities, on demand. The Commission saw a demonstration of equipment used in some southern California voting places that allows voters to choose a ballot in English, Cantonese, Japanese, Korean, Spanish, Tagalog, and Vietnamese. The Voting Rights Act requires jurisdictions to provide various forms of language assistance when that language group exceeds a threshold population in the country. The statutory thresholds reflect a balancing of voter need and administrative burden. With shifting technology and accelerating demographic change, jurisdictions will have opportunities to consider, on a voluntary basis, striking a different balance. The same technologies offer potential advantages to people who are blind or visually impaired, because audio equipment can be readily incorporated.

Many of the problems that occur in elections are caused or exacerbated by poll workers who were not fully educated about the rights of voters. We heard testimony that the electoral system works most effectively when poll workers are well educated about the rights of voters and the procedures for handling voters with special needs. Additionally, when all states implement the provisional balloting recommendation made by the Commission, no voter will ever need to be turned away from a polling place again.

Of course, administration of elections is likely to be more effective, and the effectuation of voting rights more complete, if voters understand both their rights and their obligations. The Commission heard witnesses describe the importance of educating voters about how the process works.

We heard abut the lack of effective civics education in our schools, which should be providing the bedrock of citizens' knowledge about the electoral process, as well as providing some inoculation against the civic cynicism that leads too many citizens to opt out of democratic participation. Election officials should continue their efforts to educate voters through the use of sample ballots, voter pamphlets, demonstration equipment, and public outreach in a broad and diverse range of settings.

No one should believe, however, that poll worker training and voter education alone will eliminate the disparities in the performance of election systems across communities. Nor can campaigns to promote voter awareness, especially when framed as obligations of the individual voter, substitute for concerted efforts by officials to obey the law.

V

A Democratic Process That Uses Equipment That Reliably Clarifies and Registers the Voter's Choices

In the 2000 presidential election, more than two million voters went to the polls but did not have any vote counted in the race for president. Specialists call these votes in which no choice is counted "residual votes." These millions of voters either spoiled their ballots by over voting (appearing to vote for more than one candidate), or by under voting, i.e., they marked their choice in a manner that could not be counted, or they marked no choice at all—accidentally or intentionally.

In addition to those two million voters, some further, unknown number of voters may have had their votes counted, but voted for a different candidate than the one they were trying to choose. No one can know how often this happens. But some initial research disturbingly suggests that a significant number of voters commit errors simply because some voting systems are badly designed.[47] In addition, large numbers of disabled individuals encounter difficulty in using certain kinds of voting equipment at all, or cannot do so without disclosing their vote to others.

Every analyst of voting equipment agrees that the number of residual votes and the rate of voter error is greatly affected by the kind of equipment that is used. An important precept in "human usability engineering" (to use a technical term) is that predictably high levels of user error are evidence of system failure, just as constant complaints that people cannot seem to "follow instructions" are usually symptoms of flawed instructions or faulty system design.[48]

These effects matter. They matter in principle, since the choice of voting equipment should not be the reason why hundreds of thousands of votes will not be counted. They also matter in practice, since elections are frequently very, very close.

VERY CLOSE ELECTIONS HAPPEN—OFTEN

Some might wonder if the extraordinary closeness of the 2000 vote in Florida was just a unique anomaly in American politics. But elections where the margin of error is as little as one percent or less are common.

In presidential elections since 1948, nearly half of all the states have had at least one occasion when the winner of their electoral votes was decided by less than one percent of the vote. In 1948 Truman carried California and Illinois each by margins of less than 1%; had he lost both states the election would have gone to the House of Representatives for decision. In 1960 the winner in six states was decided by this tiny margin, more than enough to have changed the outcome.[49] In 2000 the winners in four other states, in addition to Florida, were decided by less than 1% of the vote.[50] In a given election, past experience indicates a 90% chance that at least one state will have a presidential election decided within such a 1% technological margin of error. Very close elections are also common in elections for other federal offices or for governor. Since 1948 half of the states have had at least one senatorial race decided by less than 1% of the vote; some have had as many as three such narrowly decided senatorial races.

BENCHMARKS, NOT MANDATES

Voting equipment is generally selected by local election jurisdictions, usually counties. Different kinds of systems are therefore used all over the country. There are five basic kinds of systems. In order of the percentage of people using them in 2000, they are:

Punch card	34.4%
Mark sense (optical scan)	27.5
Lever	17.8
Electronic (DRE)	10.7
Paper ballots	1.3
Mixed (within county)	8.1

During the last twenty years the biggest technological trend has been the shift away from lever machines toward newer electronic equipment, specifically optical scan types and the Direct Read Electronic (DRE, or touch-screen, ATM-like) machines. Punch card usage has held steady.[51] Various fixes have been proposed for improving voting equipment. One of the most popular is the idea of abolishing or buying out punch card voting machines.

We do not think, however, that the federal government can effectively pick winners and losers in rapidly evolving competition among private sellers of voting equipment. Nor do we think one size will fit all—for several reasons:

- The performance of voting systems is affected by several inputs that go beyond the equipment. Some of the most important are ballot design, voter education, and the skill and training of poll workers. Some administrators believe, with cause, that they can get more improvements, dollar for dollar, from voter education and poll worker training than they can from investments in new equipment.
- Punch card systems sometimes serve specific local needs. With a punch card machine, each voter just needs a blank punch card. With an optical scan machine, each voter needs a separate ballot. In Los Angeles County, with its 4 million voters, long ballots with many offices and propositions, and requirement to offer ballots in seven different languages (soon to be ten), punch cards thus make much more sense than optical scanners—at least unless enough money can be found to upgrade to high quality DRE (touch-screen) machines.
- Punch card systems can be very different. The Datavote system, for instance, seems to have a much better performance record than the Votomatic-style systems most familiar from the television coverage of the Florida election.[52]
- Optical scan systems and DRE (touch-screen) systems can also be quite different. The different brands of optical scan systems vary, especially between those that are centrally counted and the precinct count systems that allow voters to correct errors. The earliest DRE systems had relatively high rates of voter error, which are now apparently being significantly reduced by more modern hardware and more sophisticated software designs that improve the user interface.[53]

These considerations lead us to favor a strategy of focusing on outputs rather than inputs for measuring improvements in the accuracy with which votes are counted. A benchmark expressed as a maximum acceptable percentage of residual votes would allow each state to set a standard for reliable performance and require election jurisdictions to disclose and be accountable to the public for how they did. This strategy lets state and local managers decide how they want to tackle the problem but gives citizens and their elected representatives a clear standard for judging the results.

POLICY RECOMMENDATION

Each state should set a benchmark for voting system performance, uniform for that state in each local jurisdiction that conducts elections. The benchmark should be expressed as a percentage of residual vote (the combination of over votes, spoiled votes, and under votes) in the contest at the top of the ballot and should take account of deliberate decisions of voters not to make a choice.

1. Benchmarks should consider the results obtained by best practices within that state, taking local circumstances into account. In general, we suggest that the benchmarks in the next election cycle should be set no higher than 2%, with the goal of further reductions in succeeding cycles.
2. Each state should require its election jurisdictions to issue a public report on the number of residual votes after every statewide election, including the probable causes of error, if any.
3. Each state should determine for itself how to hold its election jurisdictions accountable for achieving the benchmarks.

In considering an appropriate benchmark, officials must make allowance for the voters' right to choose no one at all. Some portion of the residual vote number comes from such intentional under votes, which can vary considerably from place to place along with local culture and traditions.

Scholars have made progress, however, in suggesting how often this practice occurs. Survey questions from the National Election Studies indicate that on average, between 1980 and 2000, about three-quarters of 1% of voters (0.73%) deliberately made no choice in the presidential race. Exit polling data from the Voter News Service allows another check on this estimate. In 1992, the only year of sufficient data on this point, again about three-quarters of 1% of voters (0.77%) said they had chosen not to cast a vote for president. The number of candidates on the ballot and the availability of straight ticket voting appear to make no difference in these numbers. Voters are more likely to pass on the presidential contest when there is a senatorial or governor's race on the ballot, or when the presidential race was not competitive in that state. Based on these data, ethnic and partisan differences were unimportant, but older and poorer voters were more likely to skip a presidential race. Even where intentional under votes were more frequent, the rate was still under 1%.[54]

Another way of bounding the problem is to look at the same jurisdictions as they move from one voting technology to another. Where, as in Detroit, the rate of invalid presidential ballots goes from 3.1% in 1996 to 1.1% in 2000, after a shift from punch card to precinct-count optical scan technology, observers can see that machines make a difference. A broader study of many counties across the country that changed from lever machines to other technologies between 1988 to 2000, after controlling for several variables, indicates that the underlying residual vote rate, the percentage unrelated to the type of technology, is no higher than 2%.[55]

Since there is bound to be some understandable variation in local conditions, we are reluctant to mandate any single federal benchmark. States should set their own standards. We encourage states (and their citizens) to judge performance at four levels. Residual vote rates at or below 1% should be considered good. Residual vote rates between 1 and 2% can be viewed as adequate, but citizens should consider local circumstances and decide what is possible. Rates between 2 and 3% should be viewed as worrying. Rates higher than 3% should be considered unacceptable.

BENCHMARKS APPLIED— THE FORTY MOST POPULOUS COUNTIES

For a concrete illustration of how transparency and accountability can work, we apply this scale below to the forty most populous election jurisdictions in the United States. In judging performance it is better to assess particular counties or cities, rather than look at statewide averages that wash out the differences between jurisdictions that are using different types of machines. This list is ranked by percentages of residual vote in the 2000 election, from lowest to highest.[56]

Good Zero to 1%		**Adequate** 1–2%	
Hennepin County, Minnesota (Minneapolis)	0.3%	Clark County, Nevada (Las Vegas)	1.1%
		Nassau County, New York	1.2
City of Milwaukee, Wisconsin	0.3	Wayne County, Michigan (Detroit)	1.3
St. Louis County, Missouri (St. Louis)	0.3	Alameda County, California (Oakland)	1.5
Dallas County, Texas (Dallas)	0.4	Tarrant County, Texas (Fort Worth)	1.6
King County, Washington (Seattle)	0.7	Erie County, New York (Buffalo)	1.7
Oakland County, Michigan	0.7	Maricopa County, Arizona (Phoenix)	1.7
Suffolk County, New York	0.7	Sacramento County, California (Sacramento)	1.7
Bergen County, New Jersey	0.7		
Franklin County, Ohio (Columbus)	0.8	Santa Clara County, California (San Jose)	1.8
Orange County, California	0.8		
Bexar County, Texas (San Antonio)	0.9	Westchester County, New York	1.9
Fairfax County, Virginia	0.9	San Bernardino County, California	2.0
Riverside County, California	0.9	San Diego County, California (San Diego)	2.0
Middlesex County, Massachusetts	1.0		

Worrying 2–3%		**Unacceptable** Above 3%	
Pinellas County, Florida (St. Petersburg)	2.1%	Manhattan County, New York	3.2%
Harris County, Texas (Houston)	2.2[57]	Queens County, New York	3.5
Broward County, Florida (Fort Lauderdale)	2.5	Kings County, New York (Brooklyn)	4.0
		Miami-Dade County, Florida (Miami)	4.4
Cuyahoga County, Ohio (Cleveland)	2.7	Bronx County, New York	4.7
Los Angeles County, California (Los Angeles)	2.7	Cook County, Illinois (Chicago)	6.2
		Palm Beach County, Florida	6.4

Philadelphia County, Pennsylvania (Philadelphia) and Allegheny County, Pennsylvania (which includes Pittsburgh) did not report total voter turnout.

This table highlights only forty out of the hundreds of counties in the United States. It also lists only urban counties, yet some of the most serious residual vote problems are in rural counties that are often especially short of resources. There are many counties in the United States with double-digit percentages of residual votes.

Setting benchmarks always has a downside. People may try hard to meet them. Sometimes they try too hard and create new problems. For instance, legislators will need to be more careful to be sure the data they receive are accurate. They should be watchful for any efforts that discourage less capable voters from attempting to cast a ballot. Officials will also have a strong incentive to count every vote. That is good. But, given that incentive, it is vital to be sure that election jurisdictions in a state share common, reasonably objective definitions of just what constitutes a vote—an issue we will take up in Chapter VI of this report.

STANDARDS FOR MORE EFFECTIVE AND ACCESSIBLE VOTING TECHNOLOGY

As computer technology was used more and more in voting, the FEC's small Office of Election Administration prepared a set of Voting System Standards, approved in 1990, to guide the certification of machines by state and local administrators. The standards have been adopted by 32 states. The National Association of State Election Directors chooses independent testing authorities (ITAs) to examine systems and determine whether they meet the federal standards. Implementation of the standards through the ITAs has been going on since 1995. The FEC is now preparing an updated set of standards for adoption this year.

This system provides a good foundation. But every aspect of it needs to be built up. Overhauling and simplifying the system is vital to encouraging innovation in the research and development of voting technology. Indeed, an able task force made up exclusively of state and local election administrators, organized under the auspices of the Elections Center, took "an unprecedented leap in recommending a more active federal involvement in developing standards for the processes involved in conducting elections." "[W]ith some trepidation" this task force of administrators decided in favor of "a major departure from an historic 'hands-off' attitude toward the federal government" and called for active federal involvement "in development and maintenance of, not only vote counting system standards, but operational standards and guidelines as well."[50] We agree.

POLICY RECOMMENDATION

The federal government should develop a comprehensive set of voting equipment system standards for the benefit of state and local election administration.

1. Congress should grant statutory authority to an appropriate federal agency to develop such standards in consultation with state and local election officials.
2. The scope of the voting system standards should include security (including a documentary audit for non-ballot systems), procedures for decertification as well as certification of both software and hardware, assessment of human usability, and operational guidelines for proper

use and maintenance of the equipment. The agency should maintain a clearinghouse of information about experience in practice.

3. Voters should have the opportunity to correct errors at the precinct or other polling place, either within the voting equipment itself or in the operational guidelines to administrators for using the equipment.

4. Each voting tally system certified for use should include, as part of the certification, a proposed statement of what constitutes a proper vote in the design and operation of the system.

5. New voting equipment systems certified either by the federal government or by any state should provide a practical and effective means for voters with physical disabilities to cast a secret ballot.

6. In addition to developing the voting system standards, the federal agency should provide its own certification and decertification of hardware and software, including components in voter registration systems. These federal certifications and decertifications, like the remainder of the standards, will be recommendations to states which they can adopt or not.

7. This federal service should include selection and oversight of a federally supervised set of independent testing authorities who will apply the standards in assessing equipment. After the federal agency develops and approves the relevant voluntary voting system standards in consultation with state and local administrators, this further, technical task should be delegated to the highly regarded and relatively independent National Institute of Standards and Technology (NIST) of the Department of Commerce.

Our recommendation does not just expand the scope of the standards. We stress the importance, borne out in practice, of insuring that systems permit second-chance voting in some suitable form. We note that voting equipment designers should place on the record their assumption about what should be tallied as a vote under their system.

The accessibility of voting technology by disabled individuals is a serious problem. In an earlier section of the report we discussed the issue of physical access to polling places. Here we address the issue of whether voting machines are accessible to those who can actually get to them. Of particular concern is access for the millions of people who are blind or visually impaired. Our solution, in point five of this recommendation, is modeled on the Texas statute signed into law by then-Governor Bush in 1999. Senior election officials in Texas are satisfied so far with this statute, as are advocates for the blind and disabled.

Like the Texas law, this recommendation for accessible voting technology will tend to promote the future acquisition of DRE (touch-screen) electronic systems equipped with an audio feedback device. Such systems are already on the market. Local jurisdictions can also opt to buy just one such system for each polling place, although that may be administratively inconvenient. The standard can be met with mark sense (optical scan) or even lever machines, but the adaptation is not easy.[59]

Finally, and very important to the reform of the research and development system in voting technology, we think the federal government should offer to relieve each state of the burden of performing a separate testing and certification of whether a system meets the guidelines, which in principle can require a system to be tested again and again and force dozens of individual states to acquire the technical expertise to oversee such a process. Now this task is coordinated by the National Association of State Election Directors. We recommend instead that a technically expert institution of the federal government perform this service capably and transparently. Many states may find this service extremely helpful. Private firms may also prefer this simpler and more expeditious process. Other states need not heed the federal conclusions and can run their own testing and certification processes. But citizens and their representatives may then ask proper questions about why or how their election administrators were persuaded to buy systems that NIST-supervised testers found unacceptable.

VI

A Democratic Process That
Handles Close Elections in a
Foreseeable and Fair Way

Everyone who observed the 2000 election crisis was struck by the sheer unreadiness of every part of the system to deal with a close election. Recount and contest laws were not designed for statewide challenges. The relevant state deadlines did not mesh well with the federal schedule. Each county made its own decisions about what, when, or whether to recount. In performing the recounts the definition of a vote varied from county to county, and from official to official within the counties. Lawsuits materialized across Florida, urging judges to construct law that would overcome the alleged deficiencies of the statutes. The principal television networks also found themselves unready to deal with a very close election. Unable to handle extremely close results carefully and accurately, they dealt with them negligently and inaccurately—and loudly too—erring assertively again and again during the course of Election Night and thereby affecting the course of the very history they were supposedly only trying to report.

OBJECTIVE VOTE DEFINITIONS AND
FORESEEABLE POST-ELECTION PROCEDURES

A major part of the problem in Florida was that the vote counting process was so subjective and variable. The Supreme Court of the United States found such a standardless process to be unconstitutional, a violation of the Equal Protection Clause of the Constitution. Florida is not alone. Most state statutes do not specify a legal standard for election officials to follow in recounting votes. Amorphous statutory references to the "intent of the voter" invite still more divinations.

To the maximum extent possible, partisans on either side should be able to foresee, before a recount, how a vote will be defined by the recounters. In other words, the definition of a vote should be as objective as possible and spelled out in clear language before Election Day.[60]

POLICY RECOMMENDATION

Each state should adopt uniform statewide standards for defining what will constitute a vote on each category of voting equipment certified for use in that state. Statewide recount, election certification, and contest procedures should take account of the timelines for selection of presidential electors.

1. Statewide standards for defining a vote in advance of an election should be uniform and as objective as possible.
2. Each state should reevaluate its election code to consider adopting a predictable sequence of: a) vote tabulation and retabulation; b) machine or manual recounts to encompass the entire jurisdiction of the office being recounted, triggered by whatever threshold the state may choose; c) certification of a final count; followed then by d) contests of the certification limited to allegations of fraud or other misconduct.
3. In such a sequence, each state should allow at least 21 days before requiring certification of the final count. But we recommend retention of a federal deadline under which the "safe harbor" for conclusive state determination of presidential electors will expire.
4. Each state should also develop a uniform design for the federal portion of the state ballot, for use in each of that state's certified voting equipment systems.

The Florida Election Reform Act of 2001 rewrote the rules for manual recounts of ballots. Its approach to the problem of statewide definitions of a vote, if there is a manual recount, was to start with a sound general principle, to count a vote if there is "a clear indication on the ballot that the voter has made a definite choice." The Department of State is then commanded to adopt specific rules for each certified voting system prescribing what will constitute such clear indications. The law provides two boundaries for such rulemaking. On the one hand, the Department of State may not "exclusively provide that the voter must properly mark or designate his or her choice on the ballot." On the other, the rules may not "contain a catch-all provision that fails to identify specific standards, such as 'any other mark or indication clearly indicating that the voter has made a definite choice.'"[61]

In other words, the Florida law requires that some allowance be made for at least some voter errors that nonetheless indicate a clear choice, while it also warns that the varieties of voter error that will be tallied in a manual recount must still be specified, and specified statewide, before such a recount begins. This strikes us as a reasonable and necessary balance that states should endeavor to find in drafting their own standards, either in statute or in published administrative rules.

In examining the procedures for recounts and contests, we are struck— like practically all others who have taken such inventories—by the bewildering variety of procedures, criteria, and deadlines found around the country. We are opposed to any uniform federally imposed system. But in our mobile society, with national elections and media scrutiny, we think some rudimentary consistency of approach from one state to another may make the workings of an inherently contentious process more foreseeable and understandable.[62]

Our evaluation of best practices envisions the following model sequence:

- Initial machine tabulation (and retabulation) of ballots, including the tabulation of all absentee and provisional ballots. Given our recommendation of greater use of provisional ballots and the timeline for counting overseas votes, we think that at least 14 days should be allocated for this process, even if states call for more immediate transmission of unofficial machine tabulations.
- Manual recounts, triggered by criteria set by each state (Florida's new law has a suggestive set), that should extend throughout the area in which the contest was on the ballot. These recounts would be guided by the uniform statewide standards mentioned above. The U.S. Supreme Court decision in *Bush* v. *Gore* appears to require this reform. Nonpartisan appointees should supervise them. We believe at least 7 days should be allocated for this process, especially if the recount is statewide.
- Certification of the final vote count. In large election jurisdictions, at least 21 days should be allowed before requiring certification. But at this point all issues regarding the tabulation of votes should be settled.

▪ Contests. These contests would concede the accuracy of the count, hence they are different from recounts. In a contest the argument should instead be that the votes that were counted should be invalidated because of fraud or other misconduct in the electoral process. Under Florida's old law, and the law of thirteen other states, the distinction between recounts and contests is blurred by allowing a contest for any reason that casts the election outcome in doubt. Florida has now adopted the distinction we recommend. Since contests can involve extensive litigation and taking of evidence about possible misconduct, however, we think the contest phase should clearly be separated from the vote count and certification process itself.

Congress has established a deadline of December 12, about five weeks after the election, by which states should resolve controversies about the appointment of a state's electors if they want their resolution to be binding on the Congress's own consideration of the dispute.[63] That due date allows enough time for counting and recounting ballots and some time for resolution of contests as well. The December 12 date was adopted at a time when presidents were not inaugurated until March of the following year. Presidents are now inaugurated on January 20, as a result of the 20th Amendment to the Constitution. Though we do not recommend pushing the "safe harbor" deadline even earlier than December 12, we also do not recommend setting this date any later. A new president needs a decent opportunity to get the minimally necessary elements of a new administration into place.

MEDIA PROJECTIONS OF ELECTION RESULTS

On Election Night 2000 the major television news organizations (ABC, CBS, NBC, CNN, and Fox) and Associated Press made a series of dramatic journalistic errors. While polls were still open in Florida's panhandle, they projected that Vice President Gore had won the state. They later had to retract this projection. They also projected that Bush had won Florida and, with it, the presidency. Gore then moved to concede the election, beginning with a call to Governor Bush. He then had to retract that call, and the news organizations had to retract theirs. (Associated Press did not; it had not made the second error.) The first set of errors may have influenced voters in Florida and in other states where the polls were still open. The second set of errors irretrievably influenced public perceptions of the apparent victor in the election, which then affected the subsequent controversy over the outcome in Florida.

These problems are not new and are not limited to close elections. Early projections of Johnson's victory in 1964 came well before the polls closed in the West. The same was true in 1972. In 1980, as a result of the media projections, President Carter felt obliged to concede his defeat while polls were still open in the West. In all these cases candidates further down the ballot felt the effect. In 1980 the estimated voter turnout was about 12% lower among those who had heard the projections and not yet voted when compared with those who had not heard them.

For decades, public opinion surveys have disclosed abiding irritation with early projection of election results by the news media—and that was when the news organizations projections were accurate. Then came the 2000 election. The media projection errors on Election Night 2000 highlight a foolish race for momentary bragging rights and a tiny ratings advantage.

The Commission condemns the controversial practice by which national news networks declare a projected winner in the presidential election before all polls close within the contiguous 48 states of the United States.

This practice demeans democracy. It discourages citizens from participating in the most basic and enriching aspect of self-government—voting. It robs candidates, from the White House to the state house to the courthouse, of votes they have a right to expect. It mocks the most salient lesson of the November election—that every vote is important and should be counted

The assertion by network executives that it would be dangerous or wrong to delay calling the outcome of the presidential election until all polls close at 11:00 p.m. (EST) is disingenuous and dishonest. In fact, the networks in the last several presidential elections voluntarily have withheld calling the projected presidential winner in Eastern Time Zone states until after 7:00 p.m. (EST). In addition, as a result of the erroneous news reporting in Florida on the night of November 7, the networks now voluntarily have agreed to withhold calling the projected presidential winner in states with two time zones until all polls have closed in those states. Networks contend there is no evidence that early reporting of a presidential winner deters voters from going to vote or remaining in line at the precincts. As the decisions recited above clearly indicate, they know better. The networks' refusal to adopt a national policy to withhold declaring a presidential winner until all polls close is knowingly inconsistent and discriminates against citizens and candidates in much of the nation.

Government cannot prohibit news organizations from irresponsible political reporting. It cannot bar the exit polls on which networks largely rely for their early calls of a projected winner. The Commission notes the body of evidence that has mounted since November documenting the unreliability of exit polls. The networks now know, from their internal investigations and from studies by their paid consultants that exit polling is seriously flawed. The dirty little secret of the last campaign was that exit polls conflicted with the actual final results in many states—and in five specific instances by as much as seven to sixteen percent.

Network officials acknowledge that these exit polls have become more fallible over the years as more and more voters have refused to participate in them. The Commission was shocked by reports that network interviewers at polling precincts have offered tawdry inducements, such as small sums of money or cigarettes, as enticements to citizens to participate in exit polling. Such conduct cheapens journalism and creates an unhealthy polling place environment. The Commission strongly encourages citizens not to participate in exit polling. If candidates, political parties and election officials actively encouraged voters not to participate in the exit polling game, it could further erode the credibility of exit polls and network reliance on them.

At the same time, Congress and the states may not be completely powerless in making it difficult for the networks to call prematurely a projected winner in presidential elections. In addition to exit polls, networks rely for their early projections on official vote tallies from carefully selected precincts across a state and preliminary raw vote tallies from the state as a whole. Government officials need not be so cooperative. Statutes prohibiting public disclosure of official presidential election tallies until all polls close could limit the news media's ability to project an early winner and be consistent with the First Amendment. At the very least, withholding official vote tallies would leave the networks relying on unreliable exit polls.

POLICY RECOMMENDATION

News organizations should not project any presidential election results in any state so long as polls remain open elsewhere in the 48 contiguous states. If necessary, Congress and the states should consider legislation, within First Amendment limits, to protect the integrity of the electoral process.

1. In practice, this would mean that news organizations would voluntarily refrain from projecting the outcomes of the presidential elections in any state until 11:00 p.m. Eastern Standard Time (8:00 p.m. Pacific Standard Time). Voluntary restraint is preferable to government action.
2. If news organizations refuse to exercise voluntary restraint, Congress and the states should consider prohibiting any public disclosure by government entities of official election tallies in the race for president and vice president at the precinct level and above until 11:00 p.m. EST (8:00 p.m. PST), where such regulations are consistent with existing provision for public observation of the vote tabulation process.
3. If news organizations refuse to exercise voluntary restraint and other measures cannot protect the integrity of the electoral process, Congress should impose a plan for uniform poll closing hours in the continental United States for presidential elections.
4. National television broadcasters should provide, during the last thirty days of the presidential campaign, at least five minutes each night of free prime television time to each presidential candidate who has qualified for federal matching funds. They or their local affiliates should further make free time available for state and local election officials to provide necessary voter education.

Government cannot prohibit exit polls, or even do very much to constrain them. But the First Amendment does allow government to control what its own officials do.

Even if the states do not act on their own, we believe Congress may be able to legislate directly in the limited fashion we have suggested under the Elections Clause (protecting the integrity of congressional elections by ensuring that turnout is not depressed by announcements of results for the top of the ballot). Or Congress can rely on Article II, Section I's power to set the "the time of choosing" electors and the Spending Clause. The networks could still discuss their polls, as they do before an election, but their capacity to call elections— already somewhat shaken—will erode still further.

These legislative remedies are not a sure cure. Deprived of or constrained in getting official tallies, the news organizations—through the Voter News Service—might choose to redouble their exit polling efforts. That source has become more fragile, though, as survey response rates fall and the prevalence of early and absentee voting rises. Nevertheless, by doubling or tripling or quadrupling the polling effort, VNS might offset some of these lost data. This approach would shift the burden in spending from media projections right back to where it belongs—to the television industry that hopes to profit from making them.

The most popular idea for discouraging media projection of presidential election results is to adopt a plan of uniform poll closing times. This Commission cannot summon much enthusiasm for this approach. For such a law to work, polls must stay open later in the East or close earlier in the West. Several problems arise. Extending poll closing hours can be very costly, especially if polls must remain open for 15 hours (currently true in New York). If polls end up being open longer in the East, Western voters could complain about the differential treatment. Closing polls earlier in the West is a bad option; many Western voters turn out in the hours between 6 and 8 p.m. local time. Obtaining conformity of poll closing times in the Central and Mountain time zones is also no easy task. Some bills call for easing this burden by setting up special daylight savings time arrangements that would operate in presidential election years. This approach seems too complicated and disruptive.

In general, uniform poll closing time proposals would make voters and financially strapped counties pay the price because the television industry prefers to chase an ephemeral ratings edge. However, it may be the final option available to Congress as a last resort if voluntary restraint or prohibiting disclosure of tallies fails to protect the integrity of the electoral process.[64]

VII

A Democratic Process That
Reflects Limited but
Responsible Federal Participation

A PATTERN OF NEGLECT

Election administration gets so few resources from American governments that we do not even know how much is spent. The sums are literally too trivial to merit national accounting. The smallest general expenditure category listed in the Census of Government for the Statistical Abstract of the United States is garbage disposal (solid waste management), on which the many units of government spend a total of about $14 billion. The Caltech/MIT Voting Technology Project has worked this year to figure out how much money is spent on running elections. Their best estimate, for operating expenditures just by counties, comes to a nationwide total of only about $1 billion. As we reflect that the general election of 2000 alone involved more than 100 million voters going to more than 190,000 polling places staffed by 1.4 million poll workers, we can hardly be surprised that there are problems. It is amazing, and a tribute to dedicated professional election administrators and many poll workers who practically volunteer their time, that the system works as well as it does.

The costs of election administration are borne almost entirely by the level least able to afford them: county and city governments. These elections compete for funding every day against police and fire protection or solid waste management. The election infrastructure of democracy loses. It is commonplace to find local budgets that spend ten times more on parks and recreation, or on solid waste, than on running elections.

Thinly populated rural counties are even harder pressed. They must build and staff far-flung polling places. Measured simply as a rule of thumb against 2000 presidential voter turnout, the national average of county operating expenditures for elections, per capita, is about $10. Rural counties (less than 25,000 in population) spend anywhere from $2–32 per voter—a large proportion spends more than $15–20 per voter to provide the needed service.

Thanks again to the Caltech/MIT work, we can estimate that about a third of the operating costs of administering elections goes to voter registration, another third goes to administrative overhead, and the remainder is split about equally between equipment costs and actually running the elections on Election Day.

These numbers begin to let us put the costs of modernization into context. Recall that we are estimating average operating expenditures of about $10 per voter who turned out in the 2000 presidential election. The cost to buy modern DRE electronic (touch-screen) voting equipment is about $20–$25 per voter, or more than double an average county's entire operating budget for elections. Mark sense (optical scan) machines cost less up front ($8–10 per voter) but add more to operating expenditures each year because of the extra ballot printing costs. These costs can be spread out and financed over time. But since the operating budgets are so low, even an increment of $1–2 per year is a 10–20% increase in the continuing budget that these low priority agencies can rarely claim.

The products of the election equipment industry have recently received considerable attention. Seldom in the course of human events have so many expected so much from such a small group of firms. As the Caltech/MIT scholars have observed, with annual revenues of about $150–200 million per year the election equipment industry is less than one-tenth the size of, say, the residential lawn mower business.

ESTIMATING AND ALLOCATING THE COSTS OF IMPROVEMENT

The good news is that relatively modest public investments can effect significant improvements. But there is no objective methodology to spell out how much is needed. A few principles nonetheless stand out:

- Costs should be calculated on a long-term basis, either in the financing or leasing of capital equipment, or in added operating expenditures.
- The system has been chronically underfunded for a very long time.
- State governments should assume a major responsibility in election administration.

■ The national government should become a limited partner in financing our federal election system.

Local, county, and state governments presently run congressional and presidential elections for the benefit of the national government. As they do so they must comply with a variety of unfunded federal mandates that instruct them on who can vote, how voters should be registered, how certain kinds of votes can be cast, which polling places are suitable, and other topics. There are no hard estimates of what factor these costs play as a total of local election expenditures. One thoughtful official put together a personal calculation that placed the federally imposed share of his costs at about twenty percent of the total.[65]

Our rough estimate is that overall spending on election administration nationwide should rise by about $300–400 million per year, or about a 30–40% increase above current levels. We reach this figure in the following way:

■ With the creation of statewide registration systems, much of the cost of voter registration should shift to the state level, or about $50–75 million per year above current state spending on this problem. Some economies of scale will be achieved but new (though relatively inexpensive) capital purchases will be needed that, again spread over time, may cost another $15–20 million per year, especially when the costs of networking local jurisdictions into the system are taken into account.
■ Net county expenditures on election administration should increase by about 10%, or about $100 million per year. States relieving counties of some of the burden of building and operating voter registration can free up more operating funds for necessary tasks like voter education and poll worker recruitment and training that can yield large payoffs in public satisfaction. But, in addition, counties need to make added investments in handling their end of maintaining and updating accurate voter files, handling an increase in provisional voting, and improved training of increasingly nonpartisan and professional officials.
■ Purchases of new voting equipment, spread over time and averaged across the country, should cost about another $150 million per year. This increased spending should remain constant as systems are regularly renewed and the focus of spending evolves more to software improvements and service support for relatively inexpensive computer hardware.
■ The federal government will need to build up the agency that develops and oversees voting system standards and the national clearinghouse of

election administration information. This still should be a modestly sized national institution, with an annual budget of about $5–10 million per year.

If all levels of American government together were to spend about $1.4 billion on election administration each year, and if this represented an addition of about $300–400 million to the current spending level, what are the appropriate shares of the state and federal governments? We believe those two levels of government should furnish all of the added spending.

POLICY RECOMMENDATION

The federal government, on a matching basis with the governments of the 50 states, should provide funds that will add another $300–400 million to the level of annual spending on election administration in the United States. The federal share will require a federal contribution totaling $1–2 billion spread out over two or three years to help capitalize state revolving funds that will provide long-term assistance.

1. These responsibilities should be apportioned about 50–50 between the federal government and the states, so that the federal contribution has the effect of raising the annual federal and state level of spending on election administration by an added $150–200 million. This is a modest sum, lower than some other current estimates about what is needed.
2. The federal expenditures should be made in the form of matching grants to the states, and the states should directly administer the disbursement of funds for administration at the state, county, and local level.
3. Instead of planning on permanent expenditures of federal funds, Congress should instead consider leveraging temporary funding over a two- or three-year period in an amount, totaling perhaps $1–2 billion, that will be sufficient to capitalize the federal share of state revolving funds. These funds can leverage the initial federal contribution, after it has been matched by the states, to create a long-term source of federal and state support to election administration. The capitalization should be sufficient to sustain our proposed federal increment of $150–200 million of continued additional spending on election administration that, when matched by state contributions to the funds, will reach the $300–400 million annual nationwide target.[66]

4. Such state revolving funds would be used to carry out flexible state programs, allowing the states to support a variety of election administration activities undertaken by state, county, and local governments and do so with a variety of financing options that can include grants, loans at or below market rates, loan guarantees, and other arrangements.[67] States would assess relative needs among their election jurisdictions and be accountable for maintaining the fund.
5. Federal funds should be allocated among the states in proportion to the electoral votes that each state will cast in the presidential election of 2004. This reflects a slight per capita weighting toward rural states. Such a modest weighting is appropriate, given the greater average per capita cost of election administration in rural counties.

THE FEDERAL INSTITUTIONAL ROLE

Some legislation now pending in Congress calls for creation of a federal blue-ribbon investigatory commission as well as a new federal administrative agency. We do not see the need for another blue-ribbon commission or task force. Several bodies are providing a wealth of information and ideas to the Congress. If another year is spent deliberating what can be done, little or nothing will happen that can benefit voters who will go to the polls in 2002 or 2004.

But overall responsibility for the federal aspect of national election administration needs a better home. It is currently lodged in the Office of Election Administration in the Federal Election Commission. This office, with a staff of about five people, does a good job with what it has. But a new and larger entity is needed.

POLICY RECOMMENDATION

The federal responsibilities envisioned in this report should be assigned to a new agency, an Election Administration Commission (EAC).

1. The number of governing commissioners in this agency should be small; the members should be distinguished citizens with a reputation for integrity.
2. The commission should: a) develop federal voting system standards in consultation with state and local election administrators; b) oversee the

implementation of these standards in conjunction with the National
Institute of Standards and Technology; c) maintain a national clearinghouse of information on best practices in election administration; and
d) administer the limited federal assistance program to the states.
3. Enforcement of other federal election laws should remain a separate
   function, centered in the Civil Rights and Criminal Divisions of the
   Department of Justice.
4. States that do not have them should also consider establishing nonpartisan election commissions.

STRUCTURING FEDERAL LEGISLATION AND FINANCIAL ASSISTANCE

Although we agree on the merits of what should be done, we have also disagreed about how or even if Congress should try to make these things happen. We considered several broad approaches.

- Rely entirely on state action. Though we have endorsed state primacy in
  rhetoric and substance throughout this report, all members of the
  Commission have concluded that at least some limited federal role is
  appropriate given the mixed, interdependent character of the federal
  election system. Having already required services (the election of federal
  officers) and issued mandates, the federal government does have a
  responsibility to help pay the bill.
- Rely on conditions attached to federal grants. Some members of the
  Commission believe that in return for accepting federal funds states
  should be required to adopt a limited number of critical reforms.
- Rely more heavily on federal requirements. Some members of the Commission believe that with respect to some critical reforms, greater
  uniformity and certainty are needed. Yet the day-to-day field work of
  election administration will remain at more local levels.
- Defer the hard choices to federal administrative rulemaking. This
  view would announce broad goals but leave the exact specification of
  conditions for federal assistance to be developed by the responsible
  federal agency in a rulemaking process. We believe that, if there are to
  be conditions, they should be clear, general, and imposed directly by
  Congress.

We therefore have struck a careful balance among mandates, conditional assistance, and voluntary standards.

POLICY RECOMMENDATION

Congress should enact legislation that includes federal assistance for election administration, setting forth policy objectives for the states while leaving the choice of strategies to the discretion of the states. The Commission as a whole takes no position on whether Congress should use the powerful incentive of conditional grants or instead establish requirements or mandates wholly independent of funding. A majority of the Commission members suggests the approach described below. However, a minority suggests a more direct federal role as detailed in an additional statement of views appended to this report.

1. Congress should enact legislation to create a new federal election administration agency, to facilitate military and overseas citizen voting, to address a national election holiday, to constrain—if necessary—premature official disclosure of presidential election results, and to appropriate federal assistance in election administration.
2. To be eligible for federal assistance, states shall:
   a. match the federal assistance with an added contribution of their own in the proportion fixed by Congress;
   b. adopt legislation that will establish a statewide voter registration system networked to every local jurisdiction in that state, with provisions for sharing data with other states;
   c. permit on-site provisional voting by every voter who claims to be qualified to vote in that state, or adopt an alternative that achieves the same objective;
   d. set a uniform statewide benchmark for voting system performance in each local jurisdiction administering elections expressed as a percentage of residual vote in the contest at the top of the ballot, and require local jurisdictions to report data relevant to this benchmark;
   e. either agree to comply with the federal voting system standards and certification processes or develop their own state voting system standards and processes that, at a minimum:
      i. give voters the opportunity to correct errors, either within the voting equipment itself or in the operational guidelines to administrators for using the equipment at a precinct or other polling place and
      ii. require that new voting systems should provide a practical and effective means for voters with physical disabilities to cast a secret ballot; and

    f. adopt uniform statewide standards that define what will constitute a vote on each category of voting equipment certified for use in that state;

    g. certify that they are in compliance with existing federal voting rights statutes.

3. Specific choices on how to comply with these conditions should be left to the discretion of the states.

4. States that qualify for federal assistance should have broad discretion in how they disburse this money, so long as the money is expended on: a) establishing and maintaining accurate lists of eligible voters; b) encouraging eligible voters to vote; c) improving verification of voter identification at the polling place; d) improving equipment and methods for casting and counting votes; e) recruiting and training election officials and poll workers; f) improving the quantity and quality of available polling places; and g) educating voters about their rights and responsibilities.

In most of our policy recommendations, we have suggested specifics for possible policy design. But we have deliberately set conditions on assistance that are general, not detailed. The federal legislation should give states room to adapt to local circumstance, remaining open to managerial and technical possibilities that future developments and experience may suggest.

ENDNOTES TO THE
REPORT

1. The data are from the American National Election Studies for 1996 and 2000, with interviews completed in November and December of the election year, along with the Comparative Study of Electoral Systems. For more details, see the Background Papers prepared for this Commission by its Task Force on the Federal Election System.
2. Joseph P. Harris, *Election Administration in the United States* (Washington, DC: Brookings Institution, 1934), p. 1.
3. *Cook v. Gralike*, 531 U.S. 510 (2001).
4. Alexander Hamilton, Federalist No. 59 [1788], in *The Federalist Papers*, ed. Clinton Rossiter (New York: Penguin, 1961), pp. 362–63.
5. The major cases are *Ex Parte Siebold*, 100 U.S. 371 (1879); *Ex Parte Yarbrough*, 110 U.S. 651 (1884); *Smiley v. Holm*, 285 U.S. 355 (1932); *United States v. Classic*, 313 U.S. 299 (1941); and *Foster v. Love*, 522 U.S. 67 (1997). For a fuller discussion, see the Background Papers prepared for this Commission by its Task Force on Legal and Constitutional Issues; see also U.S. General Accounting Office, *Elections: The Scope of Congressional Authority in Election Administration*, GAO-01-470 (Washington, DC: GAO, 2001).
6. On the limits of state power over federal elections see, most recently, *Cook v. Gralike*, 531 U.S. 510 (2001). In *Foster v. Love* the Supreme Court considered it settled that Congress could override state regulations, if it wished, "by establishing uniform rules for federal elections, binding on the States." 522 U.S. at 69.
7. Michigan, California, and Illinois, among other states, refused at first to comply with the NVRA. Their refusals were struck down in *ACORN v. Miller*, 129 F.3d 833 (6th Cir. 1997); *Voting Rights Coalition v. Wilson*, 60 F.3d 1411 (9th Cir. 1995), *cert. denied*, 516 U.S. 1093 (1996); and *ACORN v. Edgar*, 56 F.3d 791 (7th Cir. 1995).

8. *Bush* v. *Gore*, 125 S.Ct. 525, 529 (2000). The landmark cases establishing congressional authority to legislate on state as well as federal voting practices using the authority of the 14th and 15th Amendments were *South Carolina* v. *Katzenbach*, 383 U.S. 301 (1966) and *Katzenbach* v. *Morgan*, 384 U.S. 641 (1966). Again, for a fuller discussion see the Background Papers prepared for this Commission by its Task Force on Legal and Constitutional Issues.

9. Current calls to amend the Electoral College system mainly argue that it does not adequately mirror the population or the popular vote. For an articulate presentation of the critique, see the testimony of Stanford University historian Jack Rakove to the Commission in the transcript of its March 26 hearing in Atlanta.

10. Recognizing this point, a group of smaller states actually attempted to bring a case contesting the constitutionality of the Electoral College, but the Supreme Court held that it did not have jurisdiction to hear such a complaint. *Delaware* v. *New York*, 385 U.S. 895 (1966).

11. The compromise was crafted late in the Convention by Pierce Butler, one of South Carolina's delegates. For a concise summary see Forrest McDonald, *The American Presidency: An Intellectual History* (Lawrence: University Press of Kansas, 1994), pp. 160–91.

12. Federalist No. 39, in *The Federalist Papers*, Rossiter ed., p. 244; see also Hamilton's comments in Federalist No. 68.

13. Political professionals hire private firms to produce winnowed voter lists so that, unlike governments, they do not waste money trying to contact nonexistent voters. According to information supplied to the Commission, these private lists tend to show that an average of 16% of the names on all state rolls are "deadwood."

14. Vote fraud is difficult to discover and prosecute. But, for illustrations of ghost voting and "repeater"schemes, see *United States* v. *Olinger*, 759 F.2d 1293 (7th Cir.), *cert. denied*, 474 U.S. 839 (1985); *United States* v. *Morado*, 454 F.2d 167 (5th Cir.), *cert. denied*, 406 U.S. 917 (1972). For an example of how ballot box stuffing is done with absentee ballots, see *United States* v. *Boards*, 10 F.3d 587 (8th Cir. 1993). For the closely related practice of "nursing home" fraud (obtaining and voting the ballots of mentally incompetent individuals), see *United States* v. *Odom*, 736 F.2d 104 (4th Cir. 1984).

15. The Qualifications Clause of Article I states that "the Electors in each state [for congressional elections] shall have the Qualifications requisite for Electors of the most numerous branch of the State Legislature."

16. The main effect of the power shift was to lower the barriers to voting that had been erected by many cities. "Almost everywhere, between 1790 and the 1850s, state suffrage laws and municipal suffrage laws became identical. Behind this convergence were two important, and related, shifts in law. The first was the early nineteenth-century deterioration and then collapse of the notion that municipal charters were inviolable. The second was the ascent of

a broad concept of state supremacy, the idea that municipalities legally ought to be regarded as administrative creatures of the state, rather than as separate sovereignties of any type. . . . One of its implications was that state legislatures could set the franchise in municipal elections and compel cities and towns to adopt the same suffrage provisions as the state." Alexander Keyssar, *The Right to Vote: The Contested History of Democracy in the United States* (New York: Basic Books, 2000), p. 31.

17. Some other countries, notably Canada, chose systems early in the 20th century that do not rely on voters to initiate registration. Instead the federal government registers voters as part of a nationwide census. Beyond that, however, Canada's successful list maintenance practices are analogous to those recently adopted in Michigan, and discussed below.

18. For the most recent report on population mobility, see U.S. Census Bureau (Jason Schachter), "Geographical Mobility: March 1999 to March 2000," Current Population Reports P20-538, May 2001. The data are reaffirmed by responses on residential duration in separate studies of voting behavior conducted as part of the Census Bureau's Current Population Surveys after the 1996 and 1998 elections.

19. More information on the various voter registration systems is collected and can be found in the Background Papers prepared for this Commission by its Task Force on the Federal Election System. The National Conference of State Legislatures (NCSL) is also an invaluable source of up-to-date information on practices and pending legislation in the different states. On the problem of agency data exchange see also the idea of developing a common Election Markup Language discussed in note 20.

20. State governments are also better positioned to solve the sometimes difficult problems that have arisen in trying to exchange accurate data on deaths, felony convictions, and the like within a state. It is promising that the international Organization for the Advancement of Structured Information Standards (OASIS), which creates industry specifications for structured information processing, has formed an Election and Voter Services Technical Committee to develop Election Markup Language (EML), based on XML (extensible markup languages). Such an innovation will facilitate interchange of data among the agencies with information relevant to voter eligibility. Establishment of an open industry standard, independent of any particular vendor, will help states modernize their systems more effectively at a lower cost and lower the barriers of entry to possible software developers.

21. For more details on state identification practices, see the Background Papers prepared for this Commission by its Task Force on the Federal Election System.

22. According to Michigan officials it cost seven and a half million dollars to develop their system. That figure includes hardware and software for the local jurisdictions, building a network, and building the street index (which the state

now also uses for many other useful tasks). Because the local offices are not tethered to the state in a traditional Internet network, there was a higher cost in providing the 400 counties with the necessary hardware. It was also necessary to build a special server for Detroit. The system cost the state only $1.5 million a year in operating expenditures. The system opens up new opportunities. Michigan is now working on an online database where voters can check their information, use a mapping program to get directions to the polling place, and even take a virtual tour of the polling place and its machines.

23. The Privacy Act prohibits most states from requiring voter applicants to provide a full SSN. It does not keep states from requesting that voters provide this information (which may be in the voter's own interest) and it does not preclude either a request or a requirement that applicants provide the last four digits of the SSN. Michigan does not need to request any SSN data because it uses the individual's driver's license number, which is different from the SSN, as a separate numeric identifier.

24. Some evidence was presented on this problem in the state and congressional investigations of the contested 1996 election in California's 46th Congressional District in which Loretta Sanchez defeated Robert Dornan by 984 votes. Both investigations concluded that the number of verifiably illegal votes was fewer than 984; hence Congresswoman Sanchez retained her seat. She defeated Dornan by more than 14,000 votes in a 1998 rematch. The evidence indicated that, just in Orange County, about a thousand prospective jurors whose names were drawn from the voter list are excused from jury service every year because they are not citizens. The evidence also included records seized from an immigrant advocacy organization showing that 61% of the voters this organization had registered were aliens. More than 300 of these new Orange County voters had voted in the contested election.

25. Political professionals also believe that some unofficial deputy registrars solicit registration applications and then discard those which have come in from voters whom they think will not support their party or candidate. This is illegal, of course.

26. States that experience disfranchisement caused by the negligence or misconduct of unofficial third-party voter registrars should be able to establish a system for licensure of deputy registrars, analogous to the licensure and accountability of notaries public. Any private individual qualified to register voters under NVRA should be able to receive a license as a deputy registrar. Such a license could be revoked on proof to the local election supervisor of negligent performance or other specified misconduct. If necessary to permit states to consider this option, Congress should amend the NVRA.

27. See Federal Election Commission, *Implementing the National Voter Registration Act of 1993: Requirements, Issues, Approaches, and Examples* (1994), Chapter Six. None of these problems apply in the same way to the six states that allow voters just to register on election day at the polling place or have no

registration of voters at all. These states, to which the NVRA does not apply, are Idaho, Minnesota, New Hampshire, North Dakota, Wisconsin, and Wyoming.

28. Michigan utilizes a version of this alternative, requiring photo identification as well as an affidavit, and then issuing a regular ballot. Illinois uses an analogous yet less satisfactory alternative, in which the voter executes an affidavit of eligibility, in some cases with a supporting affidavit, but no photo ID is required and, lacking a statewide registration system, the voter list may not be corrected.

29. For more detail, see the discussions of this issue in both the Background Paper prepared for this Commission by the Task Force on the Federal Election System and the Background Paper prepared by the Task Force on Legal and Constitutional Issues.

30. It is possible that, as electronic voting technology evolves, voting machines may be able to display the appropriate ballot for the local jurisdiction where the voter is registered, regardless of where in the state the voter chooses to cast that ballot.

31. A useful summary of the scholarship is Michael W. Traugott, "Why Electoral Reform Has Failed: If You Build It, Will They Come?," in *After 2000: The Politics of Election Reform*, ed. Ann N. Crigler and Marion R. Just (forthcoming).

32. On the relative significance of the ADA requirements, see the discussion of this law in the Background Papers prepared for this Commission by its Task Force on Legal and Constitutional Issues.

33. Some local jurisdictions are reluctant to use schools as polling places while school is in session. Some officials, usually privately, cite concerns about the security and liability issues presented when large numbers of adults shuttle in and out of areas being used by schoolchildren.

34. Holidays could be very costly to hourly workers who lack benefits that include paid holidays. But many of these workers are in retail and service jobs and will be asked to help keep these businesses open on the holiday anyway. Depending on their employment agreements, employers may be obliged to shoulder the extra cost of paying them overtime.

35. In 1968 Veterans Day was moved to the 4th Monday of October. In 1975 it was moved back to November 11. 5 U.S.C. § 6103. The United States also sets aside Memorial Day to honor those who sacrificed their lives in the nation's wars. This holiday originated after the Civil War, when May 30 was designated for honoring the graves of the war dead. Most states now conform to the federal practice, adopted in 1971, of observing the holiday on the last Monday of May.

36. 2 U.S.C. §§ 1, 7.

37. Testimony of David Walker, Comptroller General of the United States, before the House Armed Services Committee, May 9, 2001.

38. Under Executive Order 12642 (1988), the Secretary of Defense is the agent responsible for implementing UOCAVA and handling the federal responsibili-

ties under that Act. The Director of the Federal Voting Assistance Program administers this program for the Secretary of Defense.

39. Military personnel should not lose their residency in a state if they are living elsewhere under orders, regardless of whether the person intends to return to that state.

40. States should permit provisional voting, and the effective waiver of a prior registration deadline (such as 30 days), if the service member (or relative) has recently moved through separation from the service 60 days or less before the election.

41. The weight of the evidence leans toward a conclusion that early voting and vote-by-mail have slightly increased turnout among committed partisan voters or in low interest local elections. Unrestricted absentee voting probably has not increased turnout at all. See the Background Papers prepared for this Commission by its Task Force on the Federal Election System.

42. "The Congress may determine the Time of chusing the Electors, and the Day on which they shall give their Votes; which Day shall be the same throughout the United States." Article II, Section 1.

43. For recent illustrations, see *United States* v. *Cole,* 41 F.3d 303 (7th Cir. 1994); and *United States* v. *Salisbury,* 983 F.2d 1369 (6th Cir. 1993).

44. See, for example, the testimony of David Jefferson, chair of the California Secretary of State's Internet Voting Task Force, in the transcript of the Commission hearing in Simi Valley, California, on April 12.

45. To trace the evolution of laws disfranchising criminals between 1790 and 1920, see Tables A.7 and A.15 in Keyssar, *The Right to Vote.* On current practice, see ibid., pp. 302–03, and the Background Paper of this Commission's Task Force on the Federal Election System.

46. The Supreme Court case was *Richardson* v. *Ramirez,* 418 U.S. 24 (1974). For further discussion, see the Background Paper of this Commission's Task Force on Legal and Constitutional Issues.

47. In one experimental study, 15% of the voters committed errors in casting their ballots. Poor ballot design and punch-card voting technology appeared to be the source of many of the errors. Susan King Roth, "Disenfranchised by Design: Voting Systems and the Election Process," *Information Design Journal,* vol. 9 (1998).

48. This point was made to us by representatives from the Committee on Communications and Information Policy of the Institute of Electrical and Electronics Engineers (IEEE).

49. Nixon won his home state of California by less than 1%. But Kennedy won Hawaii, Illinois, Missouri, New Jersey, and New Mexico by this thin margin (with 63 total electoral votes in an election where his margin of electoral victory was 33).

50. They were Iowa, New Mexico, Oregon, and Wisconsin—all of which were carried by Gore, thus making Florida so pivotal for Bush.

51. The data are from the helpful Caltech/MIT Voting Technology Project, "Residual Votes Attributable to Technology: An Assessment of the Reliability of Existing Voting Equipment," Version 2, March 30, 2001. The data do not distinguish between the voting equipment used at polling places and the voting equipment used in counties for absentee ballots.

52. Using relatively reliable data for all of California from the Secretary of State's office and the University of California's Statewide Database, Henry Brady and Gray Chynoweth (in an informal report provided to the Commission) found a mean spoiled vote of only 0.85% for communities using the Datavote punch card system, while the Votomatic-style systems had spoiled vote rates of 1.83% (Pollstar), 2.36% (Votomatic), and 2.23% (mix of Votomatic and Pollstar).

53. For more detail on the varieties and issues related to the different technologies, see the initial report of the Caltech/MIT Voting Technology Project, *Voting: What Is, What Could Be,* July 2001.

54. Stephen Knack and Martha Kropf, "Roll Off at the Top of the Ballot: Intentional Undervoting in American Presidential Elections," April 2001 (unpublished manuscript made available to the Commission).

55. On Detroit, see "Technology Slashes Detroit Voting Error," *Washington Post,* April 5, 2001; the broader study of underlying residual vote is the Caltech/MIT report, "Residual Votes Attributable to Technology." That study concludes, in essence, that new machines in counties should be expected to have no more residual votes than they had experienced in recent elections with their older lever machines. This equated to "a performance standard in practice—an average residual vote *not in excess* of 2 percent of total ballots cast" (emphasis added).

56. Data provided by the Caltech/MIT Voting Technology Project, gathered from state election sources.

57. Harris County decided in 2001 to change its voting system from punch cards to a DRE electronic model.

58. Report of the Election Center's Task Force on Election Reform (2001).

59. For an explanation of how these alternatives can work, see sections 81.56 and 81.57 of the Texas Administrative Code (2000).

60. In this context, we mean *objective* both in the sense of a physical fact that exists regardless of anyone's attitude about it, and *objective* in the sense that— to the maximum extent possible—the judgment of what physical markings constitutes a vote should not depend on the stance, feelings, or opinions of the individual observers. See generally John R. Searle, *The Construction of Social Reality* (New York: Free Press, 1995), p. 66.

61. Section 42 of the Florida Election Reform Act of 2001, adding new subsection (5) to section 102.166 of the Florida Statutes.

62. On the variety of state schemes, see the paper on "Recounts and Contests" prepared for this Commission by its Task Force on Legal and Constitutional

Issues. On the desirability of some standardization across states, see the report of the Subcommittee on Governance and Administration in the Report of the Election Center's Task Force on Election Reform (2001).

63. See 3 U.S.C. § 5 and *Bush* v. *Palm Beach County Canvassing Bd.*, 121 S.Ct. 471, 474 (2000).

64. Our recommendation does not adequately address the concerns of the 0.6% of the voting age population that lives in Alaska and Hawaii, where the polls close another two hours later. But it would allow presidential election results to be reported on Election Night while adding to the integrity of the election process for the 52.4% of the electorate who live in the Central, Mountain, and Pacific time zones.

65. See the transcribed testimony of Ernest Hawkins, Clerk and Registrar of Sacramento County, California, at the Commission's June 7 hearing in Ann Arbor, Michigan.

66. The June 2001 report of the Governor of New York's bipartisan election modernization task force has recommended state capitalization of such a fund in that state, to be called an "Election Modernization Fund," with an initial investment of $25 million.

67. A successful precedent is the State Revolving Fund administered by the Environmental Protection Agency. Created by the 1987 Amendments to the Clean Water Act, this system effectively replaced a long-running but often unsatisfactory federal grants-in-aid program.

ADDITIONAL STATEMENT

CONCURRING IN PART AND DISSENTING IN PART BY
Christopher Edley

JOINED BY
*Leon Panetta, Deval Patrick, Bill Richardson,
John Seigenthaler,* AND *Kathleen Sullivan*

Federal Requirements and Enforcement

The quality of our democracy's infrastructure should not depend on class or color, on party or precinct. "One person, one vote" is not a principle for local officials to trade off against potholes or jails, nor should it be conditioned on the willingness of Congress to appropriate an incentive in any given budget cycle. Finally, Congress is honor bound—perhaps in this field as in no other—to ensure that the promises it makes through law to the American people will indeed be kept. For these reasons we must offer additional views on the Commission's recommendations and report.

The Commission majority declined to endorse a limited number of specific federal requirements for the administration of elections for federal office, trusting that the states will adopt vital reforms to fulfill conditions, or as quid pro quo, for receiving new federal grants. While we largely agree with the policy goals adopted by the Commission for federal legislation, certain reforms are fundamental enough to stand on their own as requirements, independent of any federal largesse.

We have several concerns with the incentive or "conditionality" approach. First, will the carrot be enticing enough? Even if Congress passes legislation to authorize a grant program, Congress may, after another bruising political battle, decline to appropriate the money, or enough of it. As the memory of 2000 fades, election financing could easily become just another game piece in the perennial battle over taxes and spending. Then some states may decline to take the bribe out of reluctance to pay the required 50-50 match, or because the federal funding may be too little to dissolve objections to all the strings and inevitable regulations. Second, if a state breaks or bends the conditions, experience teaches that the federal government will only slowly initiate enforcement and almost never press all the way to a meaningful sanction, like cutting off funds or seeking a court injunction. Third, if the funding will be limited in time, as the Commission proposes, then so will the conditions and the rights the legislation purports to ensure.

Our fourth and final concern is the most important. With the experiences of November 2000 fresh in mind, many Americans consider election reform a moral imperative because confidence in the fairness of our democracy must be made as deep and widespread as possible. At their core, these reforms are intended to vindicate our civil and constitutional rights. They are too fundamental to be framed as some intergovernmental fiscal deal, bargained out through an appropriations process.

What requirements should Congress insist upon, regardless of funds granted? We suggest at least the following, drawn from the Commission's recommendations to state officials:

1. **Residual votes or "spoiled" ballots.** Voting technologies and administrative practices should produce low rates of uncounted ballots, as the Commission argues in its Recommendation 6 and Chapter V. The right to vote means little if there is no right to have your vote counted. Therefore, at least for federal offices, Congress or the new agency should establish a maximum level of spoiled ballots considered acceptable, including overvotes and an estimate of unintended undervotes. Each state should be required to pick and achieve a benchmark, applicable in every precinct, no greater than the federal maximum. By federal law, states should be required to make every effort to make every vote count.

2. **Statewide provisional voting.** No voter who believes he or she is registered in the state should be denied a ballot at the polling place. Federal law should require all polling places to offer a provisional ballot to any voter who believes he or she is registered in that jurisdiction. Election officials should adopt procedures to count such ballots, after confirming the voter's registration status, before they certify the vote count. This requirement should be implemented regardless of whether a state has developed a statewide voter registration list, although that would make implementation easier.[1]

---

1. The National Voter Registration Act, or "Motor Voter," already mandates a "failsafe" balloting procedure as a protection against erroneous purging of registra-

3. **Accessibility.** Congress should insist that states purchase and use voting technologies that are accessible to voters with disabilities, that are readily adaptable to non-English speakers, and that permit all voters, including those who are illiterate or visually impaired, to cast a secret ballot.[2]

4. **Basic voter information.** Every jurisdiction should provide every voter, in advance of the election, a sample ballot and basic information about voting procedures. This should include an understandable description of rights and responsibilities, and of how to make a complaint. (The Voting Rights Act already requires that whenever a jurisdiction subject to the act's language provision distributes sample ballots or other information, it must do so in all languages necessary for compliance.)

In elections for the Senate and House of Representatives, the Constitution provides Congress full authority to demand that these goals be honored. The Framers recognized the practical need to rely on local administration and state oversight. But they assigned ultimate authority in such matters to Congress because they foresaw dangers in leaving the mechanisms of national governance utterly at the mercy of state politics and peculiarities. The recent election should have made clear to everyone that the basic fairness and effectiveness of federal elections should not be left to local accident or parochial preference. Furthermore, the Supreme Court's reasoning in *Bush* v. *Gore* suggests that there may be a compelling interest and constitutional authority for the Congress to impose certain

---

tion lists. It is focused on problems of disputed changes of address, and applies only to voters who move within a county. It is burdensome to the voter and has not proven very workable. The Commission's proposal, Recommendation 2, is broader.

2. The 1975 amendments to the 1965 Voting Rights Act include certain protections for non-English speaking voters in counties above a population trigger. (Congress extended those provisions in 1982 for a period of ten years and in 1992 for fifteen years). Reports of jurisdictions failing to carry out the necessary procedures for complying with these provisions are widespread, and whether this is a matter of intent or negligence is unclear. However, in addition to enforcement difficulties, current law does not require technologies that will allow a secret ballot for voters needing assistance because they are illiterate or visually impaired. Nor is a secret ballot required by the Voting Accessibility for the Elderly and the Handicapped Act. In practice, jurisdictions often comply with current law by forcing voters with disabilities to use absentee ballots.

requirements for non-federal elections as well, lest a state deny its residents the equal protection of the laws by having materially inferior elections systems for some voters or communities in comparison with others. Nevertheless, we recommend only that the legislation formally apply these requirements to elections for Congress, putting this urgent legislation beyond constitutional dispute. As a practical matter, of course, states will likely adopt the same processes and technology for their votes on presidential electors and on state and local matters.

Some will view these federal requirements as a heavy-handed imposition on state and local governments, but we believe they represent a limited and respectful assertion of Congress's responsibility under the Constitution to safeguard the election of federal officeholders, and a measured corrective for all too commonplace violations of the most fundamental of civil rights.

The Commission's Recommendation 8, calling for intensified efforts to enforce existing antidiscrimination statutes, is important. Combined with the new obligation that states certify their compliance with those laws (see Recommendation 13), the Report gives much-needed voice to legitimate frustrations felt by many. Congress made promises in the 1965 Voting Rights Act, and extended those promises in a series of statutes over the decades. Yet, after all these years, violations continue.

This leaves us all with a difficult but deeply important question: What is wrong with current laws that has made it possible for so many violations to continue, and why should our citizens feel confident that this time the promises Congress makes will be kept? What, in actual practice, will make the new promises truly enforceable?

No laws have perfect compliance. We take the Commission's report and the Commission's very existence, however, to mean we all agree more needs to be done. It is no answer to say that the U.S. Department of Justice (DOJ) will try harder, because it is inconceivable that any plausible increase in appropriations will give DOJ the resources to do its job at an acceptable level relative to the need. Surely the decades have taught us that. Therefore, we urge Congress to consider a range of possibilities for new legislation, including:

1. ensure that private individuals, not just DOJ, can bring private actions to enforce all relevant voting rights and antidiscrimination laws with the absolute minimum of technical legal barriers, such as restrictions

(other than any required by the Constitution) on who may bring suits, on class actions, and on remedies;

2. reverse the judicial misinterpretations of earlier statutes whereby courts have imposed restrictions on attorneys' fees, making it more difficult for aggrieved voters to find capable lawyers and experts;

3. provide grants to state attorneys general to support new efforts on their part to enforce antidiscrimination laws in registration and voting; and

4. provide grants to community-based organizations to investigate and if necessary litigate, as the Department of Housing and Urban Development has long done, to support fair housing and combat housing discrimination.

The Commission's report points the way forward with many sound recommendations and much useful analysis. Strong legislation is vitally important now because many of our citizens feel their confidence in our election system at a low ebb. America's challenges and America's increasing diversity should make us redouble our efforts to include people in the basic process of democracy. We cannot do that in the face of news accounts of precincts where 20 percent of ballots are not counted in an excruciatingly close presidential election. We cannot do it when voters are turned away because their names are inexplicably missing from some computer printout and the phone lines to county offices are busy for hours on end. We cannot do it when citizens with poor eyesight cannot track the columns of complex ballots, when citizens with disabilities are faced with barriers or humiliation, or when proud new citizens are made to feel second class in their own, new land.

ADDITIONAL STATEMENT

CONCURRING BY
Colleen C. McAndrews

JOINED BY
Slade Gorton AND *Leon Panetta*

W e in the West have experienced firsthand the effects of premature network election projections on voter turnout in down ballot races as
well as the presidential race. Respect for the First Amendment, shared by
all Commissioners, caused caution in our recommendations to Congress to
address this controversial practice. No unanimity was achieved for a radi-
cal approach such as federal legislation to ban outright early projections
until such time as the polls had closed in all the contiguous 48 states.

We do not urge this approach immediately. We support the Commission's incremental steps as set forth in Policy Recommendation 10. We also
are wary of First Amendment challenges if an outright ban on network
projections were attempted.

However, we wish to bring to the attention of Congress a line of legal
reasoning that holds that a carefully crafted direct ban might withstand
constitutional challenge. The Supreme Court has recognized some limitations on free speech in connection with elections in a line of cases culmi-
nating in *Burson* v. *Freeman,* 504 U.S. 191 (1992), which upheld a zone
free of campaigning and electioneering within 100 feet of a polling place.
The Court held that this intrusion on free speech was narrowly tailored to
serve a compelling government interest in preventing intimidation and election fraud. The Court grappled with "a particularly difficult reconciliation:
that accommodation of the right to engage in political discourse with
the right to vote—a right at the heart of our democracy." Id. at 198. The
Court cited earlier cases in which it "upheld generally applicable and
evenhanded restrictions that protect the integrity and reliability of the elec-

toral process itself," and found these to be "indisputable compelling interests." Id. at 191 (citing to *Anderson v. Celebrezze,* 460 U.S. 780, 788, n.9 (1983); *Eu v. San Francisco Cty. Democratic Central Comm.,* 489 U.S. 214, 228–229 (1989)).

If the broadcast media are merely delayed for a short period of time (no more than three hours) from projecting election results, it may be that the courts would agree that such restrictions on the networks' speech from 8 p.m. EST to 8 p.m. PST is outweighed by the need to protect the integrity of federal elections. These limits do not involve discourse on issues or limitations on particular viewpoints but only a practical delay of the announcement of the aftermath of the campaign, the networks' educated guessing about who won or lost the horse race.

The polling place campaign-free zone in *Burson* passed the Court's test of strict scrutiny by comparing the exercise of free speech rights with another fundamental right, the right to cast a ballot in an election free from intimidation. Id. at 211. Perhaps the Court would view the early projections of a presidential race as intimidation or suppression of West Coast voters who believe their votes no longer count.

ADDITIONAL STATEMENT

CONCURRING IN PART AND DISSENTING IN PART BY
John Seigenthaler

JOINED IN PART BY
Griffin Bell

On Point 2 of Policy Recommendation 10. The Commission's proposal for a law is wrongheaded and unrealistic. I dissent on three grounds. First, local election officials certainly have a First Amendment right to engage in political speech—and discussing election results clearly is political speech. I cannot believe that the Congress should or would seek to make a law that gags local officials from giving citizens and the news media—in their communities or in their state—presidential or Congressional election returns the moment they are available. Second, such a law, if enacted, surely would result in news media lawsuits challenging government action to directly and blatantly interfere with the First Amendment right of journalists to gather and report the news when it is news.

The legal theory on which some of my colleagues rely ignores the constitutional protection a free press enjoys to report without government interference news of great moment. They know it is a stretch. Their well-intended effort to protect West Coast voters from early presidential election projections is a bluff that the news media will call. It is a wasted effort.

Finally, the First Amendment aside, the bluff won't work. It is impractical and unrealistic. The relationship between local election officials at the precincts, and at places where votes are counted and reported, is long-standing and mutually beneficial. Elected and appointed local election officials feel a duty to get returns to the public—their constituents who elect them and pay their salaries—at the earliest possible moment on election night. Members of the news media are their allies in fulfilling this duty. In many polling and vote-counting places news media representatives serve dual journalistic roles: they collect the returns and report them to their news organizations, and also serve as monitors on the integrity of the process.

The Commission is proposing a law that will never be enforceable. Election officials will be working to let voters—again, their constituents—know the outcome of races for governor, mayor, state legislator, and city council seats, etc. At the same time the Commission would gag them from reporting who won the congressional seat in their district and the U.S. Senate race in their state. They will be pressured by voters to release that information as soon as possible and to let local citizens know, as well, how their state and congressional districts voted in the presidential election. This stratagem won't intimidate the news media. The Commission should not pretend that this is a serious recommendation.

At the same time, the news media's reliance on exit polling is seriously flawed, as the Commission accurately states. Only about half the voters asked to participate at polling places now agree to do so. That percentage is too low to assure exit poll reliability. Only twenty percent of absentee and early voters agree to participate in telephone "exit" poll interviews. If the Commission wishes to halt early network projections in the presidential race, based on exit polls, it should urge Secretaries of State, political parties, and civic groups sharing that concern to engage in voter education programs advising citizens that they contribute to possible election night chaos by participating in exit polling, either in person or by telephone.

On Point 4 of Policy Recommendation 10. I concur. This would be a great public service by the networks. They should voluntarily provide the time. The Commission is indebted to President Carter for urging the Commission to adopt it. I would oppose a law requiring the networks to provide time as violating the First Amendment.

Griffin Bell does not join in the following portion of John Seigenthaler's statement.

On Point 1 of Policy Recommendation 11. We are seeking to reform a serious ill in the most basic aspect of self-governance. The vitality and credibility of our democracy is at risk. Our funding proposal should be described as "adequate," not "modest." We can only hope that the $2 billion we recommend (hardly a modest sum) is sufficient to restore faith in the system.

On Policy Recommendation 13. The Commission recommends the establishment of a new federal agency that will provide grants and oversight to states receiving this $2 billion in funding. The federal dollars are to be matched by the states. Our recommendation falls far short of requiring strict accountability as to how the funding is expended. Nothing in our policy recommendation here bars, for example, states and local governments from diverting funds simply to defray costs created by the federal government's mandating Motor-Voter registration; nothing requires ongoing reporting statements from local and state election officials receiving money; nothing requires any prioritization of state reform efforts. Indeed, Part 4 of this policy recommendation "grants broad discretion to the states" with no suggestion that there will be strict accountability. If we are to ask Congress to give states $2 billion in federal money, to restore trust in the system, taxpayers are entitled to know that the new federal agency will demand accountability on every dollar spent. The fuzzy nature of this policy recommendation will invite abuse, diversion of funds, partisan favoritism, and the risk of fraud. Not a word here suggests what sanctions will result if states fail to keep faith with the spirit of reform. And nothing gives the new agency the needed power to enforce the law we ask Congress to pass.

The Electoral College Controversy. From the outset, members of our Commission agreed that we would not wade into this constitutional quagmire. The Commission's commentary in this section violates our agreement. In effect, it states the Founders got it right at the Constitutional Convention by creating the Electoral College. For all their wisdom and vision, the Founders got it wrong in the convention by ignoring George Mason's plea for a Bill of Rights and by creating a chaotic situation as to the selection of a vice president. Within a decade, both of those flaws of the Founders were corrected. Public opinion polls tell us that a majority thinks the Founders got it wrong with the Electoral College. In my view, the Commission should not have so obviously taken sides on a matter we agreed to avoid.

On Motor-Voter Registration. The majority of the Commission agreed to leave this issue without critical comment. Readers certainly will find the commentary here as negative comment on this subject. In fact, Motor-Voter registration has added many thousands of legitimate, qualified voters to the rolls. We should acknowledge that the complaint that Motor-Voter registration has added millions of dollars in "unnecessary costs" comes, for the most part, from local governments unhappy that Congress mandated the Motor-Voter system without funding it. We should acknowledge that Motor-Voter registration has brought significantly more citizens into the system.

On Early Voting. The Commission did not look with favor on a policy recommendation that restricts early voting now effective in fourteen states. Nor did we take a position against relatively new and more permissive absentee voting procedures. Our rhetoric suggests that we are opposed to both early and absentee voting. Many states, including my own of Tennessee, report positive experiences with the early voting experiment. Nothing the Commission has heard from those states—or from Oregon, where in the last election all voters were "absentee"—justifies our statement that early voting "threatens the right to a secret ballot." In my view, we should commend efforts by local election officials who have sought to eliminate crowding and confusion at the polls on Election Day.

ABOUT THE
NATIONAL COMMISSION ON
FEDERAL ELECTION REFORM

The National Commission on Federal Election Reform was organized in early 2001 by the Miller Center of Public Affairs at the University of Virginia and The Century Foundation. The goal of the Commission is to formulate concrete proposals for election reform that will help ensure a more effective and fair democratic process in elections to come.

Presidents Jimmy Carter and Gerald Ford are honorary co-chairs of the Commission, and former White House Counsel Lloyd Cutler and former Senator Howard Baker initially served as co-chairmen. When Senator Baker was named Ambassador to Japan, former House Minority Leader Robert Michel assumed his position as co-chairman. The members of the Commission are:

Honorary Co-Chairs

President Gerald R. Ford served as the 38th President of the United States. In 1948 he was elected to the U.S. House of Representatives and was reelected twelve times by his district in Michigan.

President Jimmy Carter served as the 39th President of the United States. He served in the Georgia Senate and was elected governor of Georgia in 1971.

Co-Chairs

Robert H. Michel served in the United States House of Representatives as a congressman from Illinois from 1956 to 1994. He currently works as senior adviser for corporate and governmental affairs at the Washington, D.C., law firm of Hogan & Hartson.

Michel served as Republican House leader from 1980 to 1994 and also as minority whip from 1975 to 1980. He began his political career as administrative assistant to Congressman Harold Velde, also of Illinois, who held office from 1949 to 1956. Michel entered military service in 1942 as a private in the U.S. Army. He was discharged in 1946 as a disabled veteran after serving as combat infantryman in England, France, Belgium, and Germany, earning two Bronze Stars, a Purple Heart, and four Battle Stars.

Lloyd N. Cutler served as the White House counsel for Presidents Carter and Clinton and was special counsel to President Carter on the ratification of the SALT II Treaty. He is a founding partner of the Washington, D.C., law firm Wilmer, Cutler and Pickering and maintains an active practice in several fields that include international arbitration and dispute resolution, constitutional law, appellate advocacy, and public policy advice.

Cutler has served on numerous government commissions and committees. He served as senior consultant on the President's Commission on Strategic Forces (the Scowcroft Commission) from 1983 to 1984, and as the President's Special Representative for Maritime Resource and Boundary Negotiations with Canada from 1977 to 1979.

Vice-Chairs

Slade Gorton was a United States Senator from Washington state for eighteen years. Gorton began his political career in 1959 as a member of the Washington House of Representatives. He served in this capacity until 1969 and held the post of majority leader from 1967 to 1969.

Gorton was elected attorney general of Washington state in 1968. During his tenure, he argued fourteen cases before the Supreme Court. He held this position until 1981, when he was elected to the Senate. Gorton served in the United States Army and was in the Air Force Reserve with the rank of colonel from 1956 to 1981.

Kathleen M. Sullivan was named dean of the Stanford Law School in 1999 and is nationally known for her work in constitutional law. She began teaching at Harvard Law School in 1984 and has been a member of the Stanford faculty since 1993. Sullivan received her J.D. from Harvard in 1981 and then clerked for Judge James L. Oakes, U.S. Court of Appeals, Second Circuit, from 1981 to 1982. Sullivan practiced constitutional appellate law from 1982 to 1984.

She is co-author with Gerald Gunther of the 14th edition of *Constitutional Law,* the leading casebook in the field. Her other books include *First Amendment Law,* also with Gunther, and *New Federalist Papers: Essays in Defense of the Constitution.*

Commission Members

Griffin Bell was attorney general of the United States from 1977 to 1979. He is senior partner at the law firm of King & Spalding in Atlanta. In 1961, President Kennedy appointed him to serve as a United States circuit judge on the Fifth Circuit Court of Appeals, a position he held until 1976.

Following his tenure as attorney general, he returned to King & Spalding. A principal focus of his law practice in recent years has been corporate crime.

Bell has served on numerous government commissions and committees for both Democratic and Republican administrations. From 1985 to 1987, Judge Bell served on the U.S. secretary of state's Advisory Committee on South Africa, and in 1989, he was appointed vice chairman of President Bush's Commission on Federal Ethics Law Reform. During the Iran-Contra investigation, he was counsel to President Bush.

Rudy Boschwitz was a United States Senator from Minnesota from 1978 to 1991. In the Senate, he was a member of the Agriculture, Foreign Affairs, Budget, Small Business, and Veterans Committees. In 1991, he was President Bush's Emissary to Ethiopia, where he negotiated Operation Solomon—the airlift of the Ethiopian Jewish community to Israel—a project that in turn helped bring an end to the Ethiopian civil war. President Bush awarded him the Citizen's Medal for his achievements in the Horn of Africa. Senator Boschwitz is a businessman and is Chairman of Home Valu Interiors, Inc., a company he founded in 1963. The company retails remodeling materials for interiors of homes throughout the Middle West.

John C. Danforth was elected to the United States Senate from Missouri in 1976 and served until he retired from the Senate in 1994. Currently, he is a partner at the firm of Bryan Cave, LLP in St. Louis and practices in the areas of international real estate development, construction, and project finance.

Danforth began his career practicing law at the firm of Davis, Polk, Wardwell, Sunderland & Kiendl in New York. He returned to Missouri and joined the firm Bryan, Cave, McPheeters and McRoberts as a partner from 1966 to 1968. Danforth was elected to serve as attorney general of Missouri in 1969, a position he held until 1976. In 1999, he led the independent investigation into the federal government's actions during the 1993 siege of the Branch Davidian compound in Waco, Texas. Danforth is an ordained deacon and priest in the Episcopal Church.

Professor Christopher Edley Jr. has taught at Harvard Law School since 1981. He is the founding co-director of The Civil Rights Project at Harvard, a multidisciplinary think tank on racial justice policy and law, and a member of the U.S. Commission on Civil Rights. He was a domestic policy aide in the Carter White House, a part-time member of *The Washington Post* editorial board, vice chairman of the Congressional Black Caucus Foundation, and national issues director in the 1988 Dukakis presidential campaign. In the Clinton White House, he served as Associate Director for Economics and Government at the Office of Management and Budget, and then as Special Counsel to the President. He led the White House review of affirmative action, described in his book, *Not All Black & White: Affirmative Action, Race and American Values*. He is also the author of a treatise on administrative law.

Hanna Holborn Gray is President Emeritus of the University of Chicago. She is a specialist in the history of humanism, political and historical thought, and European history. She joined the history faculty at Chicago in 1961 and taught there until 1972, when she became dean of the College of Arts and Sciences at Northwestern University. In 1974, Gray was named provost of Yale University and was acting president there from 1977 to 1978, when she became president of the University of Chicago, a position she held for fifteen years. She is the chair of the board of trustees of the Howard Hughes Medical Institute, one of the nation's largest philanthropic organizations, as well as chair of the board of the Andrew W. Mellon Foundation.

Colleen C. McAndrews practices political and election law at the firm of Bell, McAndrews, Hiltachk & Davidian in California. She was appointed a commissioner on the California Fair Political Practices Commission in 1977, serving in that position for six years. McAndrews has served as legal counsel and treasurer to state and local political action committees, as well as candidates and ballot measure committees. She served as an official United States observer of the Russian elections in 1993. She also trained emerging political parties in Kazakhstan and the Kyrgyz Republic prior to their first democratic elections. She recently concluded service on the Speaker's Commission on the California Initiative.

Daniel Patrick Moynihan served as a United States senator from New York from 1977 to 2000. He is now at the Woodrow Wilson International Center in Washington, D.C. He served as U.S. ambassador to India from 1973 to 1975 and as U.S. representative to the United Nations from 1975 to 1976. In 1966, Moynihan became director of the Joint Center for Urban Studies at the Massachusetts Institute of Technology and Harvard University. He was also a professor of government at Harvard and other universities and has served in the Department of Labor. Prior to his service in the Senate, he was a member of Averell Harriman's staff in his campaign for governor of New York in 1954 and served on the governor's staff in Albany until 1958.

Leon Panetta currently codirects the Leon & Sylvia Panetta Institute for Public Policy, based at California State University, Monterey Bay. In 1993, President Clinton asked him to serve as director of the Office of Management and Budget, and in 1994, he was appointed White House chief of staff, a position he held until 1997.

Panetta won a seat in the U.S. House of Representatives in 1977 and served sixteen years. During this period, he served four years as chairman of the Budget Committee. He has worked as chief legislative aide to the minority whip of the U.S. Senate and then as director of the U.S. Office for Civil Rights. In 1971–72, he served as Executive Assistant to the Mayor of New York City. From 1971 to 1976, he practiced law at the firm of Panetta, Thompson and Panetta in Monterey, California.

Deval L. Patrick is executive vice president and general counsel of The Coca Cola Company. Prior to this he was vice president and general counsel of Texaco, Inc., where he had been since 1999. He served as assistant attorney general of the United States and chief of the U.S. Justice Department's Civil Rights Division from 1994 until 1998.

From 1983 to 1986, Patrick was a staff attorney with the NAACP Legal Defense Fund, following service as a law clerk on the U.S. Court of Appeals for the Ninth Circuit in Los Angeles. He also has taught at the Harvard School of Law and served as a visiting professor at the Stanford School of Law in 1997.

Diane Ravitch is a historian of American education and a Research Professor of Education at New York University. She holds the Brown Chair in Education Policy at the Brookings Institution, where she is a senior fellow and edits the Brookings Papers on Education Policy. From 1991 to 1993, she was assistant secretary of education, responsible for the Office of Educational Research and Improvement in the Department of Education.

She is a member of the National Assessment Governing Board, to which she was appointed by Secretary of Education Richard Riley in 1997 and reappointed in 2000. Before entering government service, she was adjunct professor of history and education at Teachers College, Columbia University.

Bill Richardson held the post of secretary of the Department of Energy beginning in 1998. Prior to this, Richardson served as U.S. ambassador to the United Nations from 1997 to 1998, where he focused his work especially on securing the release of hostages and prisoners in Croatia, Burma, Cuba, Iraq, North Korea, and Sudan. Richardson served New Mexico's 3rd Congressional District in the U.S. House of Representatives for eight terms. In Congress, he served as chief deputy whip, one of the highest ranking posts in the House Democratic leadership. He served as chairman of the Congressional Hispanic Caucus and on the Subcommittee on Native American Affairs. He also was a member of the Resources Committee, the Permanent Select Committee on Intelligence, and the Helsinki Commission on Human Rights.

John Seigenthaler is the founder of the First Amendment Center at Vanderbilt University. A former president of the American Society of Newspaper Editors, Seigenthaler served for forty-three years as a journalist for *The Tennessean* in Nashville, where he began as a cub reporter and retired as editor, publisher, and CEO. In 1982, Seigenthaler became founding editorial director of *USA Today* and served in that position for a decade, retiring from both the Nashville and national newspapers in 1991. He served in the U.S. Justice Department while Robert F. Kennedy was attorney general. Seigenthaler's work in the field of civil rights led to his service as chief negotiator with the governor of Alabama during the Freedom Rides.

Michael Steele is the first African-American chairman of Maryland's Republican Party. He works as a corporate securities attorney and is president of A Brighter Future Educational Foundation. Currently he serves on the Republican National Committee's Executive Committee and is also a member of the Prince George's County Chapter of the NAACP and the Johns Hopkins Society of Black Alumni. He is a former member of the Johns Hopkins University Board of Trustees and a current member of the Board of Directors of the Hospice of Prince George's County.

He has recently led successful bipartisan grassroots efforts in Prince George's County to maintain term limits and to retain the county's property tax cap and was a delegate to the 2000 Republican National Convention in Philadelphia.

Senior Staff of the Commission

Philip Zelikow, Executive Director of the Commission, is director of the Miller Center of Public Affairs and White Burkett Miller Professor of History at the University of Virginia. Initially a trial lawyer in Texas, he served as a career diplomat in the Department of State, and worked on the staff of the National Security Council in the George H. W. Bush White House. He was a professor at Harvard University's John F. Kennedy School of Government from 1991 until 1998.

John Mark Hansen, coordinator of the Task Force on the Federal Election System, is a professor of political science at the University of Chicago. As of the fall of 2001, he will be a professor of government at Harvard University.

David King, coordinator of the Task Force on Election Administration, is an associate professor of public policy at Harvard University's John F. Kennedy School of Government.

Daniel Ortiz, coordinator of the Task Force on Legal and Constitutional Issues, is the John Allan Love Professor of Law and Joseph C. Carter, Jr. Research Professor at the University of Virginia School of Law.

Senior Advisor to the Commission

Richard Leone is president of The Century Foundation. From 1988 to 1994, he was commissioner, and then chairman of the Port Authority of New York and New Jersey. In the 1980s, Leone was the president of the New York Mercantile Exchange and then a managing director at the investment banking firm of Dillon Read & Co., Inc. He has served in federal and state government, including a term as New Jersey's state treasurer. He earned his Ph.D. and served on the faculty at Princeton University.

ORGANIZING AND SPONSORING INSTITUTIONS

The University of Virginia's Miller Center of Public Affairs

The Miller Center is a nonpartisan research center founded in 1975 whose mission is to study, inform, and influence the national and international policymaking of the United States—past, present, and future—with a special emphasis on the American presidency. It is directed by Philip Zelikow. This Commission is the ninth in a series of nonpartisan national commissions. The earlier commissions offered advice on: The Separation of Powers (1998); The Selection of Federal Judges (1996); The Vice Presidential Selection Process (1992); The Presidency and Science Advising (1989); Presidential Disability and the 25th Amendment (1988); Presidential Transitions and Foreign Policy (1986); The Presidential Nominating Process (1982); and The Presidency and the Press (1981).

The Century Foundation

The Century Foundation (formerly the Twentieth Century Fund), founded in 1919, endowed by Edward A. Filene and now directed by Richard C. Leone, is a research foundation that undertakes timely and critical analyses of major economic, political, and social institutions and issues. A not-for-profit, nonpartisan institution based in New York City, with an additional office in Washington, D.C., it works to bridge the gap between the world of ideas and the world of affairs. It concentrates on four primary areas of research: the aging of America; governance, politics, and the media; inequality and other economic issues; and American foreign policy. The Century Foundation produces books, reports, papers and websites, and convenes task forces of citizens and experts all with an eye toward finding fresh approaches to address the major issues of the day.

The following three foundations are the financial sponsors for the National Commission on Federal Election Reform.

The William and Flora Hewlett Foundation was established by the Palo Alto industrialist William R. Hewlett, his late wife, Flora Lamson Hewlett, and their eldest son, Walter B. Hewlett. The Foundation's broad purpose is to promote the well-being of mankind by supporting selected activities of a charitable nature, as well as organizations or institutions engaged in such activities. The Foundation concentrates its resources on activities in education, performing arts, population, environment, conflict resolution, family and community development, and U.S.-Latin American relations.

The David and Lucile Packard Foundation is a private family foundation created in 1964 by David Packard, co-founder of the Hewlett Packard Company and Lucile Walter Packard. The Foundation provides grants to nonprofit organizations in the following broad program areas: conservation; population; science; children, families, and communities; art; and organizational effectiveness and philanthropy. The foundation makes grants at the national and international level, and also has a special focus on the Northern California counties of San Mateo, Santa Clara, Santa Cruz, and Monterey.

The John S. and James L. Knight Foundation was established in 1950 as a private foundation independent of the Knight brothers' newspaper enterprises. It is dedicated to furthering their ideals of service to community, to the highest standards of journalistic excellence, and to the defense of a free press. In both their publishing and philanthropic undertakings, the Knight brothers shared a broad vision and uncommon devotion to the common welfare. The Knight Foundation's trustees have elected to focus on two signature programs, Journalism and Knight Community Partners, each with its own eligibility requirements. In a rapidly changing world, the Knight Foundation remains flexible enough to respond to unique challenges, ideas, and projects that lie beyond its identified programs areas, yet would fulfill the broad vision of its founders.

CONTRIBUTORS TO THE COMMISSION'S WORK

The following individuals directly contributed their expertise to the work of this Commission. Forty-eight of these individuals testified at one of our four public hearings. Others participated in the work of the task forces. Still more offered written submissions to our work. We acknowledge them below.

The Commission wishes to express its gratitude to these experts, as well as to the hundreds of citizens from across the country who, in the democratic tradition, generously contributed their opinions for this report. For those individuals who testified in a public session of the Commission, we have noted the date and place of their testimony so that interested researchers can locate the transcripts of what they said. All of the hearing transcripts are available at www.reformelections.org.

Jim Adler
VoteHere.net

Kim Alexander
California Voter Foundation
Ronald Reagan Library, April 12, 2001

Howard Allen
Southern Illinois University

R. Michael Alvarez
California Institute of Technology
Ronald Reagan Library, April 12, 2001

John Anderson
Center for Voting and Democracy
written submission

Stephen Ansolabehere
Massachusetts Institute of Technology

Peter Argersinger
Southern Illinois University

Tim Augustine
Maryland State Board of Electors

Larry Bartels
Princeton University

Robert Bauer
Perkins Coie LLP

Chris Beem
Johnson Foundation

Robert Bell
Democrats Abroad Canada
written submission

William Boone
Clark Atlanta University
The Carter Center, March 26, 2001

Kimball Brace
Election Data Service, Inc.

Henry Brady
University of California, Berkeley

Bill Bradbury
Oregon Secretary of State
Ronald Reagan Library, April 12, 2001

Philip Breen
United States Department of Justice

Polli Brunelli
Federal Voting Assistance Program

Walter Burnham
University of Texas

Dianne Byrum
Michigan State Senator
written submission

David Capozzi
The United States Access Board

Jo-Anne Chasnow
Human SERVE Campaign

David Chaum
SureVote, Inc.

Ryan Chew
Office of the County Clerk, Cook County, Illinois

Charlotte Cleary
Registrar, Arlington, Virginia

Jennifer Collins-Foley
Los Angeles County, Registrar-Recorder/County Clerk

Cathy Cox
Georgia Secretary of State
The Carter Center, March 26, 2001

Gary Cox
University of California, San Diego

Kristen Cox
National Federation of the Blind

Paul Crafts
Florida Department of State

Charles Crawford
American Council of the Blind

Henry Cuellar
Texas Secretary of State
LBJ Library, May 24, 2001

Alan Davidson
County Clerk, Marion County, Oregon

Donetta Davidson
Colorado Secretary of State

Michael Davidson
The Constitution Project

Rodolfo de la Garza
University of Texas
LBJ Library, May 24, 2001

Alan Dechert
University of California, Berkeley
written submission

Daniel DeFrancesco
New York City Board of Elections
written submission

Karen Delince
American Civil Liberties Union
written submission

Jim Dickson
*American Association
of People with Disabilities*
Gerald R. Ford Library, June 5, 2001

Christopher Dodd
*United States Senator
for the State of Connecticut*
Gerald R. Ford Library, June 5, 2001

Craig Donsanto
*United States Department of
Justice, Election Crimes Branch*

John Dowlin
*Elections Division, Hamilton
County, Ohio*

Jennie Drage
*National Conference of State
Legislatures*

Maria Echaveste
Democratic National Committee
LBJ Library, May 24, 2001

David Elliott
*Office of the Washington
Secretary of State*

Kathy Fairley
*District of Columbia Board of
Elections and Ethics*

Margaret Fung
*Asian-American Legal Defense
and Education Fund*

Curtis Gans
*Committee for the Study of the
American Electorate*

James Gashel
National Federation for the Blind
LBJ Library, May 24, 2001

James Gimpel
University of Maryland

Rosalind Gold
*National Association of Latino
Elected and Appointed Officials
(NALEO)*
Ronald Reagan Library, April 12, 2001

Stephen Gold
Disabilities Law Project

Ralph Goldman
Center for Party Development
written submission

Lance Gough
*Chicago Board of Election
Commissioners*

Gary Greenhalgh
Election Systems and Software
written submission

Michele Grgich
General Accounting Office

Kenneth Gross
*Skadden Arps Slate Meagher &
Flom LLP*

Scott Harshbarger
Common Cause
LBJ Library, May 24, 2001

David Hart
Hart InterCivic

Ernest Hawkins
*National Association of
County Recorders and Clerks*
Gerald R. Ford Library, June 5, 2001

Jeffrey Hayes
Market Strategies

Kris Heffron
*City of Los Angeles Elections
Division*

Andrew Hernandez
*Southwest Voter Registration
Education Project*

Hendrik Hertzberg
Center for Voting and Democracy
LBJ Library, May 24, 2001

Steny Hoyer
*Member of the United States
Congress for the Fifth District of
Maryland*
Gerald R. Ford Library, June 5, 2001

Zoe Hudson
The Constitution Project

J. Kenneth Huff Sr.
AARP
LBJ Library, May 24, 2001

Asa Hutchinson
*Member of the United States
Congress for the Third District of
Arkansas*
The Carter Center, March 26, 2001

Bob Irvin
Georgia General Assembly
The Carter Center, March 26, 2001

Maxine Issacs
*John F. Kennedy School of
Government, Harvard University*

John Jackson
University of Michigan

Gary Jacobson
*University of California, San
Diego*

Alvin Jaeger
North Dakota Secretary of State

David Jefferson
*California Internet Voting Task
Force/Compaq Systems Research
Center*
Ronald Reagan Library, April 12, 2001

Carolyn Jefferson-Jenkins
League of Women Voters
LBJ Library, May 24, 2001

William Jenkins
General Accounting Office

Kathy Johnson
The United States Access Board

Bill Jones
California Secretary of State
Ronald Reagan Library, April 12, 2001

Pamela Karlan
Stanford Law School
LBJ Library, May 24, 2001

Stephen Kaufman
Smith Kaufman LLP

Kevin Kennedy
Wisconsin Elections Board

Alexander Keyssar
Duke University
The Carter Center, March 26, 2001

Brad King
Office of the Minnesota Secretary of State

Jean-Pierre Kingsley
Elections Canada
Gerald R. Ford Library, June 5, 2001

Stephen Knack
American University

Joan Konner
Columbia University Graduate School of Journalism
Gerald R. Ford Library, June 5, 2001

Jon Krosnick
The Ohio State University

Linda Lamone
Maryland State Board of Electors

Richard LaVallo
Advocacy Inc.

Jan Leighley
Texas A&M University

R. Doug Lewis
The Election Center
Gerald R. Ford Library, June 5, 2001

Matt Lilly
Danaher Controls

Keith Long
Hart InterCivic

Susan MacManus
University of South Florida
The Carter Center, March 26, 2001

Ruth Mandel
Eagleton Institute of Politics
The Carter Center, March 26, 2001

Sheilah Mann
American Political Science Association

Jeff Manza
Northwestern University

Mitch McConnell
United States Senator for the State of Kentucky
written submission

Conny McCormack
Los Angeles County, Registrar-Recorder/County Clerk
Ronald Reagan Library, April 12, 2001

Gary McIntosh
Office of the Washington Secretary of State

Leigh Middleditch, Jr.
McGuire Woods

Alice Miller
District of Columbia Board of Elections and Ethics

Julie Moore
Elections Operations, King County, Washington

John Mott-Smith
Office of the California Secretary of State

Michael Neblo
University of Chicago

Peter Neumann
SRI International

Bob Ney
Member of the United States
Congress for the Eighteenth
District of Ohio
written submission
Gerald R. Ford Library, June 5, 2001

Stephen Nickelsburg
Hunton & Williams

Colm O'Muircheartaigh
National Opinion Research
Center

Norman Ornstein
American Enterprise Institute for
Public Policy Research
LBJ Library, May 24, 2001

Lee Page
Paralyzed Veterans Association

Robert Pastor
Emory University
Gerald R. Ford Library, June 5, 2001

R. Hewitt Pate
Hunton & Williams

Cathy Pearsall-Stipek
Auditor, Pierce County,
Washington

Carol Petersen
General Accounting Office

Katherine Pettus
Columbia University

Deborah Phillips
Voting Integrity Project
The Carter Center, March 26, 2001

Trevor Potter
Caplin & Drysdale

G. Bingham Powell
University of Rochester

Sharon Priest
Arkansas Secretary of State
LBJ Library, May 24, 2001

Mark Pritchett
Collins Center for Public
Policy, Inc.
The Carter Center, March 26, 2001

Cameron Quinn
State Board of Elections,
Commonwealth of Virginia

Wendy Rahn
University of Minnesota

Jack Rakove
Stanford University
The Carter Center, March 26, 2001

Joseph Rich
United States Department of
Justice, Civil Rights Division
LBJ Library, May 24, 2001

Eric Riedel
University of Minnesota

Ron Rivest
Massachusetts Institute of
Technology

Susan Roth
The Ohio State University
Ronald Reagan Library, April 12, 2001

Eric Royal
United Cerebral Palsy

Janet Ruggiero
Office of the Rhode Island
Secretary of State

Larry Sabato
University of Virginia
The Carter Center, March 26, 2001

Roy Saltman
Independent Elections Consultant
written submission

Anthony Salvanto
University of California, Irvine

Paul Schumaker
University of Kansas

Ted Selker
Massachusetts Institute of Technology

Hilary Shelton
National Association for the Advancement of Colored People
LBJ Library, May 24, 2001

W. Phillips Shively
University of Minnesota

Howard Silver
Consortium of Social Science Associations (COSSA)
written submission

Margaret Sims
Federal Election Commission

Liz Smith
Furman University

Richard Soudriette
International Foundation for Election Systems
Gerald R. Ford Library, June 5, 2001

Alfred Speer
State of Louisiana House of Representatives

Martin Stephens
State of Utah House of Representatives

Eliot Spitzer
New York Attorney General
written submission

Ralph Tabor
National Association of Counties

Clyde Terry
New Hampshire Developmental Disability Council

Abigail Thernstrom
United States Commission on Civil Rights
written submission

Christopher Thomas
Michigan Department of State Bureau of Elections
Gerald R. Ford Library, June 5, 2001

Rosita Thomas
Thomas Opinion Research

Scott Thomas
Federal Election Commission
Gerald R. Ford Library, June 5, 2001

Daniel Tokaji
American Civil Liberties Union Foundation

Mischelle Townsend
Registrar of Voters, County of Riverside, California
Ronald Reagan Library, April 12, 2001

Michael Traugott
University of Michigan
Gerald R. Ford Library, June 5, 2001

Fran Ulmer
Alaska Lieutenant Governor
written submission

James Villiesse
City Clerk of New London,
Wisconsin

Lance Ward
Oklahoma State Election Board
LBJ Library, May 24, 2001

Tracy Warren
The Constitution Project

Geraldine Washington
Los Angeles NAACP

Maxine Waters
Member of the United States
Congress for the Thirty-Fifth
District of California
Ronald Reagan Library, April 12, 2001

Martin Wattenberg
University of California, Irvine

Bob Williams
United Cerebral Palsy

Brit Williams
Kennesaw State University

Raymond Wolfinger
University of California, Berkeley

Stephen Yusem
Rear Admiral (Ret.), Reserve
Officers Association of the United
States
Gerald R. Ford Library, June 5, 2001

Bob Zeni
Voting Experience Redesign
Initiative
written submission

THE MICHIGAN QUALIFIED VOTER FILE:
A BRIEF INTRODUCTION

A new era in the administration of elections has been opened in Michigan through the realization of the state's Qualified Voter File (QVF) project. While the QVF project was originally conceived as a response to the inefficiencies of the state's highly decentralized voter registration system (Michigan's voter registration files are managed by nearly 1,700 local officials), the implementation of the National Voter Registration Act (NVRA) greatly heightened the need for such an initiative. Mandated under Public Act 441 of 1994 and placed into operation for the 1998 election cycle, the QVF links election officials throughout the state to a fully automated, interactive statewide voter registration database to achieve a wide variety of significant advantages including:

- The elimination of duplicate voter registration records in the system.
- The streamlining of the state's voter registration cancellation process.
- The elimination of time-consuming record maintenance activities.
- The elimination of registration forwarding errors and duplicative tasks.
- Sizable cost gains on the local level.

The QVF was populated with every registered elector appearing in the voter registration files held by the state's city and township clerks. The local voter registration files were electronically matched with the Department of State's driver license/personal identification card file. This process assigned driver license numbers to voter registration files. The system then removed the older record wherever duplicate registration records were found. It is important to note that a voter does NOT have to have a Michigan driver

113

license or personal identification card. When a voter registration record does not match any driver license record, the system generates an identification number. For voter registration purposes, the identical number is for internal use and is not issued to the voter. Data on the voters is maintained on a UNIX-based computer located in Lansing.

Beyond the voter registration file management functions of the QVF, the system offers Michigan's election officials a full array of election management features including components created to assist with absent voter ballot processing; petition and candidate tracking; election planning; and election inspector tracking. The election management components, designed in consultation with a special task force of county and local officials, have introduced a new level of convenience to the administration of elections in Michigan. The election management components have also worked to standardize many of the election related forms and procedures employed throughout the state.

All counties, cities, and townships play a role in the QVF program and all will enjoy ongoing benefits through the project's implementation. Michigan's 83 county clerks and the clerks of all local jurisdictions with a voting age population over 5,000 were provided with the hardware and software needed to establish a direct link with the QVF. Smaller cities and townships (i.e., those with a voting age population under 5,000) have either purchased the hardware and software needed for a direct link with the QVF or access the QVF through the local county clerk's office. In addition, jurisdictions with a voting age population under 5,000 were reimbursed for their assistance with the data validation process. (Each jurisdiction eligible for the reimbursement program received $.45 multiplied by the jurisdiction's voting age population)

Michigan's Qualified Voter File System

Transmitting Voter Registration Data to Local Clerks Instantly and Efficiently

175 Secretary of State Branch Offices

electronically enter all "motor/voter" voter registration transactions (approximately 85% of all voter registration transactions in state). The electronic data are transferred daily and are immediately available to the local clerks. The hard copy voter registration application form signed by the voter is forwarded by mail within a week.

County, city, and township clerks

electronically enter all other voter registration transactions such as registrations submitted by mail or in person at the clerk's office.

Qualified Voter File

6.8 million voter registration records

83 counties

363 cities and townships

(VAP > 5,000) online (approximately 80% of Michigan's voting age population).

1,151 cities and townships

(VAP < 5,000) share QVF resources available at county level (approximately 20% of Michigan's voting age population).

Additional Details

QVF System Components

The QVF System comprises three primary components:

Lansing file server: The heart of the QVF system is the file server located in Lansing, the state capitol. The file server holds the voter registration database for the entire state. It also holds all system software (QVF application software and Oracle database software). The file server exchanges information with the driver file database (new registrations originating in branch offices) through a series of "server processes" (automated computer programs). The file server exchanges information with local system users through the replication process.

County/local QVF installations: All of Michigan's 83 counties and 246 of Michigan's largest cities and townships (voting age population over 5,000) were provided with QVF installations at state expense. One hundred seventeen additional cities and townships opted to purchase QVF installations at their own expense. A total of 545 PC's and 512 printers are employed by the 446 counties and local jurisdictions on-line with the QVF server in Lansing. (Multiple PC's and printers are employed by the state's major cities.)

Telecommunications network: The QVF system uses the Internet as its telecommunications network. Each QVF jurisdiction was provided with an Internet account (Merit is the Internet provider) and Internet software (Netscape Communicator) which includes e-mail and web searching capabilities. To initiate the replication process, the local QVF users simply establish an Internet connection. Replication updates the Lansing server with new information provided by the local jurisdiction and updates the local jurisdiction with new information provided by the file server (usually branch office transactions). An average replication takes 20–60 minutes and is generally initiated two or three times per week.

QVF Data

The QVF is administered through the Department of State's Qualified Voter File Division. The Qualified Voter File Division is organized under the Department's Bureau of Elections. The staff members employed with the Qualified Voter Division work in four general areas:

Data entry: The data entry staff are responsible for entering data received from Michigan's city and township clerks into the QVF database as needed to build the QVF file. The data entry staff is also responsible for entering "problem records" received from the branch offices.

Data reconciliation: The data processing staff is in the final phase of completing the data reconciliation processes which had to be accomplished to implement the QVF. Over 1,500 cities and townships submitted voter registration records to the state for inclusion in the QVF database. Those records submitted electronically were matched against the driver file. Matching discrepancies (generally address or birth date conflicts) are resolved during this procedure.

Street index reconciliation: The QVF street index ensures that each voter is assigned to his or her proper precinct and voting districts. If there is not a street index entry for a voter's address, an error report is created. The data processing staff adds or changes street index entries to ensure that any errors are corrected. While the bulk of this work has taken place during the data reconciliation process, this will be an ongoing function of the Qualified Voter File Division.

QVF Help Desk

The Qualified Voter File Division maintains a Help Desk to assist the county and local clerks throughout the state with any questions they have regarding the operation of the QVF.

The Help Desk offers assistance in the following areas:

Replications: The replication process involves the transfer of data between the QVF server in Lansing and the remote QVF installations throughout the state. If there is a problem with the replication process, it generally stems from a user error, an equipment failure, or a network failure. The Help Desk is able to trace such problems, find the source and offer corrective measures.

Equipment problems: The Help Desk troubleshoots all equipment related problems. In some cases, a contract vendor is sent to the site. In other cases, the Help Desk staff members pick up the equipment for in-house problem solving.

Training: The Help Desk provides training and on-site consultations to QVF users throughout the state. The Help Desk is also responsible for updating all user guides and training materials.

Software support: The Help Desk offers QVF users advice and instruction on using the QVF software and documents requests for QVF software enhancements. The majority of all inquiries received by the Help Desk involve questions over the operation and functions of the QVF software.

Additional Information

Further information on Michigan's Qualified Voter File project can be obtained by contacting the Department of State's Bureau of Elections.

Michigan Department of State
Bureau of Elections
Qualified Voter File Division

208 North Capitol Avenue, Third Floor
Lansing, MI 48918-1591

Telephone: 517-373-2542
QVF Help Desk: 800-310-5697
Fax: 517-241-1591

—June 5, 2001

Task Force on the Federal Election System

John Mark Hansen, COORDINATOR
WITH *Michael A. Neblo*

Contents

PREFACE

The National Commission on Federal Election Reform charged the Task Force on the Federal Election System with two responsibilities: first, to provide information about current practices in federal elections and, second, to analyze the effects of current practices and the possibilities for reform. With a substantive mandate that ranged from voter registration to polling hours, the work of the task force seemed best divided into a series of reports on discrete topics. Accordingly, the final product comprises nine reports. The longest address voter registration and early, mail, and unrestricted absentee voting; the shortest consider felony disfranchisement and verification of voter identity in polling places. All of the reports combine a description of current practice with an overview of the best scholarly research into election systems and voter behavior.

The task force enjoyed the cooperation of numerous scholars, analysts, and election officials who took our phone calls, answered our e-mails, and in some cases plied us with data. Often they did not realize that in so doing they became task force participants. Raymond E. Wolfinger of the University of California at Berkeley, Stephen Ansolabehere of the Massachusetts Institute of Technology, Tracy Warren of the Constitution Project, and Conny McCormack, the registrar-recorder and county clerk of Los Angeles County, made sustained contributions to our work. We especially thank about 20 people who took time from busy schedules on short notice to participate in a critically informative conference on voter registration conducted jointly with the Task Force on Election Administration. Nothing has been more valuable in this work than to see elections from the vantage point of the people who administer them. We have emerged with a new appreciation of their talents and their patience.

The staff of the Task Force on the Federal Election System tracked and compiled and culled and summarized and helped to figure it all out. The chief responsibilities for implementing our inquiry fell to Michael A. Neblo, now a Robert Wood Johnson Fellow in Health at the University of Michigan and assistant professor at the Ohio State University. Neblo helped to shape every task force report with his research and his critical eye, and he wrote one himself. Meredith Rolfe and Nealon Scoones provided careful and timely assistance with the research. Thad Hall and Tova Wang of the Century Foundation and Leonard Shambon of Wilmer, Cutler & Pickering contributed significant help and insight.

Finally, the University of Chicago and especially its provost, Geoffrey R. Stone, allowed us the time to contribute to an effort that will, we hope, make elections work a little better.

John Mark Hansen
Coordinator

SIZING THE PROBLEM

Summary of Conclusions

1. If an election for which the margin of victory is less than a percentage point is within the current technological margin of error, then elections within the error margin are common occurrences. In an average presidential election, the results in two or three states are within the margin of error. Razor-close races for the Senate are just as common, and extremely close contests for governor are even more common. In the last half-century, every state but two has had at least one federal or gubernatorial election that was within the one-percent margin of error.

2. Elections that are within the margin of error tax the legitimacy of the federal election system. Overall, Americans express levels of satisfaction with the conduct of democracy that are among the highest in the democratic world. Americans are much less convinced, however, that elections in the United States are conducted fairly. In 2000, in fact, Americans' rating of the fairness of the election was nearly the lowest of all democratic countries. Unsurprisingly, the perceived fairness of the election is influenced by partisanship. But substantial numbers of Republicans questioned the fairness of the 2000 election, as did women and a majority of blacks. Large margins of error in close elections put a strain on the electoral system that undermines public confidence in the electoral process.

Frequency of Close Federal and Statewide Elections

The 2000 presidential election exposed to the nation what local election administrators have long known—that the process of casting and counting ballots is riddled with error. In most circumstances, the error is inconsequential because it is too small to have any plausible effect on the outcome. Most elections in the United States are simply not very close. In a very tight election, however, even a small margin of error in the balloting can mean the difference between winning and losing, as it was in Florida in the 2000 presidential contest.

In Florida and after, the nation learned that a voter's choice cannot readily be determined from something between 1.5 and 2.5 percent of the ballots cast in federal elections. The technical problems involve choices that did not register—the "undervote"—and multiple choices that did—the "overvote." As a matter of determining the election outcome, neither problem would be very worrisome if the candidate preferences of voters ensnared by technical problems in the balloting simply paralleled the preferences of all the other voters.[1] But the events in Florida and other analyses suggest otherwise. No matter what the method of balloting, less educated voters will find it harder to cast a ballot correctly than better educated voters. Moreover, depending upon the type of balloting and the availability of assistance, marking a ballot correctly will present special problems for language minorities, the elderly, and persons with physical disabilities.

As a way to size the problem of Election Day mistakes in casting and counting ballots, let us adopt one percent as the level of error that might be consequential in federal elections. If the true "residual vote" (undervote plus overvote) is 1.5 percent, a one percent margin of victory might produce an incorrect outcome if the people whose votes were not counted preferred one candidate over the other by a ratio of five to one. If the true residual vote is 2.5 percent, a 1 percent margin of victory might produce an incorrect outcome if people affected by the undervote and overvote preferred one candidate over the other by a ratio of 3 to 2. Supposing, then, that an election decided by less than 1 percent of the votes cast is within the technical margin of error, how widespread is the potential problem?

As the table following shows, the incidence of federal elections decided by less than a percentage point is far more widespread than Florida in 2000. Since 1948 elections for presidential electors have been decided by less than one percent of votes cast 31 times (and by less than 2 percent 70 times). In 1968, 1972, and 1988 presidential electors were chosen in no states by a margin of less than 1 percent, but in 1960 six were, and in 1948 and 2000 five were. In the 14 presidential elections since 1948, 22 states have seen presidential contests decided within a percentage point (and 40 states have had presidential contests within two points). In a given year, there is a 90 percent likelihood that at least one state will have a presidential election within the one-percent technical margin of error (table 1).

Razor-close elections are no less common in elections for other federal offices or for governor. Over 50 years, about 4 percent of all senatorial elections, and about 2 percent of all congressional elections, have been decided

---

1. As a matter of public satisfaction with the electoral process, even randomly distributed errors in the balloting may be consequential. People who have gone to the trouble of voting do not like to hear that their votes may not have been counted.

Table 1 Federal and Statewide Elections Decided by Less than 1 Percent (in Bold) and 2 Percent of Votes Cast, 1948–2000

State	Presidential	Senatorial	Congressional	Gubernatorial
Alabama	1980	1962, **1986**	**5,** 6	**1994**
Alaska	1960		**0,** 0	1960, **1974**
Arizona	**1964,** 1992	1980	2, 1	1950, 1970, **1974, 1990, 1994**
Arkansas	**1980**		**0,** 0	
California	**1948, 1960,** 1976	1986	9, 20	1982
Colorado	1996	**1956,** 1972, 1980, 1986	**5,** 3	**1998**
Connecticut	1948	**1988**	**10,** 7	**1948,** 1950, **1952**
Delaware	1948, 1960	1960, 1972	2, 1	1968
Florida	1992, **2000**	**1988**	2, 5	1994
Georgia	**1992,** 1996	1980, 1986, 1992, 1996	**3,** 1	**1966**
Hawaii	**1960,** 1980		2, 0	1998
Idaho	1964	1948, **1980**	**3,** 1	1958, 1982, **1986**
Illinois	**1948, 1960,** 1976	1984	**11,** 8	**1956,** 1972, **1982**
Indiana	**1948**	**1962, 1970**	**13,** 7	1960
Iowa	1976, **2000**	**1968**	4, 6	
Kansas		1974	1, 4	1974
Kentucky	**1952,** 1980, **1996**	**1956, 1984**	**5,** 3	1963
Louisiana		**1996**	**0,** 1	
Maine	**1976**		**3,** 0	**1962, 1970**
Maryland	1948, 1968	1958	**3,** 2	**1994**
Massachusetts	**1980**	1954	4, 2	**1952, 1962, 1964**
Michigan	1948	1952, 1954, 2000	7, 6	**1950, 1952,** 1960, 1970, **1990**
Minnesota	1960, **1984**		**6,** 6	1960, **1962**
Mississippi	1976, 1980		**0,** 2	
Missouri	1952, **1956, 1960,** 1968	1982	4, 4	**1976, 2000**
Montana		**1954,** 1960	1, 5	1952
Nebraska			2, 1	**1958,** 1982, **1990**
Nevada	1996	**1964, 1974, 1998**	2, 1	
New Hampshire	1992, 2000	**1974**	2, 0	1970
New Jersey	**1960**	**1954**	2, 5	1961, **1981, 1993,** 1997
New Mexico	**1960, 2000**		**6,** 2	**1958, 1960, 1968,** 1974, 1978
New York	**1948**	1970, 1980, 1992	**11,** 9	
North Carolina	1956, **1992**	**1980**	7, 7	
North Dakota		**1974, 1986**	2, 4	**1962**
Ohio	**1948, 1976,** 1992	**1964**	4, 10	**1974,** 1978
Oklahoma	1976	**1974**	2, 1	**1970**
Oregon	**1976, 2000**	**1954, 1968**	2, 2	
Pennsylvania		**1956,** 1964	**15,** 11	1958
Rhode Island	1952		**0,** 2	**1956, 1962, 1970**

(Continued)

Table 1   Federal and Statewide Elections Decided by Less than 1 Percent (in Bold) and 2 Percent of Votes Cast, 1948–2000 (*Continued*)

State	Presidential	Senatorial	Congressional	Gubernatorial
South Carolina	1952, 1980		**0**, 0	
South Dakota	1976	1956, **1962**	**1**, 0	1960
Tennessee	**1952, 1956, 1980**		**1**, 4	
Texas	1968	**1978**	2, 2	**1978**
Utah		**1978**	2, 2	1988
Vermont		1980	**0**, 0	**1958**, 1984
Virginia	1976, 1996	**1978**	5, 9	1973
Washington	1988	1986, **2000**	6, 4	1960
West Virginia		**1978**	2, 0	1968
Wisconsin	1976, **2000**	1980	**0**, 5	**1962**, 1964
Wyoming		1958, **1988**	**1**, 1	**1954**, 1978
Total				
Less than 1% margin	**31** elections in 22 states	**32** elections in 26 states	**182**	**41** elections in 25 states
Less than 2% margin	70 elections in 40 states	63 elections in 40 states	365	75 elections in 40 states

by less than 1 percent of the popular vote.[2] Over 50 years, about 5 percent of gubernatorial elections have had victory margins below 1 percent. In any given election year, the likelihood that there is at least one election within the 1 percent technical margin of error is 71 percent for senatorial elections and more than 99 percent for congressional elections. In the last half-century only two states, Mississippi and South Carolina, have not had a federal or gubernatorial election decided by less than one percent of ballots cast. It is frequently the case in federal and statewide elections that technical problems in the balloting could be consequential to the outcome.

Effect of Close Elections on the Legitimacy of the Federal Election Process

Of course, what was unusual in the 2000 presidential election was not only that the contest in Florida was so excruciatingly close, but also that the 2000 election pivoted on Florida and its 25 electoral votes. The 2000 presidential election revealed nearly every imperfection in the federal election

---

2. The counts for senatorial, congressional, and gubernatorial elections do not include special elections, which tend to be more competitive than scheduled elections because they almost never involve an incumbent.

system to the nation. What effect did the news have on the American people and their confidence in the democratic process in the United States?

As it happens, Americans as a people express an unusual level of satisfaction with the conduct of their democratic government. As table 2 shows, Americans stand near the top of the world's democracies in the pleasure they express in the way their government works. Although the less fortunate tend to feel less satisfaction with American democracy than the most fortunate, Americans nonetheless express high levels of satisfaction across class, race, and gender lines. The difficulties of the 2000 election had no real effect on Americans' attitudes toward their democratic system as a whole. Events such as occurred in Florida seem not to have had any bearing on the American people's regard for the democratic system, at least in the short run.

Americans' confidence in the electoral process is a different matter. In 1996 three-quarters of the public expressed confidence that the last election was conducted "fairly," and only 10 percent described it as having been "unfair." In 2000, on the other hand, barely a majority of the elec-

Table 2 Satisfaction with the Democratic Process in 19 Democracies
Percent

Nation	Satisfied or fairly satisfied	Satisfied
Norway	90.3	28.2
Netherlands	88.3	13.0
United States, 2000	80.7	32.1
United States, 1996	80.5	27.7
Australia	78.0	30.9
Great Britain	74.8	16.4
New Zealand	68.5	19.3
Japan	63.5	5.3
Germany	63.4	6.4
Poland	63.1	5.8
Spain	62.8	13.9
Czech Republic	61.1	3.7
Israel	53.4	26.8
Republic of China	46.9	36.7
Romania	43.9	20.4
Argentina	42.4	10.1
Hungary	42.2	1.4
Mexico	41.6	9.7
Lithuania	34.5	12.9
Ukraine	9.2	2.2

Source: Comparative Study of Electoral Systems and American National Election Studies, 1996 and 2000.

torate concluded that the election had been very fair, and 37 percent decided that it had been unfair.[3] The events in Florida had a clear impact on the faith Americans have in the electoral process (table 3).

To be sure, one part of people's perception of fairness was agreement with the outcome. In 1996 Democrats were about nine percentage points more likely to conclude that the election was fair than Republicans were, presumably because the Democratic candidate had won. In 2000 the partisan divisions turned in the other direction, but much more sharply, with Republicans 24 percentage points more likely to think the election fair than Democrats. But Republicans had their qualms about the fairness of the process in 2000 also. In 1996 just 12 percent of Republicans branded the election unfair; in 2000 nearly twice as many did.[4] Among Independents, concerns about fairness increased more than threefold (table 4).

But questions about the legitimacy of the federal election process in the wake of the 2000 campaign were not only, or even primarily, partisan sour grapes. In 1996 the most prominent difference between people who believed the election fair and people who did not was not partisanship (which had only a small effect on beliefs) but participation in the electoral system. Voters were more satisfied with the process than nonvoters.[5]

Table 3 Was the Last Election in the United States Conducted Fairly?

Percent

Response	1996	2000
Very fair	49.3	22.7
Somewhat fair	26.0	29.3
Neither fair nor unfair	15.0	10.9
Somewhat unfair	6.1	21.8
Very unfair	3.6	15.3
Total	100.0	100.0
(N)	(1,513)	(1,418)

Source: American National Election Studies, 1996 and 2000.

3. The questions were asked as part of the 1996 and 2000 American National Election Studies, a nationwide sample of eligible voters. In both years, the interviews were completed in November and December.
4. We do not know, however, whether Republicans, Democrats, and Independents all thought that the election was unfair in the same way.
5. This paragraph and the next report result from an analysis that takes into account the other characteristics of individuals, such as their partisanship. In 1996, and again in 2000, people with higher incomes and higher levels of education also professed more faith in the fairness of the electoral process than people with lower levels. Society's haves find more to like in the electoral process than society's have-nots.

Table 4 Fairness of the Last United States Election, by Partisanship

Percent

Response	1996			2000		
	Demo-crats	Independents	Republicans	Demo-crats	Independents	Republicans
Very fair	55.5	44.0	47.3	15.7	20.2	37.0
Somewhat fair	26.1	26.3	25.6	29.8	26.7	32.9
Neither fair nor unfair	12.0	18.3	15.2	9.9	12.3	9.3
Somewhat unfair	4.2	7.3	7.0	24.5	25.1	12.9
Very unfair	2.2	4.2	4.9	20.1	15.8	8.0
Total	100.0	100.0	100.0	100.0	100.0	100.0
(N)	(593)	(480)	(429)	(477)	(551)	(365)

Source: American National Election Studies, 1996 and 2000.

In 2000 partisanship still had only a small effect on beliefs, and voters were still more convinced than non-voters that the process was fair. But women and blacks in 2000 found the process deeply suspect. As the following tables show, women and men and blacks and whites scarcely differed in their assessments of the fairness of the election in 1996. But in 2000, they differed dramatically. Women were about 14 percent more likely than men to conclude that the process was unfair (table 5). Blacks were 22 percent more likely than whites to question the fairness of the process (table 6). In fact, as one of the latest instances of the perceptual divide between blacks and whites in America, beliefs about the fairness of the 2000 election were perfectly symmetric: 55 percent of whites believed that the 2000 election was conducted fairly and 56 percent of blacks believed that it was conducted unfairly. The 2000 election undermined the public's

Table 5 Fairness of the Last United States Election, by Gender

Percent

Response	1996		2000	
	Men	Women	Men	Women
Very fair	49.8	48.9	29.7	17.3
Somewhat fair	25.8	26.3	31.3	27.7
Neither fair nor unfair	14.6	15.4	9.2	12.3
Somewhat unfair	6.6	5.6	16.3	26.0
Very unfair	3.2	3.8	13.4	16.8
Total	100.0	100.0	100.0	100.0
(N)	(679)	(834)	(619)	(799)

Source: American National Election Studies, 1996 and 2000.

Table 6   Fairness of the Last United States Election, by Race

Percent

Response	1996 Whites	1996 Blacks	2000 Whites	2000 Blacks
Very fair	48.6	54.8	24.8	8.3
Somewhat fair	26.9	19.6	30.5	24.8
Neither fair nor unfair	14.8	16.0	11.1	11.0
Somewhat unfair	6.2	5.4	21.6	21.4
Very unfair	3.5	4.2	12.0	34.5
Total	100.0%	100.0%	100.0%	100.0%
(N)	(1,302)	(168)	(1,132)	(145)

Source: American National Election Studies, 1996 and 2000.

Table 7   Public's View of the Fairness of the Most Recent Election in 18 Democracies

Percent who say

Nation	Somewhat unfair or very unfair	Very fair or somewhat fair
Netherlands	1.9	91.7
Germany	2.0	90.6
Norway	3.1	93.2
Great Britain	4.2	80.5
Czech Republic	4.6	79.8
Hungary	4.9	81.9
New Zealand	6.7	76.9
Romania	9.2	81.6
United States, 1996	9.7	75.3
Poland	9.7	72.0
Spain	11.2	80.0
Republic of China	14.0	62.2
Argentina	17.4	48.8
Mexico	23.0	56.1
Lithuania	26.7	55.3
Japan	27.2	42.3
Ukraine	34.8	37.0
United States, 2000	37.1	52.0
Israel	62.6	19.7

Source: Comparative Study of Electoral Systems and American National Election Studies, 1996 and 2000.

faith in the electoral process, at least temporarily, and especially within the more disadvantaged segments of American society.[6]

Already in 1996, the United States was only in the middle among democracies in measuring citizens' faith in the fairness of its elections. But in 2000 the United States dropped nearly to the bottom, the dissatisfaction of its citizenry exceeded only by the monumentally disgruntled citizens of Israel (table 7).

Americans' faith in the electoral process will surely survive the 2000 election. But 2000 also makes clear just how much the public legitimacy of the process depends on the circumstances of the election and, in particular, on how well federal elections appear to be conducted.

---

6. Latinos were also less convinced that the election was fair, but the divisions were not as dramatic.

VOTER REGISTRATION

Summary of Conclusions

1. Registration to vote is widespread but far from universal. In 1996, 71 percent of voting age citizens were registered to vote.
2. Voter registration is the mechanism of balance between two types of errors: the inclusion in the electorate of people who are not eligible to vote and the exclusion from the electorate of people who are. The trend since enactment of voter registration has been to scale back restrictions on access. Even so, the registration laws in the United States are among the most demanding in the democratic world.
3. Voter registration laws depress voter turnout by raising the cost of the exercise of the franchise. The National Voter Registration Act has mitigated many of the most restrictive voter registration practices. The most significant restriction that remains is the lengthy closing period, although it too has been capped at 30 days.
4. The primary sufferers of voter registration are migrants and the less educated. Sixteen percent of the population changes residence each year, and the registrants among them must reregister at new addresses. The young, the poor, and renters are more likely to move and less likely to register. The less educated are less likely to be motivated to register and less likely to have the skills to manage it, giving rise to sizable differences in voter registration by education.
5. The National Voter Registration Act has complicated voter list management. In response, states have taken administrative steps to deter registration by noncitizens, to overcome the problems caused by delegation of voter registration responsibilities to driver's license bureaus, government service agencies, and third-party registrars, and to eliminate duplicate and lapsed registrations. The measures include the incorporation of separate check-offs for citizenship on voter registration applications, the adoption of statewide voter registration systems, and the use of numeric identifiers for voter registration.

Registration as a voter is the first step toward the exercise of the franchise in every state except North Dakota. Participation in that first step is broad, but far from universal. In November 1996, 71 percent of American citizens of voting age reported that they were currently registered to vote. Of registrants, 82.3 percent reported that they had voted in the 1996 presidential elections.[1] Together with voter turnout, rates of reported voter registration have fallen steadily since 1968.

Voter registration and voter turnout vary markedly across states. Registration tops 80 percent in Maine, Minnesota, and Wisconsin, all of which have Election Day registration.[2] Less than 65 percent of voting age citizens are registered to vote in Hawaii and Arkansas.[3]

A Brief History

Voter registration has a long history in the United States. Massachusetts in 1800 was the first state to require registration of voters, but the idea did not spread very far or very fast. Until 1860 voter registration was found almost exclusively in New England. After the Civil War and accelerating at the end of Reconstruction in 1877, voter registration spread rapidly.

---

1. Survey self-reports of voter registration exhibit the same sawtooth pattern as voter turnout: higher in presidential election years and lower in midterm election years. In 1998, 67.1 percent of the voting age citizen population reported registration. Sixty-eight percent of the registrants reported voting.
2. North Dakota respondents report 91.0 percent registration, even though North Dakota does not have voter registration. Either 9 percent do not realize this, or the question is confusing in a state with no voter registration.
3. The rates of registration and turnout reported in the text come from the Current Population Survey 1996 Voter Supplement. Based on people's self reports to census interviewers, the CPS estimates of both registration and turnout are probably inflated slightly. Tables at the end of this report also calculate registration and turnout from official statistics reported to the Federal Election Commission (FEC) by the states. For reasons discussed later, rates of registration calculated from official statistics are probably significantly inflated. Turnout rates calculated from official statistics, on the other hand, are probably deflated. First, voter turnout is usually calculated on the denominator of voting age population, which includes non-citizens who are not eligible to vote. Second, voter turnout is usually calculated on the basis of votes cast for president, but not everybody who turns out at the polls in fact casts a vote in the presidential contest. In the state estimates reported in the table, the numerator is the larger of the vote for president, the vote for senator, or the vote for U.S. representative. In 1996 more votes were cast for senator than for president in eight states (Delaware, Idaho, Kansas, Maine, Montana, North Carolina, South Carolina, and South Dakota); more votes were cast in total for U.S. representative than for president in one state, Missouri.

Between 1876 and 1912, nearly half of the northern states wrote registration requirements into their constitutions, and many more adopted it by statute. By 1929 only three states, Arkansas, Indiana, and Texas, lacked any form of voter registration, although eleven others limited its application to cities above a specified size.[4]

In the North and West, voter registration was typically a "progressive" measure, promoted as an antidote to the corrupt practices of urban political machines. It was an important piece of a larger set of progressive governmental and electoral reforms, which also included the civil service, direct primaries, and the secret ballot (often called the "Australian" ballot, after the country of origin). In the South, registration became part of the far-reaching system of electoral Jim Crow that included the white primary, literacy tests, and the poll tax.

The effect of the set of electoral reforms on voter turnout in the United States was dramatic. In the South, where registration was one of the milder restrictions on the exercise of the franchise, voter participation dropped from 64.2 percent of the adult male population in 1888 to 29 percent in 1904.[5] Outside the South, where registration was the major new burden on voters, turnout fell from 86.2 percent in 1888 to 67.7 percent in 1912. Nationwide, voter participation in presidential elections fell from its historic peak of 82.6 percent in 1876 to its historic low of 48.9 percent in 1924.

The effect of the electoral reforms on the incidence of vote fraud is the subject of a lively debate among historians and political scientists. One side argues that voter registration lowered voter turnout in part by excluding ineligibles and phantoms from illegal participation in elections. The other side counters that voter registration lowered voter turnout by deterring the

---

4. Application of voter registration only to urban areas was common in the earliest legislation. The first registration law in Pennsylvania, for example, applied only to Philadelphia. In 1929 the last states that limited registration to urban areas were predominantly agricultural and midwestern: Iowa, Kansas, Kentucky, Minnesota, Missouri, Nebraska, North Dakota, Ohio, Tennessee, Wisconsin, and Wyoming.

5. Turnout in the South was even more dismal in some of the individual states. Between 1920 and 1944, on average, less than 25 percent of the voting age population participated in presidential elections in Alabama, Arkansas, Georgia, Mississippi, South Carolina, and Virginia. South Carolina's voter turnout was the lowest in the nation: just under 10 percent. During this period, of course, the greatest part of the African American population was denied the franchise, but turnout calculated on the base of the voting age white population was little better.

legitimate participation of voters deemed by the middle-class progressive reformers of the era to be ignorant and manipulable. Nobody has a very good method for assessing the extent of vote fraud either before or after the reforms, but the cleverest inquiry into the issue suggests that both sides may be right. Using stories from upstate New York newspapers from 1870 to 1916, Gary W. Cox and J. Morgan Kousser found that the electoral reforms—in particular, they say, the Australian ballot—changed the mode of electoral corruption but not the fact. Before the reforms, they argue, parties engaged in "inflationary" corruption—they bought votes and recycled voters. After the reforms, however, parties pursued "deflationary" corruption—they either paid opponents to stay home or they kept opponents away from the polls. Voter registration was just as much a weapon in partisan electoral conflict as vote fraud.

Throughout the last century, voter registration laws have been a mechanism of balance between two kinds of errors: the inclusion in the electorate of people who are not eligible to vote and the exclusion of people who are. The earliest registration laws were so restrictive that they seem decidedly draconian viewed from 2001. In 1929, 18 states still required voters to reregister periodically, typically every one, two, or four years. In 1962, 38 states required at least one year of residency in the state as a condition of voter registration. In 1972, 17 states purged voters from the registration rolls if they had not voted within the last two years, and 23 others purged voters if they had not voted within a period ranging from two and one half to eight years. Finally, in 1960, 23 states with 40 percent of the eligible electorate required voters to register more than 30 days before the election, and no states had yet adopted Election Day registration.

Through time, the trend has been to scale back restrictions on access to voter registration. By 1972 periodic registration had nearly disappeared—only two states, Arizona and South Carolina, still mandated it, every 10 years—and now every state makes registration permanent. The Voting Rights Act Amendments (VRAA) of 1970 and a succeeding decision of the Supreme Court effectively mandated a maximum 30-day residency requirement for participation in federal elections in the 50 states. The National Voter Registration Act (NVRA) of 1993, better known as "Motor Voter," prevented states from purging voters from the rolls for not voting. The 1970 VRAA mandated a registration closing date no more than 30 days before Election Day, and the 1993 NVRA prompted three more states to adopt same-day voter registration (to gain exemption from the provisions of the act), bringing the total to six: Idaho, Maine, Minnesota, New Hampshire, Wisconsin, and Wyoming. Access to voter registration is now more liberal than it has been since registration's widescale adoption a century or more ago.

Still, the registration laws in force throughout the United States are among the world's most demanding. In the United States, the burdens of voter registration fall primarily on the voters themselves. In most of the rest of the democratic world, the government takes responsibility for the creation of voter rolls. In the United Kingdom, registration officers either send a form to every residential address or conduct a door-to-door canvass. In most of continental Europe, governments require citizens to register their addresses, from which information they generate voter rolls. The restrictiveness of American voter registration is one reason why voter turnout in the United States is near the bottom of the developed world. The rate of voting among registrants in the United States, about 80 percent, is just about average for the world's established democracies. The rate of voting among all eligible citizens, however, about 55 percent, is well below (see tables 8, 9, and 10).

Effect of Voter Registration on Voter Turnout

Social scientists who have examined the relationship between registration requirements and voter participation agree that registration depresses turnout. Registration depresses turnout because it imposes a cost on voters. Before the NVRA expanded the availability of voter registration sites, registration required a special trip to the registrar's office, often during business hours only. It often required the completion of a complicated form and the presentation of proof of identity and residence. Finally, it had to be—and still must be—accomplished well before Election Day. Writing in 1978, the authors of the pioneering study of the effects of voter registration, Steven J. Rosenstone and Raymond E. Wolfinger, put it this way: "Registration is often more difficult than voting. It may require a longer journey, at a less convenient hour, to complete a more complicated procedure—and at a time when interest in the [election] campaign is far from its peak."

Rosenstone and Wolfinger examined a variety of voter registration requirements for their effect on voter participation, employing survey data gathered by the Current Population Survey in its 1972 Voter Supplement. They found that regular registrar's office hours, evening and Saturday registrar's office hours, and the availability of absentee registration each contributed a small but discernible amount—2 to 5 percentage points—to the likelihood of voter turnout. Consistent with findings from other studies, they found that the single most important impact on voter turnout was the length of the closing period. By their estimates, residents of states with 30-

Table 8   Rates of Voter Registration and Turnout, by State, from Survey Self-Reports, 1996

Percent

State	Eligible voters who registered	Registered voters who turned out	Eligible voters who turned out
Alabama	74.9	75.2	56.3
Alaska	76.8	79.0	60.7
Arizona	67.2	80.8	54.3
Arkansas	64.9	80.0	53.1
California	70.9	86.4	61.3
Colorado	72.7	84.1	61.1
Connecticut	74.5	83.7	62.3
Delaware	65.6	85.4	56.1
District of Columbia	77.8	81.6	63.5
Florida	68.8	82.0	56.4
Georgia	67.8	75.1	50.9
Hawaii	60.8	78.2	47.5
Idaho	70.5	87.9	62.0
Illinois	72.0	82.1	59.1
Indiana	69.3	81.5	56.5
Iowa	75.3	83.7	63.0
Kansas	70.5	89.9	63.4
Kentucky	69.7	76.0	53.0
Louisiana	74.5	84.2	62.7
Maine	83.6	82.9	69.3
Maryland	69.2	85.3	57.2
Massachusetts	71.9	84.5	60.8
Michigan	74.2	80.8	59.9
Minnesota	80.7	85.4	69.0
Mississippi	72.2	77.0	55.6
Missouri	76.2	80.8	61.6
Montana	75.9	89.7	68.1
Nebraska	67.1	82.3	62.6
Nevada	65.8	81.0	53.3
New Hampshire	78.2	83.8	61.0
New Jersey	70.1	86.4	60.6
New Mexico	68.9	80.5	55.5
New York	70.2	83.5	58.7
North Carolina	70.3	78.9	55.5
North Dakota	91.0	72.8	66.2
Ohio	69.5	85.8	59.6
Oklahoma	70.9	83.5	59.2
Oregon	76.0	83.7	63.6
Pennsylvania	67.2	83.9	56.4
Rhode Island	76.1	84.4	64.3
South Carolina	68.4	79.9	54.7
South Dakota	75.1	86.2	64.7
Tennessee	66.5	80.5	53.6

(Continued)

Table 8   Rates of Voter Registration and Turnout, by State, from Survey Self-Reports, 1996 (*Continued*)

Percent

State	Eligible voters who registered	Registered voters who turned out	Eligible voters who turned out
Texas	69.0	74.7	51.5
Utah	67.6	82.1	55.5
Vermont	73.1	82.8	60.5
Virginia	68.8	84.9	58.4
Washington	72.6	85.8	62.3
West Virginia	65.2	77.5	50.6
Wisconsin	80.6	80.4	64.8
Wyoming	71.9	92.7	66.7
United States	71.0	82.3	58.4

Source: Current Population Survey, 1996 Voter Supplement.

Table 9   Rates of Voter Registration, by State, from State Reports, 1996

Percent

State	Voting age population		Voting age citizen population	
	On register	On register as active	On register	On register as active
Alabama	84.9	76.9	88.3	80.0
Alaska	110.4	97.6	118.1	104.5
Arizona	79.6	71.5	91.2	81.9
Arkansas	73.1	73.1	74.9	74.9
California	73.1	68.6	92.3	86.6
Colorado	82.0	66.8	85.2	69.5
Connecticut	79.7	75.9	87.4	83.2
Delaware	76.6	73.2	80.3	76.7
District of Columbia	93.8	85.6	104.8	95.5
Florida	73.2	67.9	82.6	76.5
Georgia	70.3	70.3	73.6	73.6
Hawaii	63.2	61.2	73.7	71.5
Idaho	81.6	81.6	86.4	86.4
Illinois	85.2	76.1	92.3	82.4
Indiana	79.8	79.8	83.3	83.3
Iowa	83.1	81.5	86.6	85.0
Kansas	75.9	75.9	80.7	80.7
Kentucky	81.8	81.7	82.8	82.6
Louisiana	81.7	79.2	83.8	81.2
Maine	106.0	106.0	110.9	110.9
Maryland	70.4	67.5	75.0	71.9
Massachusetts	82.3	75.2	90.5	82.6
Michigan	94.4	94.4	98.1	98.1
Minnesota	89.7	89.7	93.7	93.7
Mississippi	92.8	88.1	94.8	89.9
Missouri	83.7	83.7	86.0	86.0
Montana	90.1	90.1	92.1	92.1
Nebraska	83.8	83.8	88.3	88.3

Table 9 Rates of Voter Registration, by State, from State Reports, 1996 (*Continued*)

Percent

State	Voting age population		Voting age citizen population	
	On register	On register as active	On register	On register as active
Nevada	64.3	59.6	73.8	68.5
New Hampshire	86.7	86.7	88.9	88.9
New Jersey	71.4	68.1	80.3	76.6
New Mexico	68.5	60.3	74.2	65.4
New York	74.9	70.5	87.3	82.2
North Carolina	78.2	76.6	82.7	80.9
North Dakota	No voter registration			
Ohio	82.0	82.0	84.8	84.8
Oklahoma	81.8	81.8	85.2	85.2
Oregon	87.2	81.4	91.5	85.3
Pennsylvania	74.0	73.4	77.5	76.9
Rhode Island	80.3	80.3	88.3	88.3
South Carolina	73.2	65.5	75.0	67.1
South Dakota	89.5	86.5	92.3	89.2
Tennessee	76.7	74.6	77.8	75.6
Texas	77.5	70.2	87.5	79.3
Utah	80.3	80.3	84.1	84.1
Vermont	86.6	86.6	90.0	90.0
Virginia	65.4	62.6	69.4	66.5
Washington	78.4	74.8	82.5	78.7
West Virginia	68.5	67.1	68.8	67.4
Wisconsin	Registration not reported to FEC			
Wyoming	67.6	67.6	69.9	69.9
United States	76.3	72.8	83.3	79.5

Source: Federal Election Commission, *Implementing the National Voter Registration Act,* March 1998, Appendix A; U.S. Bureau of the Census, *Reported Voting and Registration among Citizens, by Gender, for States,* August 1998.

Table 10 Rate of Voter Turnout, by State, from State Reports and Election Returns, 1996

As percent of

State	Voting age population	Voting age citizen population	Registrants	Active registrants
Alabama	47.7	49.6	56.2	61.9
Alaska	56.9	61.0	51.5	58.3
Arizona	44.7	51.2	56.1	62.5
Arkansas	47.2	48.3	64.6	64.6
California	43.9	55.4	60.0	64.0
Colorado	52.8	54.9	64.4	79.0
Connecticut	56.2	61.6	70.5	74.0
Delaware	50.4	52.8	65.7	68.8
District of Columbia	44.0	49.2	46.9	51.4
Florida	48.1	54.2	65.7	70.9

(Continued)

Table 10   Rate of Voter Turnout, by State, from State Reports and Election Returns, 1996 (*Continued*)

Percent

State	Voting age population	Voting age citizen population	Registrants	Active registrants
Georgia	42.4	44.4	60.3	60.3
Hawaii	40.5	47.2	64.1	66.1
Idaho	57.9	61.4	71.0	71.0
Illinois	49.3	53.3	57.8	64.7
Indiana	48.8	51.0	61.2	61.2
Iowa	57.7	60.2	69.5	70.8
Kansas	58.9	62.6	77.6	77.6
Kentucky	47.4	48.0	58.0	58.1
Louisiana	57.1	58.4	69.7	71.9
Maine	64.1	67.1	60.5	60.5
Maryland	46.6	49.7	66.3	69.1
Massachusetts	55.0	60.5	66.9	73.2
Michigan	54.4	56.5	57.6	57.6
Minnesota	64.1	66.9	71.5	71.5
Mississippi	45.4	46.4	49.0	51.6
Missouri	58.2	59.8	69.6	69.6
Montana	62.1	63.4	68.9	68.9
Nebraska	55.9	58.9	66.7	66.7
Nevada	38.3	44.0	59.6	64.3
New Hampshire	57.1	58.8	66.1	66.1
New Jersey	51.0	57.3	71.4	74.8
New Mexico	45.4	49.2	66.4	75.3
New York	46.6	54.3	62.2	66.0
North Carolina	46.3	48.9	59.2	60.5
North Dakota	57.7	58.7	No voter registration	
Ohio	54.3	56.2	66.3	66.3
Oklahoma	49.7	51.8	60.8	60.8
Oregon	57.1	59.5	65.5	70.2
Pennsylvania	49.0	51.3	66.2	66.8
Rhode Island	52.0	57.1	64.8	64.8
South Carolina	41.9	42.9	57.3	64.0
South Dakota	60.5	62.4	67.6	70.0
Tennessee	46.9	47.6	61.2	62.9
Texas	41.3	46.6	53.2	58.8
Utah	49.9	52.3	62.2	62.2
Vermont	58.1	60.3	67.1	67.1
Virginia	47.5	50.5	72.8	76.0
Washington	54.8	57.6	69.9	73.2
West Virginia	44.9	45.0	65.6	66.9
Wisconsin	57.4	61.1	Registration not reported to FEC	
Wyoming	59.4	61.5	87.9	87.9
United States	49.1	53.7	64.4	67.5

Source: Federal Election Commission, *Implementing the National Voter Registration Act,* March 1998, Appendix A; Federal Election Commission, *1996 General Election Votes Cast for President, Senate, and House,* October 1997; U.S. Bureau of the Census, *Reported Voting and Registration among Citizens, by Gender, for States,* August 1998.

day closing periods were between 3 and 9 percentage points less likely to vote than people who could register on Election Day. Taking all the registration requirements in effect in 1972 together, they estimated that voter turnout nationwide was about 9 percentage points lower than it could have been had all the states adopted the most generous voter registration provisions. Registration laws, they found, were especially burdensome for voters with less education, who had less interest in participation and smaller stores of skills and knowledge with which to negotiate the bureaucratic task of registration.

Since 1972, the legal structure of voter registration has changed markedly, particularly owing to the implementation of the National Voter Registration Act. NVRA broadened access to voter registration by requiring states to

1. make voter registration applications available in driver's license bureaus and social service agencies, and
2. design procedures for registration by mail, either by allowing application by mail or by allowing requests for applications by mail,

which, taken together, essentially solve the problems of availability—of office hours, of office locations, and of absentee registration—that Rosenstone and Wolfinger found to discourage voter turnout. Indeed, of the 41.5 million applications for voter registration reported by the 43 states affected by the provisions of NVRA in 1995–96, 33.1 percent originated in motor vehicle offices and 29.7 arrived by mail.[6] Voter registration has risen by about 4 percentage points because of greater access under NVRA, according to the Committee for the Study of the American Electorate.

NVRA left the patchwork of state closing periods largely unchanged. It caused three additional states to adopt same-day voter registration, bringing to seven the total number of states that do not require voters to take action before Election Day. The six states with Election Day registration—and the one state, North Dakota, without voter registration—are smaller, more rural northern tier states with histories of clean elections. Residents of the seven states are 5.6 percent of the voting age citizen population (table 11).

In the 43 other states, closing periods range from 10 days in Alabama, Iowa, and Vermont to 31 days in Nevada. Thirty states with 63.3 percent

---

6. The 1998 Current Population Survey found that 35.6 percent of new registrants said they had registered at motor vehicle agencies. Another 10.0 percent registered by mail. About 16 percent registered at an official registrar's office.

Table 11 Voter Registration Closing Period, by State
Number of days

State	Days before election	State	Days before election
Alabama	10	Nebraska	28
Alaska	30	Nevada	31
Arizona	29	New Hampshire	0
Arkansas	30	New Jersey	29
California	15	New Mexico	28
Colorado	29	New York	25
Connecticut	14	North Carolina	25
Delaware	20	North Dakota	No registration
District of Columbia	30	Ohio	30
Florida	29	Oklahoma	25
Georgia	29	Oregon	21
Hawaii	30	Pennsylvania	30
Idaho	0	Rhode Island	30
Illinois	28	South Carolina	30
Indiana	29	South Dakota	15
Iowa	10	Tennessee	30
Kansas	15	Texas	30
Kentucky	28	Utah	20
Louisiana	30	Vermont	10
Maine	0	Virginia	29
Maryland	29	Washington	30
Massachusetts	20	West Virginia	30
Michigan	30	Wisconsin	0
Minnesota	0	Wyoming	0
Mississippi	30		
Missouri	28	U.S. average	22.1
Montana	30	U.S. median	28

Source: Democratic National Committee.

of the eligible population have closing periods of four weeks or more. On the other end of the scale, seven states with 15.7 percent of the eligible population require closing periods of 15 days or less. On the whole, closing periods have shortened over the last 25 years, but not dramatically. Twenty-three states have reduced their registration closing periods, most notably by 21 days in Arizona and Georgia and by 15 days, just this year, in California.[7] But in the same period, 10 states have moved up the date by which citizens must register to vote.

---

7. California's county registrars opposed the shortening of the closing period on the grounds that 15 days left too little time to enter new registrants on the rolls and to generate accurate registrations lists for Election Day. As one registrar told us, to shorten the closing period will necessarily be to make greater use of provisional ballots.

Voter Registration and Residential Mobility

By its nature, because voter registration is linked to residence, it has its greatest impact on people who have moved. In the United States, that is a substantial number. Between March 1999 and March 2000, 16.1 percent of the population over the age of one, or 43.4 million people, changed residences.

Before NVRA, in most states, the voting age citizens among migrants would have needed to reregister in order to vote in their new jurisdictions of residence. (Under the 1970 Voting Rights Act Amendments, movers could still vote by absentee ballot at former addresses.) NVRA required states to devise "fail-safe" procedures to accommodate registrants who had moved within county but who had not yet reregistered at new addresses. States were required to issue a full ballot, whether regular or provisional, to registrants who had moved within the same precinct. For registrants who had moved within county but to new precincts, states had to allow voting either in new precincts or in old precincts or give voters the option of voting in some combination of old precinct, new precinct, or central location. For the 2000 election, 15 states allowed voting only at the old polling place, 16 allowed voting at the new polling place, and 10 gave voters options for where to vote.[8] NVRA's fail-safe provisions cover the majority of movers. In 1999–2000, 56.2 percent of all migrants, or 24.4 million people, relocated to new homes within the same county.

The National Voter Registration Act did nothing, however, to back up registrants who move out of county or out of state. The eligible voters among the 20.3 percent of migrants who move into a new county in the same state (8.8 million people) and the 19.4 percent who move out of state (8.4 million people) must still reregister before they can vote.[9] Because of the availability of registration in government service agencies and registration by mail, reregistration is easier since NVRA than it was before. But it is still a step that citizens must take in order to exercise the franchise.

The difficulty of reregistration is distinctly more acute for citizens who relocate to new counties and new states within the registration closing period. The median state has a closing period of 28 days, and 63.3 percent of the electorate cannot register for at least the 28 days before the election. Because Election Day must be no earlier than November 2 and no later

---

8. The remaining states are the six exempted from NVRA—Idaho, Minnesota, New Hampshire, North Dakota, Wisconsin, and Wyoming—two states that did not respond to the FEC survey, and Oregon, which votes by mail.
9. The remainder is 4 percent of migrants who move abroad.

than November 8, the people who are blocked from reregistration by the closing period are predominantly people who relocate in October, when 10.4 percent of all moves occur. In 1993, the year from which these data derive, 485,000 citizens of voting age moved to a new county during October, and 535,000 eligible citizens moved to a new state during October. Therefore, a reasonable estimate of the number of eligible voters who are not accommodated by fail-safe and who cannot reregister at their new address because of moves during the closing period is a little over one million, or about 0.6 percent of the voting age citizen population.[10]

Everybody who moves into a new county or into a new state may vote in person or by absentee ballot at her former address, as specified under the 1970 Voting Rights Act Amendments. The logistical difficulties of obtaining an absentee ballot from afar during the chaos of a move probably mean that relatively few migrants who are blocked from registration by the closing period actually vote. Two other legal provisions go further in accommodating citizens caught in this predicament. The first is Election Day registration, which removes the impediment of the closing period for both intercounty and interstate migrants. The second, which helps in-state migrants alone, is an expanded use of provisional ballots. Under Washington law, registrants who move to a new county within Washington may cast a provisional ballot. Election officials send the provisionals to the jurisdictions of most recent registration, which accept votes cast for offices in common.

Characteristics of Movers and Registrants

The complications of voter registration affect people differently. As we will see, some of the demographic differences between people who are registered and people who are not trace to differences in interest in the electoral process and differences in the possession of the skills necessary to complete the task. But some of the differences trace as well to the characteristics of people who move and people who stay put.

First, residential mobility is greatest for young adults. One-third of people in their twenties, but only one-twentieth of people in and beyond their

---

10. Another population that is ensnared by registration closing periods is members of the armed forces who are discharged within the closing period. We have been unable to find data on either the number of annual discharges from active duty or their distribution through the year. But the number of people affected is certainly much smaller. In 1998 only about 1.4 million Americans were on active duty in the armed forces, 1.1 million of whom were posted stateside.

sixties, move in a year (table 12). Voter registration, accordingly, affects the young more than the old. Barely more than half of young adults were registered to vote in 1996, versus nearly 80 percent of adults over 65 years of age. Residential mobility is one of the most important factors in the low rates of voter participation among young adults.

Second, people who rent their homes are vastly more likely to move than people who own their homes (see table 13). Nearly a third of renters move in a year, versus only a tenth of owners. The greater mobility of renters makes a dramatic difference in voter registration. Nearly three-quarters of people who live in owner-occupied housing, but not even half of people who live in rental housing, are registered to vote.

Not every demographic difference in voter registration traces to mobility, however. People with advanced degrees are 20 percentage points more likely than people educated through high school and 50 percentage points more likely than people educated into grammar school to be registered to vote. To be sure, the better educated enjoy greater residential stability than the less educated. But the better educated are also better equipped to take on the task of voter registration. After years in a classroom, they are more likely to know that they must register to vote. They are more likely to know how, when, and where to register. They are more likely to be interested in politics, more likely to feel effective in politics, and more likely to be part of groups that encourage them to take part in the electoral process.

Table 12 People Who Moved within the Year, by Age, Race, and Homeownership

Percent

Characteristic	Movers
Age	
20–24	35.2
25–29	32.4
30–44	22.0
45–54	9.3
55–64	7.0
65–84	4.3
85 +	4.7
Race and ethnicity	
White	15.3
Black	19.2
Hispanic	21.0
Ownership	
Homeowners	9.1
Renters	32.5

Source: Current Population Survey, 2000.

Table 13 Voter Registration, by Age, Race, Education, and Homeownership

Percent

Characteristic	Of voting age citizen population
Age	
18–24	53.5
25–44	68.1
45–64	77.8
65 +	79.5
Race and ethnicity	
White	72.0
Black	66.4
Hispanic	58.6
	Of voting age citizen and noncitizen population
Education	
Less than 5 years	28.4
5 to 8 years	44.2
9 to 12 years	47.9
High school graduate	62.2
Some college	72.9
Bachelor's degree	78.9
Advanced degree	83.7
Homeownership	
Reside in owner-occupied unit	73.0
Reside in rental unit	49.2

Source: Current Population Survey, 1996 Voter Supplement.

In short, they are more likely to be motivated to register and more likely to have the skills to manage it.

Because of the mix of circumstances, motivation, and skills that go into decisions to register to vote, voter registration is skewed modestly toward the more advantaged parts of American society, overrepresenting older, wealthier, better educated, residentially stable whites and underrepresenting younger, poorer, less educated, residentially mobile blacks and Latinos.

Administration of Voter Registration

The successes of the National Voter Registration Act in easing access to voter registration have come at a definite cost: by their own testimony, NVRA has complicated the professional lives of elections officers. Some worry that NVRA has made it easier both for people who are eligible to vote to register legally and for people who are ineligible to vote to register illegally, increasing the risk of election fraud. More voice the concern that NVRA has put a large part of administration of voter registration in the hands of agencies that are not responsible for conducting it conscientiously and correctly. Finally, many contend that NVRA has complicated voter list management, making it more difficult to eliminate duplicates and to delete the records of people who have left the jurisdiction by migration or by death.

During the congressional debate over NVRA, critics charged that the act increased the probability of election fraud, and especially the probability of illegal registration and voting by people who are not citizens of the United States. None of the election administrators with whom the commission has spoken seems preoccupied with noncitizen registrants, but they freely admit the likelihood that noncitizens appear on registration lists, albeit, in their judgment, in small numbers. Voter registration has been made easier just as the immigrant population has soared. The foreign-born population of the United States rose from 6.2 percent in 1980 to 7.9 percent in 1990 to 10.4 percent in 2000, the largest proportion since 1930. The foreign-born make up 24.9 percent of the population of California and 19.6 percent of the population of New York.

To require proof of citizenship for voter registration would raise objections from civil libertarians and advocates for ethnic communities, especially the fastest growing, Latin American and Asian. It would also be notably burdensome for the vast majority of Americans who are either native or naturalized citizens. None of the most common forms of identification, such as driver's licenses and Social Security cards, are restricted to U.S. citizens. Definite proof of citizenship requires certified birth certificate or naturalization papers, neither of which is necessarily close at hand. In fact, given the relative difficulty of access, proof of citizenship would probably be more easily accomplished by naturalized citizens than by native-born citizens, many of whom would need to obtain a certified birth certificate from the county of their nativity.

Twelve states have recently taken less burdensome steps to deter registration by noncitizens. In every state, applications for voter registration include the applicant's signed affirmation of qualification for voter registration under the laws of the state. The attestation of a false affidavit is a felony and a deportable offense. But the twelve states go further, requiring applicants to check a separate box to indicate whether they are a citizen of the United States or not.[11] (Most warn applicants to proceed no further if

---

11. Nine of the twelve, however, also accept the national mail-in voter registration form, available from the Federal Election Commission. The national form does not include a check-off for citizenship status.

they checked "no.") Significantly, the twelve states that require a citizenship check-off include the six with the largest percentages of noncitizens in the nation (table 14).[12]

The delegation of voter registration responsibilities to agencies other than registrars has been a more active concern among election administrators. They cite an array of problems. Motor vehicle bureaus and public service agencies fail to forward applications in time for them to be entered onto the public registry.[13] Third-party registrars—political parties, advocacy groups, and citizens' groups that conduct registration drives—delay to send applications or fail to send them at all, sometimes inadvertently and sometimes deliberately. Agencies and third-party registrars take applications that are incomplete or inadmissible: applications with postal box addresses rather than street addresses, applications that are unsigned. Finally, election officials cite public confusion. People arrive at the polls convinced that they are registered to vote by virtue of having obtained a driver's license.

Table 14 States with Citizenship Check-off for Voter Registration

Percent

State	Noncitizens of voting age population, 1996	Foreign born, 1997
Alabama	1.4	1.3
Arizona	12.9	14.4
California	20.9	24.9
Connecticut	6.1	7.5
Florida	10.2	16.4
Maryland	4.8	8.6
Michigan	3.0	4.5
New York	13.2	19.6
Texas	10.3	11.3
Utah	4.5	5.9
Vermont	1.6	3.0
Virginia	3.4	6.6

Source: Offices of the Secretary of State, individual states; U.S. Census Bureau, "Profile of the Foreign-Born Population in the United States, 1997," *Current Population Report Special Studies,* Series P23-195; 1996 Current Population Survey Voter Supplement.

---

12. Four of the states that have a permanent bar on felons' voting rights include such a check-off on voter registration applications: Alabama, Florida, Tennessee, and Virginia.

13. The most recent FEC report to Congress on the implementation of NVRA noted that the incidence of such problems had increased threefold since the commission's last survey.

A number of states have adopted measures to meet these administrative challenges. Closer integration of voter registration with other government records is one solution. In the late 1990s, for example, Michigan created its Qualified Voter File (QVF), which is so closely linked to motor vehicle records that the driver's license number became the registration ID number, and the voter registration address became the driver's license address. Changes to one record automatically cause changes to the other. In other states, broader use of provisional ballots creates an audit trail for problem points.

Finally, election officials contend that NVRA has created new problems of voter list maintenance. NVRA set new and stricter standards for purging voter registration rolls. It allowed registrars to remove registrants from the rolls (subject to particular safeguards) only at their own request, because of criminal convictions, death, or mental incapacity or because of a change of address. It prohibited registrars from deleting registrations on the sole basis of extended nonparticipation in elections or on the basis of relocation within jurisdiction. It required registrars to retain "inactive" registrants who did not vote and did not respond to mailed inquiries on the list for a period of two general elections.

Because of these stricter list maintenance provisions, NVRA by all accounts has caused voter registration rolls to swell. The official number of registrants, active and inactive, exceeds the voting age population of numerous counties and two states, Alaska and Maine.[14] To be sure, registration rolls have never been lean: most jurisdictions purged their lists less frequently and less completely than they could.[15] But where informed estimates placed lapsed registrations at 15 percent of total registrations before NVRA, they now place lapsed registrations at 25 percent of the total.[16]

---

14. After a recent purge, registration in Maine is now below 100 percent of voting age population.
15. According to Election Data Services, 218 counties reported registrations in excess of 100 percent of county population in 1992. In 1996, 219 reported the same. (See Federal Election Commission, "Implementing the National Voter Registration Act," March 1998: 5–15.)
16. The problem of oversubscribed lists is not peculiar to voter registration. Thirty states currently have more driver's licenses on issue than they have population over the age of 16. The largest overage is Wyoming's, where licensed drivers are 158 percent of population.

The list maintenance provisions of NVRA have given a substantial boost to efforts to create statewide voter registration lists, which have doubled in number since 1993. Statewide lists permit election officials to eliminate duplicate registrations more easily, in that 76.5 percent of residential relocations occur within the same state. They also enable better integration of voter lists with other governmental databases, such as motor vehicle registrations, vital records, and corrections records.

According to officials who administer voter registration, however, the greatest current impediment to efficient list management is the lack of a unique numeric identifier for each registrant. Names, addresses, and dates of birth of the same people listed in two different sources frequently do not match because of alternative forms, abbreviations, similarities to others' names, or simple data reporting or data entry errors. (Death records, for instance, originate in hospitals, where hospital staff take reports from family members in a time of bereavement.) While still subject to mistakes in data reporting and data entry, numeric identifiers would vastly reduce the number of ambiguous matches and simplify list maintenance.

The most obvious numeric identifier, the Social Security number (SSN), is prohibited from new use in voter registration by the Privacy Act of 1974. The eight states that currently require Social Security numbers for registration adopted them for use before the passage of the act. Four additional states require the last four digits of the Social Security number. Sixteen states, in New England, the Upper Midwest, and the Pacific Northwest, do not use numeric identifiers.[17] Of the rest, sixteen request full SSNs, three request the last four digits, and five request driver's license or state ID numbers (table 15). Although large numbers of registrants comply with the request for an identifying number, provision of the information is not universal.[18]

Previous proposals to allow broader use of Social Security numbers for purposes of identification have met strong opposition. On the grounds of an abstract right to privacy, civil libertarians have resisted turning the Social Security number into a national identity number. Many citizens would be uneasy about broader and more public use of a number that is already linked to financial and credit records.

---

17. This list includes five of the six states with Election Day registration. The exception is Idaho.
18. Moreover, most states have only recently begun to request numeric identifiers, and they lack them for nearly everybody who registered before the request.

Table 15 Numeric Identifiers for Voter Registration, by State

State	Request			Require	
	Full Social Security number	Last four digits of Social Security number	Driver's license number	Full Social Security number	Last four digits of Social Security number
Alabama	■				
Alaska	■				
Arizona		■			
Arkansas	■				
California			■		
Colorado	■				
Connecticut					
Delaware	■				
District of Columbia	■				
Florida					■
Georgia				■	
Hawaii				■	
Idaho	■				
Illinois	■				■
Indiana	■				
Iowa	■				
Kansas	■				
Kentucky				■	
Louisiana	■				
Maine					
Maryland	■				
Massachusetts					
Michigan			■		
Minnesota					
Mississippi	■				
Missouri					■
Montana					
Nebraska					
Nevada				■*	
New Hampshire					
New Jersey					
New Mexico				■	
New York					
North Carolina			■		
North Dakota		No voter registration			
Ohio	■				
Oklahoma					■
Oregon					
Pennsylvania					
Rhode Island					
South Carolina				■	
South Dakota	■				
Tennessee				■	
Texas	■		■		

(Continued)

Table 15 Numeric Identifiers for Voter Registration, by State (*Continued*)

	Request			Require	
State	Full Social Security number	Last four digits of Social Security number	Driver's license number	Full Social Security number	Last four digits of Social Security number
Utah		■	■		
Vermont					
Virginia				■	
Washington					
West Virginia		■			
Wisconsin					
Wyoming					
United States	16 states + D.C.	3 states	5 states	8 states	4 states

Source: Federal Election Commission, National Voter Mail-In Registration Instructions.
*Nevada allows use of a driver's license number or state-issued voter ID number as an alternative.

Selected References

Argersinger, Peter H. "New Perspectives on Election Fraud in the Gilded Age," *Political Science Quarterly* 100 (Winter 1985–86): 669–87.

Burnham, Walter Dean. "The Turnout Problem," in James A. Reichley, ed., *Elections American Style* (Brookings Institution, 1987): 97–133.

Cox, Gary W., and J. Morgan Kousser. "Turnout and Rural Corruption: New York as a Test Case," *American Journal of Political Science* 25 (November 1981): 646–63.

Federal Election Commission, Office of Election Administration. "Implementing the National Voter Registration Act: A Report to State and Local Election Officials on Problems and Solutions Discovered 1995–1996," March 1998.

————. "The Impact of the National Voter Registration Act of 1993 on the Administration of Elections for Federal Office, 1999–2000," final draft, June 2001.

Hansen, Kristin A. "Seasonality of Moves and Duration of Residence," United States Bureau of the Census, Current Population Reports P70–66, October 1998.

Harris, Joseph P. *Registration of Voters in the United States* (Brookings Institution, 1929).

Keyssar, Alexander. *The Right to Vote: The Contested History of Democracy in America* (Basic Books, 2000).

Rosenstone, Steven J., and Raymond E. Wolfinger. "The Effect of Registration Laws on Voter Turnout," *American Political Science Review* 72 (March 1978): 22–45.

Wolfinger, Raymond E., and Jonathan Hoffman. "Registering and Voting with Motor Voter," *PS: Political Science and Politics* 34 (March 2001): 85–92.

Statewide Voter Registration Systems

Summary of Conclusions

1. Twenty states currently have statewide voter registration systems in place or in process, and all but 11 states now have some form of periodic centralized statewide voter list.

2. Improved computing and data networking capabilities have made statewide registration systems possible, but the most important impetus to the adoption of statewide systems was the National Voter Registration Act (NVRA). The act made voter registration available through driver's license bureaus and other government offices, and states have turned to centralized voter lists to achieve better coordination between local registrars and state and local governmental service agencies. NVRA also set stricter standards for voter list management, and states have found centralized registration lists to help in list maintenance, for instance, in identifying duplicate registrations and in facilitating reregistrations by people who have moved within state.

3. Statewide voter registration systems require standardization of data formats and computing platforms, which has been a challenge to achieve in large states and in states with radically decentralized voter registration responsibilities. Michigan is the largest and most complex state yet to implement a statewide voter registration system.

Historically, voter registration has been administered, except in Alaska and Oklahoma, almost exclusively on the local level, by city, town, and township registrars in much of New England and the Great Lakes and by county registrars almost everywhere else. Recently, as computerization has opened new possibilities and voter list management has become more difficult, states have begun to coordinate voter registration through centralized voter lists.

South Carolina was the first to create a computerized statewide registration list, a compilation of local registries, in 1968. Kentucky followed suit in 1973, consolidating local voter registration records in an active statewide database. Louisiana piloted a centralized list in 1983 and extended it statewide in 1987.

By now, 11 states and the District of Columbia have already implemented statewide registration systems that cover all their jurisdictions. Seven more states are midstream in implementation, and three more states are on the verge of adoption. The 20 states with full statewide systems in place or in process are able to give local election officials access to complete statewide registration lists, often but not always in real time. Altogether, these 20 states and the District of Columbia account for 39.2 percent of the voting age citizen population of the United States (table 16).

Most of the rest of the states are moving toward better coordination of local voter registries. Fourteen states (with 17.8 percent of the voting age population) have or plan minimal systems to collect local voter lists and to

Table 16 Voter Registration Systems, by State

State	Local voter registration systems	State periodically collects local voter registries	State has some local registries on line	State has all local registries on line
Alabama	11 current		Yes	Implementing
Alaska				Yes
Arizona		Yes		
Arkansas				Yes
California		Yes	Implementing	
Colorado			Yes	Nearing passage
Connecticut				Implementing
Delaware				Yes
District of Columbia				Yes
Florida		Implementing		Nearing passage
Georgia				Implementing
Hawaii				Yes
Idaho	Yes			
Illinois		Yes		
Indiana		Yes		Nearing passage
Iowa			Yes	
Kansas		Yes		
Kentucky				Yes
Louisiana				Yes
Maine	Yes			
Maryland			Yes	Implementing
Massachusetts				Implementing
Michigan				Yes
Minnesota				Yes
Mississippi	Yes			
Missouri			Yes	
Montana		Yes		
Nebraska			Implementing	
Nevada	Yes			
New Hampshire	Yes			
New Jersey		Yes		
New Mexico		Yes		
New York	Yes			
North Carolina				Implementing
North Dakota		No voter registration		
Ohio		Yes		
Oklahoma				Yes

Table 16 Voter Registration Systems, by State (*Continued*)

State	Local voter registration systems	State periodically collects local voter registries	State has some local registries on line	State has all local registries on line
Oregon	Yes			
Pennsylvania	Yes			
Rhode Island		Yes		
South Carolina				Yes
South Dakota	Yes			
Tennessee		Implementing	Planned	
Texas			Yes	
Utah			Yes	
Vermont	Yes			
Virginia				Yes
Washington		Yes		
West Virginia		Implementing		
Wisconsin	Yes			
Wyoming			Implementing	
United States	11 current	11 current 3 implementing	7 current 3 implementing 1 planned	12 current 7 implementing 3 nearing passage

Source:"Statewide Voter Registration Systems," Election Data Services, May 31, 1997, updated from Mary M. Janicki,"Statewide Voter Registration Systems," Connecticut Office of Legislative Research, January 17, 2001; Council of State Governments Elections Task Force,"Innovative Election Practices," 1999; and "2001 Legislative Scan on Election Reform," Center for Policy Alternatives, May 9, 2001.

check them for duplicate registrations. In between are 11 states that have coordinated systems with partial coverage of election jurisdictions. Altogether, 80.8 percent of the adult citizen population lives in one of the 39 states and the District with at least rudimentary statewide capacity for administration of voter registration.

Many factors have promoted the development of statewide voter registration systems. Computerization of records and faster communications technologies made effective statewide systems imaginable in the 1980s, and the pioneering systems in Kentucky and Louisiana worked on the model of one-way local access to mainframe databases. With innovations in networked computing and database management software, the mainframe systems were soon considered obsolete. Kentucky in fact overhauled its system in 1995, in response to the National Voter Registration Act. The new systems are superior in their capacity for interactivity. Michigan's Qualified Voter File (QVF), for instance, works on a model of two-way local access to centralized servers in Lansing via the Internet. New information is communicated from local QVF offices to Lansing, and updated data are communicated back in less than an hour.

The passage of the National Voter Registration Act in 1993 provided a major impetus for the adoption of statewide registration systems.[1] First, NVRA required states to allow voter registration through driver's license bureaus and social service agencies. Statewide registration systems were an adaptation that made possible better coordination and data sharing between voter registration agencies and the other registration offices specified by the act. In the Michigan system, for example, voter registration records and motor vehicle records are fully integrated. Michigan turned the driver's license number into the registration ID number and changed its motor vehicle license code so that the voter registration address became the driver's license address. Changes to one record automatically cause changes to the other.

Second, NVRA set new and stricter standards for voter list maintenance. It allowed registrars to remove citizens from the rolls (subject to particular safeguards) only at their own request, because of criminal convictions, death, or mental incapacity or because of a change of address. In the new management environment, statewide registration systems had attractive list maintenance capabilities. They slimmed voter registration rolls by allowing identification of existing duplicate registrations. They improved processing of in-state changes of address by pairing the incorporation of new voter registration records with deletion of the old records. If integrated successfully with motor vehicle registers, statewide systems also improved detection of changes of address to out of state, triggered by driver's license cancellations. With its new system, Michigan claims to have eliminated 600,000 duplicate and ineligible registrations. Integration with corrections records and vital records, which so far has proven difficult, may bring still greater efficiencies in list management.

An examination of the states that have yet to attempt statewide systems provides insight into the difficulties. Clearly, one challenge to the development of statewide registration is sheer size. To date, the largest state to implement a statewide system is Michigan, with about 6.8 million citizens of voting age, the nation's eighth largest electorate. If Florida goes forward with its plans, it will become the largest state to undertake the task, with an electorate of 9.8 million, the fourth largest. Prominent among the states that have not yet adopted even a partial system of statewide registration

---

1. Interestingly, South Carolina's first-in-the-nation system was a response to the 1965 Voting Rights Act, which put pressure on the state to ensure uniform and scrupulous administration of voter registration.

are New York, Pennsylvania, Illinois, and New Jersey, the third, fifth, sixth, and ninth most populous jurisdictions. In addition, the systems in California (largest) and Texas (second) are not very far advanced. Texas's system has only 109 of its 256 counties on line, and California's does not yet include Los Angeles County.

For the largest states, the challenge is just the absolute size of the task. For statewide systems to work, local records must be converted to common format and made to work on common platforms. The administrative obstacles of database conversion and system conversion are formidable. And, as Maryland has discovered, experienced vendors with turnkey systems in hand are in short supply.

A second obvious challenge to the implementation of statewide voter registration systems is the number and diversity of the local voter registration offices that must be coordinated. Also prominent among states that have not yet adopted even a partial statewide system are Maine, New Hampshire, Vermont, and Wisconsin, all states in which elections are administered by city, town, and township governments rather than county governments. Statewide systems in radically decentralized states require reconciliation of many, vastly different local voter registration practices.

In both respects, in size and complexity, Michigan represents an attractive model. Michigan is a large state with a large city, Detroit. It is also the state with the largest number of jurisdictions that manage federal elections, 273 city and 1,242 township governments. The Michigan QVF was accomplished at a considerable expense (which was spread out, in part, over a much-needed overhaul of its motor vehicle system). The state provided both hardware and software, at state expense, to 83 county clerks and to 236 clerks of cities and townships of over 5,000 population. Ninety-four smaller jurisdictions opted to purchase the infrastructure at their own expense. As a result, 83 counties and 363 larger cities and townships, with about 80 percent of the Michigan electorate, have direct, real-time access to the Qualified Voter File. The remaining 1,151 cities and townships share access through county QVF sites. Now that the start-up costs are paid, Michigan believes that local governments realize considerable cost savings in voter list management. The most recent Federal Election Commission report on the implementation of NVRA notes that many other states have found their investments in statewide computerized voter registration lists worthwhile.

As technology develops, statewide registration systems hold even greater promise. First, statewide voter registration systems might facilitate statewide provisional balloting. After Election Day, election officials could quickly verify registration in other counties and accept votes cast for common offices. Second, statewide voter registration systems with real-time access on Election Day might make same-day registration possible even in states with histories of "early and often" voting. By entering Election Day registrations directly into registration databases, election administrators could prevent the same person from voting at multiple sites.[2] Finally, statewide registration systems coupled with electronic voting systems might make it possible for voters to cast their ballots not only at their home precincts but at any precinct in the state. As of 1990, 17.7 percent of employed persons worked outside their county of residence, and 30.5 percent lived more than 30 minutes away from their workplace. The numbers of commuters and the distance of commutes continue to rise. If it were technologically possible to verify registration and call up the correct ballot anywhere in the state, citizens could vote near work, near school, or near errands and not only near home. Statewide registration systems, that is, might make it possible to make participation in elections more convenient for legitimate voters without adding to the risk of election fraud.

Selected References

Election Data Services and AutoGenesis Systems. "Developing a Statewide Voter Registration Database: Procedures, Alternatives, and General Models," Office of Election Administration, Federal Election Commission, August 1997.

Federal Election Commission, Office of Election Administration. "The Impact of the National Voter Registration Act of 1993 on the Administration of Elections for Federal Office, 1999–2000," final draft, June 2001.

InfoSentry Services. "Needs and Requirements for an Oregon Centralized Voter Registration System," report prepared for the Secretary of State of Oregon, 18 March 1999.

Michigan Department of State. "Michigan's Qualified Voter File System," typescript, June 5, 2001.

---

2. Virginia already treats the entire state as a single jurisdiction for registration purposes, so that in-state migrants need not reregister in order to vote.

CIVIC EDUCATION PROGRAMS

Summary of Conclusions

1. Americans' engagement in civic affairs is low and declining. Voter turnout dropped 15 percentage points between 1964 and 1996. The lowest levels of engagement are found among the youngest voters. Over two thirds of voters over 45, but only a third of voters under 25, cast ballots in 1996.
2. Scholars find that participation in a civics curriculum has only a small and indirect effect on political involvement later in life. The possibility that exposure to civic education is elective, either by students or by school districts, complicates the assessment of its effect.
3. Several recent civic education curricula seem to hold promise. The most successful programs involve students—and occasionally their parents—directly in governmental processes, either through participation in mock elections or through cooperation and debate. So far, the evidence of their long-term impact on civic engagement in adulthood is limited. None appears likely to restore civic participation to the levels achieved a generation ago, but they may produce modest improvement.

By a variety of measures, the engagement of the American public in government and elections is low and declining. Public interest in public affairs "most of the time" averaged 35 percent from 1964 to 1976 but has not exceeded 30 percent even once ever since. Likewise, "very much" public interest in the current election campaign hovered around 36 percent from 1952 to 1976 but since has dropped under 30 percent, with the singular exception of 1996 (when it was 39 percent). Finally, as is well known, voter turnout has declined from 69.3 percent of the voting age population in 1964 to 54.2 percent in 1996.[1]

The lowest levels of engagement are found among the youngest voters. In 1996, as shown below, the percentage of voters 70 years old and over who were interested in public affairs "most of the time," at 30 percent, was double the percentage of voters 37 and under who were interested most of the time, 14 percent. The percentage of the most senior voters

---

1. The source for interest in public affairs and interest in the current campaign is the 1952 through 1996 American National Election Studies. The source for voter turnout is the U.S. Census Bureau, Current Population Report, Series P20–504, July 1998.

who had "very much" interest in the current campaign, 38 percent, was more than double the percentage of the most junior voters who were very interested, 17 percent. Voter turnout among citizens aged 65 and over was 69.1 percent, but voter turnout among citizens 24 and younger was just 35.6 percent:

Age in years	Turnout of voting age citizen population
18 to 24	35.6
25 to 44	54.2
45 to 64	68.2
65 or more	69.1

The two observations are connected. Interest in public affairs, interest in elections, and voter turnout have been lowest among young adults throughout postwar American history. Accordingly, a substantial part of the decline in interest and turnout in the electorate from the 1960s to the 1980s occurred because of the movement of the enormous postwar baby boom generation through the electorate (in Raymond Wolfinger's vivid phrase) "like a pig through a boa constrictor."[2] The connection may be still deeper. Several scholars have argued that civic engagement among the most recent generations is lower than civic engagement among older generations even at the same point in the life cycle, although others have disputed the claim.

Concern over low and declining civic participation in America has created a strong interest in civic education as a means of reversal. Advocates for greater civic education contend that basic civic knowledge is a precondition for effective participation and that early practical experiences in civic life whet the appetite for sustained engagement into adulthood.

The best and largest study to date on civic engagement, by Sidney Verba, Kay Lehman Schlozman, and Henry E. Brady, finds that formal instruction in civics plays, at best, a small and indirect role in fostering active citizenship. The effect of exposure to civics courses is dwarfed by the impact of educational attainment, in general, and dwarfed as well by the effect of other demographic characteristics and other life experiences. Exposure to civics education does seem to foster attitudes that later promote political involvement, but civics education does not contribute directly to greater civic engagement in adulthood.

---

2. Using survey data from 1952 to 1996, Rosenstone and Hansen estimated that the younger electorate accounted for 2.7 percentage points of the 11.3 percentage point decline in voter turnout from the 1960s to the 1980s.

Even with this evidence, it is difficult to tell whether civics instruction per se contributes to greater political engagement in adulthood. If civics courses are optional, they will be taken as electives mostly by students who are already more interested in government and therefore already more likely to participate upon achieving the age of suffrage. Moreover, if civics curricula are offered by some school districts but not by others, the relationship between civics education and civic engagement may not reflect the impact of the curricula themselves but rather the effect of other characteristics of the communities that adopt them. Civics curricula, that is, may be just one manifestation of the community's broader interest in promoting the civic engagement of its young people. In this and other studies, the possibility that exposure to civic education is elective (either by school districts or by students themselves) complicates the assessment of the program's effect on civic engagement.

The Verba, Schlozman, and Brady study interviewed thousands of people who were exposed to hundreds of different kinds of civic education. A few recent studies have focused on particular civic education curricula. They suggest that three recent initiatives may hold particular promise.

The Kids Voting USA curriculum originated in Arizona, and several communities across the nation have adapted it to their needs as well. Students research and discuss the issues and candidates leading up to an election and then, on Election Day, actually cast replica ballots, oftentimes in real booths alongside the adults in the precincts serviced by their schools. One study on a diverse population in California found that the short and medium (six-month) term effects on political knowledge, interest, and motivation were quite substantial and held across demographic groups.[3] Even more remarkable, the curriculum had a significant and positive effect on the attitudes and behavior of the students' *parents*, particularly among Latinos. One activity in the curriculum had students pose questions to their parents about their own views on political issues and their own experiences with politics. Parents' engagement with the curriculum through their children may well have raised their interest in politics and increased their knowledge of election practices.

---

3. Martin Wattenberg tells us that his data show that young people who register to vote immediately on turning 18 are more likely to turn out and remain registered than people who wait to register until later. Wattenberg's finding may suggest that programs to enroll high school students as voters at the time of graduation may be worthwhile. Or the finding may indicate that young people who are very interested in civic affairs just cannot wait to become registrants.

The Center for Civic Education has developed another promising curriculum, Project Citizen, which is based on ideas offered originally by John Dewey. In many ways it is similar to Kids Voting USA. Project Citizen, however, places more emphasis on engaging ongoing public policy questions, as opposed to getting ready for periodic elections. In addition, the general approach emphasizes cooperation and group involvement, rather than the friendly debate and individual decisionmaking that is the focus of Kids Voting USA. Research on the effectiveness of the curriculum is encouraging, demonstrating improvements in political knowledge, interest, and sense of effectiveness in politics.

Finally, some evidence suggests that well-designed civic education courses that incorporate sustained and substantial amounts of "service learning" can significantly reinforce classroom-based civics. Service learning is a form of community service that is designed to work in tandem with classroom work in furthering various learning objectives, for example, understanding the process of public administration. In addition to making book learning more vivid and relevant, students gain concrete skills to serve them later in life. What is more, advocates claim that service learning adds to the community's stock of "social capital." Since private forms of community service are one of the few types of social capital to have increased over the last several decades, advocates see integrated civics and service learning programs as an exciting opportunity to redirect such activities in an explicitly civic direction.

Unfortunately, the evidence on service learning suggests that short-term and small-scale programs have no effect. Participation must be sustained and substantial in addition to being tightly integrated with classroom activity. Thus, effective programs are resource intensive and, under current funding conditions, are probably not practical as a widespread remedy for the decline in civic engagement. Nonetheless, where resources are available, service learning might be a valuable adjunct to traditional classroom-based civics.

Many more educators and scholars have put forth interesting programs and proposals to improve civic education. They have less empirical research to support them than those discussed above. In general, there is a dearth of reliable knowledge to indicate what works and what does not in civic education. While researchers and educators have collected the data, much of it cannot speak to the question of what actually causes increased civic engagement and, therefore, what would happen if we redirected resources and implemented policy changes. Many service learning courses, for example, are electives, making it difficult to tell whether the course had a real effect, or whether instead the students who enrolled were those who were going to become more engaged in politics anyway. If we changed the elective into a required course, we may see no change among the new, less motivated students.

Even more important, there currently is only thin evidence to assess the effects of civic education initiatives on civic involvement in adulthood. Given their recent vintage, very few programs have produced evidence of long-term efficacy, which is the ultimate question of interest. Even the three programs discussed above cannot claim that when the students who participated in them become adults they will behave any differently from their peers who did not participate. Of course, such research takes time and may prove that modern "best practices" are quite effective and will contribute to a resurgence of civic participation. Certainly it is worth the effort and resources to conduct such research on a large scale and in a rigorous way. For now, however, we should probably moderate our expectations. Better civic education may help to promote greater civic involvement, but it is unlikely to erase the decline in civic engagement that has occurred over the last generation.

Selected References

Atherton, Herbert M. "We the People . . . Project Citizen," in *Education for Civic Engagement in Democracy: Service Learning and Other Promising Practices*, Sheilah Mann and John J. Patrick, eds. (Bloomington, Ind.: ERIC Clearinghouse for Social Studies/Social Science Education, 2000).

Blyth, Dale A., Rebecca Saito, and Tom Berkas. "A Quantitative Study of the Impact of Service-Learning Programs," in *Service Learning: Applications from the Research*, Alan S. Waterman, ed. (Mahwah, N.J.: Lawrence Erlbaum, 1997).

Chaffee, Steven. "Education for Citizenship: Promising Effects of the Kids Voting USA Curriculum," in *Education for Civic Engagement in Democracy: Service Learning and Other Promising Practices*, Sheilah Mann and John J. Patrick, eds. (ERIC Clearinghouse for Social Studies/Social Science Education, 2000).

Eyler, Janet, and Dwight Giles Jr. "The Importance of Program Quality in Service Learning," in *Service Learning: Applications from the Research*, Alan S. Waterman, ed. (Mahwah, N.J.: Lawrence Erlbaum, 1997).

Honnet, Ellen P., and Susan J. Poulsen. *Wingspread Report: Principles of Good Practice for Combining Service and Learning* (Racine, Wisc.: Johnson Foundation, 1989).

Mann, Sheilah. "What the Survey of American College Freshman Tells Us about Their Political Interest," *PS: Politics and Political Science* 32 (June 1999): 263–68.

McDevitt, Michael, and Steven Chaffe. "Second Chance Political Socialization: Trickle-Up Effects of Children on Parents," in *Engaging the Public: How Government and the Media Can Reinvigorate American Democracy*, Thomas J. Johnson, Carol E. Hays, and Scott P. Hays, eds. (Lanham, Md.: Rowman and Littlefield, 1998).

Melchior, Alan. "National Evaluation of Learn and Serve America and Community-based Programs: Final Report" (Brandeis University Center for Human Resources and Abt Associates, 1998).

Miller, Warren E., and J. Merrill Shanks. *The New American Voter* (Harvard University Press, 1996).

Robert D. Putnam. *Bowling Alone: The Collapse and Revival of American Community* (Simon and Schuster, 2000).

Rosenstone, Steven J., and John Mark Hansen. *Mobilization, Participation, and Democracy in America* (Macmillan, 1993).

Tolo, K. W., ed. "An Assessment of We the People . . . Project Citizen: Promoting Citizenship in Classroom and Community" (University of Texas, Lyndon B. Johnson School of Public Affairs, 1998).

Verba, Sidney, Kay Lehman Schlozman, and Henry E. Brady, *Voice and Equality: Civic Voluntarism in American Politics* (Harvard University Press, 1995).

Youniss, James, Jeffrey A. McLellan, and Miranda Yates. "What We Know about Engendering Civic Identity," *American Behavioral Scientist* 40 (March/April 1997): 620–31.

Early Voting, Unrestricted Absentee Voting, and Voting by Mail

Summary of Conclusions

1. In the last 20 years, states have expanded the availability of early voting, voting by mail, and absentee voting. Twenty-six states with 45 percent of the voting age citizens of the United States offer one or more. Voters' use of opportunities to vote before Election Day has doubled since 1980.

2. Older voters, younger voters, retirees, students, disabled persons, and members of the armed forces make greater use of absentee balloting. Whites are about twice as likely as blacks to vote by absentee. Early voters are older, more interested, and more partisan than Election Day voters.

3. Ten years' experience with voter participation outside Election Day suggests that early voting and voting by mail have boosted voter turnout, though modestly. Unrestricted absentee voting by and large has not, or has but by less. It is unclear whether the gains will endure, because voters could be responding more to the novelty and the publicity than the convenience. Both might ultimately increase turnout by a small amount, by making it less likely that habitual voters will fail to turn out because of Election Day exigencies.

4. Early voting, voting by mail, and unrestricted absentee voting have won enthusiastic endorsement from the public. The evidence of savings in elections costs, however, is mixed.

5. In the longer term, some argue, early voting, voting by mail, and unrestricted absentee voting might undercut voter participation by discouraging campaigns and advocacy groups from efforts to mobilize voter turnout. Widespread voting before Election Day might alter the dynamics of election campaigns. Finally, early voting, voting by mail, and unrestricted absentee voting might undermine the public's sense of participation in common in one of our few important civic rites.

In the last decade, states have adopted a number of measures to allow citizens to vote more easily on days other than Election Day. Many states, especially in the West, have followed the lead of California in 1978 and liberalized access to absentee ballots. Altogether, 22 states now make an absentee ballot available to any registered voter who requests one, without need to show cause. Thirty-two percent of the voting age citizen population lives in a state that provides an absentee ballot automatically on request.

Fourteen other states have adopted what has come to be called "early voting." Pioneered in Texas in 1991, early voting evolved from in-person absentee voting but is now distinct from it. In-person absentee voters must apply for an absentee ballot; early voters must simply report to an early voting station, sign the poll book, and have registration verified. Absentee ballots cast in person are usually enclosed in a sealed and signed envelope; early voting ballots cannot be identified individually. In-person absentee voting, finally, takes place only within the regular hours of the elections office; early voting programs often provide extended hours on both weekdays and weekends. Twenty-five percent of the voting age citizen population lives in a state with early voting.

Finally, in 1995, Oregon became the first state to implement voting by mail (VBM) in statewide elections, employing it first in special partisan primary elections and soon after in a special general election to fill a vacant U.S. Senate seat. In 1998, by more than a two-to-one margin, Oregon voters approved an initiative to extend voting by mail permanently to statewide primary and general elections.

Early voting programs overlap significantly with liberalized absentee laws. All but four of the states that provide early voting also provide absentee ballots automatically upon request. Taking the three provisions together, 26 states with 44.5 percent of the voting age citizen population make it easy for voters to cast their ballots before Election Day.[1]

The effect of early voting and liberalized absentee voting has been dramatic. In 1980, just as the movement toward liberalization of access to absentee ballots was begun, five percent of voters nationwide cast their votes by absentee ballot. In 1996, 10 percent nationwide voted prior to Election Day, either by mail (8 percent), mostly by absentee voting, or in-person before Election Day (3 percent), mostly by early voting. In states with liberal access to voting before Election Day, the percentages are still higher. Thirty-nine percent of the 2000 presidential vote in Texas was

---

1. Among the states that do not offer unrestricted absentee voting, Oliver names Michigan and Ohio as the two that have "expanded" eligibility for absentees. Michigan and Ohio provide an absentee ballot for any voter over the ages of 62 and 65, respectively, who requests one. As table 19 at the end of this section shows, Michigan and Ohio are the two states among those without "liberalized" absentee voting that have the highest rates of absentee voting. Adding Michigan and Ohio to the list brings the percentage of the voting age citizen population that lives in a state that makes it easy to vote before Election Day to 52.8.

cast early, and 24.6 percent of the 2000 vote in California was by absentee.[2] And in Oregon, of course, every statewide election since 1995 has used a mail-in ballot. (See tables 18, 19, and 20 at the conclusion of this section.)

Who Votes Early, by Absentee, and by Mail?

Even though both are means by which voters can cast their ballots prior to Election Day, early voting and absentee voting make significantly different demands on voters.

First, absentee voting requires that voters exercise foresight. Registered voters must file an application for an absentee ballot anywhere from a day to five days in advance of Election Day, on average, and up to three weeks in advance in one state.[3] Second, in most states, voters who wish to obtain an absentee ballot must give a reason for needing to vote absentee, most often on the grounds of travel, disability, and educational and occupational circumstances. In contrast, early voting requires only the voter's conviction that he has made up his mind already.

The difference suggests that absentee voting will be highest among people who meet the conditions for use of an absentee ballot and who have the resources to know to arrange to vote in advance. And indeed, as table 17 shows, use of absentee voting is highest among the oldest voters, who often have physical infirmities that make it difficult to turn out in person, followed closely by the youngest voters, who often are in school. One of every six voters over the age of 75 votes absentee.

Certain types of people are very prone to vote absentee out of sheer necessity. Students, retirees, persons with permanent disabilities, and mem-

---

2. Texas law requires early voting only in the larger jurisdictions in the state and requires satellite polling stations with extended hours only in the largest jurisdictions. Accordingly, early voting is even more common in the larger counties. In 1992, 52.5 percent of the vote in Bexar County (San Antonio) and over 40 percent in El Paso, Jefferson (Beaumont), Travis (Austin), and Galveston were by early ballot.

3. Ten states maintain "permanent" absentee voter lists. In four of the states, Oregon, Washington, New Jersey, and selected jurisdictions in Utah, the list is unrestricted, that is, any voter can ask to be placed on it. In the other six states, Kansas, Missouri, New York, Rhode Island, Tennessee, and California, the list is restricted and voters must show cause to be entered onto it. See Maryland League of Women Voters, "LWVMD Voter Participation Study 1999–2000," 2000.

bers of the armed forces are all several times more likely to vote absentee than other Americans.

Use of absentee ballots also has a class bias. People with better educations, higher incomes, and more prestigious jobs are more likely to vote absentee. The highest rates of absentee usage are among holders of graduate and professional degrees and among persons with the very highest family incomes. Finally, in analysis not shown, people in managerial and professional occupations are the most likely to use absentee voting. Citizens of higher social and economic status are not only more likely to need to vote absentee—because they are traveling on business, for instance—but also more likely to know that they will have to plan ahead to obtain an absentee ballot.

Finally, use of absentee ballots varies by race. Blacks are only half as likely as whites to vote absentee. Absentee usage among Latinos is right about in between.[4] Usage of absentee ballots is highest among Americans of Asian descent, which probably owes to the concentration of the Asian population on the Pacific Coast, where unrestricted absentee balloting has the longest history and the greatest popularity.[5]

As the table shows, fewer patterns in usage of early voting present themselves. Early voting is still fairly rare.[6] A better sense of the demographic composition of early and Election Day voters comes from a study of Texas by Robert Stein. The Texas investigators interviewed voters as they exited polling sites on Election Day and as they exited early voting stations during the three-week period of early voting in 1994.

Stein found some significant differences between early and Election Day voters. The most important was age: just as older voters tend to vote absentee so they also tend to vote early. In fact, more than a third of the early voters in 1994 were over the age of 60 and more than half were over 50. In contrast, the youngest voters, who are overrepresented among absentee

---

4. Absentee usage among Latinos was much closer to usage among blacks in 1980. Presumably, the increase owes to the concentration of the Latino population in states that have liberalized absentee voting and implemented early voting.

5. Thirty-seven percent of the Asian population of the United States resides in California. The Pacific Coast states together account for 41.5 percent of the Asian population.

6. The only difference that looks at all striking is the peak rate of in-person voting before Election Day by Latinos. Most probably, this small difference emerges because of a heavy concentration of Latinos—19.3 percent of all Americans of Hispanic descent—in Texas, the state with the most extensive program of early voting.

Table 17 Use of Absentee (by Mail) and Early (in Person) Voting, by Demographic Characteristics, 1996

Percent

Characteristic	Voted in person on election day	Voted in person before election day	Voted by mail
Age			
18–24	87	2	11
25–34	93	2	5
25–64	91	3	6
65–74	85	3	12
75 +	81	3	16
Education			
No diploma	90	3	7
High school diploma	91	2	7
Some college	89	3	8
Bachelor's degree	89	3	8
Graduate degree	87	3	9
Family income			
< $20,000	89	3	8
$20–29,999	90	2	8
$30–49,999	91	2	7
$50–74,999	90	3	7
$75,000 +	87	3	10
Race			
White	89	3	9
Black	95	2	4
Latino	90	4	6
Asian	87	2	11
Other	92		8

Source: Bureau of the Census, 1996 Current Population Survey Voter Supplement, courtesy of Raymond E. Wolfinger.

voters, were underrepresented among early voters. The circumstances that cause absentee usage among the youngest voters, absence from the jurisdiction during Election Day, are also the circumstances that preclude early voting. Stein also found some small differences in early voting by gender, with men more likely to be early voters than women, and by income, with poorer voters more likely to turn out early (the opposite of the pattern for absentee voters).[7]

The main factors that discriminated between early voters and Election Day voters, however, were motivational. People who professed a great deal

---

7. Stein found no racial differences, although blacks were slightly more represented among early voters than among Election Day voters. He also found no appreciable differences in partisan identification or candidate choice, although early voters tended to be more conservative than Election Day voters.

of interest in politics were more likely to turn out early than people who professed little. More strikingly, people who were strong partisans—in Stein's study, people who claimed identification with the Republican or Democratic party and who reported having voted a straight ticket—were overrepresented among early voters. Both interest in politics and strong identification with a political party foster voter turnout, suggesting that early voting simply allows people who are highly motivated to vote to vote sooner. But strong partisans are also much more likely to make their election choices early on the basis of their partisanship and regardless of the particular candidates and the particular circumstances of the campaign. Strong partisans vote early because they have already made up their minds and see nothing to gain from waiting.

Voting by mail differs significantly from early voting and absentee voting. Voting by mail requires no extraordinary action on the part of registered voters, to whom the state of Oregon mails the ballot.[8] Analysis of the Oregon experience by Michael Traugott of the University of Michigan suggests that vote by mail increased the representation in the electorate of newer residents and registrants with a weaker sense that they could affect what government does, but in both cases only slightly. Because vote by mail was the only election game going in Oregon, the overall vote by mail electorate did not differ markedly from the electorate that voted in person on Election Day.

Effect of Early Voting and Liberalized Absentee Voting on Voter Turnout

The stated rationale for the extension of early voting, vote by mail, and the liberalization of access to absentee voting was to make it easier for people to vote. Studies of voter turnout and surveys of nonvoters have both found that large numbers of people do not vote because it is costly or inconvenient for them. By making it easier to vote, the argument went, participation in elections would surely increase.

By the standard of promoting turnout, however, the innovations have been either a modest success or a modest disappointment, depending on expectations. The consensus among analysts is that liberalized absentee voting has had a very small positive effect on voter participation, at best.

---

8. The only exception is people who cannot receive mail at their registration address, but they have the option of specifying a different address to which the ballot may be mailed.

The most careful study of the effect of liberalized absentee voting, by Eric Oliver of Princeton University, found increases in voter turnout in states that had liberalized. But the increases in turnout depended wholly upon the ability of political parties to mobilize voters. In states with closed primaries and therefore with registration of voters by partisanship, turnout increased modestly, by just over 2 percent. In states with open primaries and therefore no easy identification of voters by partisanship, turnout increased far less and maybe even not at all. All in all, liberalized access to absentee balloting increases voter turnout by perhaps a small amount.

Studies of early voting have tended to find larger but still modest effects on voter participation. A study of Tennessee found a 5 percentage point increase in turnout in the first early voting election, 1994, compared to nine earlier midterm congressional election years. Another study of Texas found that increases in levels of early voting across counties in 1992 correlated positively with increases in voter turnout. These studies, at best, are suggestive of a relationship between early voting and voter turnout, but there is still much to be learned. It is hard to tell whether increases in voter turnout, if there are some, are the permanent result of greater ease of early voting or instead are the temporary result of the novelty of early voting. Moreover, it is difficult to assess whether the increases in turnout that analysts have seen in aggregate turnout figures are the result of early voting or the result of other steps that states have taken simultaneously to promote voter turnout (for example, easing access to voter registration or more strongly encouraging people to vote in publicizing early voting) or the result of other features of the counties or elections that were compared (for example, more competitive elections coincident with the introduction of early voting or political characteristics of counties that cause them to have higher rates of early voting and higher rates of voter turnout). In fact, a recent report of the Committee for the Study of the American Electorate makes the contrary claim for the 2000 election. Basing its argument on the same kind of aggregate, state-level voter turnout data, the committee contends that early voting and liberalized absentee voting have actually depressed voter turnout.[9]

---

9. The CSAE study illustrates some of the difficulties of evaluating the effect of early and absentee voting by comparing aggregate voter turnout between elections. The committee found that states with early and liberalized absentee voting posted smaller increases in voter turnout in 2000 than states without. But two problems hamper the interpretation of this comparison. First, the commit-

The adoption of vote by mail statewide in Oregon followed a very successful experiment with VBM in substate and local elections in Oregon and elsewhere. In these low-interest and low-stimulus contests, with notoriously low voter participation, vote by mail often produced double digit increases in turnout. Unsurprisingly, the effects on turnout have been much more modest in elections that draw more interest from voters, parties, mobilizers, and the mass media. In the statewide mail-in balloting of the last six years, Traugott and other analysts have found significant but small increases in voter turnout in Oregon, with the estimates in the range of 5 or 6 percent, although he also found signs that the stimulus of vote by mail might be wearing off as the publicity over its implementation fades.

Using survey data, Traugott found that mail-in balloting had the greatest influence on voters who were less likely to turn out, on recent residents and citizens with a weak sense of their ability to influence government. But in the main, vote by mail stimulated voter turnout by making it easier for people who tend to participate to continue to participate rather than by moving people who tend not to participate to enter the electorate. The demographic composition of early and absentee voters suggests that the same is also true of early and liberalized absentee voting. By making it easier to vote, early voting, mail-in voting, and unrestricted absentee voting make it easier for habitual voters to carry through on their intentions to exercise their franchise. But the greater ease of voting does little to bring people who are less interested in elections or people who feel little obligation to vote into the electorate.

In sum, the balance of the evidence indicates that opportunities to vote before Election Day are associated with a positive but modest increase in voter turnout. But it is not clear that the increase is due entirely to early,

---

tee calculated turnout as votes cast in the presidential race divided by voting age population. Because the voting age population includes noncitizens who are not eligible to vote, the ratio underestimates the increase in turnout in states in which the noncitizen population is increasing rapidly, like Texas, an early voting state, and California, a liberalized absentee state. Second, the committee did not take into account the competitiveness of the presidential races in states with and without early and liberalized absentee voting. As happened in 2000, the competitive presidential races (and other competitive races) were in more and bigger states without early and liberalized absentee voting—for example, Michigan, Pennsylvania, and Florida—than in states with them. (Oliver counts Michigan as a state with "expanded" eligibility for absentee voting, but CSAE counts it as a state that has not liberalized.)

mail, and absentee voting per se. Implementation of early voting and voting by mail has been accompanied by an unusual level of publicity, and voters may also have been stimulated either by the publicity itself or by the desire to try something new. Liberalized absentee voting appears to have had very little effect on voter turnout, except possibly in states in which it has become a strategy of campaign mobilization.

Considerations for and against the Options

Early voting, vote by mail, and unrestricted absentee voting spread rapidly in the 1990s. In 1992 Oliver counted two states with early voting, Texas and Oklahoma. In 2000 the Committee for the Study of the American Electorate (CSAE) found 14. In 1992 Oliver identified 10 states with "universal" eligibility for absentee voting and six more states (plus the District of Columbia) with "expanded" eligibility. In 2000 CSAE found 20 states (and the District) with liberalized absentee requirements, even missing Nevada and not counting two states with "expanded" eligibility, Michigan and Ohio. And Oregon in 1998 went entirely to voting by mail in statewide elections.

A key factor in the spread of early, mail, and absentee voting has been the enthusiasm of the public. Despite the misgivings of many election administrators, nobody seems to believe there is any chance of repeal in the states that now have the provisions, so popular are they with voters. Voters appear to appreciate the convenience of early, mail, and absentee voting.

A second factor in the adoption was the genuine desire to promote voter participation in the electoral process, which experiment has, as indicated, been either a cautious success or a limited disappointment.

A third significant argument for expansion of opportunities to vote before Election Day was to economize on election costs. By dispensing entirely with staffed polling sites in the 2000 primary, Oregon claims to have saved about a half million dollars in election expenses after implementing VBM, or about 17 percent, compared to the 1998 primary. The experience with early voting in Texas is apparently more mixed. A 1994 Federal Election Commission (FEC) study found that early voting actually increased election costs in the largest counties, which offered extended hours and satellite stations, but maintained or decreased costs in counties that did not have to make such accommodations. A 1987 FEC report notes that per-vote processing costs for absentee ballots are several times the expense for ballots cast at the polls. All three systems help to spread administrative effort from a single Election Day into a couple of weeks, with savings in aggravation if not in cost.

On the other side, critics voice three prominent concerns. The first is a worry that early, mail, and absentee voting might ultimately erode voter turnout by discouraging campaigns, parties, and advocacy groups from making the effort to get people to the polls. A considerable body of research has found that mobilization has a significant positive effect on voter participation, but campaigns, parties, and groups undertake it only when the benefit, to them, is greater than the cost at the margin. The concentration of mobilization on a single day plausibly allows campaigns, parties, and groups to realize economies of scale in their efforts. By having to sustain mobilization efforts over a longer period of time for early, mail, and absentee voting, groups might be dissuaded from investing as much as they do in stimulating voter turnout.

The argument that greater access to voting before Election Day might discourage mobilization of voters is difficult to assess. In many states, and especially in those states where third parties can request an application for an absentee ballot on a voter's behalf, liberalized absentee laws have fostered the development of sophisticated efforts, mostly partisan, to acquire, distribute, and in some cases collect and return absentee ballots. In other cases, the argument seems plausible. In states with early voting, for instance, the expense of standing at the ready to ferry voters to the polls must be greater when the election is spread over weeks rather than concentrated in a single day.

Critics also voice a second concern, that early, mail, and absentee voting allow people to make their choices before campaigns have run their full course. By making their choices early, voters make selections that they might not have made had they been exposed to information that issued only at the very end of the campaign. This line of argument assumes, of course, that the voters who make their decisions early could still be influenced by late campaign developments, an assumption that is by no means obvious. People who decide early in the campaign tend, as Stein shows of early voters, to have stronger partisan attachments than people who decide at the last minute. It is less likely the case that the rock-ribbed Republicans and yellow-dog Democrats who make their choices early could so easily be swayed from them by information that arises late in the campaign.

But this possibility leads to a second variant on the same argument: that early, mail, and absentee voting might change the dynamics of campaigns themselves, in particular to insert the pattern of early gestures to the partisan base followed by late moves to the center into the last few weeks of the race. It is unclear, however, that campaigns could make such a strategy work: it is difficult enough to soften strident partisan images over a period of months, let alone over a few days. Moreover, even if they could, it is not obvious that a change in campaign dynamics would necessarily be a bad thing.

Finally, the most forceful argument made against the extension of opportunities to vote before Election Day emphasizes the way in which early, mail, and absentee voting undermine participation in common in an important civic ritual. Election Day is one of the few opportunities Americans have to do something important together as a nation. It is the one time when the American people come together to govern themselves through the choice of their leaders. To critics, to make participation in this important civic rite a matter to be pursued at an individual's convenience is to undermine the sense of our nationhood, our common experience in the government of, by, and for the people.

Early, Mail, and Absentee Voting Compared

There are serious arguments for and against broadening the opportunities of Americans to vote before Election Day. For liberalization, the strongest argument is the popularity of early, mail, and unrestricted absentee voting. The citizens of states that have adopted these policies show broad enthusiasm for them. Against liberalization, the most compelling argument is that the freedom to vote other than on Election Day might loosen Americans' attachments to each other and to the common purpose of self-government.

If, on balance, greater opportunities to vote before Election Day are deemed desirable, the relative attractiveness of early, mail, and unrestricted absentee voting might be evaluated on three different dimensions, in addition to those discussed already.

First, early voting and mail voting place fewer demands on voters than participating by absentee. Except in a few states that allow registrants to apply for an absentee ballot even on Election Day itself, voters must exercise forethought to obtain and vote an absentee ballot. In contrast, early voting and mail voting require no more of voters than is demanded by voting on Election Day.

Second, early voting and its close cousin, in-person absentee voting, typically offer greater administrative support for voters as they cast their ballots. Early and in-person absentee voters make their decisions in election offices and satellite sites staffed by election workers, who can offer immediate assistance to voters who encounter difficulties. In fact, one election administrator told us that she liked unrestricted participation in in-person absentee voting because she could serve voters with her own elections staff, who are much more experienced and much better trained than Election Day poll workers.

Finally, early voting and in-person absentee voting occur in controlled sites under the supervision of elections officials, diminishing the opportunities for fraud. Critics of voting by mail and absentee voting by mail raise two concerns about security. The first is absentee ballots obtained and completed by someone other than the voter herself. The second is absentee and mail voters' being coerced or influenced in settings that lack the fundamental privacy of the voting booth.

The election officials from whom the National Commission on Election Reform has heard, all from states with expanded eligibility for absentee and mail voting, have felt confident that the first concern is not very serious. Oregon describes a rigorous protocol by which officials check return signatures on VBM ballot envelopes against registration signatures. As of 1987 seven states required that signatures on absentee ballots be checked against registration signatures, and fourteen states required that ballot signatures be checked against signatures on absentee applications. According to the National Conference of State Legislatures, five states require absentee ballots to bear the signature of a witness, and another eight states require that absentee ballots either be witnessed or notarized.[10] But in fact, for practical reasons, most states do not routinely check signatures either on applications or on returned ballots, just as most states do not verify signatures or require proof of identity at the polls. Judging from what the commission has heard, the consensus among election administrators in states that promote absentee voting and voting by mail is that absentee ballots are no less secure against fraud than in-person voting. Administrators in other states, and Justice Department investigators, are less sanguine. Certainly, the potential for fraud is present, and all the more so because so much of the process is beyond the supervision of election officials.

The potential for violation of privacy in vote choices is also difficult to assess. Oregon cites a survey study that found only a tiny proportion of VBM voters who felt they had been subject to pressure in marking their ballots. The 1987 FEC study of absentee voting suggested that the potential for invasion of privacy was greatest in states that allowed public access to applications for absentee ballots. In the last twenty years, during which access to absentee ballots has been expanded, political parties in many

---

10. Fifteen states require a witness's signature if the absentee voter has been assisted in voting.

Table 18 Days in Advance of Election Day That Absentee Ballots Must Be Requested, by State

State	Days in advance	State	Days in advance
Alabama	5/5	Nebraska	2 after/4
Alaska	8/4	Nevada	8/7
Arizona	12/4	New Hampshire	0/3
Arkansas	8/1	New Jersey	8/1
California	8/7	New Mexico	3/3
Colorado	4/4	New York	8/1
Connecticut	8/1	North Carolina	1/4
Delaware	3/1	North Dakota	None specified/1
District of Columbia	8/1	Ohio	3/3
Florida	12/0	Oklahoma	6/1
Georgia	18/1	Oregon	22/vote by mail
Hawaii	8/7	Pennsylvania	4/7
Idaho	0/1	Rhode Island	22/21
Illinois	5/1	South Carolina	3/1
Indiana	9/1	South Dakota	0/0
Iowa	1/0	Tennessee	0/0
Kansas	4/1	Texas	8/7
Kentucky	8/7	Utah	4/4
Louisiana	1/1	Vermont	1/1
Maine	8/0	Virginia	5/3
Maryland	9/7	Washington	0/1
Massachusetts	1/1	West Virginia	6/3
Michigan	6/1	Wisconsin	1/1
Minnesota	1/1	Wyoming	NA/1
Mississippi	1/3		
Missouri	6/1	U.S. average	5.4/2.8
Montana	0/1	U.S. median	5/1

Note: Information is discrepant. Before slash: www.election.com/us/deadlines.htm. After slash: League of Women Voters Education Fund, "Absentee Voting: Vote: The First Steps," 1996. NA = not ascertained.

states have undertaken concerted efforts to mobilize their partisans to vote absentee, with the purpose, critics charge, of exercising influence over vote choices. The potential for violations of privacy is obviously greater for mail and absentee ballots than for ballots cast in voting booths at polling sites.

Selected References

Committee for the Study of the American Electorate. "Two Pro-Participation Reforms Actually Harm Voter Turnout," January 9, 2001.

Election.com. "Voter Registration and Absentee Ballot Requirements," www.election.com/deadlines.htm (June 17, 2001).

Feigenbaum, Edward D., and James A. Palmer. "Absentee Voting: Issues and Options," Federal Election Commission, Autumn 1987.

League of Women Voters Education Fund. "Absentee Voting: Vote: The First Steps," 1996.

National Conference of State Legislatures. "Absentee Ballots," Elections Reform Task Force, www.ncsl.org/programs/legman/elect/taskfc/absentee.htm (July 1, 2001).

Oliver, J. Eric. "The Effects of Eligibility Restrictions and Party Activity on Absentee Voting and Overall Turnout," *American Journal of Political Science* 40 (May 1996): 498–513.

Rosenfield, Margaret. "Early Voting," *Innovations in Election Administration*, vol. 9, Federal Election Commission, April 1994.

Stein, Robert M. "Early Voting," *Public Opinion Quarterly* 62 (1998): 57–69.

Stein, Robert M., and Patricia Garcia-Monet. "Voting Early, but Not Often," *Social Science Quarterly* 78 (September 1997): 657–77.

Traugott, Michael W. "Why Electoral Reform Has Failed: If You Build It, Will They Come?" typescript, University of Michigan, October 2000.

Wolfinger, Raymond E. "Fraud, Deadwood, and Purging," typescript, 2001.

Table 19 Early Voting and Liberalized Absentee Voting Provisions, by State

State	Total percentage of votes cast before Election Day, 1996	Early voting, 2000	Percentage of votes cast in person before Election Day, 1996	Liberalized absentee voting (CSAE), 2000	Percentage of votes cast by absentee ballot, 1996
Alabama	3		0		3
Alaska	9		4	■	5
Arizona	24	■	2	■	22
Arkansas	14	■	9	■	5
California	19		0	■	19
Colorado	20	■	11	■	10
Connecticut	7		0		7
Delaware	6		0		6
District of Columbia	4		1		3
Florida	7		1		7
Georgia	3		1		2
Hawaii	12	■	1	■	11
Idaho	7	■	1	■	6
Illinois	4		1		4
Indiana	6		1		5
Iowa	11	■	3	■	9
Kansas	15		5	■	11
Kentucky	6		1		5

Table 19 Early Voting and Liberalized Absentee Voting Provisions, by State (*Continued*)

State	Total percentage of votes cast before Election Day, 1996	Early voting, 2000	Percentage of votes cast in person before Election Day, 1996	Liberalized absentee voting (CSAE), 2000	Percentage of votes cast by absentee ballot, 1996
Louisiana	3		1		2
Maine	5		1	■	5
Maryland	3		1		3
Massachusetts	4		1	■	3
Michigan	14		1	**	14
Minnesota	7		1		6
Mississippi	3		1		2
Missouri	3		1		3
Montana	9		1	■	8
Nebraska	6		0	■	6
Nevada	11	■	5	■*	6
New Hampshire	7		1		6
New Jersey	3		0		3
New Mexico	15	■	10	■	6
New York	3		0		3
North Carolina	4	■	1	■	3
North Dakota	6		1		5
Ohio	9		2	**	7
Oklahoma	5	■	2	■	3
Oregon	46	Vote by mail	0	Vote by mail	46
Pennsylvania	4		0		4
Rhode Island	3		0		3
South Carolina	2		0		2
South Dakota	8		3		6
Tennessee	21	■	19		2
Texas	26	■	23		4
Utah	4		1	■	3
Vermont	7		1	■	7
Virginia	5	■	1		3
Washington	37		0	■	37
West Virginia	3		1		2
Wisconsin	3	■	0	■	3
Wyoming	13		1	■	12
United States	10	14 states	3	22 states	8

Source: Committee for the Study of the American Electorate, "Two Pro-Participation Reforms Actually Harm Voter Turnout," January 9, 2001; J. Eric Oliver, "The Effects of Eligibility Restrictions and Party Activity on Absentee Voting and Overall Turnout," *American Journal of Political Science* 40 (May 1996): 501–02; Bureau of the Census, 1996 Current Population Survey Voter Supplement, courtesy of Raymond E. Wolfinger.
*Oliver classifies Michigan and Ohio as states with "expanded" eligibility for absentee voting.
**This omission is in error in the original source.

Table 20   Accepted Reasons for Requesting Absentee Ballots, by State, 1996

State	No reason necessary	Absent on business	College student	Disabled or ill	Prevented by employment	Religious reasons	Elderly	Out of jurisdiction for any reason
Alabama		■	■	■	■			■
Alaska	■							
Arizona	■							
Arkansas	■							
California	■							
Colorado	■							
Connecticut		■	■	■		■		■
Delaware		■	■	■	■	■	■	■
District of Columbia		■	■	■			■	■
Florida			■	■	■	■		■
Georgia			■	■	■			■
Hawaii	■							
Idaho	■							
Illinois		■	■	■	■	■	■	■
Indiana			■	■			■	■
Iowa	■							
Kansas	■							
Kentucky			■	■			■	
Louisiana			■	■	■	■		■
Maine	■							
Maryland		■	■	■				■
Massachusetts	■							
Michigan		■	■	■		■	■	■
Minnesota		■	■	■				■
Mississippi		■	■		■			■
Missouri			■	■		■	■	■
Montana	■							
Nebraska	■							
Nevada	■							
New Hampshire		■	■	■		■		■
New Jersey		■	■	■	■			■
New Mexico	■							
New York				■				■
North Carolina	■							
North Dakota		■	■	■				■
Ohio				■		■	■	■
Oklahoma	■							
Oregon	■							
Pennsylvania		■	■	■	■			■
Rhode Island		■	■	■		■		■
South Carolina		■	■	■	■	■		■
South Dakota		■	■	■	■	■		■
Tennessee			■	■		■	■	■

Table 20 Accepted Reasons for Requesting Absentee Ballots, by State, 1996 (*Continued*)

State	No reason necessary	Absent on business	College student	Disabled or ill	Prevented by employment	Religious reasons	Elderly	Out of jurisdiction for any reason
Texas				■			■	■
Utah	■							
Vermont	■							
Virginia		■	■	■	■	■		■
Washington	■							
West Virginia		■	■	■		■	■	■
Wisconsin	■							
Wyoming	■							
United States	22 states	18 states	23 states	27 states	13 states	18 states	12 states	28 states

Source: League of Women Voters Education Fund, "Absentee Voting, Vote: The First Steps," 1996, updated from Committee for the Study of the American Electorate, "Two Pro-Participation Reforms Actually Harm Voter Turnout," January 9, 2001.

VERIFICATION OF IDENTITY

Summary of Conclusions

1. States use three methods to verify voter identity in the polling place. The largest number require voters to sign their names in an official registry or on a ballot application; just more than half also require that poll officials check signatures against those provided at the time of registration. About a third of the states demand that voters produce some form of identification. Finally, all states rely on the familiarity that election officials and partisan judges have with the residents of precincts, and 11 states rely on familiarity exclusively.
2. States that have histories of strong party organization and election improprieties employ more rigorous methods of identity verification: signature validation and official proof of identity. Among the states with more rigorous requirements, northern states by and large validate signatures, while southern states also require proof of identity.
3. Signature validation imposes some significant costs on election administrators. Proof of identity places burdens on voters, especially those who are poor and urban. At least five percent of the voting age population does not have photo identification. Identification requirements might also be applied selectively in polling places.

In the United States, there is a long and well-developed notion of an individual right to privacy. This commitment to privacy is the traditional barrier to proposals suggesting national identity cards, which are common in most of the world. Abroad, national identity cards are sufficient proof of identity for purposes of participation in elections. In the United States, with its different traditions, states have had to verify the identities of voters in different ways.

Methods of Verification of Identity

In polling places, a voter's identity is verified in essentially three ways. One widespread method is by providing a signature. In 39 states and the District of Columbia, voters must sign their names on an official registry or on a ballot application. In most states, the signature completes an affidavit sworn under penalty of law. In an additional 17 states, voters' signatures are compared to signatures provided at the time of registration; in three other states, voters' signatures may be compared.

Fourteen states require voters to produce a form of identification, and an additional six allow local election officials to ask for it. All but four of the states that require a form of identification also require a signature. In most states, the specified type of identification is broad, from driver's licenses to employee ID cards to (in some instances) birth certificates and Social Security cards, and where the requirements could be ascertained only Florida seemed to specify identification with a photograph. Several of the states that require identification, for example Virginia and Louisiana, also allow voters who lack it to vote after signing an affirmation of identity. The states that require identification are disproportionately in the South. (See table 21, which identifies verification procedures by state.)

Table 21   Identity Verification, by State

State	Voter required to show identification	Voter required to give signature	Voter's signature verified
Alabama		Yes	
Alaska	Yes	Yes	
Arizona		Yes	
Arkansas	Yes	Yes	Yes
California		Yes	
Colorado		Yes	Varies
Connecticut	Yes		
Delaware	Yes	Yes	Yes
District of Columbia		Yes	
Florida	Yes	Yes	Yes
Georgia	Yes	Yes	
Hawaii	Yes	Yes	
Idaho		Yes	
Illinois		Yes	Yes
Indiana		Yes	Yes
Iowa	May	Yes	
Kansas		Yes	
Kentucky	Yes	Yes	
Louisiana	Yes	Yes	Yes
Maine			
Maryland		Yes	
Massachusetts	May		
Michigan		Yes	Varies
Minnesota	May	Yes	For absentees
Mississippi		Yes	
Missouri	Yes	Yes	Yes
Montana		Yes	
Nebraska		Yes	
Nevada		Yes	Yes
New Hampshire			
New Jersey		Yes	Yes

(Continued)

Table 21   Identity Verification, by State (*Continued*)

State	Voter required to show identification	Voter required to give signature	Voter's signature verified
New Mexico		Yes	
New York		Yes	Yes
North Carolina			
North Dakota			
Ohio		Yes	Yes
Oklahoma	May	Yes	Yes
Oregon		Yes	Yes
Pennsylvania		Yes	Yes
Rhode Island		Yes	
South Carolina	Yes	Yes	Yes
South Dakota			
Tennessee	Yes	Yes	Yes
Texas	May when voter does not present valid voter's registration certificate	Yes	May
Utah	May	Yes	
Vermont			
Virginia	Yes		
Washington		Yes	
West Virginia	Yes, for first election after mail registration	Yes	Yes
Wisconsin	May		
Wyoming			
United States	14 states, yes; 6 may	39 states + District	17 states, yes; 1 may; 2 varies; 1 absentee only

Source: Federal Election Commission.

Finally, every state relies on the efforts of poll workers and partisan election judges to challenge voters whom they believe not to be qualified. Seven states, all but one lacking major urban centers, rely solely on poll officers' familiarity, demanding neither identification nor signature.

In sum, very few states have chosen to rely solely on the knowledge of polling place officials to verify voters' identity. But at the same time, few states have seen it necessary to require voters to produce identification. Most states depend on voters' positive affirmation of their identity with a signature.

State Histories and Verification of Identity

The states that have adopted more rigorous methods for verifying voter identity have instructive similarities. The states that require voters to show identification or that check voters' signatures are disproportionately states with histories of strong party organizations based on patronage and the ability to control nominations. David Mayhew of Yale University has researched party organization in the states and assigned each a score ranging from 1, for minimal organization, to 5, for very strong organization. As table 22 shows, almost all of the states with histories of any party organization at all—80 percent of them—require either identification or signature verification. Of the states with histories of powerful party organization, only Maryland and Rhode Island do not. States that need to exercise greater care, because they have historically been vulnerable to election improprieties, have adopted more stringent methods for certifying voter identity.

The other pattern in table 22 is the contrast between the northern states and the southern and border states. Whatever their experience with party

Table 22 Histories of Strong Party Organization and Verification of Voter Identity

State	Requires identification	Verifies signature
Very powerful party organizations (5)		
Connecticut	Yes	No
Illinois	No	Yes
Indiana	No	Yes
Maryland	No	No
New Jersey	No	Yes
New York	No	Yes
Pennsylvania	No	Yes
Rhode Island	No	No
Powerful party organizations (4)		
Delaware	Yes	Yes
Kentucky	Yes	No
Missouri	Yes	Yes
Ohio	No	Yes
West Virginia	After mail registration	Yes
Significant party organization (3)		
Louisiana	Yes	Yes
Modest party organization (2)		
Arkansas	Yes	Yes
Georgia	Yes	No
New Mexico	No	No
Tennessee	Yes	Yes
Texas	May	May
Virginia	Yes	No
Weak party organization (1)		
30 states	Require: 5	Require: 6
	May require: 7	Varies: 2

Source: Federal Election Commission and David R. Mayhew, *Placing Parties in American Politics* (Princeton University Press, 1986).

organization, the southern states as a group require more stringent methods of verification than the northern states. The list of weak organization states that require proof of identity or signature verification or both includes every southern and border state in the category except for Alabama and Mississippi. Among states with histories of at least modest strength of party organization, the northern states favor signature verification for establishing voter identity—Connecticut is the exception—while the southern and border states demand identification in addition.[1]

Costs of Methods of Identity Verification

Identification requirements and signature verification have clearly been strategies states have adopted to deter election fraud. Each has its downside, however. For signature verification, election administrators must make signatures (or facsimiles) from voter registration available for comparison at polling sites. At the polls, signature verification slows the process of voting, as poll workers search through the registry and make the comparison, potentially lengthening lines. Finally, signatures change over time, making signature verification an inexact art, placing a great deal of responsibility and discretion in the hands of officials at the polls. The costs of signature verification are primarily administrative, but they potentially affect voters through slower lines.

Identification requirements present two problems for voters. First, the costs of proof of identity fall more heavily on the voters themselves. Even if states do not require it, those that demand identification clearly prefer photo IDs. But photo identification is not universal. In the early 1990s the United States Department of Transportation estimated that 87 percent of

---

1. In most statistical analyses of voter turnout, residence in the South has a significant negative impact on voter participation. Wolfinger and Rosenstone found that southerners were about 6 percent less likely to turn out in 1972, even after taking account of personal characteristics like education and systemic characteristics like registration laws. Rosenstone and Hansen estimated that southerners were between 10 and 16 percent less likely to participate in the period from 1952 to 1988, controlling for an even broader array of individual, systemic, and social characteristics. Analysts have long attributed lower turnout in the South to the cultural residuum of Jim Crow: culturally, voter participation was not very much encouraged in the South. But it is also possible that lower turnout in the South traces to the accumulation of minor barriers to voting, like identification requirements, that do not amount to much individually but sum to substantial.

the voting age population held a driver's license and another 4 percent held an identification card issued by a state driver's license agency. A Gallup Poll in October 2000 found that 93 percent of Americans over age 16 held a motor vehicle operator's license, an estimate that comports with the ratio of driver's licenses issued to the voting age population of the United States, 92 percent. Accordingly, some 6 to 10 percent of the American electorate does not have official state identification, and while other kinds of photo identification are available—student IDs, military IDs, employee IDs, passports—they probably broaden the number of holders of photo identification only slightly. We have not been able to locate information about the characteristics of adults who lack driver's licenses, but they probably parallel the characteristics of people who do not own automobiles: they are poorer (and cannot afford a car) or urban (and do not need a car).

Consequently, while photo IDs are certainly more secure, to require them for voting would be to impose an additional expense on the exercise of the franchise, a burden that would fall disproportionately on people who are poorer and urban. The expense and trouble of obtaining a photo identification card could be a significant deterrent to their participation in the electoral process, unless states were to issue official identification at state expense and on state initiative.

A second drawback to the requirement that voters present identification is the possibility of selective enforcement in polling places. Poll workers with the best of motives might still dispense with the requirement when voters are known to them. Poll workers with the worst of motives might deliberately use the requirement to confront and intimidate "strangers." Either way, voters who were asked to show identification when others were not might come to feel that they were singled out.

Selected References

Maybury, Kelly. "Most Americans Favor Tougher Drunk Driving Law," Gallup News Service, October 26, 2000.

Mayhew, David R. *Placing Parties in American Politics* (Princeton University Press, 1986).

Rosenstone, Steven J., and John Mark Hansen. *Mobilization, Participation, and Democracy in America* (Macmillan, 1993).

Wolfinger, Raymond E., and Steven J. Rosenstone. *Who Votes?* (Yale University Press, 1980).

U.S. House of Representatives, Committee on House Administration. "National Voter Registration Act of 1993," Report 103–9, February 1993.

PROVISIONAL BALLOTING

Summary of Conclusions

1. Nineteen states with 51 percent of the voting age citizen population of the United States issue provisional ballots to voters whose names do not appear on the precinct voter registry, at least in the narrow circumstances required by the "fail-safe" provisions of the National Voter Registration Act.
2. Washington makes use of provisional ballots in the broadest range of circumstances. Uniquely, Washington requires county election officials to accept votes cast in other jurisdictions by voters who are legal registrants of their counties for the offices that are common to the two ballots.
3. Provisional ballots help to speed operations in polling places. They help election administrators to identify and correct voter registration mistakes. Finally, they make it possible not to have to turn away voters at the polls. On the other hand, provisional balloting is labor intensive and therefore expensive. It also slows official election counts.

The 2000 presidential election made abundantly clear that mistakes occur, mistakes that cause some eligible voters to be denied the right to vote and some ineligible citizens to believe they were denied the right to vote. As a general principle, most Americans would surely agree that honest administrative errors should not contravene a voter's right to participate in an election. Most Americans would surely also agree that false or mistaken claims of administrative error should not entitle a citizen to vote despite ineligibility. Provisional balloting is one way to advance both principles.

What are most commonly called "provisional" ballots go by many other names as well. They are "special" ballots in Washington State and the District of Columbia, "affidavit" ballots in New York and Mississippi, and "conditional" ballots in Oklahoma and Virginia. Whatever the name and whatever the state practice, provisional ballots have three common characteristics:

1. Issuance to voters whose names do not appear on the voter registry. Poll officials provide a voter with a provisional ballot if her name does not appear on the precinct voter registration roll. Almost all states that have adopted provisional ballots issue them in other circumstances as well, but the absence of the voter's name from the registry triggers issue in all states.

2. Identification of provisional ballot. The voter places the provisional ballot inside an unmarked ballot envelope and in turn inside an envelope that bears information about the circumstances of the provisional vote and the voter's signature.
3. Postelection determination of eligibility. After the election, officials use the information on the outer envelope to research the voter's eligibility. If the voter is found to be eligible, election officials enter the vote into the tally.

These three characteristics helpfully distinguish provisional voting from other balloting practices. Postelection determination of eligibility distinguishes voting by provisional ballot from voting by affidavit in states like Illinois and Michigan. In Illinois and Michigan, voters whose names do not appear on the registry are required to swear an affidavit, under penalty of law, that they are qualified to vote in the precinct under the laws of the state. Upon execution of the affidavit, however, they cast a regular ballot. Their ballots are not segregated and their eligibility is not researched later by election officials. Upon execution of the affidavit, in short, their ballots count.

Provisional ballots differ from challenged ballots as well. In most states, partisan election observers may bring a challenge to a voter on a variety of grounds, among them invalid registration at the address given. In some states challenges are adjudicated on the spot, often by another voter's sworn affirmation that the challenged voter is qualified under the laws of the state. In other states, challenged ballots are segregated and researched after the election. Voting by provisional ballot, however, is a process that is originated administratively and automatically rather than upon challenge.

The provisional ballot was pioneered by Washington and California, which have used it for more than a decade. Provisional voting spread rapidly following the passage of the National Voter Registration Act (NVRA, or "Motor-Voter") in 1993. Nineteen of the 44 states covered by NVRA use provisional ballots to comply with the "fail-safe" provisions of the act. The 19 states that provide provisional ballots in at least some circumstances account for 51 percent of the voting age citizen population of the United States (see table 23).

In most of the states that have adopted provisional balloting—in fact, as nearly as we can tell, in most states other than California and Washington—poll workers offer the provisional ballot only in the fail-safe circumstances

Table 23 States with Provisional Balloting

State	FEC survey: provisional balloting for fail-safe voting	Election Center survey
Alabama	Yes	Yes
Alaska	Yes	No response
Arizona	Yes	Yes
Arkansas	Yes	Yes
California	Yes	Yes
Colorado	No response	No
Connecticut	No	No
Delaware	No	No response
District of Columbia	Yes	No response
Florida	Yes (new)	No response
Georgia	No	No
Hawaii	No	No
Idaho	NVRA exempt	No response
Illinois	No	Challenge
Indiana	No	No
Iowa	Yes	Yes
Kansas	Yes	Yes
Kentucky	No	No
Louisiana	No	No response
Maine	No	Same day VR
Maryland	Yes (new)	Yes
Massachusetts	No	No response
Michigan	No	No
Minnesota	NVRA exempt	No
Mississippi	Yes	Yes
Missouri	No	No
Montana	No	No
Nebraska	Yes	Yes
Nevada	No	No
New Hampshire	NVRA exempt	No response
New Jersey	Yes	Yes
New Mexico	Yes	Yes
New York	Yes	Yes
North Carolina	Yes	Yes
North Dakota	NVRA exempt	No VR
Ohio	Yes	Yes
Oklahoma	No	No
Oregon	Yes	Yes
Pennsylvania	Some counties	No response
Rhode Island	No	No response
South Carolina	Yes	Yes
South Dakota	No	No
Tennessee	No	Challenge
Texas	No	Challenge
Utah	No	No
Vermont	No	No
Virginia	Yes	Yes
Washington	Yes	Yes

Table 23 States with Provisional Balloting (*Continued*)

State	FEC survey: provisional balloting for fail-safe voting	Election Center survey
West Virginia	No	No response
Wisconsin	NVRA exempt	No
Wyoming	NVRA exempt	No
United States	19 states, yes	19 states, yes

Source: Federal Election Commission, "State Fail-Safe Voting Procedures," revised May 31, 2001; Election Center, "Provisional Ballot Survey," March 5, 2001.
Notes: NVRA = National Voter Registration Act of 1993; VR = voter registration.

mandated by NVRA. The act required that states provide the opportunity to cast a vote when voters have failed to register at a new address

- within the same precinct, or
- outside the precinct but within the jurisdiction of the registrar.

In the first circumstance, when voters have moved within the precinct, most states in fact issue a regular ballot for all offices. Six states and the District of Columbia issue a provisional ballot for all offices. In Kansas, Nebraska, New Mexico, and the District, poll workers provide a provisional ballot immediately. In Alaska, Arizona, and Washington, they first try to determine eligibility and issue a provisional ballot only if eligibility remains a question.

In the second fail-safe circumstance, when voters have moved out of the precinct but elsewhere within the jurisdiction, 17 states and the District of Columbia issue a provisional ballot for all offices. Two states, Mississippi and South Carolina, provide a provisional ballot limited to federal offices.

States such as California and Washington make more expansive use of provisional ballots, employing them in circumstances beyond those required under NVRA. In California poll workers issue a provisional ballot to a voter who has not moved but whose name does not appear on the voter registration list. In Washington, if a voter's name cannot be found on the registry, poll workers call the central administrative elections office to try to verify registration. But if registration cannot quickly be sorted out, or if a voter cannot wait, or if a voter cannot go back to the precinct in which he is registered, poll workers provide a provisional ballot. Moreover, in Washington poll workers issue a special ballot if registration has been cancelled, for change of address or for conviction for a felony, but the voter claims that the cancellation is in error. In both states, finally, poll workers give a provisional ballot if a voter is listed as having requested an absentee ballot but claims not to have received it or claims to have lost it.

The most expansive use of provisional ballots is in Washington. Uniquely, Washington issues a special ballot to voters who have moved to a new county or even into Washington from another state. After the election, election officials research the eligibility of voters of provisional ballots. If they determine that a voter is legally registered in another jurisdiction, whether another Washington county or out of state, they mail the ballot to the election office in that jurisdiction. County election officials in Washington are obligated, by law, to accept votes cast in other jurisdictions by voters who are legal registrants of their counties for the offices that are common to the two ballots.

Voter registration problems are common enough that substantial numbers of voters receive provisional ballots in each election. In the majority of cases, election officials find provisional voters to be qualified, as determined from official records.[1] In the 2000 general election in Los Angeles County, California, voters cast 100,168 provisional ballots, about four percent of the total, of which 61,521 (62 percent) were ultimately recognized as valid. King County, Washington (Seattle), received 17,082 special ballots in 2000, about 2 percent of all cast. With Washington's more liberal provisions, election officials determined 13,307 (78 percent) to be valid.

Arguments for Provisional Balloting

No matter how well election officials manage voter registration lists, some voters will inevitably be left off the rolls. Often, the fault is the voters' own. Americans move often, and many neglect to reregister at their new address, or they do not realize that they must. Every year, 16.4 percent of the U.S. voting age population changes residence. Fifty-seven percent of the movers (8.8 percent of the voting age population) relocate within the same county and therefore fall mostly within the fail-safe requirements of the NVRA. Another 21 percent (3.2 percent of the population) move to a different county within the same state and accordingly would be covered by an expansive system of provisional balloting such as is offered in Washington.

In other cases, the fault lies in election administration. With the press of activity, poll workers overlook names that in fact are on the registry. Staff in registrars' offices make clerical errors. Driver's license bureaus and service agencies either fail to elicit required information from registrants or fail to forward applications in time. Third-party registrars—for example, political parties and citizens' groups—do not turn the applications they

---

1. In an unknown proportion of the other cases, voters might in fact have made the attempt to register but do not appear on the voter registration rolls because of purely administrative errors.

receive into the county registrars' offices. Late closing dates for registration make it impossible for registrars to put all the new registrants onto the official rolls. For all these reasons, in every election, people appear at the polls who believe, quite reasonably, that they are legally registered to vote. But they are not on the rolls.

Because of the inevitability of errors in voter registration, provisional balloting has several attractive features. First, provisional ballots help to speed operations in the polling place. Because voter registration problems can be resolved after the voter casts a provisional ballot, everybody need not be required to wait while poll workers research the status of a voter's registration.[2] Several county elections officers have commented that they find provisional balloting attractive because it smooths operations in polling places on Election Day.

Second, provisional ballots make it possible not to have to turn away voters at the polls. People who have been told that they cannot vote because there is no record of their registration tend to react with disappointment and anger, given the time and effort they have already invested in a trip to the polls and given their often-reasonable belief that they are indeed registered. The 2000 Current Population Survey found that 7.4 percent of registrants who did not vote said they were prevented from voting by problems with voter registration. The group of registrants who encountered registration difficulties numbers 1.5 to 3 million people. By providing an outlet for participation, provisional ballots reduce voter frustration and probably also lessen the wear and tear on poll workers, the front line of contact with voters.

Third, provisional ballots help election administrators to catch voter registration mistakes. Neither California nor Washington requires election officials to notify provisional voters of the outcome of their investigation, but it appears that most do anyway. In the 60 to 80 percent of the cases for which the investigation finds a valid voter registration, and the provisional ballot counts, election officials amend the registration administratively and inform the voter of the changes. In the remaining cases, election officials send an application for voter registration so that the provisional voter might be registered or registered correctly. Provisional balloting provides another opportunity to register people who clearly intend to be registered.

---

2. Moreover, because registration problems are left for later resolution, polling processes are less sensitive to the availability of communications with central elections offices and data servers.

To be sure, the provisional ballot is not the only way that election administrators might identify and correct errors in voter registration. In many of the states that comply with the NVRA by allowing voters to cast a regular ballot, fail-safe voters must first complete a new application for voter registration at the current address.

Nevertheless, the provisional ballot seems to be a superior tool for managing voter registration lists, and for two reasons. First, to the extent that the circumstances that trigger the issue of a provisional ballot are broader than the requirements of the NVRA, election administrators are able to find and fix more errors in registration. Second, because provisional ballots receive a full investigation, election officials can better tell whether the problems are the doing of voters, poll workers, clerical staff, service agency personnel, or third party registrars. They can use the knowledge gained to intervene in administrative processes so as to reduce the number of problems going forward.

Arguments against Provisional Balloting

The obvious downside to provisional balloting is its labor intensity. Research into the registration status of provisional voters takes significant amounts of staff time in county elections offices. The assistant superintendent of the King County, Washington, Department of Records and Elections estimated that the 17,000 provisional ballots in 2000 had occupied 15 staff for nine days. (Because of the interest in closely contested races for president and the U.S. Senate, the 2000 election produced roughly three times the usual number of provisional ballots in King County.) On a per-ballot basis, provisional ballots probably consume no more resources than absentee ballots, and in most states there are significantly fewer provisional ballots. Still, provisional balloting requires a noticeable expense.[3]

Second, the process of researching provisional ballots slows official election counts. In most contests, the delay has little consequence because the election is not close enough to hinge on the provisional votes. But in close elections, provisional ballots add to the time until an election can be considered decided. In states that issue a provisional ballot to absentee voters who appear in person, the investigation of provisional ballots cannot be completed until all the absentee ballots have been received. In Washington,

---

3. As noted earlier, however, some part of this expense might properly be understood as list maintenance.

where absentee ballots need be postmarked but not received by Election Day, the count can stretch for quite a long time.

Third, the use of provisional balloting in broader circumstances might encourage voters to exploit it as a more convenient opportunity for registration or change of address. Many states currently use provisional ballots to comply with the fail-safe requirements of NVRA, which pertain only to registered voters who move within jurisdiction. With broader use, voters might treat provisional balloting as a back-door form of Election Day registration, albeit with a crucial difference: voters who had not preregistered could not use provisional balloting to participate in the *current* election. But we have no evidence to indicate that states that already make provisional ballots available in circumstances beyond fail-safe, like California and Washington, have encountered this problem in practice.[4]

Finally, the practice of provisional balloting has encountered scattered resistance from voters themselves. According to a 1997 Federal Elections Commission (FEC) survey, Tennessee election officials found that their fail-safe voters were reluctant to vote by provisional ballot, evidently concerned that their votes might not ultimately be allowed. As a result, Tennessee abandoned provisional voting and instead allows fail-safe voters who have moved within counties to vote by regular ballot.[5]

The same FEC report also noted concerns that provisional balloting might be used to discriminate against minority voters. It did not elaborate the concerns, nor did it provide any instances. One can see the basis for the fear: biased election officials might use provisional ballots to segregate minority votes that they will later, quietly, disallow. On the other hand, minority voters with registration problems (of whoever's making) might find voting by provisional ballot preferable to not being allowed to vote at all. Provisional balloting leaves a paper trail—the ballot envelopes that election officials use to investigate eligibility—which might be concrete evidence to support legal action under the Voting Rights Act.

---

4. In 2000, according to the FEC, North Carolina election officials discovered that political parties had mustered unregistered people to the polls to demand to vote by provisional ballot. It is not clear what this tactic's purpose was, unless to hope that the provisionals would simply be counted without investigation.

5. Voters in very small jurisdictions might also resist provisional ballots because they are segregated from regular ballots. In smaller, rural districts, the employment provisional ballots may be so infrequent that voters can be identified even after the provisionals have been shorn of the outer, identifying envelopes.

Selected References

Federal Election Commission, Office of Election Administration. "Implementing the National Voter Registration Act: A Report to State and Local Election Officials on Problems and Solutions Discovered 1995–1996," March 1998.

————. "The Impact of the National Voter Registration Act of 1993 on the Administration of Elections for Federal Office, 1999–2000," final draft, June 2001.

DISFRANCHISEMENT OF FELONS

Summary of Conclusions

1. States currently deny the right to vote to 4.2 million people on account of current or prior felony conviction. Every state but two disfranchises felons in current incarceration. Eleven states disfranchise felons for life.
2. One third of the people denied the franchise because of a felony conviction have already completed their sentences. The disfranchisement rate in the 11 states that permanently deny voting rights, 5.1 percent, is three times the rate in states that impose no disability beyond the period of incarceration, probation, and parole, 1.7 percent.
3. Felony disfranchisement has particular impact on the African American electorate. Nearly 7 percent of black Americans cannot participate in the electoral process because of a felony conviction.

States currently deny the franchise to nearly 4.2 million people, about 2.1 percent of the voting age population, on account of current or prior felony conviction. Every state but two, Maine and Vermont, disfranchises those currently serving prison or jail sentences for felony offenses. Twenty-nine states prevent felons from voting during the period of their parole or probation, or both. Fourteen states, primarily in the South and West, impose civil disability on felons beyond the term of their incarceration, probation, and parole. Eleven disfranchise felons for life, nine for a single felony conviction [table 24].[1]

In states that permanently deny to felons the right to vote, the impact on the electorate is sizable.[2] The percentage of the voting age population dis-

---

1. According to the Center for Policy Alternatives, within the last six months Kentucky and New Mexico have approved legislation to repeal permanent disfranchisement of felons. Legislation in Maryland awaits the governor's signature. Repeal of permanent disfranchisement has cleared one chamber in Alabama and Nevada.
2. The estimates reported here owe to the work of Jeff Manza, Christopher Uggen, and Marcus Britton, sociologists at Northwestern University and the University of Minnesota. Estimates of the number of felons currently in custody, on parole, or on probation are straightforwardly derived from the reports of state departments of justice. Manza and his colleagues estimated the number of felons no longer under sentence using careful and standard demographic techniques. The estimates reflect the numbers of felons newly discharged from sentence, the number returned to custody on subsequent felony convictions, and the number who have died.

Table 24 Felony Disfranchisement Provisions, by State, as of January 1, 1999

State	Circumstances of disfranchisement					Disfranchised as percentage of voting age population		
	Currently imprisoned for felony conviction	Currently jailed for felony conviction	On parole after felony conviction	On probation for felony conviction	Previously convicted of felony	Black	White, Latino, and other	All
Alabama	■	■	■	■	■	12.41	4.26	6.21
Alaska	■	■	■	■		5.65	1.55	1.70
Arizona	■	■	■	■	2d conviction	11.75	3.29	3.58
Arkansas	■	■	■	■		7.60	1.78	2.61
California	■		■			4.84	0.87	1.18
Colorado	■		■			4.07	0.55	0.69
Connecticut	■	■	■	■		6.42	1.73	1.85
Delaware	■	■	■	■	For 5 years	15.60	3.45	5.63
District of Columbia	■					4.18	0.58	2.44
Florida	■	■	■	■	■	13.77	5.07	6.24
Georgia	■	■	■	■		6.08	1.62	2.80
Hawaii	■	■				0.26	0.42	0.42
Idaho	■	■		■		4.05	0.47	1.40
Illinois	■	■				2.39	0.21	0.51
Indiana	■	■				5.24	0.07	0.46
Iowa	■	■	■	■	■	22.52	3.81	4.14
Kansas	■		■			5.22	0.50	0.76
Kentucky	■	■	■	■	■	14.96	3.46	4.24
Louisiana	■	■	■	■		2.87	0.36	1.10
Maine								
Maryland	■	■	■	■	2d conviction	7.57	1.62	3.20
Massachusetts	■*							
Michigan	■	■				2.72	0.34	0.65
Minnesota	■	■	■	■		7.54	0.91	1.07

State				48 states + D.C.	41 states + D.C.	35 states	29 states	14 states
Mississippi	9.71	3.06	5.28	■	■	■	■	■
Missouri	6.56	1.31	1.84	■	■	■	■	
Montana	3.33	0.43	0.44	■	■	■		
Nebraska	3.83	0.42	0.56	■	■	■	■	
Nevada	16.53	3.66	4.56	■	■	■	■	■
New Hampshire	1.91	0.25	0.26	■				
New Jersey	9.73	1.25	2.40	■	■	■	■	
New Mexico	24.78	5.00	5.52	■	■	■	■	■
New York	3.11	0.57	1.00	■	■	■		
North Carolina	3.72	0.68	1.31	■	■	■		
North Dakota	1.04	0.20	0.20	■				
Ohio	3.10	0.30	0.60	■				
Oklahoma	8.00	1.47	1.93	■	■	■	■	
Oregon	2.74	0.32	0.38	■				
Pennsylvania	2.56	0.19	0.40	■				
Rhode Island	11.68	1.65	2.09	■	■	■	■	
South Carolina	3.90	0.88	1.72	■	■	■	■	
South Dakota	2.64	0.46	0.47	■				
Tennessee	5.86	1.36	2.03	■	■	■	■	**
Texas	8.77	2.95	3.64	■	■	■	■	
Utah	5.01	0.53	0.57	■				
Vermont								
Virginia	13.82	3.35	5.33	■	■	■	■	■
Washington	12.32	3.01	3.33	■	■	■	■	**
West Virginia	2.70	0.54	0.60	■	■	■		
Wisconsin	10.61	0.86	1.32	■	■	■		
Wyoming	14.94	4.46	4.55	■	■	■	■	■
United States	6.57	1.49	2.09	48 states + D.C.	41 states + D.C.	35 states	29 states	14 states

*In November 2000, Massachusetts voters approved an initiative to disfranchise persons currently imprisoned for a felony conviction.

**Tennessee and Washington deny voting rights to felons convicted before they eased their laws in the mid-1980s.

Source: Jeff Manza, Christopher Uggen, and Marcus Britton, "The Truly Disfranchised: Felon Voting Rights and American Politics," Northwestern University, January 3, 2001.

franchised by felony conviction in states that disfranchise forever ranges from 3.2 percent in Maryland (which disfranchises permanently only on a second felony conviction) to 6.2 percent in Alabama and Florida. Every state that currently practices permanent disqualification has a higher rate of felony disfranchisement than any state that does not. Of people currently disqualified by a felony conviction across the United States, one-third are felons who have already completed their sentences.

As is well known, a disproportionate number of African Americans pass through the justice system, and consequently, the impact of disqualification for felony conviction is especially dramatic for the black electorate. Nearly 7 percent of black Americans cannot participate in the electoral process because of felony convictions. Because 95 percent of felons are male, the felony disfranchisement rate for black men is almost double. All but one state, Hawaii, records felony disfranchisement rates for blacks that are larger than disfranchisement rates for whites and others, in most cases several times larger.

The impact of permanent disqualification is especially striking. The only states with African American disfranchisement rates that exceed the least of the rates in permanent disfranchisement states are states that disqualify felons during the term of their probation or parole. In states with small African American populations and lifetime disqualification, such as Iowa and New Mexico, disfranchisement rates for black males exceed 40 percent. The lowest felony disfranchisement rate for blacks among the permanent disqualification states still surpasses the highest felony disfranchisement rate for whites and others, Florida's 5.1 percent.

The impact of the separate provisions for felony disqualification can be seen in estimates of the effect of rescission (table 25). Repeal of permanent disfranchisement would reduce the number excluded from the electorate on account of felony convictions by about a third. Repeal of disfranchisement during probation and parole would have a somewhat larger effect, mostly because it is current policy in more and larger states. Repeal of both provisions would benefit white and other felons a little more than blacks. Overall, felony disfranchisement rates would fall to just 0.6 percent, about 1.2 million people, were disqualifications imposed only on felons in current custody. Felony disfranchisement rates would remain at 2.5 percent for blacks, well above the felony disqualification rate for whites and others under current law, 1.5 percent.

In 28 of the 39 states that do not permanently bar felons from the franchise, restoration of voting rights occurs automatically on completion of sentence, probation, or parole. About a third of felons eligible for restora-

Table 25 Effect of Repeal of Disfranchisement Provisions on Percentage Disqualified by Felony Disfranchisement

State	Circumstances of disfranchisement					Disfranchised as percentage of voting age population		
	Currently imprisoned for felony conviction	Currently jailed for felony conviction	On parole after felony conviction	On probation for felony conviction	Previously convicted of felony	Black	White, Latino, and other	All
State laws as of January 1999	47 states + D.C.	42 states + D.C.	35 states	30 states	14 states	6.57	1.49	2.09
If disabilities beyond imprisonment probation, and parole repealed	47 states + D.C.	42 states + D.C.	35 states	30 states		4.63	0.95	1.38
If all provisions repealed except disqualification for current incarceration	47 states + D.C.	42 states + D.C.				2.46	0.35	0.60

Source: Jeff Manza, Christopher Uggen, and Marcus Britton, "The Truly Disfranchised: Felon Voting Rights and American Politics," Northwestern University, January 3, 2001.
Note: In November 2000 Massachusetts voters approved an initiative to disfranchise persons currently imprisoned for a felony conviction.

tion of voting rights, about 700,000 people, face some minimal barrier or complication for reinstatement (for example, filing a legal document formally requesting restoration). In states that mandate permanent loss of voting rights for felons, restoration can be accomplished only through an executive pardon or a successful petition for restoration of rights.

The enforcement of a permanent disqualification for felony conviction is a difficult administrative task. Felons are easily identified as long as they remain in the justice system. Once discharged, they cannot as readily be barred from participation in the electoral process. As recent events in Florida demonstrate, enforcement is especially difficult, if not impossible, when felons relocate to a state that denies voting rights to felons indefinitely.

Selected References

Cloud, David S. "Felons Make up a Large Chunk of the Missing Electorate in U.S.," *Wall Street Journal*, December 18, 2000.

Fellner, Jamie, and Marc Mauer. *Losing the Vote: The Impact of Felony Disenfranchisement Law in the United States* (Washington and New York: Sentencing Project and Human Rights Watch, 1998).

Manza, Jeff, Christopher Uggen, and Marcus Britton. "The Truly Disfranchised: Felon Voting Rights and American Politics," typescript, Northwestern University, January 3, 2001.

U.S. Department of Justice, Office of the Pardon Attorney. "Civil Disabilities for Convicted Felons: A State-by-State Survey," October 1996.

UNIFORM POLL CLOSING AND REPORTING

Summary of Conclusions

1. The effect of most early projections on voter turnout is small. In most cases, the early projections simply confirm what voters expected to happen. In some circumstances, however, the effect of projections may be large enough to influence outcomes further down the ticket. The effect is concentrated in the western region of the country.

2. Uniform poll hours, such as exist in Canada, would probably meet resistance from western states, where polls would have to close earlier than they now do, and from eastern states, where polls would have to open later. Resistance would arise partly from concerns about convenience for voters and partly from potential difficulties in staffing polling places and conducting the count, which could range far into the night in the East.

3. A uniform closing would tend to restrict turnout opportunities for workers in blue collar occupations, who tend to vote Democratic. A uniform opening would restrict opportunities for white collar workers, who tend to vote Republican. Most voters so affected would find ways to vote at other times, but uniform poll times would probably have a greater effect on lower status and less educated citizens, who typically are less motivated to vote and therefore more sensitive to convenience.

4. Restrictions on the official reports of election outcomes could probably not prevent early projections absolutely, but they could raise the cost of a projection of a close election considerably. In closer races, exit pollsters could defeat restrictions on official reports by increasing the size of exit poll samples, by polling in more precincts, and, as they already do, by observing counts in precincts, which activity by law is open to public scrutiny in most states.

Every close election brings with it concerns about the effects of election projections from exit polls on voter turnout and election outcomes. The 2000 election certainly fit the pattern. On the basis of exit polls and early counts, several of the national networks called the state of Florida for Al Gore just before 8:00 p.m. Eastern Standard Time (EST), after the polls had closed in the Florida peninsula but a bit before they were to close in the panhandle. Shortly before 10 p.m. EST, with an hour left for the balloting on the West Coast, the networks withdrew their projections. Early the next morning they called Florida, and by now the 2000 election, for

George W. Bush, and only a couple hours later they retracted their calls for a second time.

The broadcast media faced a barrage of criticism almost immediately. Media executives and exit poll analysts were called before a House panel, where they took stands that ranged from defiant to contrite.

Once again, a close election has put election projections in the spotlight. Once again, the issues are far from straightforward.

Evidence of Effects of Early Calls on Voter Turnout

As most people recognize, it stands to reason that authoritative news that the election is decided might affect whether people turn out to vote. The rationale is not that people have lost the chance to influence the outcome. Even in a close election, the likelihood that an individual voter will change the outcome with his own single vote is vanishingly small. Rather, the concern is that people who wish to be part of an event will no longer care to participate in an election that is already in the history books. And the concern is that campaigns, parties, and advocacy groups will ease up in their efforts to bring people out to the polls.

For these reasons, early projections of election results are likely to depress voter turnout. But the magnitude of the effect is limited for four reasons. First, early calls can only affect people who live in areas where the polls have not yet closed. Because nearly a majority of the American electorate resides in the Eastern time zone, and about a third resides in the Central, early calls can have an impact only on a subset of eligible voters. Second, early projections can only affect the turnout decisions of people who still intend to vote but who have not yet voted. Calls made 30 minutes before poll closing must necessarily have a smaller effect on turnout than calls made two hours before poll closing. Third, early projections can only affect the turnout decisions of people who were exposed to them. Voters who do not hear the early calls cannot be affected by them. Finally, early projections can only affect the turnout decisions of people whose intention to vote depended predominantly on a desire to participate in the presidential race. Some fraction of voters who have not already voted will turn out, despite the futility of affecting the presidential race, simply because they care a great deal about races that are further down the ticket.

Taken together, these four considerations imply that the effect of early projections on voter turnout will be modest in the context of the nation. Nevertheless, the effects on individuals who live in the West, who have not already voted and who still intend to vote, might be quite large. Even small decrements in turnout might be consequential in close races, and the depressing effects on turnout will be concentrated mostly in the states in the West.

The best study of the effect of early projections on voter turnout is based on an examination of the 1980 election. In November 1980, after a presidential campaign that was too close to call even the weekend before the election, one network made the first formal projection for Ronald Reagan very early, at 8:15 p.m. EST. Soon after, at 9:50 p.m. EST, President Carter appeared on national television to concede. At the time of the call, the polls remained open in most of the states in the Mountain and Pacific time zones, in many of the states in the Central zone, and even in a couple states in the Eastern zone. But informal forecasts of a substantial Republican victory began even earlier, with the opening of election night coverage at 6:00 p.m. EST, at which time the polls were still open throughout the nation. Critics of the networks' actions charged that the early calls of the presidential race had depressed voter turnout and caused the defeat of Democratic candidates, particularly in the West.

After the election, John E. Jackson of the University of Michigan secured funds to reinterview participants in the 1980 American National Election Study, a survey of a national sample of about 2,000 persons. Jackson's follow-up survey asked the time respondents had voted, the election night news they had heard, and the time they had heard the news of a projected winner. The earlier survey had gathered a large amount of additional information, such as respondents' preferences in the presidential race. Each respondent's turnout was verified by an examination of official voting records.

Sizable numbers of voters in 1980 had been exposed to election night coverage before their polls had closed. Fourteen percent had heard about Carter's concession before the local polls had closed (29 percent more could not recall the time), and 26 percent had found out that Reagan had been projected the winner before the local balloting ended (30 percent could not recall the time). Overall, nearly half of the electorate, 49 percent, had been exposed to some kind of news about the election results, intimations if not projections, before their polls closed (17 percent could not recall the time).[1]

---

1. These percentages are based on self-reports, which are sometimes mistaken, but they seem plausible. In 1980 about 14 percent of the voting age population resided in the Pacific time zone, about 5 percent in the Mountain zone, and 29 percent lived in the Central zone.

Having heard the election projections or Carter's concession did in fact depress turnout in 1980, and noticeably. In the West, the region most affected, the estimated turnout of those who had heard the projections and had not voted as of 6:00 p.m. EST (3:00 p.m. PST) was about 12 percentage points lower than the estimated turnout of those who had not heard the projections and had not yet voted. The impact on the total turnout, however, was much smaller, even in the West: not everybody heard of the projections before the polls closed, not everybody still intended to vote, and nearly half of the electorate had already cast ballots.[2] Though small in the aggregate, the effect was certainly large enough to have affected outcomes in close races further down the ticket.[3]

Jackson's study provides good evidence that early reports of election outcomes suppress turnout among those citizens who have heard the news, who intend to vote, and who have not yet voted. Given the special circumstances of the 1980 election, his estimates probably represent an upper bound on the effect that projections might have. The 1980 calls and concession were made much earlier than they have been made either before or since, meaning that larger numbers of intended voters might have been affected by them. Moreover, the 1980 projections were more informative than the projections either before or since, because the magnitude of Reagan's victory was simply not anticipated by the pre-election polls. In most elections, early calls only confirm what voters expected to happen already.[4] Accordingly, in most elections, early calls have even more limited effect on voter turnout.

_____

2. Jackson does not break these out by region, so it is impossible to reconstruct the total effect on turnout across the population.

3. Jackson also ventured some guarded conclusions about the differential effects of the early calls on the turnout of Republicans and Democrats. (None of the effects were sufficiently strong to give much confidence that they were not the result of sampling error.) He found that in fact the early projections lowered the likelihood of turnout more among Republicans than Democrats. Apparently, the information that the election was decided had more effect on the turnout of the winners than the losers. He also found that more Democrats than Republicans had yet to cast ballots at 6:00 p.m. EST. But because of their higher socioeconomic status, Republicans are more likely to turn out. Jackson does not indicate exactly how these three partisan differences play out, although he implies that the early projections probably hurt Republican turnout more than Democratic turnout.

4. Of course, exit poll results and early vote tallies that vary from the pre-election polls produce surprise, and surprise is newsworthy. Consequently, competition to be first with the result of the election is even greater in elections that are closer than expected or in elections that are not as close as expected.

Effects of a Nationwide Poll Closing Time

One proposal often offered to solve the problem that early projections might depress turnout is a uniform nationwide poll closing time. For such a law to achieve its purposes, polls would need to stay open later in the East and close earlier in the West. Otherwise, reports from states that had closed earlier than the statutory closing hour—in the East, only New York and Rhode Island currently stay open until 9:00 p.m.—would be available before the polls close in the West.

If the closing time were established at 10:00 p.m. EST, table 26 shows, polls in five western states with roughly 14 percent of the nation's population would need to close an hour earlier, at 7 p.m. PST or 8 p.m. MST, than they currently do.[5] Conversely, every state in the Eastern time zone and every state but one in the Central zone (Iowa) would need to keep its polls open longer, most by two to three hours. If, on the other hand, the closing time were set earlier, at 9 p.m. EST, every state in the Pacific time zone would have to shorten polling hours, and in the East only New York and Rhode Island would not have still to extend their hours.[6]

One obvious problem with such a proposal is that it would considerably extend the hours of operation of the polls in most of the Atlantic states and in many of the central states. If the states in the Eastern time zone wished to begin the balloting as early as they do currently, most would have to keep their precincts in operation for 15 hours and, after the closing, count ballots well into the night. (Currently, only New York's largest counties operate their precincts for 15 hours. Connecticut, Iowa, Louisiana, and Rhode Island maintain 14 hours.) Uniform poll closing would in fact have the greatest effect not on the western states but on the eastern states. The states in the Eastern time zone, home to 47 percent of the nation's population, would surely be concerned by the additional administrative costs of the extended precinct hours that would need be maintained.

---

5. All of the references to population percentages are approximations, although reasonably good approximations. Many states give discretion to local election jurisdictions to set polling times, and eleven states cover two time zones. In making the estimates for these states, we allocated all of a state's population to the time zone with the largest share of its population.
6. All of the analyses set aside the issue of polling times in Alaska and Hawaii, both two hours behind Pacific Standard Time.

Table 26 Uniform Closing Times and Their Effect on the States

Closing Time		Affected states

Polls closing at 10:00 p.m. EST

Later than current

4 hours later	EST:	Indiana (most), Kentucky (most)
3 hours later	EST:	Florida (most), Georgia, New Hampshire (most), South Carolina, Vermont, Virginia
	CST:	Indiana (some), Kentucky (some)
2 1/2 hours later	EST:	North Carolina, Ohio, West Virginia
2 hours later	EST:	Alabama, Connecticut, Delaware, District of Columbia, Florida (some), Maine, Maryland, Massachusetts, Michigan (most), New Hampshire (some), New Jersey, Pennsylvania, Tennessee (part)
	CST:	Illinois, Kansas (most), Mississippi, Missouri, North Dakota (most), Oklahoma, Texas
1 1/2 hours later	CST:	Arkansas
1 hour later	EST:	New York, Rhode Island
	CST:	Louisiana, Michigan (some), Minnesota, Nebraska, South Dakota, Tennessee (part), Wisconsin
	MST:	Arizona, Colorado, Kansas (some), New Mexico, North Dakota (some), Wyoming

Earlier than current

1 hour earlier	PST:	California, Idaho (some), Oregon (most), Washington

Polls closing at 9:00 p.m. EST

Later than current

3 hours later	EST:	Indiana (most), Kentucky (most)
2 hours later	EST:	Florida (most), Georgia, New Hampshire (most), South Carolina, Vermont, Virginia
	CST:	Indiana (some), Kentucky (some)
1 1/2 hours later	EST:	North Carolina, Ohio, West Virginia
1 hour later	EST:	Alabama, Connecticut, Delaware, District of Columbia, Florida (some), Maine, Maryland, Massachusetts, Michigan (most), New Hampshire (some), New Jersey, Pennsylvania, Tennessee (part)
	CST:	Illinois, Kansas (most), Mississippi, Missouri, North Dakota (most), Oklahoma, Texas
1/2 hour later	CST:	Arkansas

Earlier than current

1 hour earlier	CST:	Iowa
	MST:	Idaho (most), Montana, Oregon (some), Utah
	PST:	Nevada
2 hours earlier	PST:	California, Idaho (some), Oregon (most), Washington

Note: Text in parentheses indicates geographically affected areas. EST = Eastern Standard Time; CST = Central Standard Time; MST = Mountain Standard Time; PST = Pacific Standard Time.

A second option is suggested by Canada, the only other venerable democracy that spans several time zones. In Canada, both the times the polls open and the times the polls close are regulated nationally. The precincts in most of the country open at 9:30 a.m. EST and close 12 hours later, at 9:30 p.m. EST. The polls open and close two and a half hours earlier in Newfoundland, two hours earlier in the other Maritimes, and a half hour later on the Pacific coast. The balloting begins as late as 9:30 a.m. local time in the Eastern zone and ends as early as 7:00 p.m. local in the Pacific zone. Because only 8 percent of Canada's population resides in the Maritimes, the vast majority of the balloting is begun and completed at approximately the same time nationwide.

The Canadian system of uniform opening and closing would solve the problem of extended hours in the East by opening the polls later in the Eastern and Central time zones. But it would raise its own set of issues. The least of the issues is the length of polling hours. Only a third of the U.S. population lives in states that allow 12 hours or less of polling time. A majority lives in states that allow no fewer than 13 hours. Hours could easily be extended by an additional hour, but either by pushing the balloting past 9:00 p.m. in the East or before 7:00 a.m. in the West.

The second issue is the polling period itself. The population of the United States is spread more evenly across the continent than the population of Canada. The two largest Canadian provinces, Quebec and Ontario, both predominantly in the Eastern time zone, contain 62 percent of Canada's population. The third largest province, British Columbia, has 13 percent. Only about 17 percent of the population lives in the Central and Mountain time zones. In the United States, in contrast, a much smaller proportion, only 47 percent, lives in the Eastern time zone and a slightly larger fraction, 14 percent, lives in the Pacific. In between, 33 percent lives in the Central zone, as shown in the following listing of the time zone and percent of eligible citizens residing in that zone, as of 1996:

Eastern	47.0	Pacific	14.1
Central	32.9	Alaska and Hawaii	0.6
Mountain	5.4		

As a result, it is difficult to identify a polling period that would not cause some substantial dislocation from current practices in the states. As shown in the next two tables, later opening and closing times would cause the polls to open quite late for a large proportion of the eligible voters in the Eastern and Central zones. Conversely, earlier opening and closing times

Table 27   Poll Opening Times, by State, in Eastern Time

Typical or earliest opening time	States	Percent of eligible citizens, 1996
6:00 a.m. EST	Connecticut, Indiana (most), Kentucky (most), Maine (some), New York, Virginia	14.3
6:30 a.m. EST	North Carolina, Ohio, West Virginia	8.2
7:00 a.m. EST	Delaware, District of Columbia, Florida (most), Georgia, Illinois, Indiana (some), Kansas (most), Kentucky (some), Louisiana, Maine (most), Maryland, Massachusetts, Michigan, Missouri, New Jersey, Pennsylvania, Rhode Island, South Carolina, Tennessee, Vermont	39.0
8:00 a.m. EST	Arizona, Florida (some), Iowa, Kansas (some), Minnesota, Mississippi, New Hampshire, Oklahoma, Texas, Wisconsin (some)	14.0
8:30 a.m. EST	Arkansas	1.0
9:00 a.m. EST	Alabama, Colorado, Montana, Nebraska, New Mexico, Oregon (some), South Dakota, Utah, Wisconsin (most), Wyoming	8.1
10:00 a.m. EST	California, Idaho (most), Nevada, North Dakota (most), Oregon (most), Washington	14.8
11:00 a.m. EST	Idaho (some), North Dakota (some)	0.0

Source: www.cnn.com/election/1998/states.
Note: Text in parentheses indicates geographically affected areas.

would require the polls to close quite early for a large proportion of eligible voters in the Pacific and Mountain time zones.[7]

One effect of uniform hours of operation would be on election administration. On one hand, time set earlier in the day would require election officials in the western states to begin their operations much earlier than they have in the past. Precincts serving 24 percent of the electorate currently open later than 8:00 a.m. EST. On another hand, a time set later would require poll workers in the eastern states to continue their work much later into the evening and extend the count well into the night. Polling places serving 66 percent of the electorate currently close before 6:00 p.m. PST.

---

7. In many states there is local variation in opening and closing times, especially in opening times. Several states specify that the polls shall not open later than a legislated time but allow local election officials to open the polls earlier.

Table 28 Poll Closing Times, by State, in Eastern Time

Required closing time	States	Percent of eligible citizens, 1996
6:00 p.m. EST	Indiana (most), Kentucky (most)	3.9
7:00 p.m. EST	Florida (most), Georgia, Indiana (some), Kentucky (some), New Hampshire (most), South Carolina, Vermont, Virginia	13.2
7:30 p.m. EST	North Carolina, Ohio, West Virginia	8.2
8:00 p.m. EST	Alabama, Connecticut, Delaware, District of Columbia, Florida (some), Illinois, Kansas (most), Maine, Maryland, Massachusetts, Michigan (most), Mississippi, Missouri, New Hampshire (some), New Jersey, North Dakota (most), Oklahoma, Pennsylvania, Tennessee, Texas	39.1
8:30 p.m. EST	Arkansas	1.0
9:00 p.m. EST	Arizona, Colorado, Kansas (some), Louisiana, Michigan (some), Minnesota, Nebraska, New Mexico, New York, North Dakota (some), Rhode Island, South Dakota, Wisconsin, Wyoming	17.2
10:00 p.m. EST	Idaho (most), Iowa, Montana, Nevada, Oregon (some), Utah	3.2
11:00 p.m. EST	California, Idaho (some), Oregon (most), Washington	13.5

Source: www.cnn.com/election/1998/states.
Note: Text in parentheses indicates geographically affected areas.

A second effect of uniform hours of operation would be on the voters themselves. As shown in the next table, about 65 percent of all voters go to the polls before 4:00 p.m. local time, but 15 percent—one in seven—vote after 6:00 p.m. local time (see table 29).[8]

The hours that people turn out to vote vary across regions, in ways that would make uniform polling hours a greater problem on the West Coast. Voters in the middle of the country prefer to vote early, two thirds of them by 4:00 p.m. local time. Greater numbers of voters on the coasts prefer to vote later. Voters in the Pacific time zone prefer to turn out later than voters in any other part of the country: 19 percent of the voter turnout occurs

---

8. Unfortunately, the 1980s were the last time the Current Population Surveys asked for time of day voted. Since 1980 the main population trends have been the continued distribution westward, the continued aging of the population, and the sharp rise in the Latino population.

Table 29 Time of Day Voted, 1980

Percent

Hour of day voted	Voters	Voters at polls
Before 12:00 p.m.	41.4	43.6
Between 12:00 p.m. and 4:00 p.m.	20.7	21.8
Between 4:00 p.m. and 6:00 p.m.	18.7	19.7
After 6:00 p.m.	14.2	15.0
By absentee	5.0	...

Source: Current Population Survey, 1980.

after 6:00 p.m. Under a uniform closing law, late voters in the West would be at the top of the list of those affected (see table 30).[9]

Changes in the hours of voting would also affect different types of people in different ways. Later opening times would impose the greatest burdens on older voters, while earlier closing times would impose most on younger voters. Sixty-three percent of voters over the age of 65 turn out before noon, and 22 percent of voters between 18 and 25 turn out after 6:00 (see table 31).

If one factor in the times people choose to vote is age, another is work circumstances. Students, disabled people unable to work, and armed forces personnel vote in large numbers by absentee. Of those who vote in person, people who are not in the labor force either tend to vote early in the day, in the case of homemakers, retirees, and disabled persons, or in the middle of the day, in the case of students. Working people vote at the beginning of the day, before work, or at the end of the day, after work (see table 32).

Table 30 Time Voted, by Time Zone

Percent

Time voted	Eastern	Central	Mountain	Pacific
Before 12:00 p.m.	43.4	43.8	42.8	43.9
12:00 p.m. to 4:00 p.m.	21.5	23.0	24.0	17.3
4:00 p.m. to 6:00 p.m.	18.7	21.0	19.5	19.8
After 6:00 p.m.	16.5	12.3	13.8	19.0
Total	99.9	100.1	100.1	100.0
(N)	(27,155)	(20,351)	(5,699)	(6,610)

Source: Current Population Survey, 1980.

---

9. According to the Current Population Survey, the time of turnout was slightly earlier in 1984, a less competitive national election. The regional pattern was the same: later on the coasts than inland, and latest in the West. Current Population Report, Series P20-405, March 1986.

Table 31 Time Voted, by Age

Percent

Time voted	18–25	26–45	46–64	65 +
Before 12:00 p.m.	29.7	37.5	45.8	63.1
12:00 p.m. to 4:00 p.m.	23.7	20.6	20.4	25.8
4:00 p.m. to 6:00 p.m.	24.9	22.8	20.2	7.9
After 6:00 p.m.	21.8	19.1	13.6	3.3
Total	100.1	100.0	100.0	100.1
(N)	(8,414)	(26,764)	(19,502)	(12,017)

Source: Current Population Survey, 1980.

The workday differs across type of employment in ways that affect preferences for times of voting. The day for white collar workers begins later and ends later than the workday for blue collar workers. As table 33 shows, people in managerial and professional employment tend to prefer to vote early. More distinctly, so do farmers, fishers, and foresters. People employed as operators, assemblers, and handlers, on the other hand, tend to prefer to vote late. (People with higher occupational status also vote more often by absentee.) It has long been part of political lore that Republicans turn out early and Democrats turn out late; occupational differences account for the pattern.[10]

Table 32 Time Voted, by Selected Work Statuses

Time voted	Working	Looking for work	Homemaker	In school	Unable to work	Other, including retired
Before 12:00 p.m.	37.0	44.2	53.3	32.5	54.6	64.0
12:00 p.m. to 4:00 p.m.	19.1	27.8	27.5	26.4	28.2	24.9
4:00 p.m. to 6:00 p.m.	24.3	15.6	11.8	25.1	12.9	7.7
After 6:00 p.m.	18.5	12.4	7.4	15.9	4.3	3.4
Total	99.9	100.0	100.0	99.9	100.0	100.0
(N)	(39,311)	(1,892)	(11,410)	(1,011)	(443)	(7,389)

Source: Current Population Survey, 1980.

10. The partisan differences in time of voting are perhaps not as sharp as they may have been in the past. Running counter are the differences in time of voting across income and education. Better educated people vote later than less educated people, and except at the very highest levels, earners of high incomes vote later than poorer people. Republican affiliation, of course, rises with education and income. Part of the responsibility for this pattern is that the poorest and least educated in 1980 were disproportionately elderly.

Table 33 Time Voted, by Selected Occupational Classes

Time voted	Managerial, professional	Technical, sales, clerical	Operators, assemblers, handlers	Farmers, fishers, foresters
Before 12:00 p.m.	42.3	38.3	31.0	42.4
12:00 p.m. to 4:00 p.m.	17.8	19.9	18.4	23.7
4:00 p.m. to 6:00 p.m.	22.0	22.4	29.0	16.6
After 6:00 p.m.	17.9	19.4	21.6	17.3
Total	100.0	100.0	100.0	100.0
(N)	(13,229)	(14,975)	(10,655)	(1,555)

Source: Current Population Survey, 1980.

Demographically, only one more difference is worthy of note. Blacks and whites turn out throughout the day in almost equal proportion. But by about six percentage points, Latino voters prefer to vote at the end of Election Day rather than the beginning.[11] The Latino population has long been concentrated in the Southwest—a third of all Americans of Hispanic origin reside in California—and since 1980 the percentage of Americans of Latin descent has nearly doubled (table 34).

Accordingly, hours that are skewed toward the morning will tend to make it harder for younger voters and working class voters to get to the polls, and hours that are skewed toward the evening will make it harder for older and upper class voters to turn out. Compared to the current, decentralized regime of poll hours, a uniform poll closing law would reduce the number of evening hours in the western states and dampen turnout most among workers who are young, blue collar, and Latino. Conversely, a nationwide poll hours law would reduce the number of morning hours in the eastern states and dampen turnout most among people who are older, white collar, and white. Any politically feasible uniform hours

Table 34 Time Voted, for Latinos and Non-Latinos

Time voted	Latino	Non-Latino
Before 12:00 p.m.	37.9	43.7
12:00 p.m. to 4:00 p.m.	20.8	21.8
4:00 p.m. to 6:00 p.m.	20.5	19.6
After 6:00 p.m.	20.8	14.9
Total	100.0	100.0
(N)	(1,460)	(59,996)

Source: Current Population Survey, 1980.

---

11. One reason is that the Latino population is younger on average than the Anglo population.

law would probably require West Coast polls to close no earlier than 7:00 p.m. local time, which with a 13-hour Election Day would require East Coast polls to open no earlier than 9:00 a.m. local.[12] Overall, by expanding evening hours and restricting morning hours in the eastern half of the United States, a nationwide hours law would apparently make Election Day more convenient for younger voters and less convenient for older voters. By expanding morning hours and contracting evening hours in the West, however, a uniform polling time law would make Election Day less convenient for Latino voters.

To be sure, most voters who are no longer able to turn out at the time of day they previously preferred will find other times to vote. But if we imagine that voters currently make choices that offer the most convenience, any change is likely to lower the probability that they turn out at all, at least marginally. The inconvenience is unlikely to deter people who are highly motivated to vote: strong partisans, the politically engaged, the highly educated. The added trouble is more likely to deter people who are less motivated to vote. Because they tend to turn out later in the day, and because they tend to vote less often already, we might conjecture that a uniform closing law would be a particular hardship for younger voters and Latino voters.

Effects of Uniform Reporting

Because a uniform polling time seems such a draconian step, observers concerned about the effect of early projections of election results have proposed other measures. In recent hearings, representatives of exit polling organizations have outlined their protocols for election calls, which incorporate a mix of information from exit polls and from early returns. Accordingly, one suggestion put forth by critics of the media polls is that eastern states should embargo the release of election returns until the western polls have closed and thereby deny exit poll analysts the information they need to make calls. Idaho state law, for instance, forbids release of official returns from its Mountain time counties until polls close in the Pacific zone counties.

In close elections, the election returns are a very important part of the information needed to produce projections. Still, even in close elections, returns are not absolutely essential to the task of making projections. Like all sample surveys, exit polls have a statistical "margin of error" that

---

12. Or 8:30 a.m. local, if hours were staggered as in Canada.

reflects the level of confidence the analyst can have in a conclusion drawn from the survey, for example, a conclusion about who has won the election. The margin of error depends predominantly on the number of interviews (the "size of the sample"): the larger the number of interviews, the smaller the margin of error. In a very close race, the vote difference between the candidates will often be smaller than the poll's margin of error, so that an analyst does not have enough confidence in the projection to make the call. If precinct and county returns are consistent with the results of the exit poll, they can provide the additional confidence the analyst needs to project a winner. If precinct and county returns are inconsistent with the exit poll, they can instead cause the analyst to await additional information before making a projection.

When a race is close, then, the returns are important as a complement to the results from the exit polls. Analysts need precinct and county tallies when the margin of error in the survey is too large to have confidence that the candidate with the lead in the exit poll is in fact the winner. But analysts can remedy their uncertainty other than by recourse to official election returns. If the returns are unavailable to them, they can collect larger samples. As table 35 shows, for any vote margin between two candidates there is a sample that is large enough to make a projection with a high degree of confidence strictly from exit polls.

In practical terms, to call a race as close as those listed near the bottom of the table, exit poll samples would need to be considerably larger than they currently are. In 1996 the Voter News Service exit samples ranged in size from 795 in Mississippi to 2,232 in North Carolina, 2,423 in Texas, and 3,282 in California. The samples tended to be a little larger in states with competitive races for the presidency and in states with spirited contests for senator or governor.[13] In most instances, however, even these sample sizes are sufficient in themselves to make an election call: races decided by margins of less than 5 percent are not so common.

Restriction on release of official returns, accordingly, will not necessarily cause exit polling organizations to delay election projections. It could cause them instead to invest in larger exit poll samples in election districts where outcomes are expected to be close. To be sure, restriction on release of returns would raise the costs of exit polling, and significantly. As the

---

13. Washington, where Gary Locke became the first Asian American elected to the governorship of a continental 48 state, drew 1,895 interviews, and New Hampshire, where Jeanne Shaheen was the first woman elected governor of the state, attracted 2,047 interviews.

Table 35 Number of Exit Interviews Needed to Project a Winner, by Margin of Victory and Risk of Incorrect Projection

Actual margin of victory (percent)	Risk of incorrect projection			
	1 in 20	*1 in 100*	*1 in 500*	*1 in 1000*
3.0	2,986	6,026	9,272	10,599
2.0	6,721	13,567	20,872	23,861
1.5	11,951	24,123	37,112	42,435
1.0	26,893	54,284	83,513	95,471
0.5	107,581	217,150	334,076	381,914
0.25	430,333	868,619	1,336,328	1,527,686

table shows, a 50 percent reduction in the margin of error, say from 1.0 percent to 0.5 percent, requires not a twofold increase in sample size but a fourfold increase.[14] The election returns might not be essential for exit poll projections as a theoretical matter, but they might well be as a practical matter.[15]

Moreover, and more important, it is not clear that exit poll operations need access to "official" reports of election results either at the county or state level. According to Michael Traugott, who has consulted for the industry, exit poll organizations gather their information about the early returns by posting people in precincts to observe the count (see table 36). Most states require that the counts be open to public scrutiny, in large part to reassure campaigns that the count is being conducted legally and fairly.

Selected References

Jackson, John E. "Election Night Reporting and Voter Turnout," *American Journal of Political Science* 27 (November 1983): 615–35.

———. "Election Night Reporting and Voter Turnout: Issues Related to Previous Research," testimony prepared for the U.S. House of Representatives Committee on Energy and Commerce, 2001.

---

14. Mathematically, this is because the statistical margin of error diminishes by the square root of sample size.
15. Official returns might be useful for other purposes as well. Because exit polls do not sample in every precinct, they must weight the results from each precinct by precinct turnout to achieve a representative sample of the whole election district. The returns provide a cross check on assumptions about turnout. Because exit polls typically sample a set proportion of voters as they leave the polls, however, exit poll analysts already have a measure of turnout at hand in the number of interviews in each precinct.

Table 36 Provisions for Public Observation of Ballot Counts, Ten Selected States

Arizona	"…under the observation of representatives of each political party and the public"
Colorado	"…conducted under the observation of watchers"
California	"…shall be open to the view of the public"
Georgia	"…shall be open to the view of the public"
Massachusetts	"…the ballots taken therefrom and audibly counted in public view"
Montana	"…count shall be public"
New Hampshire	"…counting of votes shall be public"
Tennessee	"Each political party and any organization of citizens interested in a question on the ballot or interested in preserving the purity of elections and in guarding against abuse of the elective franchise may appoint poll watchers….A watcher may also inspect all ballots while being called and counted and all tally sheets and poll lists during preparation and certification."
Utah	"Proceedings at the counting center are public and may be observed by interested persons."
Wyoming	"After all the votes are cast and the polls are officially declared closed, only election judges shall be permitted in a polling place."

Source: State statutes, compiled by Aaron Longo.

Merkle, Daniel, and Murray Edelman. "A Review of the 1996 Voter News Service Exit Polls from a Total Survey Error Perspective," in *Election Polls, the News Media, and Democracy*, Paul J. Lavrakas and Michael W. Traugott, eds. (New York: Chatham House, 2000).

Task Force on Constitutional and Federal Election Law

Daniel R. Ortiz, COORDINATOR
WITH *Kenneth A. Gross, Pamela S. Karlan,*
Stephen M. Nickelsburg, AND *Trevor Potter*

Contents

PREFACE

These reports, developed by the Task Force on Constitutional and Federal Election Law, describe the legal background of election administration and reform. Although in some respects a primer on election law, they do not consider important issues, such as campaign finance regulation, outside the purview of the National Commission on Federal Election Reform. They also focus on those areas where discussion of the governing law would likely most help the commission's deliberations.

The task force's work rests on the unstinting efforts of its participants: Robert F. Bauer, Kenneth A. Gross, Pamela S. Karlan, Stephen M. Nickelsburg, and Trevor Potter. In addition, Marianne Holt, Kirk L. Jowers, Geremy C. Kamens, and Jason C. Rylander offered critical help on several sections. Eric Braverman, Thad Hall, Leonard M. Shambon, and Tova Wang all read the reports with a critical eye and strengthened them immeasurably. The research assistance of Melissa Cline, Kurt A. Hohenstein, Aaron Longo, Michael A. Mugmon, and David F. Olsky proved invaluable as well.

The task force, of course, owes much to the commission itself. Several members served as powerful soundboards for many of its ideas, and Philip Zelikow, executive director, provided critical guidance. The two other task forces, led by John Mark Hansen of the University of Chicago and David King of Harvard University, aided our work, and their questions focused much of our inquiry. The commission's hardworking professional staff also made the task force's work much easier. Ryan Coonerty helped furnish necessary day-to-day direction, and Wistar Morris and Lisa-Joy Zgorski handled the administrative details that made progress possible.

The Miller Center and the Century Foundation also provided much assistance. In addition to providing necessary logistical support, they gladly shared their experiences with other projects of this kind and helped keep the task force both on track and on schedule.

Daniel R. Ortiz
Coordinator

FEDERAL REGULATION OF ELECTIONS

The American electoral system falls at the intersection of many different regulatory regimes—some federal, some state; some constitutional, some statutory; some general, some specific; and some mandatory and some prohibitory. The Fourteenth Amendment's Equal Protection Clause, for example, represents a general federal constitutional prohibition against certain discriminatory electoral practices. It does not affirmatively mandate any particular practices itself. On the other hand, the federal statute setting the date of congressional elections on "[t]he Tuesday next after the first Monday in November in every even numbered year" does represent a specific federal statutory mandate.[1] Members of Congress *must* regularly be elected on that day. If election law represented only a patchwork of these different kinds of legal requirements, understanding it would be difficult enough. Unfortunately, the situation is worse still. These regulatory regimes can contradict and compete with one another. State statutory requirements, for example, may conflict not only with the state constitution but with federal statutes and the federal constitution as well.

Luckily, there is a well-recognized hierarchy of authority. In the event of a conflict, federal constitutional law trumps federal statutory law, which trumps state constitutional law, which in turn trumps state statutory law, not to mention state administrative regulation.[2] In order to understand best what the law requires and prohibits, then, it is best to move from the top down. This background report thus begins with a discussion of what the U.S. Constitution requires. Surprisingly, neither of its two prohibitory provisions most relevant to election practices—the Fourteenth Amendment's Equal Protection Clause and the First Amendment's protection of free speech and association—even mentions elections. The courts have, however, applied both to the political process in far-reaching ways.

Next the report discusses the scope of Congress's power to enact statutes regulating elections. The Constitution grants it broad power to directly regulate congressional elections, less power to directly regulate the selection of presidential electors (through election or otherwise), and less power still to directly regulate state and local elections. Still, as a practical matter, Congress has great power to regulate these other elections through other means—either collaterally through its power to directly regulate the "time, place, and manner" of congressional elections, through its power to determine how federal moneys made available to the states should be spent, or through its power to enforce certain constitutional safeguards, such as the Equal Protection Clause of the Fourteenth Amendment.

The report next takes up how Congress has actually used its power to regulate elections. In addition to regulating campaign financing—an important area not considered in the report because it falls outside the National Commission on Election Reform's agenda—Congress has enacted three different kinds of laws of particular importance: voting rights laws (the Voting Rights Act); registration and absentee voting laws (the National Voter Registration Act and the Uniformed and Overseas Citizens Absentee Voting Act); and laws protecting individuals with disabilities in many areas, including voting (the Americans with Disabilities Act, the Rehabilitation Act, and the Voting Accessibility for the Elderly and Handicapped Act). Because any reform instituted by a state would have to satisfy all these laws, their contours guide the possibilities of reform on the state level.

This background report concludes with some applications demonstrating how all these different regulatory regimes interact in practice. The task force has chosen its particular hypotheticals—a federal statute enfranchising felons who have served their time, state laws requiring voters to produce certain forms of identification at the polls, a federal statute requiring uniform voting technology within a state or across all states, and state laws regulating media election forecasting and exit polling—not because it believes the commission should adopt or even consider them but because as a group they well show how many of the different pieces of the puzzle fit together.

One important piece is missing, of course: state constitutional and statutory requirements. Because these vary so much from state to state, it was impossible to include them. But they will certainly affect how any reforms proposed by the commission are adopted. Any proposal requiring the amendment of a state constitution, for example, may be harder for a state to adopt than one requiring only an amendment to its code.

Finally, one caution. This task force report is intended only to provide the commission with a general background understanding of the laws that control in this area and how they interact. There are many specific questions it does not directly address. This is unavoidable. Unless the task force were to prepare a comprehensive treatise on election law, which time does not permit, many legal questions must remain unanswered here. That is not to say, however, that the task force is less than eager to help the commission understand them, but only to realize that this particular document has a very specific purpose—to help inform the commission so that its members may themselves see what the legal issues are and how to begin to analyze them. Needless to say, nothing in this document necessarily represents the views of the commission itself. Indeed, its various authors do not necessarily agree in every detail of each other's arguments.

Constitutional Restrictions on Federal and State Regulation of the Election Process

KENNETH A. GROSS

Federal and state authority to regulate elections, though considerable, is not absolute. Numerous federal constitutional provisions constrain it. Two constitutional provisions in particular have great reach in this area: the Equal Protection Clause of the Fourteenth Amendment and the First Amendment. In addition, a number of other constitutional provisions have a narrower but still significant impact on the election process.

Equal Protection Clause

> No State shall . . . deny to any person within its jurisdiction the equal protection of the laws.
>
> U.S. Const. Amend. XIV, § 1.

The Equal Protection Clause is typically implicated in one of two situations: (1) when a statute employs an inherently suspect or invidious classification, such as race or national origin, or (2) when a statute implicates a fundamental right. Both situations can arise in elections. In fact, elections nearly always potentially implicate the fundamental rights strand. The U.S. Supreme Court has long held the right to vote to be fundamental. As early as 1886 it declared in *Yick Wo* v. *Hopkins*:

> When we consider the nature and the theory of our institutions of government, the principles upon which they are supposed to rest, and review the history of their development, we are constrained to conclude that they do not mean to leave room for the play and action of purely personal and arbitrary power. . . . For, the very idea that one man may be compelled to hold his life, or the means of living, or any material right essential to the enjoyment of life, at the mere will of another, seems to be intolerable in any country where freedom prevails, as being the essence of slavery itself.
>
>   There are many illustrations that might be given of this truth, which would make manifest that it was self-evident in the light of our system of jurisprudence. The case of the political franchise of voting is one. Though not regarded strictly as a natural right, but as a privilege merely conceded by society, according to its will, under certain conditions, nevertheless it is regarded as a *fundamental political right*, because preservative of all rights.[3]

Whenever an election law employs a suspect classification or infringes the fundamental right to vote, the courts subject it to so-called "strict scrutiny." Under this test, the law will be declared unconstitutional unless it can be shown to bear a necessary relationship or be narrowly tailored to a compelling state interest—a very demanding requirement.[4]

Suspect Classifications. At one time some statutes straightforwardly burdened disfavored groups' right to vote. These laws would simply employ suspect classifications on their face. Although the Fifteenth Amendment, for example, barred states from restricting the franchise to whites, some states banned African American citizens outright from voting in political primaries on the theory that primaries, unlike general elections, represented a private activity rather than an act of the state. A court today would quickly strike down any statute like this that discriminated on its face against African Americans, and even a state inclined to discriminate would not be foolish enough to enact one.[5] Nowadays voters typically challenge a different kind of statute, one that although facially neutral has the effect of burdening a protected group's vote. In reviewing this kind of statute, courts employ strict scrutiny whenever voters in a protected group can show both a discriminatory impact on their vote and an intent to burden them because of their group identity.

The courts employ so-called "reduced scrutiny," on the other hand, when the voters cannot show such a discriminatory intent or when, if they can, the state can nonetheless prove it would have passed the same law even without it.[6] Thus, a law disproportionately burdening African Americans but passed for nonracial reasons or which *would* have been passed for nonracial reasons is subject to only reduced scrutiny. Under reduced scrutiny, a statute will survive so long as it bears a rational relationship to a legitimate government interest—a fairly lax requirement.[7] The courts, in fact, have never employed reduced scrutiny to strike down an election law affecting a particular group. Realistically speaking, a showing of intent is necessary to make a suspect classification challenge stick.

Hunter v. *Underwood* well illustrates how the suspect classification strand of equal protection operates in this area.[8] The Alabama Constitution of 1901 provided for the disenfranchisement of persons convicted of certain enumerated felonies and misdemeanors, including "any . . . crime involving moral turpitude." Two citizens who had been disenfranchised because they had been convicted of the misdemeanor of presenting a worthless check challenged the provision under the Equal Protection Clause. From looking at the historical record, the Supreme Court found that the state constitutional convention included this provision because it believed it would disproportionately disenfranchise blacks. In the absence of any showing that the convention would have passed the provision for other legitimate reasons, the Court applied strict scrutiny and struck the provision down. Strict scrutiny is so demanding, in fact, that the Court did not even bother to inquire whether a compelling interest might support the provision. The finding of intent alone effectively decided the case. Thus, although the Equal Protection Clause does not generally bar states from disenfranchising those convicted of crimes,[9] it does bar them from disenfranchising selectively on the basis of race or any intended racial proxy.

Fundamental Rights. The fundamental rights strand of equal protection falls into several largely discrete parts even within the field of election law. Two parts in particular—"one person, one vote" and durational residency requirements—have long received attention from courts and commentators and represent much of the doctrinal backdrop to *Bush* v. *Gore*, which itself suggests that the Supreme Court may—or may not—be interested in expanding this strand of equal protection to encompass much about how votes are cast, counted, and recounted. And some lower courts have already applied this strand to invalidate certain registration requirements. In particular, one federal court of appeals has held that a state cannot require registration applicants to disclose their Social Security numbers unless the state protects that information from further disclosure.

One Person, One Vote. Equal protection was the basis for the one person, one vote line of cases addressing malapportioned election districts. As early as *Reynolds* v. *Sims* the Supreme Court made clear that both state legislative districts and federal congressional districts had to be apportioned on a near equal population basis.[10] The courts have allowed some deviation from absolute equality, however, especially in state legislative districts, in order to serve specific governmental interests. Indeed, in *Reynolds* v. *Sims* itself, Chief Justice Earl Warren's opinion observed that "some distinctions may well be made between congressional and state legislative representation . . . [since] it may be feasible to use political subdivision lines to a greater extent in establishing state legislative districts."[11] Thus, in practice, congressional districting plans must generally strive for absolute equality in population (that is, zero deviation), and drafters must justify nearly all deviations,[12] while state and local districting plans are allowed more leeway.[13]

Durational Residency Requirements. Equal protection analysis has also been used to test state durational residency requirements for voting. Such requirements are prohibited for elections for president and vice president,[14] but are permissible for congressional elections so long as the requirements are the same as those for the more numerous branch of the state's own legislature. Nevertheless, several such durational requirements have been successfully challenged as unconstitutional burdens on the right to vote. In *Dunn v. Blumstein,* the Supreme Court invalidated a Tennessee statute imposing a one-year state and three-month county residence requirement as a prerequisite to voting. It reasoned that such long periods completely denied some residents the fundamental right to vote, and it rejected them under strict scrutiny because it found they were not necessary to promote a compelling state interest.[15] Not all durational residency requirements, however, are invalid. Courts have accepted ensuring the "purity" of the electorate, avoiding fraud, and providing time for a jurisdiction to close its registration books in advance of an election as compelling interests that can support reasonable residency requirements.[16]

Bush v. Gore. Of course, the Supreme Court's most recent application of equal protection to elections is *Bush v. Gore.*[17] In *Bush,* the Supreme Court found that the Florida Supreme Court's decision to order manual recounts in an effort to resolve the contest of the state's 2000 presidential election violated the Equal Protection Clause. Although the *per curiam* opinion was silent on the specific standard of review the Court used in evaluating the equal protection claim, it cites two cases—*Harper v. Virginia Board of Elections* and *Reynolds v. Sims*—that apply strict scrutiny to state statutes challenged on equal protection grounds, and the opinion later discusses the "fundamental right" of voters in a statewide recount, suggesting strict scrutiny as well.[18] Yet in actually reviewing Florida's recount procedures, the Court used language that looks more like reduced scrutiny's rational basis review. Specifically, the *Bush* court held that

> [t]he right to vote is protected in more than the initial allocation of the franchise. Equal protection applies as well to the manner of its exercise. Having once granted the right to vote on equal terms, the State may not, by arbitrary and disparate treatment, value one person's vote over that of another.[19]

This threshold ambiguity as to the applicable standard of review makes any prediction of how future courts will apply *Bush v. Gore* difficult. But the Supreme Court's analysis does identify several particular deficiencies in the Florida recount process to which future courts will presumably remain attentive:

- Varying standards of what counts as a vote. Because Florida used a general "intent of the voter" standard in determining for whom a ballot should count and left the application of this general standard up to individual county canvassing boards, a ballot counted for a candidate in one county might not be counted at all in another. In fact, as the Court noted, "[t]he standards for accepting or rejecting contested ballots might vary not only from county to county but within a single county from one recount team to another."[20] While one team in a particular county might count a dimpled chad, for example, as a vote for a particular candidate, another team might not. The Court thought such disuniformity in recount standards across and within jurisdictions represented unconstitutional "uneven treatment."[21] If *Bush* v. *Gore* stands for nothing else, it stands for this: standards for what counts as a vote have to be reasonably uniform in application, not just in theory, across the whole jurisdiction for a particular race. For statewide races, this effectively points to a single, specific statewide standard for each type of voting machinery used.
- Overvotes versus undervotes. The Florida recounts were focused exclusively on undervotes (ballots that failed to register any choice in the presidential race) and did not focus on overvotes (ballots that registered more than one choice in the contest, rendering them invalid). The Court noted that under the Florida Supreme Court's order, "the citizen who failed to vote for a candidate in a way readable by a machine may still have his vote counted in a manual recount; on the other hand, the citizen who marks two candidates in a way discernible by a machine will not have the same opportunity to have his vote count, even if a manual examination of the ballot would reveal the requisite indicia of intent."[22] The Court's concern suggests that any recounting procedure should include both types of votes.
- Inclusion of partial counts. The Florida Supreme Court, in ordering the recounts, appeared willing to accept partial counts as of the time of final certification. The U.S. Supreme Court in *Bush* v. *Gore* disagreed, reasoning that "[t]he press of time does not diminish the constitutional concern" and observing that "[a] desire for speed is not a general excuse for ignoring equal protection guarantees."[23]

- Use of voting machinery. Noting the requirement that any recount conducted under the Florida Supreme Court's order would involve the use of voting machines in an unapproved manner (for example, screening out undervotes and overvotes), the *Bush* court observed that such use of machines would possibly require the state to design new software, which under state law would need to be evaluated for accuracy. Without this "substantial additional work," the *Bush* court concluded that "the recount cannot be conducted in compliance with the requirements of equal protection."[24]
- Education. Similarly, the *Bush* court observed that the recount would require the use of "ad hoc teams comprised of judges . . . with no previous training in handling and interpreting ballots." In conjunction with other aspects of the recount, the *Bush* court found this process to "rais[e] further concerns."[25]

In addition to the ambiguity of *Bush* v. *Gore*'s general standard of review, another feature makes it difficult to say how expansively future courts will apply the case. Although the Court's general reasoning would seem to sweep broadly, the Court defined the actual constitutional violation quite narrowly: "The recount process . . . is inconsistent with the minimum procedures necessary . . . in the special instance of a statewide recount under the authority of a single state judicial officer."[26] It immediately cautioned, moreover, that *"[o]ur consideration is limited to the present circumstances, for the problem of equal protection in election processes generally presents many complexities."*[27] And it took care to point out all that it was *not* deciding:

> The question before the Court is not whether local entities, in the exercise of their expertise, may develop different systems for implementing elections. Instead, we are presented with a situation where a state court with the power to assure uniformity has ordered a statewide recount with minimal procedural safeguards. When a court orders a statewide remedy, there must be at least some assurance that the rudimentary requirements of equal treatment and fundamental fairness are satisfied.[28]

The Court's opinion points to three particular features of Florida's scheme that might limit the future reach of the case. First, the case focuses only on recounts, not on other features of the election process in which differences of treatment might be justified. As two justices often supportive of equal protection claims stated in dissent:

the Equal Protection Clause does not forbid the use of a variety of voting mechanisms within a jurisdiction, even though different mechanisms will have different levels of effectiveness in recording voters' intentions; local variety can be justified by concerns about cost, the potential value of innovation, and so on.[29]

Second, the Court suggests that its standard might apply only to statewide, not local, procedures. The Court carefully distinguishes between local and statewide procedures several times in the *per curiam* opinion, twice remarks that the Florida Supreme Court's remedy in *Bush* was statewide, and clearly indicates that it is not speaking to the issue of non-statewide races. Third, the Court expressly focuses on the situation "where a state court [has] the power to assure uniformity." This focus leaves open the possibility that equal protection might require less from an executive actor, such a secretary of state, particularly if the secretary has under state law no "power to assure uniformity" through promulgating rules or issuing opinions. In short, the Court in *Bush* reasoned broadly in a way that leaves hope for those who would challenge many existing election procedures but at the same time hedged its opinion with enough cautions and special circumstances that future courts, if they want, can limit the case to its facts. It is safe to say only that *Bush* v. *Gore*'s future is unclear.

Privacy and Social Security Numbers. One U.S. Court of Appeals has applied the fundamental rights strand of equal protection to protect a voter's privacy. Before 1993 Virginia required registration applicants to provide their Social Security numbers to voting registrars and allowed any other qualified voter, along with candidates, incumbents, political parties, and certain nonprofits, to obtain that information. Because Social Security numbers are protected from disclosure (and the "alarming and potentially financially ruinous" harm of identity theft) under the Privacy Act and the Freedom of Information Act, the court found that the two provisions together imposed a substantial, indeed "intolerable," burden on the fundamental right to vote.[30] That finding, in turn, obliged it to apply strict scrutiny, which asked whether the provisions were narrowly tailored to advance a compelling state interest. Virginia argued that the provisions prevented voter fraud and promoted participation in the electoral process. The court, however, concluded that the provisions together were not narrowly tailored to fulfill those interests. In particular, it saw no reason for the second provision, which allowed disclosure to the public. It did, however, find that the first provision by itself would "unquestionably" have passed constitutional muster.[31] It thus gave Virginia two choices. The state could either stop demanding that registration applicants provide their Social Security numbers as a condition of voting or it could continue to require that information and use it internally but not allow members of the public to see it. The state now prohibits disclosure of Social Security numbers to anyone other than election officials and courts.

First Amendment

> Congress shall make no law respecting an establishment of religion, or prohibiting the free exercise thereof; or abridging the freedom of speech, or of the press; or the right of the people peaceably to assemble, and to petition the Government for a redress of grievances.
>
> U.S. Const. Amend. I.

Although the election process is fraught with First Amendment issues (most notably in the context of campaign finance regulation and political speech), the First Amendment is most relevant to the commission's work in two general areas: (1) political parties' freedom of association and (2) the media's freedom of the press, especially with respect to the collection of exit poll data and the use of such data to forecast the outcome of elections. Each of these is discussed below.

Political Parties' Freedom of Association. In *NAACP* v. *Alabama*, the Supreme Court first recognized a right to freedom of association emanating from the First Amendment.[32] In the elections context, freedom of association has been applied to evaluate statutes that directly or indirectly affect political parties, particularly their conduct of primary elections. A state can, for example, require that parties use primaries to nominate candidates, but there are some types of primaries they cannot impose against a party's wishes. Conversely, when party activities grow to be an integral part of the overall election process, they become subject to constitutional requirements and statutory limitations to enforce them.[33]

The first case applying freedom of association to party primaries was *Tashjian* v. *Republican Party of Connecticut*.[34] In *Tashjian*, the Court invalidated a state law barring parties from allowing independents from voting in their parties. In invalidating the statute, the Court concluded that "the Party's determination of the boundaries of its own association . . . is protected by the Constitution."[35] The Court made clear, however, that strict scrutiny does not always apply in cases where a state law infringes the autonomy of political parties. "No litmus-paper test . . . separates those restrictions that are valid from those that are invidious. . . . The rule is not self-executing and is no substitute for the hard judgments that must be made."[36] As the Court made clear in a more recent case, the applicable test balances the party's associational interests against the state's interests in a complicated way:

> When deciding whether a state election law violates First and Fourteenth Amendment associational rights, we weigh the "'character and magnitude'" of the burden the State's rule imposes on those rights against the interests the State contends justify that burden, and consider the extent to which the State's concerns make the burden necessary. Regulations imposing severe burdens on plaintiffs' rights must be narrowly tailored and advance a compelling state interest. Lesser burdens, however, trigger less exacting review, and a State's important regulatory interests will usually be enough to justify reasonable, nondiscriminatory restrictions. No bright line separates permissible election-related regulation from unconstitutional infringements on First Amendment freedoms.[37]

In short, the Court applies strict scrutiny whenever a state severely burdens a party's rights of association and something like reduced scrutiny when a state does not. The commission must thus carefully think through any proposals that affect the autonomy of political parties. So far, the Court has struck down, among other things, state attempts (1) to limit the voters a party may allow to participate in its primary,[38] (2) to impose restrictions on the selection of party officials, as opposed to candidates,[39] and (3) to structure the primary system in a way that forces members to associate with voters with whom they not only disagree but who have actively declined to associate formally with the party.[40]

Media Restrictions on Exit Polling and Forecasting Election Results. The other relevant application of the First Amendment to elections concerns the always-controversial media practice of conducting exit polls and then forecasting election results before the polls have closed in all areas of the country. Because the First Amendment strongly protects the media's activities, it is inevitable that any attempt to regulate the media's collection and use of exit poll data will draw a First Amendment challenge.

Restricting Forecasts. Efforts to restrict broadcast of election forecasts would likely be subject to scrutiny under the First Amendment's highly protective approach to political speech. In *Mills* v. *Alabama*, the most relevant Supreme Court precedent, the Court struck down an Alabama statute that barred the media from publishing on election day itself editorials urging voters to vote in certain ways.[41] The Court found no need to make the controlling First Amendment standard clear because "*no* test of reasonableness" could save the statute.[42] Nowadays rules barring the media from disseminating information such as forecasts, which some voters would view as relevant to their decision as to whether or how to vote, would invoke strict scrutiny, and this would require the state to show that the rules were narrowly tailored to serve a compelling government interest—a difficult test indeed.

Restrictions on the Collection of Exit Poll Data. Another possible means to stem the forecasting of election results is to ban or restrict exit polling. If the media lacks information on how people voted, it cannot make reliable predictions. A number of states have attempted to do this and have been largely unsuccessful. In *Daily Herald* v. *Munro*, for example, the Ninth Circuit upheld a trial court's decision to overturn a Washington statute banning exit polling within 300 feet of a polling place.[43] The court found the 300-foot zone to be a public forum because of its traditional openness for press interviews and public discourse and found the restriction to be content-based because it turned on the kind of information discussed. Thus, with strict scrutiny applied, "[a] content-based statute that regulates speech in a public forum is constitutional only if it is narrowly tailored to accomplish a compelling government interest."[44]

The state argued that the statute satisfied this demanding test. The law was designed, the state claimed, to preserve order at polling places. The court recognized, however, that the unspoken goal of the statute was to restrict exit polling and election forecasts,[45] noted that the state already had a statute prohibiting "disruption" at polling places, and found that less-restrictive ways were available to address the state's asserted interest, such as a smaller zone, media identification requirements, and separate entrances and exits to the polls.[46] District courts elsewhere have followed the reasoning of *Daily Herald* to invalidate similar restrictions in other states.[47] In Georgia, however, a district court did uphold a 25-foot zone, reasoning that the state's interest in polling place decorum outweighed the media's interest in this small area and that the 25-foot figure was a fair balance between the interests of pollsters and voters.[48]

Restricting the Release of Official Polling Results to the Press. Although the First Amendment generally bars the government from restricting the press's collection and publication of publicly available data or predicting election results, it places no duty on the government to make information available to the media that it does not make available to the general public.[49] Thus, the government could, if it wanted, embargo the public release of official polling data until a certain time on election day or after. It could not, however, release such information to some members of the public while not releasing it to the press. In particular, a state could not allow some members of the public to witness the official counting and then prevent the media from asking those witnesses about the results.

OTHER CONSTITUTIONAL PROVISIONS AFFECTING ELECTIONS

Twelfth Amendment (presidential elections)

> The Electors shall meet in their respective states and vote by ballot for President and Vice-President, one of whom, at least, shall not be an inhabitant of the same state with themselves. . . .
>
> U.S. Const. Amend. XII.

The Twelfth Amendment, together with Article II, establishes the presidential selection process known popularly as the Electoral College and specifies the procedures by which electors' votes are cast and counted (that is, opening and counting in the Senate and procedures for resolving the election in the two Houses of Congress if no candidate receives a majority). Any proposal to abolish the Electoral College would require a constitutional amendment. The Constitution, however, does leave the states and Congress some flexibility. A state legislature can, for example, forgo a popular election and pick presidential electors itself subject to due process constraints. It can also change the traditional winner-take-all formula for allocating electors, as both Nebraska and Maine have done, by awarding electors by congressional district (with a bonus for winning the statewide popular vote), and it can bind electors to vote for their party's nominee. Likewise, although the Twelfth Amendment says that the electors' votes shall be counted in a joint session of Congress, it does not specify the method of counting, presumably leaving that to Congress itself.

Fifteenth Amendment (race)

> The right of citizens of the United States to vote shall not be denied or abridged by the United States or by any state on account of race, color, or previous condition of servitude.
>
> U.S. Const. Amend. XI, § 1.

Nineteenth Amendment (sex)

The right of citizens of the United States to vote shall not be denied or abridged by the United States or by any state on account of sex.

U.S. Const. Amend. XIX, § 1.

Twenty-Sixth Amendment (age)

The right of citizens of the United States, who are 18 years of age or older, to vote, shall not be denied or abridged by the United States or any state on account of age.

U.S. Const. Amend. XXVI, § 1.

These three amendments ban states and localities from discriminating against racial minorities, women, and youths aged 18 or older in the grant of the franchise. None grants the right to vote to anyone. Rather, they all prohibit states, if they grant the right to vote to others, from denying it to individuals in these groups. These amendments, together with the Fourteenth, would be the basis for any constitutional claim of discrimination in voting against a state or locality.

Seventeenth Amendment (election of senators)

The Senate of the United States shall be composed of two Senators from each State, elected by the people thereof, for six years; and each Senator shall have one vote. The electors in each State shall have the qualifications requisite for electors of the most numerous branch of the State legislatures.

U.S. Const. Amend XVII, § 1.

This amendment provides for the popular election of United States senators. Before its adoption in 1913, senators were chosen in whatever way the legislature of each state directed.[50]

Twentieth Amendment (presidential and congressional transition)

The terms of the President and Vice President shall end at noon on the 20th day of January, and the terms of Senators and Representatives at noon on the 3d day of January, of the years in which such terms would have ended if this article had not been ratified; and the terms of their successors shall then begin.

U.S. Const. Amend. XX, § 1.

This amendment specifies that the executive transition should occur on January 20th following each presidential election and the congressional transition on January 3rd following each congressional election. This deadline creates the ultimate pressure for speedy resolution of presidential election contests.

Twenty-Second Amendment (presidential term limits)

> No person shall be elected to the office of the President more than twice, and no person who has held the office of President, or acted as President, for more than two years of a term to which some other person was elected President shall be elected to the office of the President more than once.
>
> U.S. Const. Amend. XXII, § 1.

This amendment imposes a limit of two terms on the office of President of the United States and prohibits an individual who ascends to the office and serves as president for more than two years from seeking re-election more than once. The Twenty-Second Amendment effectively bars certain candidates (that is, two-term incumbents) from gaining access to the presidential ballot in the states.

Twenty-Third Amendment
(selection of presidential electors for the District of Columbia)

> The District constituting the seat of Government of the United States shall appoint in such manner as the Congress may direct:
>   A number of electors of President and Vice President equal to the whole number of Senators and Representatives in Congress to which the District would be entitled if it were a State, but in no event more than the least populous state. . . .
>
> U.S. Const. Amend. XXIII, § 1.

This amendment allows residents of the District of Columbia some voice in choosing the president. Before its adoption in 1961, the District had no representation in the Electoral College. Other territories of the United States currently have none.

Twenty-Fourth Amendment (poll taxes)

> The right of citizens of the United States to vote in any primary or other election for President or Vice President, for electors for

President or Vice President, or for Senator or Representative in Congress, shall not be denied or abridged by the United States or any state by reason of failure to pay any poll tax or other tax.

U.S. Const. Amend. XXIV.

This amendment prohibits states from requiring people to pay money in order to exercise their right to vote in federal elections. Although the amendment does not prohibit the use of such taxes in state or local elections, such practices will generally be unconstitutional under the Fourteenth Amendment's Equal Protection Clause.[51]

Congressional Authority to Regulate Elections

PAMELA S. KARLAN AND DANIEL R. ORTIZ

Since the federal government is one of delegated power, any act of Congress must rest on some affirmative grant by the Constitution. Four major constitutional provisions give Congress power to regulate how states and localities conduct elections: the Elections Clause of Article I, section 4, which governs congressional elections, and its presidential counterpart in Article II, section 1; the enforcement power conferred by section 5 of the Fourteenth Amendment; the Spending Clause of Article I, section 8, clause 1; and the Commerce Clause of Article I, section 8, clause 3.

Elections Clause and Article II, Section 1

The Times, Places and Manner of holding Elections for Senators and Representatives, shall be prescribed in each State by the Legislature thereof; but the Congress may at any time by Law make or alter such Regulations, except as to the Places of chusing Senators.

U.S. Const. Art. I, § 4.

The Congress may determine the Time of chusing the Electors, and the Day on which they shall give their Votes, which Day shall be the same throughout the United States.

U.S. Const. Art. II, § 1, cl. 4.

The Elections Clause has traditionally been interpreted to give Congress virtually plenary power over a wide range of aspects relating to congressional elections. In its most recent decision discussing this clause, *Cook* v.

Gralike, the Supreme Court stated that "in our commonsense view [the] term ['Manner of holding Elections'] encompasses matters like 'notices, registration, supervision of voting, protection of voters, prevention of fraud and corrupt practices, counting of votes, duties of inspectors and canvassers, and making and publication of election returns.' "[52] The list of practices that the Supreme Court and the lower federal courts have actually found within the scope of Congress's Election Clause power is broad indeed—ranging from registration of voters at the beginning of the federal election process to the certification of results at the end.[53] The courts, in fact, have interpreted the clause as granting Congress authority both to regulate conduct at any state or local election that coincides with a federal contest and to punish state election officers for violating state duties connected with federal elections.[54] The clause does not, however, grant Congress power to decide who may vote in congressional elections. That power belongs to the states. Under the Qualifications Clauses of the Constitution, the voters for House and Senate elections "shall have the Qualifications requisite for Electors of the most numerous Branch of the State Legislature."[55] In other words, the Constitution restricts the congressional franchise to those whom the state allows to vote for members of the lower house of its own legislature. The power to set the qualifications of voters, however, does not mean that states can set them discriminatorily on certain prohibited grounds, like race and gender. The fundamental rights strand of equal protection, moreover, limits the state's ability to restrict the franchise in other ways as well.

The Elections Clause assumes, in the first instance, that states will enact election regulations themselves. But as the Court has explained:

> The Clause is a default provision; it invests the States with responsibility for the mechanics of congressional elections, but only so far as Congress declines to pre-empt state legislative choices. Thus it is well settled that the Elections Clause grants Congress the power to override state regulations by establishing uniform rules for federal elections, binding on the States. The regulations made by Congress are paramount to those made by the State legislature; and if they conflict therewith, the latter, so far as the conflict extends, ceases to be operative.[56]

As the Court went on to say, the clause gives Congress "'comprehensive' authority to regulate the details of elections, including the power to impose 'the numerous requirements as to procedure and safeguards which experience shows are necessary in order to enforce the fundamental right involved.'"[57]

This power has a long pedigree, stretching back to the 1880s. In one of the earliest cases, the Court construed the "make or alter" language of the Elections Clause:

> [If Congress] chooses to interfere, there is nothing in the words to prevent its doing so, either wholly or partially. On the contrary, their necessary implication is that it may do either. It may either make the regulations, or it may alter them. If it only alters, leaving, as manifest convenience requires, the general organization of the polls to the State, there results a necessary co-operation of the two governments in regulating the subject. But no repugnance in the system of regulations can arise thence; for the power of Congress over the subject is paramount. It may be exercised as and when Congress sees fit to exercise it. When exercised, the action of Congress, so far as it extends and conflicts with the regulations of the State, necessarily supersedes them.[58]

Several aspects of Congress's Elections Clause power bear discussion. The first is that the states' default power to regulate congressional elections comes from the Elections Clause, rather than from their residual, Tenth Amendment-protected sovereignty. As the Supreme Court reaffirmed recently in *Cook*:

> The federal offices at stake aris[e] from the Constitution itself. Because any state authority to regulate election to those offices could not precede their very creation by the Constitution, such power had to be delegated to, rather than reserved by, the States. . . . No other constitutional provision gives the States authority over congressional elections, and no such authority could be reserved under the Tenth Amendment. By process of elimination, the States may regulate the incidents of such elections, including balloting, only within the exclusive delegation of power under the Elections Clause.[59]

Thus, federalism concerns and state sovereignty cannot trump any exercise of Congress's Elections Clause power. In fact, the lower federal courts have uniformly rejected state arguments that Congress's wide-ranging regulation of state voter registration practices under the National Voter Registration Act (or "Motor Voter" law) violates the Tenth Amendment by commandeering state personnel and resources.[60]

Second, a long series of cases, mostly involving statutes that criminalize various forms of election-related misconduct, holds that Congress's power under the Elections Clause extends to many, if not all, aspects of an election conducted even in part to select members of Congress. In the most recent reported case, a federal Court of Appeals upheld the convictions of two men charged with vote buying in primary elections for county commissioner and sheriff who appeared on the same ballot as those running in uncontested primaries for the U.S. Senate and House of Representatives. In language fairly typical of these cases, the Court of Appeals firmly rejected the defendants' claim that there was no federal jurisdiction:

> [T]he federal election fraud statutes were implemented to protect two aspects of a federal election: the actual results of the election and the integrity of the process of electing federal officials. In the present case, we agree with the government that [the defendants'] fraudulent conduct corrupted the election process, if not the election results.
>
> Moreover, the government maintains, and we agree, that the Constitution's Necessary and Proper Clause (Art. I, § 8, cl.18), along with Art. I, § 4, empowers Congress to regulate mixed elections even if the federal candidate is unopposed.[61]

This ability to regulate "mixed" elections effectively gives Congress some extra power to protect voting rights in state and local elections. Thus, for example, the federal anti-intimidation statute protects voters even if the real aim of intimidation concerns a state or local contest.[62]

The practical reach of Congress's power is wider still. Although as a formal matter the Elections Clause gives Congress power only to regulate elections for the House and Senate, states may find it easier and cheaper simply to standardize to the federally mandated congressional model for all the elections they conduct—presidential, state, or local. The exact scope of Congress's power under Article II, section 1, to regulate presidential elections, for example, is somewhat unclear. The Elections Clause grants Congress the authority to regulate "the time, place, and manner" of congressional elections while its presidential counterpart grants Congress authority to regulate only the "Time of chusing Elector[s] and the Day on which they shall give their Votes." Article II, section 1, cl. 2, also expressly gives states, not Congress, the power to "appoint in such Manner as the legislature thereof may direct, a Number of electors." Those textual differences would seem to give Congress much less power over presidential elections and the states more. The courts, however, have not been so clear. In *Burroughs* v. *United States,* for example, the Supreme Court held that Congress could regulate the *manner* of financing presidential campaigns.[63] Its reasoning sweeps broadly:

> While presidential electors are not officers or agents of the federal government . . . they exercise federal functions under, and discharge duties in virtue of authority conferred by, the Constitution of the United States. The President is vested with the executive power of the nation. The importance of his election and the vital character of its relationship to and effect upon the welfare and safety of the whole people cannot be too strongly stated. To say that Congress is without power to pass appropriate legislation to safeguard such an election from the improper use of money to influence the result is to deny to the nation in a vital particular the power of self-protection. Congress, undoubtedly, possesses that power, as it possesses every other power essential to preserve the departments and institutions of the general government from impairment or destruction, whether threatened by force or by corruption.[64]

Bush v. *Gore's* recent affirmation of the state legislature's expansive power to control the manner of selecting presidential electors, however, casts some doubt on the scope of Congress's authority. Simply put, the states' and Congress's power cannot both be expansive. One must come at the expense of the other. As a practical matter, however, there never is a presidential election that does not simultaneously select members of Congress.[65] Thus, even if Congress's power to regulate presidential elections directly is somewhat limited, any limitations may make little practical difference. Many standards and requirements that apply to congressional elections will, practically speaking, govern the presidential elections held at the same time.

The same holds true for state and local elections. Although Congress has no authority under the Elections Clause to regulate these races, states may conform them to federal standards to ease their administration. Experience under the Motor Voter law bears this out. Although in that law Congress mandated voter registration practices only for federal elections, all but a handful of states shifted to a single voter registration scheme that complied with federal law rather than maintain a dual registration system in which voters who wished to participate in state and local elections had to register differently.

In short, the broad judicial understanding of the phrase "Manner of holding Elections" and the plenary power afforded Congress to "at any time by Law make or alter" state regulations regarding the way in which elections for senators and representatives are held effectively make the Elections Clause an expansive source of federal power over all elections.

Fourteenth Amendment

> [N]or shall any State deprive any person of life, liberty, or property, without due process of law; nor deny to any person within its jurisdiction the equal protection of the laws.
>
> U.S. Const. Amend. XIV, § 1.

> The Congress shall have power to enforce, by appropriate legislation, the provisions of this article.
>
> U.S. Const. Amend. XIV, § 5.

The Fourteenth Amendment's Due Process and Equal Protection Clauses are the primary constitutional provisions protecting the right to vote. Although the Supreme Court has consistently held that the Constitution recognizes no right to vote, it has just as consistently held that voting, when allowed by a state, is a "fundamental" interest and thus that restrictions on the franchise trigger strict scrutiny.[66] In a set of cases construing critical provisions of the Voting Rights Act of 1965, the Supreme Court upheld the act as an appropriate use of Congress's power under section 5 of the Fourteenth Amendment, the "enforcement clause."[67]

There are two sorts of practices Congress might regulate using its Enforcement Clause powers, and they raise different questions. First, Congress might provide special remedies for violations of the self-executing prohibitions of section 1 of the Fourteenth Amendment. For example, Congress has provided for the award of attorney's fees in cases where plaintiffs establish a violation of their constitutional right to vote.[68] Such provisions, which modify the traditional "American rule" that each party bears its own litigation costs, clearly make it easier for plaintiffs to vindicate their rights. Similarly, Congress could provide other expedited or plaintiff-friendly procedures. With respect to this first category, however, Congress does not itself prohibit any practices that are not already prohibited by the

Equal Protection or Due Process Clauses. It leaves up to the judiciary the decision whether a particular practice in a particular jurisdiction violates the Constitution.

Second, Congress might seek to deter constitutional violations by outlawing conduct that a court has not already declared violates the self-executing prohibitions of the Equal Protection or Due Process Clauses. The question then becomes how far beyond simply outlawing practices that courts would find to violate the Fourteenth Amendment itself can Congress go? The central Supreme Court decision discussing this use of section 5's enforcement power is *City of Boerne v. Flores*.[69] In *Boerne*, the Court struck down a provision of the Religious Freedom Restoration Act of 1993 (RFRA) that prohibited state and local governments from "substantially burdening" a person's exercise of religion even if the burden resulted from a rule of general applicability that was not intended to burden religious free exercise unless the government could demonstrate that the burden "(1) is in furtherance of a compelling governmental interest; and (2) is the least restrictive means of furthering that . . . interest."[70]

The federal government defended RFRA as an appropriate use of Congress's enforcement power under section 5 of the Fourteenth Amendment. It argued that Congress's "decision to dispense with proof of deliberate or overt discrimination and instead concentrate on a law's effects accords with the settled understanding that section 5 includes the power to enact legislation designed to prevent as well as remedy constitutional violations."[71] The Supreme Court disagreed. While acknowledging that "[l]egislation which deters or remedies constitutional violations can fall within the sweep of Congress' enforcement power even if in the process it prohibits conduct which is not itself unconstitutional and intrudes into legislative spheres of autonomy previously reserved to the States," it declared that "[t]here must be a congruence and proportionality between the injury to be prevented or remedied and the means adopted to that end."[72] With respect to RFRA, the Court found no such congruity: the record before Congress did not indicate a pervasive practice of intentional discrimination against religious free exercise that would justify the prophylactic step of prohibiting conduct with a discriminatory impact absent a finding of purposeful discrimination. Given that failure, the Court saw Congress's action as an attempt to redefine the substantive scope of First and Fourteenth Amendment protections, rather than as an appropriate remedial response. The Court has followed *Boerne*'s analysis in several later cases construing Congress's authority under section 5 to abrogate states' sovereign immunity under the Eleventh Amendment[73] and in striking down a provision of the Violence against Women Act that allowed private parties to sue other individuals who engaged in gender-motivated violence against them.[74]

The "congruence and proportionality" requirement of *Boerne* thus requires asking, first, what practices violate section 1 of the Fourteenth Amendment, and, second, whether a congressional enactment that goes beyond banning simply those practices is nonetheless an acceptable response to the overall situation because such "over-inclusive" legislation is appropriate to deter or remedy constitutional violations. The Court's recent opinion in *Board of Trustees* v. *Garrett* illustrates the bite of both parts of *Boerne*'s requirement.[75] There, the Court struck down Congress's use of the Enforcement Clause to render states liable for money damages for discriminating against individuals with disabilities in employment. The Court's analysis seems to rest on the following syllogism: individuals with disabilities do not form a suspect or quasi-suspect class; therefore discrimination against them is unconstitutional only if arbitrary or capricious; the congressional findings that undergirded the Americans with Disabilities Act (ADA) may show that states have treated people with disabilities differently but not necessarily arbitrarily; thus without a basis for seeing a serious risk of unconstitutionally arbitrary differential treatment, Congress exceeded its powers because there was no section 1 violation to which the section 5 enforcement mechanism could be proportional and congruent.

Garrett poses two questions—one general and one specific—whose answers are unclear. First, how far may Congress legislate to "enforce" the equal protection principle announced in *Bush* v. *Gore*? Since both the reach and the basis of that holding are somewhat unclear, so too will be the constitutionality of many efforts to enforce it. Whether Congress may under section 5 require that states use uniform voting technologies statewide, for example, depends on whether *Bush* v. *Gore* extends to these technologies—something the five justices joining in the Court's opinion insisted they were not deciding while two dissenting justices explicitly stated the case would not.[76]

Second, *Garrett*'s holding unsettles an important antidiscrimination provision not at issue in *Garrett* itself. *Garrett* decided only that Title I of the ADA did not represent a valid exercise of Congress's section 5 power. Since Title I, which concerns discrimination in employment, also represents an exercise of Congress's power over interstate commerce, its substantive prohibitions remain in place. Only individuals' damage remedies against a state, which cannot for technical reasons be authorized by the interstate commerce power, were effectively invalidated. (Damage remedies against state officials in their official capacity and injunctive remedies against all types of parties were unaffected.) Unlike Title I, however, Title II, which prohibits discrimination on the basis of disability in the provision of public services, including voting, might not represent a valid exercise of Congress's commerce power. If it does not, some or all of its substantive prohibitions, not only some of its remedies, could prove ineffective.

In any event, one thing seems clear about the Enforcement Clause power. The Supreme Court has been looking quite closely at the evidentiary record before Congress when Congress makes its decision about how to regulate the states. So if Congress intends to use its Enforcement Clause powers, it must anticipate building a record designed to show substantial and pervasive constitutional violations and tie the remedy to them.

Overall, the fact that the Supreme Court has evinced a growing suspicion of congressional use of section 5 of the Fourteenth Amendment to ban conduct that a court would not itself hold unconstitutional suggests that Congress's power to use the Fourteenth Amendment may be less robust than its Elections Clause power.

Spending Clause

> The Congress shall have Power To . . . provide for the . . . general Welfare of the United States.
>
> > U.S. Const. Art. I, § 8, cl. 1.

Under the so-called "Spending Clause," Congress may attach conditions to the receipt of federal funds. And it has frequently used this power to induce states to undertake or forgo actions that it would otherwise lack the power to regulate. As the Supreme Court has explained, "The power of Congress to authorize expenditure of public moneys for public purposes is not limited by the direct grants of legislative power found in the Constitution."[77] Thus, even issues not within Article I's "enumerated legislative fields" may be addressed by conditionally granting or withholding federal funds.[78]

At least so far, the Spending Clause remains a robust source of congressional power.[79] In *South Dakota* v. *Dole*, the Court upheld a statute that conditioned states' receipt of certain federal highway funds on their raising the drinking age to 21.[80] The Court identified three key limitations on the scope of the spending power. First, the exercise of the spending power must be in pursuit of "the general welfare." Second, the congressional regulation must be unambiguous so that states understand the choice they are making in agreeing to receive the funds. Third, the conditions on the federal funds must be related to the purposes of the federal spending.[81]

Could the Spending Clause be used to induce states to adopt appropriate electoral practices? Certainly. But Congress would have to carefully specify the conditions imposed. The first two prongs of the *Dole* requirement would be easy to satisfy. Clearly, such congressionally imposed conditions and the underlying funding would be in pursuit of the general welfare. Similarly, making the conditional nature of the grant unambiguous is a simple matter of legislative drafting. The real question concerns the third prong. So long as the conditional spending sufficiently relates to Congress's aims, there will be no problem. Congress could, for example, simply make new funds available for state and local governments to spend on elections and impose appropriate election conditions. It could not, however, condition receipt of federal highway or Social Security funds on those same conditions. In short, Congress has great power to regulate elections under the Spending Clause provided it properly lays out its conditions and ties them to election funding. The states, however, always retain the right to refuse the funds and so can escape any federal obligations.

Commerce Clause

> The Congress shall have Power . . . [t]o regulate Commerce . . . among the Several States. . . .
>
> 　　　　　　　　　　U.S. Const., Art. I, § 8, cl. 3.

The Commerce Clause has traditionally been the source of much federal regulation, including much regulation of state and local governments that can best be described as about social policy rather than commerce in its traditional sense. The paradigmatic examples of social regulation are the cases upholding provisions of the Civil Rights Act of 1964.[82] While Congress cannot abrogate states' immunity to suit by private citizens using its commerce clause power,[83] it can regulate states directly and authorize the United States itself to sue the states as well as allow private lawsuits seeking injunctions against state officials.[84]

The real question here will be whether Congress is actually regulating "interstate commerce." Some election laws would clearly satisfy any conceivable definition. Congressional prohibition of the use of particular kinds of voting technology that had traveled across state lines would clearly be permissible. But recent Supreme Court cases suggest there are at least some limits as to what counts as regulable interstate commerce.[85] The Court has sometimes struck down congressional action when the Court perceives Congress to be using the commerce clause to reach intrastate activity that is not itself sufficiently "economic" to substantially affect interstate commerce. So if Congress wants to use its Commerce Clause powers to regulate elections more generally, it must make specific findings about both the amount of commerce involved and its interstate nexus.

Major Federal Statutes Directly Regulating Elections

STEPHEN M. NICKELSBURG

Congress has exercised its power over both federal and state elections in a variety of statutes. Some statutes, like those laying out the presidential counting rules or congressional apportionment formulas, are quite focused and regulate only one stage of a single type of election. Others, most notably the Voting Rights Act of 1965, are quite broad and regulate many stages of many different elections—from filing to run for president to recounting the votes for local school boards. Together these different federal statutes create a complex framework that states must take into account when they exercise their own power over elections.

Time, Place, and Manner Regulations

Pursuant to its authority under the Elections Clause to regulate the "time, place, and manner" of congressional elections, Congress has laid down rules governing the apportionment of representatives among the states, districting principles within each state, and the date of the election.

The Fourteenth Amendment requires congressional seats to be apportioned among the states according to their respective populations.[86] The amendment is silent, however, as to exactly what formula should be used. Through statute Congress employs the so-called "method of equal proportions," which assigns representatives among the states according to a particular mathematical formula.[87] Although other formulas are available to apportion according to population, the Supreme Court has treated congressionally selected apportionment measures with a fair degree of deference.[88] For instance, when Montana claimed that the method of equal proportions unfairly left it with a single representative for 803,655 persons, as compared to a nationwide average district size of 572,466, the Court responded that Congress had "a measure of discretion" to make a "good-faith choice of a method of apportionment of Representatives among the several States."[89] Once seats have been apportioned among the states, Congress requires each state with more than one representative to establish an individual district for each one.[90]

Beyond apportionment by equal proportions and single-member districts for the House of Representatives, Congress has imposed few time, place, and manner requirements on federal elections. It has, of course, set the date for congressional elections—"[t]he Tuesday next after the first Monday in November in every even numbered year."[91] Congress has also set that same day for the quadrennial appointment of presidential electors.[92] No federal statute, however, addresses the times polling places should remain open on election day. Congress also allows states to decide for themselves when an election may be held when a vacancy occurs or when, for some reason, a state fails to select a representative on election day.[93] Similarly, if a state fails to choose presidential electors on election day, Congress provides for them to be appointed "as the legislature of the State may direct."[94]

Presidential Counting Rules

Under Article II, section 1, and the Twelfth Amendment to the Constitution, the president and the vice president are to be elected by the electors from the states. Each state receives one elector for each senator and one elector for each representative to which that state is entitled.[95] Under the Twenty-third Amendment, the District of Columbia is entitled to the number of electors it would receive were it a state up to the number that the least populous state receives. Congress has then by statute laid down how it will receive the electors' votes and how it will handle disputes.

The Constitution gives state legislatures the authority to determine the manner of appointing the electors in the states.[96] Unlike with representatives, there is no general provision under which Congress can override state rules for appointing electors—states enjoy nearly plenary authority over the manner of appointment.[97] Congress has by statute, however, provided a safe harbor provision that applies in the event of a "controversy or contest" concerning the appointment of a state's electors.[98] If a state has provided before election day a method for the resolution of such a controversy, and if that method results in the naming of electors at least six days before the day electors are supposed to meet in each state to elect the president and vice president, then the naming of those electors will be "conclusive" in the event of further controversy.[99]

The Twelfth Amendment establishes in detail the procedures for each state's electors to cast their votes.[100] The electors are to meet in their respective states and cast separate ballots for president and for vice president. They are then to make lists of those receiving votes for president and vice president and of the number of votes those persons received. The electors must then sign and certify the lists and transmit them to the president of the Senate, who must open the certificates in the joint presence of the Senate and the House of Representatives where the votes will be counted.

It takes a majority vote of the electors to select the president.[101] If there is no majority, then the House of Representatives is entitled to select from among the three candidates who received the greatest number of votes. In casting their votes, each state delegation in the House is entitled to a single vote on behalf of their state. A majority of these votes is required to select the president.

It likewise takes a majority of the electors to select the vice president.[102] If there is no majority, then the Senate is entitled to select from among the two candidates who received the greatest number of votes. A majority vote of the Senate is required to select the vice president.

Voting Rights Act

The Voting Rights Act of 1965 (VRA), as amended, is the primary federal statute addressed to discriminatory election practices.[103] The VRA's initial aim was to use federal legislation to end decades of official state discrimination and disenfranchisement. In "covered jurisdictions" (largely the southern states), the VRA established procedures to register minority voters, including the appointment of federal election examiners and hearing officers to ensure the availability of voter registration. The VRA suspended in covered jurisdictions (and later eliminated nationwide) the use of any "tests or devices" impeding the right to vote, such as literacy tests or "good character" requirements.[104] These provisions had dramatic effects in opening the franchise and combating rank discrimination and are not a major subject of controversy today.

The Supreme Court upheld the constitutionality of the VRA in *South Carolina v. Katzenbach*.[105] Here the Court held that the passage of the VRA was within Congress's enforcement power under the Fifteenth Amendment. The Court later upheld the constitutionality of the VRA's provisions relating to voting by persons who attend non-English speaking schools as a valid exercise of Congress's enforcement power under section 5 of the Fourteenth Amendment.[106] Notwithstanding the Supreme Court's recent limitations on the scope of congressional enforcement power in *City of Boerne*, the Court has continued to reaffirm the constitutional validity of the VRA in its most recent cases.[107]

Three provisions of the VRA dwarf the others in terms of their current importance. First, section 5 imposes a "preclearance" requirement for any changes affecting voting within certain covered jurisdictions.[108] Section 5 applies primarily to the southern states as well as selected areas of other states and requires approval by the U.S. attorney general or the U.S. District Court for the District of Columbia before new measures related to voting can take effect. The second provision of particular significance, section 2, applies nationwide.[109] This section creates an affirmative cause of action by which citizens can challenge allegedly discriminatory districting or other voting practices. Section 2 was the impetus for the creation of "majority-minority" legislative districts beginning in the 1980s. The creation of those districts in turn has become the focus of constitutional litigation under the Equal Protection Clause over the legitimacy of the use by states of race in the drawing of legislative districts.[110] The third provision, section 4(f), protects certain language minorities, granting them the right to registration and voting materials in their language and triggering treatment under sections 2 and 5.

Section 2

> No voting qualification or prerequisite to voting or standard, practice, or procedure shall be imposed or applied by any State or political subdivision in a manner which results in a denial or abridgement of the right of any citizen of the United States to vote on account of race or color or in contravention of the guarantees [protecting language minorities].
>
> 42 U.S.C. § 1973.

The primary battleground with respect to section 2 of the VRA has been in the context of at-large voting systems and legislative districtings. As originally enacted, section 2 of the VRA merely restated the guarantees of the Fifteenth Amendment.[111] During the 1970s, claims of vote "dilution"— the manipulation of racial voting strength by either packing minority voters together in a disproportionately minority district or dispersing them in a way that makes their vote less effective—were litigated under the Fifteenth Amendment and the Fourteenth Amendment's equal protection guarantee.[112] After a plurality of the Supreme Court concluded that constitutional vote dilution cases required a showing of discriminatory purpose or "intent,"[113] Congress amended section 2 in 1982.[114]

The 1982 amendments adopted a "results" test that eliminated the requirement that plaintiffs show discriminatory intent in order to demonstrate that a districting scheme or other practice was racially dilutive in violation of the VRA. The operative language of amended section 2 provides a "totality of the circumstances" test under which plaintiffs may challenge a districting plan or other voting mechanism on grounds that the political processes in the jurisdiction are not equally open to participation by members of a racial, ethnic, or language group in that its members have less opportunity than others to participate in the political process and to elect candidates of their choice.[115] The statute provides that the extent to which members of a protected group have been elected to office in the relevant jurisdiction is relevant.[116] The so-called "Dole Proviso" also provides, however, that nothing in amended section 2 is meant to give rise to a right of proportional representation.[117] Under the "totality of the circumstances" test, the following factors are typically relevant:

1. the extent of any history of official discrimination in the state or political subdivision that touched the right of the members of the minority group to register, to vote, or otherwise to participate in the democratic process;
2. the extent to which voting in the elections of the state or political subdivision is racially polarized;
3. the extent to which the state or political subdivision has used unusually large election districts, majority vote requirements, anti-single shot provisions, or other voting practices or procedures that may enhance the opportunity for discrimination against the minority group;
4. if there is a candidate slating process, whether the members of the minority group have been denied access to that process;
5. the extent to which members of the minority group in the state or political subdivision bear the effects of discrimination in such areas as education, employment, and health, which hinder their ability to participate effectively in the political process;
6. whether political campaigns have been characterized by overt or subtle racial appeals;
7. the extent to which members of the minority group have been elected to public office in the jurisdiction.[118]

Two further factors can be relevant in some cases:

- whether there is a significant lack of responsiveness on the part of elected officials to the particularized needs of the members of the minority group [, and]
- whether the policy underlying the state or political subdivision's use of such voting qualification, prerequisite to voting, or standard, practice, or procedure is tenuous.[119]

Litigation under amended section 2 led to the creation of significant numbers of majority-minority districts in the 1980s. The Justice Department also used section 5 preclearance review to demand that some districting plans include significant numbers of majority-minority districts in covered jurisdictions.[120] Facing the prospect of litigation under section 2, state legislators in many cases also proposed districting plans that included majority-minority districts. In 1993, however, the Supreme Court held that the Equal Protection Clause subjects the use of race in redistricting to strict scrutiny.[121] Although this issue remains intensely controversial, the Supreme Court's current guiding principle appears to be that race may be considered in drawing districts so long as it does not "predominate" over other factors such as seeking geographical compactness, respecting the territorial integrity of political subdivisions, and politics.[122]

While the commission's work is unlikely to involve districting issues, section 2 is not limited to the arena of legislative apportionment. Section 2 also has been used to challenge other types of election mechanisms, including balloting and counting procedures,[123] appointment of registrars,[124] convicted felon disenfranchisement laws,[125] all manner of registration requirements, and other elements of the voting process that potentially could be employed to deny or abridge the right to vote. And it is currently being used in many of the post-*Bush* v. *Gore* lawsuits challenging state and local voting procedures and machinery. The courts evaluate these other mechanisms under the same general totality of the circumstances test they apply to districting claims. The courts have not, however, developed more specific standards, as they have in the districting cases, to judge these other mechanisms.

Section 5

> Whenever [a covered jurisdiction] shall enact or seek to administer any voting qualification or prerequisite to voting, or standard, practice, or procedure with respect to voting different from [before], such [covered jurisdiction] may institute an action . . . for a declaratory judgment that such qualification, prerequisite, standard, practice, or procedure does not have the purpose and will not have the effect of denying or abridging the right to vote on account of race or color, or in contravention of the guarantees [protecting certain language minorities,] and unless and until . . . such judgment no person shall be denied the right to vote for failure to comply with such qualification, prerequisite, standard, practice, or procedure.
>
> 42 U.S.C. § 1973c.

Almost any proposal by the commission that relates to voting in covered jurisdictions will be subject to the requirements of section 5 unless the federal government mandates it or provides an exemption. The VRA's original coverage provisions set out a formula by which any state or political subdivision that maintained a "test or device" that limited access to voting and where fewer than 50 percent of voting age persons were registered became a covered jurisdiction and thus subject to the preclearance requirements of the statute.[126] In theory, section 4 of the VRA provided a "bailout" procedure by which a jurisdiction that had not used prohibited tests or devices for ten years and could show that their effects had been eliminated could remove itself from coverage under section 5.[127] Debates over the extension and amendment of the VRA in 1970, 1975, and 1982 all included efforts to modify the bailout provisions to make relief under them more attainable. Nonetheless, no state and only a handful of political subdivisions have successfully made use of the bailout procedures. The list of covered jurisdictions thus has remained essentially unchanged over the last quarter century.[128]

Section 5 requires a covered jurisdiction seeking to implement a change in any "voting qualification or prerequisite, or any standard, practice, or procedure with respect to voting" to obtain "preclearance" before doing so.[129] A covered jurisdiction may meet this obligation in two ways. The most common means of compliance with section 5 is to submit a proposed change to the U.S. attorney general, who has 60 days in which to object and thereby block the change from taking effect.[130] The Civil Rights Division of the Department of Justice is responsible for reviewing proposed changes. Alternatively, a state or political subdivision may institute a declaratory judgment action in the U.S. District Court for the District of Columbia. In either case, the jurisdiction bears the burden of demonstrating that the proposed change does not have the purpose and will not have the effect of denying or abridging the right to vote.[131] As a practical matter, thousands of proposed voting changes are submitted to the Department of Justice each year, and the overwhelming majority of them are precleared in the administrative review process.[132]

In addition, private individuals may bring suit in a local U.S. district court to enjoin the implementation of any new state measure affecting voting that has not been precleared.[133] Local district courts in such private suits are limited to making a determination whether the change at issue is covered by section 5, in which case the local district court may enjoin the implementation of the change until it has been properly precleared by the attorney general or the U.S. District Court for the District of Columbia.[134]

In these "coverage" suits, local district courts cannot rule on the substantive validity of any changes.

It is important to recognize that the coverage provisions of section 5 are extremely broad. Almost any change related to voting practices or procedures, no matter how small, is subject to the section 5 preclearance requirement in covered jurisdictions.[135] From the earliest interpretations of the VRA, it has been well settled that changes in polling places, changes in voting mechanisms or procedures, changes in registration requirements, residence requirements, or any other prerequisite to voting, and any similar provision are subject to the preclearance requirement.[136] While any federal statute that results from the commission's recommendations would not itself be subject to section 5 preclearance, any state or local provisions enacted by a covered jurisdiction to implement commission proposals would be subject to preclearance. In fact, any provisions enacted by a covered jurisdiction to implement congressional requirements would also be subject to preclearance so long as the congressional act left the covered jurisdiction some residual discretion and did not expressly exempt the state choice from section 5 review.

The substantive standard governing preclearance requires that a change not have the purpose or effect of denying or abridging the right to vote of racial, ethnic, and certain language minorities. Unlike section 2, which creates a cause of action to challenge existing voting procedures as discriminatory, section 5's substantive standard is comparative—a standard of "nonretrogression."[137] In other words, section 5 forbids only changes that: (1) are intended to reduce minority participation in the electoral process below that prevailing under the existing regime, or (2) have that effect.[138] Under the nonretrogression principle, for example, a legislative districting plan will pass muster so long as it provides for no less minority representation than the existing plan does. A plan that reduces minority representation will not. In simple terms, any change to voting practices that can be demonstrated to "improve" or maintain the existing ability of racial or language minorities effectively to cast the vote they intend and to have that vote counted should be approved pursuant to section 5.

Minority Language Protections

> No voting qualification or prerequisite to voting, or standard, practice, or procedure shall be imposed or applied by any State or political subdivision to deny or abridge the right of any citizen of the United States to vote because he is a member of a language minority group.
>
> 42 U.S.C. § 1973b(f)(2).

In 1975 Congress amended the VRA to protect members of language minority groups. It extended three different protections. First, it brought language minority groups under section 2.[139] Thus, any voting practice which "results in a denial or abridgement of the right of any citizen . . . to vote" on account of that person's language status is prohibited. As with any section 2 claim, the court will look at "the totality of the circumstances" and not construe the right as one to proportional representation.[140] Second, Congress subjected any jurisdiction that in 1972 provided voting and registration information and materials only in English and that had more than 5 percent of its citizens of voting age in a single language minority group to section 5's preclearance requirement[141] and specified that section 5's "purpose or effects" test would apply to such groups.[142] In practice, this has both brought more jurisdictions within the ambit of section 5 generally and meant that changes in voting practices in covered jurisdictions could not retrogress the effectiveness of the vote of any covered language group.[143] Third, Congress required that voting and registration materials and information in these jurisdictions and others in which a single language group later came to constitute more than 5 percent of or more than 10,000 of the citizens of voting age be provided in the covered group's own language unless that language was unwritten, in which case the jurisdiction had to furnish only oral instructions and assistance.[144] In measuring compliance with this requirement, the U.S. Department of Justice looks at the extent to which "materials and assistance [have been] provided in a way designed to allow members of applicable language minority groups to be effectively informed of and participate effectively in voting-connected activit|ies| and |the extent to which the| affected jurisdiction [has] taken all reasonable steps to achieve that goal."[145]

Registration and Overseas and Military Voting

TREVOR POTTER

National Voter Registration Act

The National Voter Registration Act of 1993 (NVRA) codifies the federal government's broad authority over voter registration for federal elections. "Motor Voter," as the act was nicknamed, was written to "create procedures to increase the number of eligible citizens who register to vote, to protect the integrity of the voting process, and to ensure accurate and current voter registration records" for presidential and congressional elections.[146]

Congressional power over voter registration was affirmed by the 1932 U.S. Supreme Court case of *Smiley* v. *Holm*. [147] In *Smiley*, the court interpreted the Election Clause as allowing Congress

> to provide a complete code for congressional elections, not only as to times and places, but in relation to notices, registration, supervision of voting, protection of voters, prevention of fraud and corrupt practices, counting of votes, duties of inspectors and canvassers, and making and publication of election returns; in short, to enact the numerous requirements as to procedure and safeguards which experience shows are necessary in order to enforce the fundamental right involved.[148]

And in 1941 the Supreme Court further held that Congress could regulate not only general but also primary elections.[149]

Based on these constitutional interpretations of its powers over federal elections and voting registration, Congress enacted the Motor Voter law to regulate the election process, provide greater access to voter registration, and secure safer registration records. Motor Voter defines both state and federal responsibilities for voter registration in federal elections. NVRA imposes three different sets of obligations on any state that requires registration before election day: registration requirements, list maintenance requirements, and so-called "fail-safe" voting requirements. It imposes no obligations on states that permit same-day registration or require no registration at all.

First, NVRA requires that these states allow individuals to register for federal elections in three particular ways:

> *Driver's license applications.* States must allow driver's license applications to serve also as voting registration applications unless an applicant fails to sign the voter registration application section.[150] The voting registration portion of the joint application, moreover, (1) cannot duplicate any part of the driver's license portion; (2) may require only the minimum amount of additional information necessary to prevent duplicate voter registrations and to allow state officials to assess an applicant's eligibility under state law; and (3) shall include a statement that sets forth each eligibility requirement, including citizenship, shall require the applicant to attest that he meets each requirement, and shall require the applicant's signature under penalty of perjury.[151]

By mail. States must also allow voters to register and change their address by mail using forms prescribed by the Federal Election Commission. If a state wishes, it may also use its own mail registration forms provided that they meet certain congressionally specified minimal requirements. Mail registration must have the same effect as registration in person, except that a state may require a voter who registered by mail to vote in person for the first time if that person has not previously voted in person within the jurisdiction.

Other state services. States must also allow individuals to register in person at certain state-designated voter registration agencies. The state *must* designate all offices in the state that provide public assistance and all offices that provide state-funded services to persons with disabilities and *may* designate any other state and local government offices, such as schools, libraries, and fishing and hunting license bureaus.[152] In addition, if a state-funded agency provides disability services in a person's home, that agency must accept voter registration applications in the home during its normal course of business.[153]

Regardless of the mode of registration, the registrar must notify the applicant of whether the registration application is accepted.

Second, NVRA places certain list maintenance obligations on state officials. In particular, it requires that each state "conduct a general program that makes a reasonable effort to remove the names of ineligible voters from the official lists of eligible voters by reason of . . . death . . . or a change in residence. . . ."[154] Any such program, however, must be uniform and nondiscriminatory, must comply with the Voting Rights Act, and must not remove anyone from the list because of that person's failure to vote.[155]

NVRA establishes a safe-harbor purging procedure, which most jurisdictions now adhere to.156 It allows the state to use change-of-address information supplied by the postal service to identify registrants whose addresses may have changed. The registrar may then send the registrant a notice by forwardable mail with a prepaid, preaddressed return form on which the registrant can state his current address. The notice must say that if the registrant has not changed address or has changed address within the registrar's jurisdiction, he should so state and return the form within the time allowed for mail registration. It must also state that, if the form is not returned, affirmation or confirmation of the registrant's address may be required before the registrant can vote in any federal elections between the date of the notice and the day after the second-next federal general election and, if the registrant does not vote in any election in that period, the state then may purge him from the rolls. A registrar may, of course, immediately purge from the rolls any voter who directly affirms that he has moved outside the registrar's jurisdiction.

Third, NVRA requires covered states to allow "fail-safe" voting in federal elections to registrants who fall within certain groups:[157]

> *Those who have not actually moved.* If the registration records indicate that a registrant has moved but the registrant affirms before an election official on election day that he has not, the registrant must be permitted to vote at his usual polling place.
>
> *Those who have moved from one address to another within the area served by the same polling place.* On affirmation of their change of address, these registrants must be allowed to vote at that polling place.
>
> *Those who have moved from an area served by one polling place to an area served by another within the same registrar's jurisdiction and congressional district.* State law can specify that any registrant in this group can vote at either his old or new polling place on affirmation of his change of address. If state law does not specify either alternative, a somewhat different choice defaults to the voter. He can vote (1) at his former polling place on affirmation of his new address, (2) at a central location on written affirmation of his new address, or (3) if state law permits, at the location of the new polling place on providing verification of his new address.

Many states employ provisional voting to satisfy their fail-safe voting obligations to members of these groups, but it is not necessary to do so. NVRA allows a state to simply accept a fail-safe ballot under the appropriate conditions. It neither requires nor prohibits any subsequent verification of the voter's eligibility.

NVRA provides two different enforcement mechanisms. First, the U.S. attorney general may bring a civil action in federal district court for declaratory or injunctive relief.[158] Second, "any person aggrieved by a violation" may bring a civil action in federal district court for declaratory or injunctive relief if he has provided notice to the chief election officer of the state and the violation is not corrected within a certain amount of time.[159] NVRA waives this notice requirement, however, whenever the violation occurs within 30 days before the federal election. Although damages are not available under the act, NVRA does allow a prevailing plaintiff to recover reasonable attorney fees, including litigation expenses, and costs.[160]

Privacy Act

(a) (1) It shall be unlawful for any Federal, State or local government agency to deny to any individual any right, benefit, or privilege provided by law because of such individual's refusal to disclose his social security account number.

(2) the provisions of paragraph (1) of this subsection shall not apply with respect to—

(A) any disclosure which is required by Federal statute, or

(B) the disclosure of a social security number to any Federal, State, or local agency maintaining a system of records in existence and operating before January 1, 1975, if such disclosure was required under statute or regulation adopted prior to such date to verify the identity of an individual.

(b) Any Federal, State, or local government agency which requests an individual to disclose his social security account number shall inform that individual whether that disclosure is mandatory or voluntary, by what statutory or other authority such number is solicited, and what uses will be made of it.

Section 7 of the Privacy Act (uncodified),
Pub. L. No. 93-579

In 1974 Congress enacted section 7 of the Privacy Act. Section 7 forbids any government agency—federal, state, or local—from conditioning any right, benefit, or privilege, including voting, on an individual's disclosure of his Social Security number. It contains two exceptions. First, if an agency required disclosure before 1975 it may continue to do so. Second, an agency may condition enjoyment of a right, a privilege, or benefits upon disclosure if Congress requires it.

Congress has created one wide exception to section 7. A state may require the disclosure of Social Security numbers for identification purposes "in the administration of any tax, general public assistance, driver's license, or motor vehicle registration law within its jurisdiction. . . ."[161] Since Congress has created no exception for voting registration programs, however, section 7 effectively forbids states from requiring disclosure as a condition of registration unless they did so before 1975. Any state may require disclosure of the last four digits of a registration applicant's Social Security number, and nothing prevents the states from requesting this number as a voluntary matter. Whenever they do request the full number—whether as a voluntary matter or not—they must give the registrant certain information. In particular, they must indicate whether the disclosure is mandatory or voluntary, under what statute or other authority it is requested, and how the Social Security number will be used.

Uniformed and Overseas Citizens Absentee Voting Act

> Each State shall—
> Permit absent uniformed services voters and overseas voters to use absentee registration procedures and to vote by absentee ballot in general, special, primary, and runoff elections for Federal office. . . .
>
> 42 U.S.C § 1973ff-1.

In 1986 Congress passed the Uniformed and Overseas Citizens Absentee Voting Act (UOCAVA) to ensure that eligible service members and their families away from their voting district on election day and citizens overseas could vote in federal elections. According to the General Accounting Office, UOCAVA covers nearly 6.1 million citizens, including 3.4 million individuals living abroad and 2.7 million active military personnel and their families.[162]

UOCAVA makes several recommendations to the states but imposes only three clear requirements. Its recommendations include (1) that states waive registration requirements for absent service members and their families and for citizens overseas who do not have an opportunity to register; (2) that if they do not waive registration requirements for these people, states allow them to use a federally developed postcard form to apply simultaneously for voting registration and absentee ballots; (3) that if states do not allow use of the federally developed simultaneous application, they send out their own registration forms along with the absentee ballot itself and allow them to be returned together; (4) that states adopt a federally developed design for absentee ballot mailing envelopes; and (5) that states expedite processing of balloting material requested by these voters.[163] In the words of UOCAVA, all these recommendations aim "[t]o afford maximum access to the polls by absent uniformed services voters and overseas voters."[164]

The three requirements, of course, have more bite. Most important, they require that states permit covered voters to use absentee registration procedures and to vote by absentee ballot in all federal elections.[165] Thus, even if a state had no absentee voting process available for state and local elections, it would have to create such a process for federal ones. Since most, if not all, states already allow absentee voting, the real impact of this provision lies in the scope of voters it covers. Although its definition of absent uniformed services voters and their families is straightforward, its definition of overseas voter is expansive. It includes not only someone who resides outside the country and is still qualified to vote in the last place he was domiciled before leaving the United States, but also someone who resides outside the country and because of his absence is no longer qualified to vote in the last place he was domiciled.[166] Thus, while a state can bar a former voter who moved to another state from voting in its elections, it must allow a former voter who moved outside the country to vote in all its federal elections.

UOCAVA also partially overrides state voter registration deadlines. It requires states to accept any otherwise valid voter registration application for a federal election from a covered voter that is received no less than thirty days before an election.[167] States can on their own, of course, accept registration applications even fewer days before and closer to election.

Finally, UOCAVA requires states to accept from overseas voters a federally prescribed "back-up" write-in absentee ballot for federal general elections.[168] A state can escape this obligation either by having the federal government approve the state's own absentee ballot and by making it available to overseas voters at least sixty days before it must be received or by making the absentee ballot available to overseas military voters at least ninety days before the general election and making it available to nonmilitary overseas voters as soon as the official list of candidates in the general election is complete.[169] The federal write-in absentee ballot is a back-up ballot only. To use it, an overseas voter must have applied for a state absentee ballot no fewer than thirty days before the election and have been unable to submit it by the state deadline.[170] A completed federal write-in absentee ballot of an overseas voter will not be counted if it is submitted from within the United States.[171]

Because UOCAVA prescribes a single federal back-up ballot for federal races everywhere, the federal back-up ballot differs in one crucial respect from the state absentee ballots it replaces. The federal back-up ballot is write-in only. In other words, it does not present any list of candidates for the voter to choose from but instead allows the voter to write in the name of the candidate for a particular federal office.[172] If a voter wants, he may instead write in the name of a political party and his vote will be counted for the candidate of that party running for the particular office.[173] Any minor mistakes in indicating the candidate, moreover, will be ignored so long as "the intention of the voter can be ascertained."[174]

Disability Protections

PAMELA S. KARLAN AND DANIEL R. ORTIZ

Section 208 of the Voting Rights Act of 1965

> Any voter who requires assistance to vote by reason of blindness, disability or inability to read or write may be given assistance by a person of the voter's choice, other than the voter's employer or agent of that employer or officer or agent of the voter's union.
>
> 42 U.S.C. § 1973aa-6.

Section 208 of the Voting Rights Act of 1965, as amended, grants both people with disabilities and the illiterate the right to be assisted in voting by certain people of their choice. Until passage of the Voting Accessibility for the Elderly and Handicapped Act and the Americans with Disabilities Act, this provision was the only federal law to directly address the rights of individuals with disabilities in voting. It extends broadly to all elections—state, local, and federal—and beyond the voting booth itself. It protects, for example, the right of a voter with disabilities to appoint a person to obtain an absentee ballot application, deliver the completed application to the election board, obtain the actual ballot, and deliver the completed ballot to a mailbox or to the board itself for a state election.[175] Strictly speaking, however, this part of the Voting Rights Act is not an antidiscrimination provision. Although it grants people with disabilities a right to assistance in order to make their vote more effective, it does not require the state to remove obstacles that differentially burden people with disabilities in voting. Since the assistance provision is part of the Voting Rights Act, moreover, that act's remedial provisions, particularly its allowance of reasonable attorney's fees, are available to encourage its enforcement.

Voting Accessibility for the Elderly and Handicapped Act

> Within each State . . . each political subdivision responsible for conducting elections shall assure that all polling places for Federal elections are accessible to handicapped and elderly voters.
>
> 42 U.S.C. § 1973ee-1.

Passed in 1984, the Voting Accessibility for the Elderly and Handicapped Act (VAEH) generally requires that polling places nationwide be accessible to voters with disabilities in federal elections. If none can be made available, a political subdivision must provide individuals with disabilities a legally acceptable alternative way of voting, such as an absentee ballot. In addition to this general requirement, VAEH imposes several specific duties, including that each state (1) make available special registration and voting aids for handicapped and elderly individuals, such as large-type instructions for the visually impaired and information by telecommunications devices for the deaf, and (2) provide timely notice of the availability of such aids and the procedures for voting by absentee ballot. Either the U.S. attorney general or a "person who is personally aggrieved by noncompliance" may bring an action for declaratory or injunctive relief in federal court, but only forty-five days after the plaintiff has notified the state's chief election officer that an election authority is not in compliance.[176]

Several factors restrict the practical reach of this seemingly broad prohibition. First, by its very terms, it applies only to federal elections. Election administrators, of course, are likely to apply the same standards to other elections happening on the same day in order to reduce the cost of administration. But it is less practical to extend these standards to state and local elections occurring at other times, and the VAEH standards may, in fact, conflict with otherwise governing state law. Second, VAEH allows the states some leeway in defining what accessibility means. It states that the key term in the general prohibition, "'accessible[,]' means accessible to handicapped and elderly individuals for the purpose of voting and registration, *as determined under guidelines established by the chief election officer of the State involved.*"[177] It allows the state, in effect, to define the extent of applicable protections. Third, although any "personally aggrieved" individual may sue under the VAEH, neither damages nor attorney's fees are available.[178] This effectively discourages private parties from bringing any suit. For all these reasons, very few VAEH cases have been brought, and the courts have had few opportunities to interpret the reach of the law's provisions. Furthermore, because plaintiffs usually bring VAEH claims along with claims under other, "friendlier" disability acts, the courts have felt little need to rely on a remedy based on the VAEH even in the few cases citing the act.

Americans with Disabilities Act

> [N]o qualified individual with a disability shall, by reason of such disability, be excluded from participation in or be denied the benefits of the services, programs, or activities of a public entity, or be subject to discrimination by such entity.
>
> 42 U.S.C. § 12132.

Title II of the Americans with Disabilities Act (ADA) prohibits public entities from discriminating on the basis of disability in the provision of public "services, programs, or activities," which include voting. Title II requires public entities to make reasonable modifications to practices that would otherwise discriminate unless they can show that the modifications would fundamentally change the nature of the program involved or impose undue financial or administrative burdens.[179]

Few of the factors limiting the practical reach of the VAEH affect Title II of the ADA. First, Title II applies to all, not just federal, elections. Second, Title II empowers the U.S. attorney general, not the chief election officer of each state, to issue regulations giving definition to the central prohibition of the act.[180] Third, unlike the VAEH, Title II allows aggrieved individuals generally to sue for money damages, not only injunctions and declaratory relief, and allows successful plaintiffs to recover reasonable attorney's fees.[181] After *Board of Trustees* v. *Garrett,* an individual cannot sue a state, but only state officials in their official capacity and localities, for money damages.[182] For these reasons, Title II has proven a more popular means of vindicating claims of discrimination in voting on the basis of disability.

Given the ADA's broad language, results under it have been surprisingly few and mixed. On the one hand, all courts have agreed that Title II covers elections, and cases challenging physical access to polling places have generally been successful. In New York, for example, the state attorney general successfully brought suit against several counties requiring them to make polling places accessible to voters with physical disabilities. Although suit was brought under the ADA, the VAEH, and state law, the court felt it need reach only the ADA claim and granted a preliminary injunction requiring the counties to physically modify polling places to bring them into compliance with the ADA. A later order required them to decertify any polling places not made compliant by a certain date.[183]

Claims by the blind, on the other hand, have not met with such strong success. In Texas a group of visually impaired voters sued the Texas secretary of state claiming that voting machinery that required them to use third-party assistance violated the secrecy of their vote in contravention of the ADA. The federal district court agreed, finding that

> [h]andicapped voters presently take an assistant or are to be assisted by election judges, one from each party in the case of a general election. The Secretary of State concedes that no present system assures the secrecy of the ballot for visually-impaired

voters other than enforcement of election laws making it a crime to disclose how someone voted, which would be the same enforcement method afforded to non-handicapped voters. Likewise, under the present system there is no means by which a visually-impaired voter may verify in his own mind that his ballot is properly marked.[184]

The victory was short-lived, however. On appeal, the federal court of appeals reversed on the ground that the secretary of state was the wrong party.[185] Although state law authorized the secretary of state to supervise local elections in order to protect the voting rights of citizens from abuse, the court found that the secretary had no duty to do so. Absent such a duty, it believed, the secretary could not be held responsible under the ADA. The court of appeals later vacated the district court's opinion denying it any kind of precedential effect whatsoever. Texas did, however, subsequently pass a statute granting much of what plaintiffs had requested.[186]

In Michigan a group of blind voters brought a similar suit.[187] They claimed that the secretary of state's failure to implement a system by which they could vote without third-party assistance denied them secrecy of the ballot, which Michigan's sighted voters enjoyed. Despite a state constitutional provision that expressly directed the state legislature to "enact laws . . . to preserve the secrecy of the ballot," the federal court of appeals held that no right of secrecy was violated. Requiring third-party assistance for the blind, it found, was completely consistent with the constitutional guarantee because the legislature had passed the assistance measure and the state supreme court had never questioned it.

Rehabilitation Act

No otherwise qualified individual with disabilities . . . shall, solely by reason of his disability, be excluded from participation in, be denied the benefits of, or be subjected to discrimination under any program or activity receiving federal assistance.

29 U.S.C. § 794.

The Rehabilitation Act prohibits discrimination on the basis of disability in any program receiving federal funds. Its standards for identifying prohibited discrimination are generally the same as those under Title II of the ADA and the same remedies are generally available. The major difference between the two acts is coverage: Title II of the ADA covers public entities providing public services and benefits; the Rehabilitation Act covers all programs receiving federal money. Whereas Title II represents an exercise of Congress's powers under section 5 of the Fourteenth Amendment and perhaps the Commerce Clause, section 504 of the Rehabilitation Act represents an exercise of its spending power.

In the elections context, claims under the Rehabilitation Act often encounter difficulty on the threshold issue of coverage. Although the states, of course, receive much federal money, the Rehabilitation Act requires that the money go to the "program or activity" being sued. Since the federal government does not generally fund elections held in the states, section 504 has little effective reach here. In Texas, for example, the federal court of appeals denied a section 504 claim brought by a group of blind voters against the secretary of state on the grounds that the plaintiffs did not allege that the secretary himself received any federal assistance.[188] If the federal government were in the future to provide funds to states and localities for elections, section 504 would then, of course, apply. The operating standards and legal issues would look like those under the ADA.

Illustrative Applications

Together these various constitutional and statutory provisions create a complex legal framework, many different parts of which may apply to any particular reform proposal. In order to give a better idea of how these various provisions interact with one another and might apply to the work of the commission, this report demonstrates their application to a group of sample reform proposals. The task force has chosen these particular proposals not because it believes the commission should or is likely to propose them. Rather, we have chosen them because we believe that together they well illustrate how the law might bear on the different types of issues the commission may consider.

Enfranchising Felons

> Can Congress declare that felons who have served their time
> and otherwise qualify for the franchise may vote?

No federal law prevents states from allowing felons who otherwise qualify for the franchise from voting. Many states, however, do not permit them to do so. Could Congress declare that felons who have served their time may vote in all or just federal elections?

The answer may depend on how Congress tries to accomplish its aim. It has four possible means available to it. First, Congress might try to accomplish this result by exercising its great power under the Elections Clause to regulate the "time, places, and manner" of federal elections. Who can vote might seem to concern the "manner" of conducting elections. Another federal constitutional provision, however, clearly blocks such an interpretation. The Qualifications Clause, which states that "the Electors in each state [for the United States House of Representatives or Senate] shall have the Qualifications requisite for Electors of the most numerous Branch of the State Legislature," pegs federal voting qualifications to those set for the larger chamber of the state legislature. Thus, although Congress's Elections Clause power is broad, it does not extend to setting voter qualifications in either state or congressional elections. And, as *Bush* v. *Gore* makes clear, the states have even more power over the selection of presidential electors.

Second, Congress might try to enfranchise felons by exercising its power under section 5 of the Fourteenth Amendment to enforce equal protection. *Richardson* v. *Ramirez*, however, clouds this prospect.[189] In *Ramirez*, the Supreme Court held that the Equal Protection Clause does not generally bar the states from disenfranchising felons. It construed section 2 of the Fourteenth Amendment, which reduces a state's representation in the House of Representatives to the extent that the state denies the vote "to any . . . male inhabitants . . . , being twenty-one years of age, and citizens of the United States . . . *except for participation in rebellion, or other crime*" as expressly contemplating a state's right to disenfranchise felons.[190] Thus, Congress's section 5 powers here seem narrower than with respect to other restrictions on the franchise.

To proceed under section 5, Congress would have to identify an equal protection violation to which the remedy of enfranchising felons would be congruent and proportional. The closest candidate for a suitable equal protection violation would be the disproportionate burdening of African American citizens' right to vote. A court would clearly hold unconstitutional any state action intentionally and disproportionately burdening the vote of this group. The issue, then, is whether the congressionally mandated remedy of enfranchising felons would be considered congruent and proportional to this particular violation.

Here guidance is very thin. Disenfranchising felons has been found to have a discriminatory impact on African Americans, and the Supreme Court has recognized that in some circumstances section 5 permits Congress to remedy intentional discrimination prophylactically by prohibiting actions that have discriminatory effects. Significantly, however, the Court has never said that Congress can *always* act prophylactically by prohibiting actions that have discriminatory effects, and it has not addressed this issue since it imposed requirements of congruence and proportionality on section 5 legislation.

What result? On balance, congressional success under section 5 is doubtful. Whether the action would be constitutional depends both on how rigorously the Supreme Court will interpret the congruence and proportionality requirements and how much resistance *Ramirez* poses. In *Garrett* earlier this year, the Supreme Court indicated that it was taking the congruence and proportionality requirements seriously indeed. Under such an approach, Congress would likely encounter constitutional difficulty.

Third, Congress might try to enfranchise felons pursuant to its plenary authority over interstate commerce. In recent years, however, the Court has restricted this once capacious power in two different ways. It has pressed the requirement that the law must really regulate interstate commerce and it has given the states more leeway than before to operate without federal interference in areas of traditional state authority. Both these movements would pose difficulties for enfranchising felons through this means. Whether felons can vote would seem to have a fairly attenuated connection to interstate economic transactions, and deciding who may vote in state elections would seem central to state governance and autonomy. For both reasons, the Commerce Clause would be an unlikely source of authority for this congressional action.

Fourth, Congress might try to enfranchise felons pursuant to its spending power. Three conditions apply: (1) the exercise of the spending power must be in pursuit of "the general welfare," (2) the congressional regulation must be unambiguous so that states understand the choice they are making in agreeing to receive the funds, and (3) the conditions on the federal funds must be related to the purposes of the federal spending. Luckily for Congress, the Supreme Court has interpreted the general welfare requirement quite broadly. It would cover both federal aid to localities and states to improve elections and expand the franchise. The second requirement could easily be satisfied. Congress would just have to draft the statute to make clear that states could receive funds only on condition that they allow felons who had served their time the right to vote. Meeting the third requirement would require only the right financial hook. Congress could not condition highway funds on such enfranchisement, but it could so condition grants for purchasing or maintaining election machinery. Congress could then pass a provision allowing felons who had served their time to vote in both federal and state elections if it attached the provision to an appropriate funding program in the right way. Nothing, of course, would stop a state from refusing such funds and so escaping the federal requirements.

Identification Requirements for Voting

May a state require a voter to produce a driver's license or other form of identification before voting on election day?

According to the Federal Election Commission, thirteen states require voters to produce some form of identification at the polls and another seven either require or allow local officials to do so under some circumstances.[191] Under what circumstances does federal law permit this?

Whether a state identification requirement is permissible under federal law depends largely on what forms of identification the state allows. In general, the fewer the forms of identification the state allows and the more difficult they are for voters to obtain, the less likely the identification requirement is to pass federal muster. Allowing a voter to affirm his identity under penalty of perjury as an acceptable substitute for identification, however, makes any requirement more sustainable.

Any identification requirement must first pass federal constitutional requirements. Such a requirement would pose no real First Amendment issues, but it could pose serious questions under the fundamental rights strand of equal protection. Requiring identification as a condition of voting clearly burdens the right to vote substantially. Without an acceptable form of identification, the voter simply cannot cast a ballot. Strict scrutiny would thus apply, and a court would ask whether the identification requirement is necessary or narrowly tailored to accomplish a compelling state interest. Courts have accepted preventing voter fraud as a compelling interest. The question would be whether the particular identification requirement was necessary or narrowly tailored to achieve this goal. This would depend on the type of identification requested and perhaps the amount and type of voter fraud committed in the state.

Requiring a passport or driver's license, for example, would likely be unconstitutional. Passports are expensive to obtain, and relatively few people have reason to possess one. Driver's licenses, on the other hand, are more common, but still many people have no reason to drive a car or cannot afford to drive one. Since other forms of identification could also serve to prevent fraud while effectively disenfranchising many fewer legitimate voters, requiring one of these two forms of identification would not represent narrow tailoring, and a court would likely strike down any such requirement.

On the other hand, requiring any form of identification provided by any level of government or certain private substitutes, such as utility bills, would likely pass constitutional muster, especially if the voter were allowed the alternative of affirming his identity under penalty of perjury. Although even this wider requirement would invoke strict scrutiny, a court would likely find that the broad variety of forms of identification permitted provided acceptably narrow tailoring. Such a regime would prevent some fraud without arbitrarily excluding many legitimate voters from the franchise.

Many possible schemes range between these two extremes, of course, and courts would analyze each on its individual merits. Constitutionally speaking, the perfect identification scheme would exclude all fraudulent voters while permitting every legitimate voter to vote. No conceivable identification scheme meets this standard in practice, of course, and the Equal Protection Clause does not demand perfection. It does, however, demand that any identification scheme not burden legitimate voters unduly and that it actually work to prevent fraud. That is an empirical question that depends on the circumstances.

An identification requirement is not likely to pose any problem under the suspect classification strand of equal protection unless the particular forms of acceptable identification were chosen because they would disparately burden a protected group, like a racial minority. If the identification requirement was designed for this end, even if it did not employ any such classification on its face, it would be subject to strict scrutiny unless the state could show that it would have enacted the same requirement without such intent. Under strict scrutiny, the requirement would fall. It is impossible to imagine any constitutionally acceptable justification that such a requirement would be narrowly tailored or necessary to achieve.

Even if constitutional, an identification requirement might pose conflicts with other federal law, particularly with the Voting Rights Act. If the jurisdiction is a so-called "covered" jurisdiction under the Voting Rights Act, it must preclear any identification requirement before it can employ it. In order to preclear it, the state or political subdivision must convince either the U.S. District Court for the District of Columbia or the U.S. Department of Justice that the requirement does not have the purpose or effect of abridging the right to vote of any racial or qualifying language minority. The test is one of nonretrogression, that is, whether the requirement would reduce the vote of any of these groups within the jurisdiction, and the state itself bears the burden of persuading that the requirement would not make voting more difficult.

Once again, whether the identification requirement passed muster would depend on the circumstances. If the requirement disproportionately burdened minority voters, that is, if relatively fewer of them possessed the forms of identification that satisfied the requirement, no preclearance should be granted. If they were not disproportionately burdened, preclearance should be granted.

Even if preclearance is granted (or the jurisdiction is not "covered" and so preclearance is not required), an individual voter could challenge an identification requirement under section 2 of the Voting Rights Act. In such a challenge, the voter would bear the burden of proving that the requirement resulted in abridging the vote of a racial minority or qualified language group. In evaluating such a claim, a court would look at the "totality of the circumstances," especially the following factors:

1. the extent of any history of official discrimination in the state or political subdivision that touched the right of the members of the minority group to register, to vote, or otherwise to participate in the democratic process;
2. the extent to which voting in the elections of the state or political subdivision is racially polarized;
3. the extent to which the state or political subdivision has used unusually large election districts, majority vote requirements, anti-single shot provisions, or other voting practices or procedures that may enhance the opportunity for discrimination against the minority group;
4. if there is a candidate slating process, whether the members of the minority group have been denied access to that process;
5. the extent to which members of the minority group in the state or political subdivision bear the effects of discrimination in such areas as education, employment, and health, which hinder their ability to participate effectively in the political process;
6. whether political campaigns have been characterized by overt or subtle racial appeals;
7. the extent to which members of the minority group have been elected to public office in the jurisdiction;
8. whether there is a significant lack of responsiveness on the part of elected officials to the particularized needs of the members of the minority group; and
9. whether the policy underlying the state or political subdivision's use of such voting qualification, prerequisite to voting, or standard, practice, or procedure is tenuous.[192]

Because all these factors can play out so differently in different jurisdictions, it is dangerous to generalize about which kinds of identification requirements are permissible under section 2 and which not. It can safely be said only that the more forms of identification permitted and the more widely those forms are held across racial and language groups, the more likely the requirement is to pass muster. Again, any requirement that permits a voter to cast a ballot upon affirmation of his identity is much more likely to be acceptable under section 2.

Uniform Voting Machinery

Can Congress require the states to adopt uniform voting technologies at least in some elections?

"[T]he policy of Congress for so great a part of our constitutional life has been . . . to leave the conduct of the election of its members to state laws, administered by state officers."[193] Even after the enactment of the Voting Rights Act, Congress generally has left the mechanics of the electoral process to the states. Until recently, the fact that states employ a wide variety of voting methods has largely avoided attention.[194]

Nonetheless, Congress unquestionably has the authority to require or to induce the states to adopt uniform voting technologies for use in at least their congressional elections. First, Congress could require the states to adopt a particular technology pursuant to its authority under the Constitution's Elections Clause.[195] Under that clause, the states have the primary authority to prescribe regulations for the time, place, and manner of choosing senators and representatives, but Congress may override those regulations at any time.[196] Since regulations prescribing the type of voting technology address the "manner" of choosing senators and representatives, Congress has the authority under the Elections Clause to promulgate those regulations.[197]

Moreover, although Congress does not have the authority to override state rules for the appointment of presidential electors, Congress has exercised its authority to set the time for choosing those electors on the same day as congressional elections. Consequently, as a practical matter, the use of uniform voting technologies in congressional elections would likely result in the use of those technologies in elections for presidential electors as well.

Second, Congress could induce states to adopt uniform voting technologies by using its spending power.[198] In other words, Congress could condition the receipt of certain federal funds on a state's adoption of a particular type of technology. Spending Clause legislation has been subject only to relaxed judicial scrutiny.[199] So long as (1) Congress clearly states the condition to which it attaches the funds, (2) the condition is related to the purpose for which the funds are given, and (3) the funds serve some public purpose, Congress is within its authority to attach the condition to those funds.

Third, Congress might attempt to require uniform voting technology under section 5 of the Fourteenth Amendment to the Constitution on the ground that the use of differential voting machines violates the equal protection of the laws. Legislation under section 5 has received close scrutiny since *City of Boerne*, however, with courts examining whether a constitutional violation has in fact occurred and policing the congruence and proportionality of the remedy for any violation. It is open to debate after *Bush v. Gore* whether the use of different voting technologies from state to state or from precinct to precinct violates the Fourteenth Amendment. In short, the Elections and Spending Clauses would furnish a more solid basis for such legislation.

It should be noted that 2 U.S.C. § 9 requires voting technology used in elections for representatives to be "duly authorized by State law." Under this provision, the states would need to authorize whatever technology was selected. If it wanted to avoid this requirement, Congress could simply repeal or modify it contemporaneously with whatever legislation it promulgated. Or, under the Spending Clause option, Congress could make the receipt of federal funds conditional on the due authorization by the state.

It should also be noted that the adoption of new voting technologies would be subject to the preclearance requirements of section 5 of the Voting Rights Act if federal legislation leaves any discretion to the states. Preclearance should pose no significant hurdle, however, since uniform election technology would be designed to enhance all participation— including minority participation—in the elective process. It would be unlikely to make things worse, which is the standard for a section 5 violation.

Finally, it is at least possible that voting technology legislation may invite private actions charging that the adoption of a particular technology imposes a heightened burden on the exercise of the elective franchise by minority voters in violation of section 2 of the Voting Rights Act.[200] Again, voters could challenge only the discretionary choices among technology that Congress left to the states, not the congressional mandates themselves. Since the purpose of adopting uniform voting technology would be to ensure better counting of votes, a suit under section 2 would likely claim that some engineering, technical, or educational issue related to the technology had the effect of limiting the opportunity of minority groups to participate equally in the political process and to elect representatives of their choice. A court would apply this standard "under the totality of the circumstances" and look to much empirical evidence of the effect of the voting technology chosen by the state on different groups.

Exit Polling and Forecasting

To what extent could a state regulate or discourage exit polling and the forecasting of election results before all polls are closed?

There are no court cases ruling on the constitutionality of state laws prohibiting the forecasting of election results for good reason—no state has been foolish enough to try it. Under *Mills* v. *Alabama,* where the Supreme Court struck down a state ban on "electioneering" content in media on election day itself, a ban on media forecasting would face very high hurdles.[201] As a restriction of speech that many voters would find relevant to their decision whether and how to vote, such a ban would have to bear a necessary relationship to a compelling state interest. The state's usually robust interest in promoting democratic participation would not likely carry the day since in this context it means denying individual voters political information—how others have voted—that they deem relevant to their own democratic decisionmaking. Furthermore, even if this interest were found to be compelling, the prohibition might well fall on grounds that it is not narrowly tailored. Unless the law made an exception for forecasts appearing in areas where the polls had already closed, it would arguably spread too wide.

A law restricting exit polling, on which election forecasts are partly based, would also face high hurdles. Courts have struck down laws prohibiting exit polling in the vicinity of polls except where the distance specified is so small—25 feet—that the ban would be ineffectual. The government could, however, refuse to release its own official polling data until whatever time it wished unless the count is conducted in public. Under the First Amendment, although the press enjoys great freedom from government restraint, it enjoys no special right of access to government information. The First Amendment, in other words, generally keeps the government from barring the press from using and publishing information the press has itself collected, but it does not force the government to give the press information that is not available to the public generally.

Finally, the federal government could try to minimize the perceived adverse effects of early media forecasting on election day by enacting uniform nationwide poll closings times. Congress could surely enact such a law under the Elections Clause, and it would likely pose no First Amendment problems. Depending on the particular circumstances, however, it might possibly face an equal protection challenge. If a particular uniform closing time burdened voters in different time zones very differentially, a voter in a more inconvenient time zone might challenge it under the fundamental right strand of equal protection. For example, a national law that closed polls nationwide at 7 p.m. Eastern Standard Time would arguably place a great burden on voters working on the west coast. Most of them would have no opportunity to vote after a daytime job. On the other hand, a law that closed polls at 9 p.m. Pacific Standard Time would not pose such a great burden on any voters except perhaps those in Hawaii and Alaska. Multiple-day voting would pose even less of a burden, if any at all.

Appendix A. Constitutional Provisions

Qualifications Clause

The House of Representatives shall be composed of Members chosen every second Year by the People of the several States, and the Electors in each State shall have the Qualifications requisite for Electors of the most numerous Branch of the State Legislature.

U.S. Const. Art. I, § 2, cl. 1

Elections Clause

The Times, Places and Manner of holding Elections for Senators and Representatives, shall be prescribed in each State by the Legislature thereof; but the Congress may at any time by Law make or alter such Regulations, except as to the Places of chusing Senators.

U.S. Const. Art. I, § 4, cl. 1

Commerce Clause

To regulate commerce with foreign nations, and among the several States, and with the Indian tribes.

U.S. Const. Art. I, § 8, cl. 3

Necessary and Proper Clause

To make all Laws which shall be necessary and proper for carrying into Execution the foregoing Powers, and all other Powers vested by this Constitution in the Government of the United States, or in any Department or Officer thereof.

U.S. Const. Art. I, § 8, cl. 18

Presidential Electors Clause

Each State shall appoint, in such Manner as the Legislature thereof may direct, a Number of Electors, equal to the whole Number of Senators and Representatives to which the State may be entitled in the Congress: but no Senator or Representative, or Person holding an Office of Trust or Profit under the United States, shall be appointed an Elector.

U.S. Const. Art. II, § 1, cl. 2

Election Day Clause

The Congress may determine the Time of chusing the Electors, and the Day on which they shall give their Votes; which Day shall be the same throughout the United States.

U.S. Const. Art. II, § 1, cl. 3

First Amendment

Congress shall make no law respecting an establishment of religion, or prohibiting the free exercise thereof; or abridging the freedom of speech, or of the press; or the right of the people peaceably to assemble, and to petition the Government for a redress of grievances.

U.S. Const. Amend. I

Twelfth Amendment

The Electors shall meet in their respective states and vote by ballot for President and Vice-President, one of whom, at least, shall not be an inhabitant of the same state with themselves; they shall name in their ballots the person voted for as President, and in distinct ballots the person voted for as Vice-President, and they shall make distinct lists of all persons voted for as President, and of all persons voted for as Vice-President, and of the number of votes for each, which lists they shall sign and certify, and transmit sealed to the seat of the government of the United States, directed to the President of the Senate;—the President of the Senate shall, in the presence of the Senate and House of Representatives, open all the certificates and the votes shall then be counted;—the person having the greatest number of votes for President, shall be the President, if such number be a majority of the whole number of Electors appointed; and if no person have such majority, then from the persons having the highest numbers not exceeding three on the list of those voted for as President, the House of Representatives shall choose immediately, by ballot, the President. But in choosing the President, the votes shall be taken by states, the representation from each state having one vote; a quorum for this purpose shall consist of a member or members from two-thirds of the states, and a majority of all the states shall be necessary to a choice. And if the House of Representatives shall not choose a President whenever the right of choice shall devolve upon them, before the fourth day of March next following, then the Vice-President shall act as President, as in the case of the death or other constitutional disability of the President.—The person having the greatest number of votes as Vice-President, shall be the Vice-President, if such number be a majority of the whole number of Electors appointed, and if no person have a majority, then from the two highest numbers on the list, the Senate shall choose the Vice-President; a quorum for the purpose shall consist of two-thirds of the whole number of Senators, and a majority of the whole number shall be necessary to a choice. But no person constitutionally ineligible to the office of President shall be eligible to that of Vice-President of the United States.

U.S. Const. Amend. XII

Fourteenth Amendment

§ 1. All persons born or naturalized in the United States, and subject to the jurisdiction thereof, are citizens of the United States and of the State wherein they reside. No State shall make or enforce any law which shall abridge the privileges or immunities of citizens of the United States; nor shall any State deprive any person of life, liberty, or property, without due process of law; nor deny to any person within its jurisdiction the equal protection of the laws.

§ 2. Representatives shall be apportioned among the several States according to their respective numbers, counting the whole number of persons in each State, excluding Indians not taxed. But when the right to vote at any election for the choice of electors for President and Vice-President of the United States, Representatives in Congress, the Executive and Judicial officers of a State, or the members of the Legislature thereof, is denied to any of the male inhabitants of such State, being twenty-one years of age, and citizens of the United States, or in any way abridged, except for participation in rebellion, or other crime, the basis of representation therein shall be reduced in the proportion which the number of such male citizens shall bear to the whole number of male citizens twenty-one years of age in such State.

§ 5. The Congress shall have power to enforce, by appropriate legislation, the provisions of this article.

U.S. Const. Amend. XIV

Fifteenth Amendment

§ 1. The right of citizens of the United States to vote shall not be denied or abridged by the United States or by any State on account of race, color, or previous condition of servitude.

§ 2. The Congress shall have power to enforce this article by appropriate legislation.

U.S. Const. Amend. XV

Seventeenth Amendment

The Senate of the United States shall be composed of two Senators from each State, elected by the people thereof, for six years; and each Senator shall have one vote. The electors in each State shall have the qualifications requisite for electors of the most numerous branch of the State legislatures.

When vacancies happen in the representation of any State in the Senate, the executive authority of such State shall issue writs of election to fill such vacancies: Provided, That the legislature of any State may empower the executive thereof to make temporary appointments until the people fill the vacancies by election as the legislature may direct.

This amendment shall not be so construed as to affect the election or term of any Senator chosen before it becomes valid as part of the Constitution.

U.S. Const. Amend. XVII

Nineteenth Amendment

§ 1. The right of citizens of the United States to vote shall not be denied or abridged by the United States or by any State on account of sex.

§ 2. The Congress shall have power to enforce this article by appropriate legislation.

U.S. Const. Amend. XIX

Twenty-Second Amendment

§ 1. No person shall be elected to the office of the President more than twice, and no person who has held the office of President, or acted as President, for more than two years of a term to which some other person was elected President shall be elected to the office of the President more than once. But this article shall not apply to any person holding the office of President when this article was proposed by the Congress, and shall not prevent any person who may be holding the office of President, or acting as President, during the term within which this article becomes operative from holding the office of President or acting as President during the remainder of such term.

U.S. Const. Amend. XXII

Twenty-Third Amendment

§ 1. The District constituting the seat of Government of the United States shall appoint in such manner as the Congress may direct:

A number of electors of President and Vice President equal to the whole number of Senators and Representatives in Congress to which the District would be entitled if it were a State, but in no event more than the least populous State; they shall be in addition to those appointed by the States, but they shall be considered, for the purposes of the election of President and Vice President, to be electors appointed by a State; and they shall meet in the District and perform such duties as provided by the twelfth article of amendment.

§ 2. The Congress shall have power to enforce this article by appropriate legislation.

U.S. Const. Amend. XXIII

Twenty-Fourth Amendment

§ 1. The right of citizens of the United States to vote in any primary or other election for President or Vice President, for electors for President or Vice President, or for Senator or Representative in Congress, shall not be denied or abridged by the United States or any State by reason of failure to pay any poll tax or other tax.

§ 2. The Congress shall have power to enforce this article by appropriate legislation.

U.S. Const. Amend. XXIV

Twenty-Sixth Amendment

§ 1. The right of citizens of the United States, who are eighteen years of age or older, to vote shall not be denied or abridged by the United States or by any State on account of age.

§ 2. The Congress shall have power to enforce this article by appropriate legislation.

U.S. Const. Amend. XXVI

Appendix B. Federal Statutory Provisions

2 U.S.C. § 2b

Number of Representatives. . . . Each State shall be entitled . . . based upon the method known as the method of equal proportions, no State to receive less than one Member.

2 U.S.C. § 7

The Tuesday next after the 1st Monday in November, in every even numbered year, is established as the day for the election, in each of the States and Territories of the United States, of Representatives and Delegates to the Congress commencing on the 3d day of January next thereafter.

Electoral Count Act

3 U.S.C. § 1

The electors of President and Vice President shall be appointed, in each State, on the Tuesday next after the first Monday in November, in every fourth year succeeding every election of a President and Vice President.

3 U.S.C. § 2. Failure to make choice on prescribed day

Whenever any State has held an election for the purpose of choosing electors, and has failed to make a choice on the day prescribed by law, the electors may be appointed on a subsequent day in such a manner as the legislature of such State may direct.

3 U.S.C. § 3. Number of electors

The number of electors shall be equal to the number of Senators and Representatives to which the several States are by law entitled at the time when the President and Vice President to be chosen come into office; except, that where no apportionment of Representatives has been made after any enumeration, at the time of choosing electors, the number of electors shall be according to the then existing apportionment of Senators and Representatives.

3 U.S.C. § 5. Determination of controversy as to appointment of electors

If any State shall have provided, by laws enacted prior to the day fixed for the appointment of the electors, for its final determination of any controversy or contest concerning the appointment of all or any of the electors of such State, by judicial or other methods or procedures, and such determination shall have been made at least six days before the time fixed for the meeting of the electors, such determination made pursuant to such law so existing on said day, and made at least six days prior to said time of meeting of the electors, shall be conclusive, and shall govern in the counting of the electoral votes as provided in the Constitution, and as hereinafter regulated, so far as the ascertainment of the electors appointed by such State is concerned.

Civil Rights Crimes

18 U.S.C. § 241

If two or more persons conspire to injure, oppress, threaten, or intimidate any person in any State, Territory, Commonwealth, Possession, or District in the free exercise or enjoyment of any right or privilege secured to him by the Constitution or laws of the United States, or because of his having so exercised the same; or

If two or more persons go in disguise on the highway, or on the premises of another, with intent to prevent or hinder his free exercise or enjoyment of any right or privilege so secured—

They shall be fined under this title or imprisoned not more than ten years, or both; and if death results from the acts committed in violation of this section or if such acts include kidnapping or an attempt to kidnap, aggravated sexual abuse or an attempt to commit aggravated sexual abuse, or an attempt to kill, they shall be fined under this title or imprisoned for any term of years or for life, or both, or may be sentenced to death.

18 U.S.C. § 242

Whoever, under color of any law, statute, ordinance, regulation, or custom, willfully subjects any person in any State, Territory, Commonwealth, Possession, or District to the deprivation of any rights, privileges, or immunities secured or protected by the Constitution or laws of the United States, or to different punishments, pains, or penalties, on account of such person being an alien, or by reason of his color, or race, than are prescribed for the punishment of citizens, shall be fined under this title or imprisoned not more than one year, or both; and if bodily injury results from the acts committed in violation of this section or if such acts include the use, attempted use, or threatened use of a dangerous weapon, explosives, or fire, shall be fined under this title or imprisoned not more than ten years, or both; and if death results from the acts committed in violation of this section or if such acts include kidnapping or an attempt to kidnap, aggravated sexual abuse, or an attempt to commit aggravated sexual abuse, or an attempt to kill, shall be fined under this title, or imprisoned for any term of years or for life, or both, or may be sentenced to death.

Rehabilitation Act

29 U.S.C. § 794. Nondiscrimination under federal grants and programs

(a) **Promulgation of rules and regulations.** No otherwise qualified individual with a disability in the United States, as defined in section 7(8) [29 U.S.C. § 706(8)], shall, solely by reason of her or his disability, be excluded from the participation in, be denied the benefits of, or be subjected to discrimination under any program or activity receiving Federal financial assistance or under any program or activity conducted by any Executive agency or by the United States Postal Service. The head of each such agency shall promulgate such regulations as may be necessary to carry out the amendments to this section made by the Rehabilitation, Comprehensive Services, and Developmental Disabilities Act of 1978. Copies of any proposed regulation shall be submitted to appropriate authorizing committees of the Congress, and such regulation may take effect no earlier than the thirtieth day after the date on which such regulation is submitted to such committees.

(b) **Program or activity defined.** For the purposes of this section, the term "program or activity" means all of the operations of—

(1) (A) a department, agency, special purpose district, or other instrumentality of a State or of a local government; or

   (B) the entity of such State or local government that distributes such assistance and each such department or agency (and each other State or local government entity) to which the assistance is extended, in the case of assistance to a State or local government.

(2) (A) a college, university, or other postsecondary institution, or a public system of higher education; or

   (B) a local educational agency (as defined in section 14101 of the Elementary and Secondary Education Act of 1965 [20 U.S.C. §8801]), system of vocational education, or other school system;

(3) (A) an entire corporation, partnership, or other private organization, or an entire sole proprietorship—

   (i) if assistance is extended to such corporation, partnership, private organization, or sole proprietorship as a whole; or

   (ii) which is principally engaged in the business of providing education, health care, housing, social services, or parks and recreation; or

   (B) the entire plant or other comparable, geographically separate facility to which Federal financial assistance is extended, in the case of any other corporation, partnership, private organization, or sole proprietorship; or

(4) any other entity which is established by two or more of the entities described in paragraph (1), (2), or (3);

any part of which is extended Federal financial assistance.

(c) **Significant structural alterations by small providers.** Small providers are not required by subsection (a) to make significant structural alterations to their existing facilities for the purpose of assuring program accessibility, if alternative means of providing the services are available. The terms used in this subsection shall be construed with reference to the regulations existing on the date of enactment of this subsection [enacted March 22, 1998].

(d) **Standards used in determining violation of section.** The standards used to determine whether this section has been violated in a complaint alleging employment discrimination shall be the standards applied under Title I of the Americans with Disabilities Act of 1990 (42 U.S.C. 12111 et seq.) and the provisions of sections 501 through 504, and 510, of the Americans with Disabilities Act of 1990 (42 U.S.C. 12201-12204 and 12210), as such sections relate to employment.

29 U.S.C. § 794a. Remedies and attorney's fees

(a) (1) The remedies, procedures, and rights set forth in section 717 of the Civil Rights Act of 1964 (*42 U.S.C. 2000e-16*), including the application of sections 706(f) through 706(k) (*42 U.S.C. 2000e-5 (f) through (k)*), shall be available, with respect to any complaint under section 501 of this Act [*29 USCS § 791*], to any employee or applicant for employment aggrieved by the final disposition of such complaint, or by the failure to take final action on such complaint. In fashioning an equitable or affirmative action remedy under such section, a court may take into account the reasonableness of the cost of any necessary work place accommodation, and the availability of alternatives therefor or other appropriate relief in order to achieve an equitable and appropriate remedy.

(2) The remedies, procedures, and rights set forth in title VI of the Civil Rights Act of 1964 [*42 USCS §§ 2000d* et seq.] shall be available to any person aggrieved by any act or failure to act by any recipient of Federal assistance or Federal provider of such assistance under section 504 of this Act [*29 USCS § 794*].

(b) In any action or proceeding to enforce or charge a violation of a provision of this title [*29 USCS §§ 790* et seq.], the court, in its discretion, may allow the prevailing party, other than the United States, a reasonable attorney's fee as part of the costs.

Voting Rights Act
42 U.S.C. § 1971. Voting rights

(a) Race, color, or previous condition not to affect right to vote; uniform standards for voting qualifications; errors or omissions from papers; literacy tests; agreements between Attorney General and State or local authorities; definitions.

    (1) All citizens of the United States who are otherwise qualified by law to vote at any election by the people in any State, Territory, district, county, city, parish, township, school district, municipality, or other territorial subdivision, shall be entitled and allowed to vote at all such elections, without distinction of race, color, or previous condition of servitude; any constitution, law, custom, usage, or regulation of any State or Territory, or by or under its authority, to the contrary notwithstanding.

    (2) No person acting under color of law shall—

        (A) in determining whether any individual is qualified under State law or laws to vote in any election, apply any standard, practice, or procedure different from the standards, practices, or procedures applied under such law or laws to other individuals within the same county, parish, or similar political subdivision who have been found by State officials to be qualified to vote;

        (B) deny the right of any individual to vote in any election because of an error or omission on any record or paper relating to any application, registration, or other act requisite to voting, if such error or omission is not material in determining whether such individual is qualified under State law to vote in such election; or

        (C) employ any literacy test as a qualification for voting in any election unless (i) such test is administered to each individual and is conducted wholly in writing, and (ii) a certified copy of the test and of the answers given by the individual is furnished to him within twenty-five days of the submission of his request made within the period of time during which records and papers are required to be retained and preserved pursuant to title III of the Civil Rights Act of 1960 (*42 U.S.C. 1974-74e; 74 Stat. 88*) [*42 USCS § § 1974* et seq.]: Provided, however,

That the Attorney General may enter into agreements with appropriate State or local authorities that preparation, conduct, and maintenance of such tests in accordance with the provisions of applicable State or local law, including such special provisions as are necessary in the preparation, conduct, and maintenance of such tests for persons who are blind or otherwise physically handicapped, meet the purposes of this subparagraph and constitute compliance therewith.

(3) For purposes of this subsection—

    (A) the term "vote" shall have the same meaning as in subsection (e) of this section;

    (B) the phrase "literacy test" includes any test of the ability to read, write, understand, or interpret any matter.

(b) **Intimidation, threats, or coercion.** No person, whether acting under color of law or otherwise, shall intimidate, threaten, coerce, or attempt to intimidate, threaten, or coerce any other person for the purpose of interfering with the right of such other person to vote or to vote as he may choose, or of causing such other person to vote for, or not to vote for, any candidate for the office of President, Vice President, presidential elector, Member of the Senate, or Member of the House of Representatives, Delegates or Commissioners from the Territories or possessions, at any general, special, or primary election held solely or in part for the purpose of selecting or electing any such candidate.

(c) **Preventive relief; injunction; rebuttable literacy presumption; liability of United States for costs, State as party defendant.** Whenever any person has engaged or there are reasonable grounds to believe that any person is about to engage in any act or practice which would deprive any other person of any right or privilege secured by subsection (a) or (b), the Attorney General may institute for the United States, or in the name of the United States, a civil action or other proper proceeding for preventive relief, including an application for a permanent or temporary injunction, restraining order, or other order. If in any such proceeding literacy is a relevant fact there shall be a rebuttable presumption that any person who has not been adjudged an incompetent and who has completed the sixth grade in a public school in, or a private school accredited by, any State or territory, the District of Columbia, or the Commonwealth of Puerto Rico where instruction is carried on predominantly in the English language, possesses sufficient literacy, comprehension, and intelligence to vote in any election. In any proceeding hereunder the United States shall be liable for costs the same as a private person. Whenever, in a proceeding instituted under this subsection any official of a State or subdivision thereof is alleged to have committed any act or practice constituting a deprivation of any right or privilege secured by subsection (a), the act or practice shall also be deemed that of the State and the State may be joined as a party defendant and, if, prior to the institution of such proceeding, such official has resigned or has been relieved of his office and no successor has assumed such office, the proceeding may be instituted against the State.

(d) **Jurisdiction; exhaustion of other remedies.** The district courts of the United States shall have jurisdiction of proceedings instituted pursuant to this section and shall exercise the same without regard to whether the party aggrieved shall have exhausted any administrative or other remedies that may be provided by law.

(e) **Order qualifying person to vote; application; hearing; voting referees; transmittal of report and order; certificate of qualification; definitions.** In any proceeding instituted pursuant to subsection (c) in the event the court finds that any person has been deprived on account of race or color of any right or privilege secured by subsection (a), the court shall upon request of the Attorney General and after each party has been given notice and the opportunity to be heard make a finding whether such deprivation was or is pursuant to a pattern or practice. If the court finds such pattern or practice, any person of such race or color resident within the affected area shall, for one year and thereafter until the court subsequently finds that such pattern or practice has ceased, be entitled, upon his application therefor, to an order declaring him qualified to vote, upon proof that at any election or elections (1) he is qualified under State law to vote, and (2) he has since such finding by the court been (a) deprived of or denied under color of law the opportunity to register to vote or otherwise to qualify to vote, or (b) found not qualified to vote by any person acting under color of law. Such order shall be effective as to any election held within the longest period for which such applicant could have been registered or otherwise qualified under State law at which the applicant's qualifications would under State law entitle him to vote.

Notwithstanding any inconsistent provision of State law or the action of any State officer or court, an applicant so declared qualified to vote shall be permitted to vote in any such election. The Attorney General shall cause to be transmitted certified copies of such order to the appropriate election officers. The refusal by any such officer with notice of such order to permit any person so declared qualified to vote, to vote at an appropriate election shall constitute contempt of court.

An application for an order pursuant to this subsection shall be heard within ten days, and the execution of any order disposing of such application shall not be stayed if the effect of such stay would be to delay the effectiveness of the order beyond the date of any election at which the applicant would otherwise be enabled to vote.

The court may appoint one or more persons who are qualified voters in the judicial district, to be known as voting referees, who shall subscribe to the oath of office required by Revised Statutes, section 1757; (5 U.S.C. 16) to serve for such period as the court shall determine, to receive such applications and to take evidence and report to the court findings as to whether or not at any election or elections (1) any such applicant is qualified under State law to vote, and (2) he has since the finding by the court heretofore specified been (a) deprived of or denied under color of law the opportunity to register to vote or otherwise to qualify to vote, or (b) found not qualified to vote by any person acting under color of law. In a proceeding before a voting referee, the applicant shall be heard ex parte at such times and places as the court shall direct. His statement under oath shall be prima facie evidence as to his age, residence, and his prior efforts to register or otherwise qualify to vote. Where proof of literacy or an understanding of other subjects is required by valid provisions of State law, the answer of the applicant, if written, shall be included in such report to the court; if oral, it shall be taken down stenographically and a transcription included in such report to the court.

Upon receipt of such report, the court shall cause the Attorney General to transmit a copy thereof to the State attorney general and to each party to such proceeding together with an order to show cause within ten days, or such shorter time as the court may fix, why an order of the court should not be entered in accordance with such report. Upon the expiration of such period, such order shall be entered unless prior to that time there has been filed with the court and served upon all parties a statement of exceptions to such report. Exceptions as to matters of fact shall be considered only if supported by a duly verified copy of a public record or by affidavit of persons having personal knowledge of such facts or by statements or matters contained in such report; those relating to matters of law shall be supported by an appropriate memorandum of law. The issues of fact and law raised by such exceptions shall be determined by the court or, if the due and speedy administration of justice requires, they may be referred to the voting referee to determine in accordance with procedures prescribed by the court. A hearing as to an issue of fact shall be held only in the event that the proof in support of the exception discloses the existence of a genuine issue of material fact. The applicant's literacy and understanding of other subjects shall be determined solely on the basis of answers included in the report of the voting referee.

The court, or at its direction the voting referee, shall issue to each applicant so declared qualified a certificate identifying the holder thereof as a person so qualified.

Any voting referee appointed by the court pursuant to this subsection shall to the extent not inconsistent herewith have all the powers conferred upon a master by rule 53(c) of the Federal Rules of Civil Procedure [USCS Federal Rules of Civil Procedure, Rule 53(c)]. The compensation to be allowed to any persons appointed by the court pursuant to this subsection shall be fixed by the court and shall be payable by the United States.

Applications pursuant to this subsection shall be determined expeditiously. In the case of any application filed twenty or more days prior to an election which is undetermined by the time of such election, the court shall issue an order authorizing the applicant to vote provisionally: Provided, however, That such applicant shall be qualified to vote under State law. In the case of an application filed within twenty days prior to an election, the court, in its discretion, may make such an order. In either case the order shall make appropriate provisions for the impounding of the applicant's ballot pending determination of the application. The court may take any other action, and may authorize such referee or such other person as it may designate to take any other action, appropriate or necessary to carry out the provisions of this subsection and to enforce its decrees. This subsection shall in no way be construed as a limitation upon the existing powers of the court.

When used in the subsection, the word "vote" includes all action necessary to make a vote effective including, but not limited to, registration or other action required by State law prerequisite to voting, casting a ballot, and having such ballot counted and included in the appropriate totals of votes cast with respect to candidates for public office and propositions for which votes are received in an election; the words "affected area" shall mean any subdivision of the State in which the laws of the State relating to voting are or have been to any extent administered by a person found in the proceeding to have violated subsection (a); and the words "qualified under State law" shall mean qualified according to the laws, customs, or usages of the State, and shall not, in any event, imply qualifications more stringent than those used by the persons found in the proceeding to have violated subsection (a) in qualifying persons other than those of the race or color against which the pattern or practice of discrimination was found to exist.

(f) **Contempt; assignment of counsel; witnesses.** Any person cited for an alleged contempt under this Act shall be allowed to make his full defense by counsel learned in the law; and the court before which he is cited or tried, or some judge thereof, shall immediately, upon his request, assign to him such counsel, not exceeding two, as he may desire, who shall have free access to him at all reasonable hours. He shall be allowed, in his defense to make any proof that he can produce by lawful witnesses, and shall have the like process of the court to compel his witnesses to appear at his trial or hearing, as is usually granted to compel witnesses to appear on behalf of the prosecution. If such person shall be found by the court to be financially unable to provide for such counsel, it shall be the duty of the court to provide such counsel.

(g) **Three-judge district court: hearing, determination, expedition of action, review by Supreme Court; single judge district court: hearing, determination, expedition of action.** In any proceeding instituted by the United States in any district court of the United States under this section in which the Attorney General requests a finding of a pattern or practice of discrimination pursuant to subsection (e) of this section the Attorney General, at the time he files the complaint, or any defendant in the proceeding, within twenty days after service upon him of the complaint, may file with the clerk of such court a request that a court of three judges be convened to hear and determine the entire case. A copy of the request for a three-judge court shall be immediately furnished by such clerk to the chief judge of the circuit (or in his absence, the presiding circuit judge of the circuit) in which the case is pending. Upon receipt of the copy of such request it shall be the duty of the chief judge of the circuit or the presiding circuit judge, as the case may be, to designate immediately three judges in such circuit, of whom at least one shall be a circuit judge and another of whom shall be a district judge of the court in which the proceeding was instituted, to hear and determine such case, and it shall be the duty of the judges so designated to assign the case for hearing at the earliest practicable date, to participate in the hearing and determination thereof, and to cause the case to be in every way expedited. An appeal from the final judgment of such court will lie to the Supreme Court.

In any proceeding brought under subsection (c) of this section to enforce subsection (b) of this section, or in the event neither the Attorney General nor any defendant files a request for a three-judge court in any proceedings authorized by this subsection, it shall be the duty of the chief judge of the district (or in his absence, the acting chief judge) in which the case is pending immediately to designate a judge in such district to hear and determine the case. In the event that no judge in the district is available to hear and determine the case, the chief judge of the district, or the acting chief judge, as the case may be, shall certify this fact to the chief judge of the circuit (or, in his absence, the acting chief judge) who shall then designate a district or circuit judge of the circuit to hear and determine the case.

It shall be the duty of the judge designated pursuant to this section to assign the case for hearing at the earliest practicable date and to cause the case to be in every way expedited.

42 U.S.C. § 1973. Denial or abridgement of right to vote on account of race or color through voting qualifications or prerequisites; establishment of violation

(a) No voting qualification or prerequisite to voting or standard, practice, or procedure shall be imposed or applied by any State or political subdivision in a manner which results in a denial or abridgement of the right of any citizen of the United States to vote on account of race or color, or in contravention of the guarantees set forth in section 4(f)(2) [*42 USCS § 1973b*(f)(2)], as provided in subsection (b).

(b) A violation of subsection (a) is established if, based on the totality of circumstances, it is shown that the political processes leading to nomination or election in the State or political subdivision are not equally open to participation by members of a class of citizens protected by subsection (a) in that its members have less opportunity than other members of the electorate to participate in the political process and to elect representatives of their choice. The extent to which members of a protected class have been elected to office in the State or political subdivision is one circumstance which may be considered: Provided, That nothing in this section establishes a right to have members of a protected class elected in numbers equal to their proportion in the population.

42 U.S.C. § 1973b. Suspension of the use of tests or devices in determining eligibility to vote

(a) Action by state or political subdivision for declaratory judgment of no denial or abridgement; three-judge district court; appeal to Supreme Court; retention of jurisdiction by three-judge court.

   (1) To assure that the right of citizens of the United States to vote is not denied or abridged on account of race or color, no citizen shall be denied the right to vote in any Federal, State, or local election because of his failure to comply with any test or device in any State with respect to which the determinations have been made under the first two sentences of subsection (b) or in any political subdivision of such State (as such subdivision existed on the date such determinations were made with respect to such State), though such determinations were not made with respect to such subdivision as a separate unit, or in any political subdivision with respect to which such determinations have been made as a separate unit, unless the United States District Court for the District of Columbia issues a declaratory judgment under this section. No citizen shall be denied the right to vote in any Federal, State, or local election because of his failure to comply with any test or device in any State with respect to which the determinations have been made under the third sentence of subsection (b) of this section or in any political subdivision of such State (as such subdivision existed on the date such determinations were made with respect to such State), though such determinations were not made with respect to such subdivision as a separate unit, or in any political subdivision with respect to which such determinations have been made as a separate unit, unless the United States District Court for the District of Columbia issues a declaratory judgment under this section. A declaratory judgment under this section shall issue only if such court determines that during the ten years preceding the filing of the action, and during the pendency of such action—

   (A) no such test or device has been used within such State or political subdivision for the purpose or with the effect of denying or abridging the right to vote on account of race or color or (in the case of a State or subdivision seeking a declaratory judgment under the second sentence of this subsection) in contravention of the guarantees of subsection (f)(2);

   (B) no final judgment of any court of the United States, other than the denial of declaratory judgment under this section, has

determined that denials or abridgements of the right to vote
on account of race or color have occurred anywhere in the territory of such State or political subdivision or (in the case of a
State or subdivision seeking a declaratory judgment under the
second sentence of this subsection) that denials or abridgements of the right to vote in contravention of the guarantees
of subsection (f)(2) have occurred anywhere in the territory of
such State or subdivision and no consent decree, settlement, or
agreement has been entered into resulting in any abandonment of a voting practice challenged on such grounds; and no
declaratory judgment under this section shall be entered during the pendency of an action commenced before the filing of
an action under this section and alleging such denials or
abridgements of the right to vote;

(C) no Federal examiners under this Act have been assigned to
such State or political subdivision;

(D) such State or political subdivision and all governmental units
within its territory have complied with section 5 of this Act
[42 USCS § 1973c], including compliance with the requirement that no change covered by section 5 [42 USCS § 1973c]
has been enforced without preclearance under section 5 [42
USCS § 1973c], and have repealed all changes covered by section 5 [42 USCS § 1973c] to which the Attorney General has
successfully objected or as to which the United States District
Court for the District of Columbia has denied a declaratory
judgment;

(E) the Attorney General has not interposed any objection (that
has not been overturned by a final judgment of a court) and
no declaratory judgment has been denied under section 5 [42
USCS § 1973c], with respect to any submission by or on
behalf of the plaintiff or any governmental unit within its
territory under section 5 [42 USCS § 1973c], and no such submissions or declaratory judgment actions are pending; and

(F) such State or political subdivision and all governmental units
within its territory—

(i) have eliminated voting procedures and methods of election
which inhibit or dilute equal access to the electoral process;

(ii) have engaged in constructive efforts to eliminate intimidation and harassment of persons exercising rights
protected under this Act; and

      (iii) have engaged in other constructive efforts, such as ex-
      panded opportunity for convenient registration and vot-
      ing for every person of voting age and the appointment of
      minority persons as election officials throughout the juris-
      diction and at all stages of the election and registration
      process.

(2) To assist the court in determining whether to issue a declaratory judgment under this subsection, the plaintiff shall present evidence of minority participation, including evidence of the levels of minority group registration and voting, changes in such levels over time, and disparities between minority-group and non-minority-group participation.

(3) No declaratory judgment shall issue under this subsection with respect to such State or political subdivision if such plaintiff and governmental units within its territory have, during the period beginning ten years before the date the judgment is issued, engaged in violations of any provision of the Constitution or laws of the United States or any State or political subdivision with respect to discrimination in voting on account of race or color or (in the case of a State or subdivision seeking a declaratory judgment under the second sentence of this subsection) in contravention of the guarantees of subsection (f)(2) unless the plaintiff establishes that any such violations were trivial, were promptly corrected, and were not repeated.

(4) The State or political subdivision bringing such action shall publicize the intended commencement and any proposed settlement of such action in the media serving such State or political subdivision and in appropriate United States post offices. Any aggrieved party may as of right intervene at any stage in such action.

(5) An action pursuant to this subsection shall be heard and determined by a court of three judges in accordance with the provisions of section 2284 of title 28 of the United States Code [*28 USCS §
2284*] and any appeal shall lie to the Supreme Court. The court shall retain jurisdiction of any action pursuant to this subsection for ten years after judgment and shall reopen the action upon motion of the Attorney General or any aggrieved person alleging that conduct has occurred which, had that conduct occurred during the ten-year periods referred to in this subsection, would have precluded the issuance of a declaratory judgment under this subsection. The court, upon such reopening, shall vacate the declara-

tory judgment issued under this section if, after the issuance of such declaratory judgment, a final judgment against the State or subdivision with respect to which such declaratory judgment was issued, or against any governmental unit within the State or subdivision, determines that denials or abridgements of the right to vote on account of race or color have occurred anywhere in the territory of such State or political subdivision or (in the case of a State or subdivision which sought a declaratory judgment under the second sentence of this subsection) that denials or abridgements of the right to vote in contravention of the guarantees of subsection (f)(2) have occurred anywhere in the territory of such State or subdivision, or if, after the issuance of such declaratory judgment, a consent decree, settlement, or agreement has been entered into resulting in any abandonment of a voting practice challenged on such grounds.

(6) If, after two years from the date of the filing of a declaratory judgment under this subsection, no date has been set for a hearing in such action, and that delay has not been the result of an avoidable delay on the part of counsel for any party, the chief judge of the United States District Court for the District of Columbia may request the Judicial Council for the Circuit of the District of Columbia to provide the necessary judicial resources to expedite any action filed under this section. If such resources are unavailable within the circuit, the chief judge shall file a certificate of necessity in accordance with section 292(d) of title 28 of the United States Code [*28 USCS § 292(d)*].

(7) The Congress shall reconsider the provisions of this section at the end of the fifteen-year period following the effective date of the amendments made by the Voting Rights Act Amendments of 1982.

(8) The provisions of this section shall expire at the end of the twenty-five year period following the effective date of the amendments made by the Voting Rights Act Amendments of 1982.

(9) Nothing in this section shall prohibit the Attorney General from consenting to an entry of judgment if based upon a showing of objective and compelling evidence by the plaintiff, and upon investigation, he is satisfied that the State or political subdivision has complied with the requirements of section 4(a)(1) [subsec. (a)(1) of this section]. Any aggrieved party may as of right intervene at any stage in such action.

(b) Required factual determinations necessary to allow suspension of compliance with tests and devices; publication in Federal Register.

The provisions of subsection (a) shall apply in any State or in any political subdivision of a state which (1) the Attorney General determines maintained on November 1, 1964, any test or device, and with respect to which (2) the Director of the Census determines that less than 50 per centum of the persons of voting age residing therein were registered on November 1, 1964, or that less than 50 per centum of such persons voted on the presidential election of November 1964. On and after August 6, 1970, in addition to any State or political subdivision of a State determined to be subject to subsection (a) pursuant to the previous sentence, the provisions of subsection (a) shall apply in any State or any political subdivision of a State which (i) the Attorney General determines maintained on November 1, 1968, any test or device, and with respect to which (ii) the Director of the Census determines that less than 50 per centum of the persons of voting age residing therein were registered on November 1, 1968, or that less than 50 per centum of such persons voted in the presidential election of November 1968. On and after August 6, 1975, in addition to any State or political subdivision of a State determined to be subject to subsection (a) pursuant to the previous two sentences, the provisions of a subsection (a) shall apply in any State or any political subdivision of a State which (i) the Attorney General determines maintained on November 1, 1972, any test or device, and with respect to which (ii) the Director of the Census determines that less than 50 per centum of the citizens of voting age were registered on November 1, 1972, or that less than 50 per centum of such persons voted in the Presidential election of November 1972.

A determination or certification of the Attorney General or of the Director of the Census under this section or under section 6 or section 13 [*42 USCS § 1973d* or 1973k] shall not be reviewable in any court and shall be effective upon publication in the Federal Register.

42 U.S.C. § 1973c. Alteration of voting qualifications and procedures; action by State or political subdivision for declaratory judgment of no denial or abridgement of voting rights; three-judge district court; appeal to Supreme Court

Whenever a State or political subdivision with respect to which the prohibitions set forth in section 4(a) [*42 USCS § 1973b*(a)] based upon determinations made under the first sentence of section 4(b) [*42 USCS*

§ 1973*b*(b)] are in effect shall enact or seek to administer any voting qualification or prerequisite to voting, or standard, practice, or procedure with respect to voting different from that in force or effect on November 1, 1964, or whenever a State or political subdivision with respect to which the prohibitions set forth in section 4(a) [*42 USCS § 1973b*(a)] based upon determinations made under the second sentence of section 4(b) [*42 USCS § 1973b*(b)] are in effect shall enact or seek to administer any voting qualification or prerequisite to voting, or standard, practice, or procedure with respect to voting different from that in force or effect on November 1, 1968, or whenever a State or political subdivision with respect to which the prohibitions set forth in section 4(a) [*42 USCS § 1973b*(a)] based upon determinations made under the third sentence of section 4(b) [*42 USCS § 1973b*(b)] are in effect shall enact or seek to administer any voting qualification or prerequisite to voting, or standard, practice, or procedure with respect to voting different from that in force or effect on November 1, 1972, such State or subdivision may institute an action in the United States District Court for the District of Columbia for a declaratory judgment that such qualification prerequisite, standard, practice, or procedure does not have the purpose and will not have the effect of denying or abridging the right to vote on account of race or color, or in contravention of the guarantees set forth in section 4(f)(2) [*42 USCS § 1973b*(f)(2)], and unless and until the court enters such judgment no person shall be denied the right to vote for failure to comply with such qualification, prerequisite, standard, practice, or procedure: Provided, That such qualification, prerequisite, standard, practice, or procedure may be enforced without such proceeding if the qualification, prerequisite, standard, practice, or procedure has been submitted by the chief legal officer or other appropriate official of such State or subdivision to the Attorney General and the Attorney General has not interposed an objection within sixty days after such submission, or upon good cause shown, to facilitate an expedited approval within sixty days after such submission, the Attorney General has affirmatively indicated that such objection will not be made. Neither an affirmative indication by the Attorney General that no objection will be made, nor the Attorney General's failure to object, nor a declaratory judgment entered under this section shall bar a subsequent action to enjoin enforcement of such qualification, prerequisite, standard, practice, or procedure. In the event the Attorney General affirmatively indicates that no objection will be made within the sixty-day period following receipt of a submission, the Attorney General may reserve the right to reexamine the submission if additional information comes to his attention during the remainder of the sixty-day period which would otherwise require objection in accordance with this section. Any action under this section shall be heard and determined by a court of three judges in accordance with the provisions of section 2284 of title 28 of the United States Code and any appeal shall lie to the Supreme Court.

42 U.S.C. § 1973i. Prohibited acts

(a) **Failure or refusal to permit casting or tabulation of vote.** No person acting under color of law shall fail or refuse to permit any person to vote who is entitled to vote under any provision of this Act or is otherwise qualified to vote, or willfully fail or refuse to tabulate, count, and report such person's vote.

(b) **Intimidation, threats, or coercion.** No person, whether acting under color of law or otherwise, shall intimidate, threaten, or coerce, or attempt to intimidate, threaten, or coerce any person for voting or attempting to vote, or intimidate, threaten, or coerce, or attempt to intimidate, threaten, or coerce any person for urging or aiding any persons to vote or attempt to vote, or intimidate, threaten, or coerce any person for exercising any powers or duties under section 3(a), 6, 8, 9, 10, or 12(e) [*42 USCS § § 1973a*(a), 1973d, 1973f, 1973g, 1973h, or 1973j(e)].

(c) **False information in registering or voting; penalties.** Whoever knowingly or willfully gives false information as to his name, address, or period of residence in the voting district for the purpose of establishing his eligibility to register or vote, or conspires with another individual for the purpose of encouraging his false registration to vote or illegal voting, or pays or offers to pay or accepts payment either for registration to vote or for voting shall be fined not more than $ 10,000 or imprisoned not more than five years, or both: Provided, however, That this provision shall be applicable only to general, special, or primary elections held solely or in part for the purpose of selecting or electing any candidate for the office of President, Vice President, presidential elector, Member of the United States Senate, Member of the United States House of Representatives, Delegate from the District of Columbia, Guam, or the Virgin Islands, or Resident Commissioner of the Commonwealth of Puerto Rico.

(d) **Falsification or concealment of material facts or giving of false statements in matters within jurisdiction of examiners or hearing officers; penalties.** Whoever, in any matter within the jurisdiction of an examiner or hearing officer knowingly and willfully falsifies or conceals a material fact, or makes any false, fictitious, or fraudulent statements or representations, or makes or uses any false writing or document knowing the same to contain any false, fictitious, or fraudulent statement or entry, shall be fined not more than $ 10,000 or imprisoned not more than five years, or both.

(e) **Voting more than once.**

(1) Whoever votes more than once in an election referred to in paragraph (2) shall be fined not more than $ 10,000 or imprisoned not more than five years, or both.

(2) The prohibition of this subsection applies with respect to any general, special, or primary election held solely or in part for the purpose of selecting or electing any candidate for the office of President, Vice President, presidential elector, Member of the United States Senate, Member of the United States House of Representatives, Delegate from the District of Columbia, Guam, or the Virgin Islands, or Resident Commissioner of the Commonwealth of Puerto Rico.

(3) As used in this subsection, the term "votes more than once" does not include the casting of an additional ballot if all prior ballots of that voter were invalidated, nor does it include the voting in two jurisdictions under section 202 of this Act [*42 USCS § 1973aa-1*], to the extent two ballots are not cast for an election to the same candidacy or office.

42 U.S.C. § 1973j. Civil and criminal sanctions

(a) **Depriving or attempting to deprive persons of secured rights.** Whoever shall deprive or attempt to deprive any person of any right secured by section 2, 3, 4, 5, 7, or 10 [*42 USCS § 1973, 1973a, 1973b, 1973c, 1973e*, or *1973h*] or shall violate section 11(a) [*42 USCS § 1973i*(a)], shall be fined not more than $ 5,000, or imprisoned not more than five years, or both.

(b) **Destroying, defacing, mutilating, or altering ballots or official voting records.** Whoever, within a year following an election in a political subdivision in which an examiner has been appointed (1) destroys, defaces, mutilates, or otherwise alters the marking of a paper ballot which has been cast in such election, or (2) alters any official record of voting in such election tabulated from a voting machine or otherwise, shall be fined not more than $ 5,000, or imprisoned not more than five years, or both.

(c) **Conspiring to violate or interfere with secured rights.** Whoever conspires to violate the provisions of subsection (a) or (b) of this section, or interferes with any right secured by section 2, 3, 4, 5, 7, 10, or 11(a) [42 USCS § § 1973, 1973a, 1973b, 1973c, 1973e, 1973h or 1973i(a)] shall be fined not more than $ 5,000, or imprisoned not more than five years, or both.

(d) **Civil action by Attorney General for preventive relief; injunctive and other relief.** Whenever any person has engaged or there are reasonable grounds to believe that any person is about to engage in any act or practice prohibited by section 2, 3, 4, 5, 7, 10, 11 [42 USCS § § 1973, 1973a, 1973b, 1973c, 1973e, 1973h, or 1973i], or subsection (b) of this section, the Attorney General may institute for the United States, or in the name of the United States, an action for preventive relief, including an application for a temporary or permanent injunction, restraining order, or other order, and including an order directed to the State and State or local election officials to require them (1) to permit persons listed under this Act to vote and (2) to count such votes.

(e) **Proceeding by Attorney General to enforce the counting of ballots of registered and eligible persons who are prevented from voting.** Whenever in any political subdivision in which there are examiners appointed pursuant to this Act any persons allege to such an examiner within forty-eight hours after the closing of the polls that notwithstanding (1) their listing under this Act or registration by an appropriate election official and (2) their eligibility to vote, they have not been permitted to vote in such election, the examiner shall forthwith notify the Attorney General if such allegations in his opinion appear to be well founded. Upon receipt of such notification, the Attorney General may forthwith file with the district court an application for an order providing for the marking, casting, and counting of the ballots of such persons and requiring the inclusion of their votes in the total vote before the results of such election shall be deemed final and any force or effect given thereto. The district court shall hear and determine such matters immediately after the filing of such application. The remedy provided in this subsection shall not preclude any remedy available under State or Federal law.

(f) **Jurisdiction of district courts; exhaustion of administrative or other remedies unnecessary.** The district courts of the United States shall have jurisdiction of proceedings instituted pursuant to this section and shall exercise the same without regard to whether a person asserting rights under the provisions of this Act shall have exhausted any administrative or other remedies that may be provided by law.

42 U.S.C. § 1973l. Attorney's fees

In any action or proceeding to enforce the voting guarantees of the fourteenth or fifteenth amendment [USCS Constitution, Amendments 14, 15] the court, in its discretion, may allow the prevailing party, other than the United States, a reasonable attorney's fee as part of the costs.

42 U.S.C. § 1973aa-1. Residence requirements for voting

(a) **Congressional findings.** The Congress hereby finds that the imposition and application of the durational residency requirement as a precondition to voting for the offices of President and Vice President, and the lack of sufficient opportunities for absentee registration and absentee balloting in presidential elections—

    (1) denies or abridges the inherent constitutional right of citizens to vote for their President and Vice President;

    (2) denies or abridges the inherent constitutional right of citizens to enjoy their free movement across State lines;

    (3) denies or abridges the privileges and immunities guaranteed to the citizens of each State under article IV, section 2, clause 1, of the Constitution [USCS Constitution, Art. IV, § 2, ch. 1];

    (4) in some instances has the impermissible purpose or effect of denying citizens the right to vote for such officers because of the way they may vote;

    (5) has the effect of denying to citizens the equality of civil rights, and due process and equal protection of the laws that are guaranteed to them under the fourteenth amendment [USCS Constitution, Amendment 14]; and

    (6) does not bear a reasonable relationship to any compelling State interest in the conduct of presidential elections.

(b) **Congressional declaration: durational residency requirement, abolishment; absentee registration and balloting standards, establishment.** Upon the basis of these findings, Congress declares that in order to secure and protect the above-stated rights of citizens under the Constitution, to enable citizens to better obtain the enjoyment of such rights, and to enforce the guarantees of the fourteenth amendment [USCS Constitution, Amendment 14], it is necessary (1) to completely abolish the durational residency requirement as a precondition to voting for President and Vice President, and (2) to establish nationwide, uniform standards relative to absentee registration and absentee balloting in presidential elections.

(c) **Prohibition of denial of right to vote because of durational residency requirement or absentee balloting.** No citizen of the United States who is otherwise qualified to vote in any election for President and Vice President shall be denied the right to vote for electors for President and Vice President, or for President and Vice President, in such election because of the failure of such citizen to comply with any durational residency requirement of such State or political subdivision; nor shall any citizen of the United States be denied the right to vote for electors for President and Vice President, or for President and Vice President, in such election because of the failure of such citizen to be physically present in such State or political subdivision at the time of such election, if such citizen shall have complied with the requirements prescribed by the law of such State or political subdivision providing for the casting of absentee ballots in such election.

(d) **Registration: time for application; absentee balloting: time of application and return of ballots.** For the purposes of this section, each State shall provide by law for the registration or other means of qualification of all duly qualified residents of such State who apply, not later than thirty days immediately prior to any presidential election, for registration or qualification to vote for the choice of electors for President and Vice President or for President and Vice President in such election; and each State shall provide by law for the casting of absentee ballots for the choice of electors for President and Vice President, or for President and Vice President, by all duly qualified residents of such State who may be absent from their election district or unit in such State on the day such election is held and who have applied therefor not later than seven days immediately prior to such election and have returned such ballots to the appropriate election official of such State not later than the time of closing of the polls in such State on the day of such election.

(e) **Change of residence; voting in person or by absentee ballot in State of prior residence.** If any citizen of the United States who is otherwise qualified to vote in any State or political subdivision in any election for President and Vice President has begun residence in such State or political subdivision after the thirtieth day next preceding such election and, for that reason, does not satisfy the registration requirements of such State or political subdivision he shall be allowed to vote for the choice of electors for President and Vice President, or for President and

Vice President, in such election, (1) in person in the State or political subdivision in which he resided immediately prior to his removal if he had satisfied, as of the date of his change of residence, the requirements to vote in that State or political subdivision, or (2) by absentee ballot in the State or political subdivision in which he resided immediately prior to his removal if he satisfies, but for his nonresident status and the reason for his absence, the requirements for absentee voting in that State or political subdivision.

(f) **Absentee registration requirement.** No citizen of the United States who is otherwise qualified to vote by absentee ballot in any State or political subdivision in any election for President and Vice President shall be denied the right to vote for the choice of electors for President and Vice President, or for President and Vice President, in such election because of any requirement of registration that does not include a provision for absentee registration.

(g) **State or local adoption of less restrictive voting practices.** Nothing in this section shall prevent any State or political subdivision from adopting less restrictive voting practices than those that are prescribed herein.

(h) **"State" defined.** The term "State" as used in this section includes each of the several States and the District of Columbia.

(i) **False registration, and other fraudulent acts and conspiracies: application of penalty for false information in registering or voting.** The provisions of section 11(c) [42 USCS § 1973i(c)] shall apply to false registration, and other fraudulent acts and conspiracies, committed under this section.

Voting Accessibility for the Elderly and Handicapped Act (VAEH)

§ 1973ee. Purpose

It is the intention of Congress in enacting this Act [42 USCS § § 1973ee et seq.] to promote the fundamental right to vote by improving access for handicapped and elderly individuals to registration facilities and polling places for Federal elections.

§ 1973ee-1. Selection of polling facilities

(a) Within each State, except as provided in subsection (b), each political subdivision responsible for conducting elections shall assure that all polling places for Federal elections are accessible to handicapped and elderly voters.

(b) Subsection (a) shall not apply to a polling place—

(1) in the case of an emergency, as determined by the chief election officer of the State; or

(2) if the chief election officer of the State—

    (A) determines that all potential polling places have been surveyed and no such accessible place is available, nor is the political subdivision able to make one temporarily accessible, in the area involved; and

    (B) assures that any handicapped or elderly voter assigned to an inaccessible polling place, upon advance request of such voter (pursuant to procedures established by the chief election officer of the State)—

        (i) will be assigned to an accessible polling place, or

        (ii) will be provided with an alternative means for casting a ballot on the day of the election.

(c) (1) Not later than December 31 of each even-numbered year, the chief election officer of each State shall report to the Federal Election Commission, in a manner to be determined by the Commission, the number of accessible and inaccessible polling places in such State on the date of the preceding general Federal election, and the reasons for any instance of inaccessibility.

(2) Not later than April 30 of each odd-numbered year, the Federal Election Commission shall compile the information reported under paragraph (1) and shall transmit that information to the Congress.

(3) The provisions of this subsection shall only be effective for a period of 10 years beginning on the date of enactment of this Act [enacted Sept. 28, 1984].

§ 1973ee-2. Selection of registration facilities

(a) Each State or political subdivision responsible for registration for Federal elections shall provide a reasonable number of accessible permanent registration facilities.

(b) Subsection (a) does not apply to any State that has in effect a system that provides an opportunity for each potential voter to register by mail or at the residence of such voter.

§ 1973ee-3. Registration and voting aids

(a) **Printed instructions; telecommunications devices for the deaf.** Each State shall make available registration and voting aids for Federal elections for handicapped and elderly individuals, including—

    (1) instructions, printed in large type, conspicuously displayed at each permanent registration facility and each polling place; and

    (2) information by telecommunications devices for the deaf.

(b) **Medical certification.** No notarization or medical certification shall be required of a handicapped voter with respect to an absentee ballot or an application for such ballot, except that medical certification may be required when the certification establishes eligibility, under State law—

    (1) to automatically receive an application or a ballot on a continuing basis; or

    (2) to apply for an absentee ballot after the deadline has passed.

(c) **Notice of availability of aids.** The chief election officer of each State shall provide public notice, calculated to reach elderly and handicapped voters, of the availability of aids under this section, assistance under section 208 of the Voting Rights Act of 1965 (42 U.S.C. 1973aa-6), and the procedures for voting by absentee ballot, not later than general public notice of registration and voting is provided.

42 U.S.C. § 1973ee-4. Enforcement

(a) **Action for declaratory or injunctive relief.** If a State or political subdivision does not comply with this Act [42 USCS § § 1973cc et seq.], the United States Attorney General or a person who is personally aggrieved by the noncompliance may bring an action for declaratory or injunctive relief in the appropriate district court.

(b) **Prerequisite notice of noncompliance.** An action may be brought under this section only if the plaintiff notifies the chief election officer of the State of the noncompliance and a period of 45 days has elapsed since the date of notification.

(c) **Attorney fees.** Notwithstanding any other provision of law, no award of attorney fees may be made with respect to an action under this section, except in any action brought to enforce the original judgment of the court.

§ 1973ee-5. Relationship to 42 USCS § § 1973 et seq.

This Act [42 USCS § § 1973ee et seq.] shall not be construed to impair any right guaranteed by the Voting Rights Act of 1965 (42 U.S.C. 1973 et seq.).

42 U.S.C. § 1973ee-6. Definitions

As used in this Act [42 USCS § § 1973ee et seq.], the term—

    (1) "accessible" means accessible to handicapped and elderly individuals for the purpose of voting or registration, as determined under guidelines established by the chief election officer of the State involved;

(2) "elderly" means 65 years of age or older;

(3) "Federal election" means a general, special, primary, or runoff election for the office of President or Vice President, or of Senator or Representative in, or Delegate or Resident Commissioner to, the Congress;

(4) "handicapped" means having a temporary or permanent physical disability; and

(5) "State" means a State of the United States, the District of Columbia, the Commonwealth of Puerto Rico, and any territory or possesssion [possession] of the United States.

Uniformed and Overseas Citizens Absentee Voting Act (UOCAVA)

42 U.S.C. § 1973ff. Federal responsibilities

(a) **Presidential designee.** The President shall designate the head of an executive department to have primary responsibility for Federal functions under this title [*42 USCS § § 1973ff* et seq.].

(b) **Duties of presidential designee.** The Presidential designee shall—

(1) consult State and local election officials in carrying out this title [*42 USCS § § 1973ff* et seq.];

(2) prescribe an official post card form, containing both an absentee voter registration application and an absentee ballot application, for use by the States as recommended in section 104 [*42 USCS § 1973ff-3*];

(3) carry out section 103 [*42 USCS § 1973ff-2*] with respect to the Federal write-in absentee ballot for overseas voters in general elections for Federal office;

(4) prescribe a suggested design for absentee ballot mailing envelopes for use by the States as recommended in section 104 [*42 USCS § 1973ff-3*];

(5) compile and distribute (A) descriptive material on State absentee registration and voting procedures, and (B) to the extent practicable, facts relating to specific elections, including dates, offices involved, and the text of ballot questions; and

(6) not later than the end of each year after a Presidential election year, transmit to the President and the Congress a report on the effectiveness of assistance under this title [*42 USCS § § 1973ff* et seq.], including a statistical analysis of uniformed services voter participation, a general assessment of overseas nonmilitary participation, and a description of State-Federal cooperation.

(c) **Duties of other Federal officials.**

(1) In general. The head of each Government department, agency, or other entity shall, upon request of the Presidential designee, distribute balloting materials and otherwise cooperate in carrying out this title [*42 USCS § § 1973ff* et seq.].

(2) Administrator of General Services. As directed by the Presidential designee, the Administrator of General Services shall furnish official post card forms (prescribed under subsection (b)) and Federal write-in absentee ballots (prescribed under section 103 [*42 USCS § § 1973ff-2*]).

§ 1973ff-1. State responsibilities

Each State shall—

(1) permit absent uniformed services voters and overseas voters to use absentee registration procedures and to vote by absentee ballot in general, special, primary, and runoff elections for Federal office;

(2) accept and process, with respect to any general, special, primary, or runoff election for Federal office, any otherwise valid voter registration application from an absent uniformed services voter or overseas voter, if the application is received by the appropriate State election official not less than 30 days before the election; and

(3) permit overseas voters to use Federal write-in absentee ballots (in accordance with section 103 [*42 USCS § 1973ff-2*]) in general elections for Federal office.

42 U.S.C. § 1973ff-2. Federal write-in absentee ballot for overseas voters in general elections for Federal office

(a) **In General.** The Presidential designee shall prescribe a Federal write-in absentee ballot (including a secrecy envelope and mailing envelope for such ballot) for use in general elections for Federal office by overseas voters who make timely application for, and do not receive, States' absentee ballots.

(b) **Submission and processing.** Except as otherwise provided in this title [*42 USCS § § 1973ff* et seq.], a Federal write-in absentee ballot shall be submitted and processed in the manner provided by law for absentee ballots in the State involved. A Federal write-in absentee ballot of an overseas voter shall not be counted—

(1) if the ballot is submitted from any location in the United States;

(2) if the application of the overseas voter for a State absentee ballot is received by the appropriate State election official less than 30 days before the general election; or

(3) if a State absentee ballot of the overseas voter is received by the appropriate State election official not later than the deadline for receipt of the State absentee ballot under State law.

(c) **Special rules.** The following rules shall apply with respect to Federal write-in absentee ballots:

(1) In completing the ballot, the overseas voter may designate a candidate by writing in the name of the candidate or by writing in the name of a political party (in which case the ballot shall be counted for the candidate of that political party).

(2) In the case of the offices of President and Vice President, a vote for a named candidate or a vote by writing in the name of a political party shall be counted as a vote for the electors supporting the candidate involved.

(3) Any abbreviation, misspelling, or other minor variation in the form of the name of a candidate or a political party shall be disregarded in determining the validity of the ballot, if the intention of the voter can be ascertained.

(d) **Second ballot submission; instruction to overseas voter.** An overseas voter who submits a Federal write-in absentee ballot and later receives a State absentee ballot, may submit the State absentee ballot. The Presidential designee shall assure that the instructions for each Federal write-in absentee ballot clearly state that an overseas voter who submits a Federal write-in absentee ballot and later receives and submits a State absentee ballot should make every reasonable effort to inform the appropriate State election official that the voter has submitted more than one ballot.

(e) **Use of approved State absentee ballot in place of Federal write-in absentee ballot.** The Federal write-in absentee ballot shall not be valid for use in a general election if the State involved provides a State absentee ballot that—

(1) at the request of the State, is approved by the Presidential designee for use in place of the Federal write-in absentee ballot; and

(2) is made available to overseas voters at least 60 days before the deadline for receipt of the State ballot under State law.

(f) **Certain States exempted.** A State is not required to permit use of the Federal write-in absentee ballot, if, on and after the date of the enactment of this title [enacted Aug. 28, 1986], the State has in effect a law providing that—

(1) a State absentee ballot is required to be available to any voter described in section 107(5)(A) [42 USCS § 1973ff-6(5)(A)] at least 90 days before the general election involved; and

(2) a State absentee ballot is required to be available to any voter described in section 107(5)(B) or (C) [*42 USCS § 1973ff-6(5)(B) or (C)*], as soon as the official list of candidates in the general election is complete.

42 U.S.C. § 1973ff-3. Recommendations to the States to maximize access to the polls by absent uniformed services voters and overseas voters

To afford maximum access to the polls by absent uniformed services voters and overseas voters, it is recommended that the States—

(1) use the official post card form (prescribed under section 101 [*42 USCS § 1973ff*]) for simultaneous voter registration application and absentee ballot application;

(2) adopt the suggested design for absentee ballot mailing envelopes prescribed under section 101 [*42 USCS § 1973ff*];

(3) waive registration requirements for absent uniformed services voters and overseas voters who, by reason of service or residence, do not have an opportunity to register;

(4) if an application other than an official post card form (prescribed under section 101 [*42 USCS § 1973ff*]) is required for absentee registration, provide that registration forms be sent with the absentee ballot and may be returned with it;

(5) expedite processing of balloting materials with respect to absent uniformed services voters and overseas voters;

(6) permit any oath required for a document under this title [*42 USCS §§ 1973ff* et seq.] to be administered by a commissioned officer of the Armed Forces or any official authorized to administer oaths under Federal law or the law of the State or other place where the oath is administered;

(7) assure that absentee ballots are mailed to absent uniformed services voters and overseas voters at the earliest opportunity;

(8) assist the Presidential designee in compiling statistical and other information relating to this title [*42 USCS §§ 1973ff* et seq.]; and

(9) provide late registration procedures for persons recently separated from the Armed Forces.

§ 1973ff-4. Enforcement

The Attorney General may bring a civil action in an appropriate district court for such declaratory or injunctive relief as may be necessary to carry out this title [*42 USCS §§ 1973ff* et seq.].

§ 1973ff-5. Effect on certain other laws

The exercise of any right under this title [*42 USCS § § 1973ff* et seq.] shall not affect, for purposes of any Federal, State, or local tax, the residence or domicile of a person exercising such right.

§ 1973ff-6. Definitions

As used in this title [*42 USCS § § 1973ff* et seq.], the term—

(1) "absent uniformed services voter" means—

    (A) a member of a uniformed service on active duty who, by reason of such active duty, is absent from the place of residence where the member is otherwise qualified to vote;

    (B) a member of the merchant marine who, by reason of service in the merchant marine, is absent from the place of residence where the member is otherwise qualified to vote; and

    (C) a spouse or dependent of a member referred to in subparagraph (A) or (B) who, by reason of the active duty or service of the member, is absent from the place of residence where the spouse or dependent is otherwise qualified to vote;

(2) "balloting materials" means official post card forms (prescribed under section 101 [*42 USCS § 1973ff*]), Federal write-in absentee ballots (prescribed under section 103 [*42 USCS § 1973ff-2*]), and any State balloting materials that, as determined by the Presidential designee, are essential to the carrying out of this title [*42 USCS § § 1973ff* et seq.];

(3) "Federal office" means the office of President or Vice President, or of Senator or Representative in, or Delegate or Resident Commissioner to, the Congress;

(4) "member of the merchant marine" means an individual (other than a member of a uniformed service or an individual employed, enrolled, or maintained on the Great Lakes or the inland waterways)—

    (A) employed as an officer or crew member of a vessel documented under the laws of the United States, or a vessel owned by the United States, or a vessel of foreign-flag registry under charter to or control of the United States; or

    (B) enrolled with the United States for employment or training for employment, or maintained by the United States for emergency relief service, as an officer or crew member of any such vessel;

(5) "overseas voter" means—

    (A) an absent uniformed services voter who, by reason of active duty or service is absent from the United States on the date of the election involved;

    (B) a person who resides outside the United States and is qualified to vote in the last place in which the person was domiciled before leaving the United States; or

    (C) a person who resides outside the United States and (but for such residence) would be qualified to vote in the last place in which the person was domiciled before leaving the United States.

(6) "State" means a State of the United States, the District of Columbia, the Commonwealth of Puerto Rico, Guam, the Virgin Islands, and American Samoa;

(7) "uniformed services" means the Army, Navy, Air Force, Marine Corps, and Coast Guard, the commissioned corps of the Public Health Service, and the commissioned corps of the National Oceanic and Atmospheric Administration; and

(8) "United States," where used in the territorial sense, means the several States, the District of Columbia, the Commonwealth of Puerto Rico, Guam, the Virgin Islands, and American Samoa.

National Voter Registration Act ("Motor Voter Act")

§ 1973gg. Findings and purposes

(a) **Findings.** The Congress finds that—

    (1) the right of citizens of the United States to vote is a fundamental right;

    (2) it is the duty of the Federal, State, and local governments to promote the exercise of that right; and

    (3) discriminatory and unfair registration laws and procedures can have a direct and damaging effect on voter participation in elections for Federal office and disproportionately harm voter participation by various groups, including racial minorities.

(b) **Purposes.** The purposes of this Act are—

    (1) to establish procedures that will increase the number of eligible citizens who register to vote in elections for Federal office;

    (2) to make it possible for Federal, State, and local governments to implement this Act in a manner that enhances the participation of eligible citizens as voters in elections for Federal office;

    (3) to protect the integrity of the electoral process; and

(4) to ensure that accurate and current voter registration rolls are maintained.

§ 1973gg-1. Definitions

As used in this Act—

(1) the term "election" has the meaning stated in section 301(1) of the Federal Election Campaign Act of 1971 (*2 U.S.C. 431*(1));

(2) the term "Federal office" has the meaning stated in section 301(3) of the Federal Election Campaign Act of 1971 (*2 U.S.C. 431*(3));

(3) the term "motor vehicle driver's license" includes any personal identification document issued by a State motor vehicle authority;

(4) the term "State" means a State of the United States and the District of Columbia; and

(5) the term "voter registration agency" means an office designated under section 7(a)(1) [*42 USCS § 1973gg-5*(a)(1)] to perform voter registration activities.

42 U.S.C. § 1973gg-2. National procedures for voter registration for elections for federal office

(a) **In general.** Except as provided in subsection (b), notwithstanding any other Federal or State law, in addition to any other method of voter registration provided for under State law, each State shall establish procedures to register to vote in elections for Federal office—

(1) by application made simultaneously with an application for a motor vehicle driver's license pursuant to section 5 [*42 USCS § 1973gg-3*];

(2) by mail application pursuant to section 6 [*42 USCS § 1973gg-4*]; and

(3) by application in person—

(A) at the appropriate registration site designated with respect to the residence of the applicant in accordance with State law; and

(B) at a Federal, State, or nongovernmental office designated under section 7 [*42 USCS § 1973gg-5*].

(b) **Nonapplicability to certain States.** This Act does not apply to a State described in either or both of the following paragraphs:

(1) A State in which, under law that is in effect continuously on and after August 1, 1994, there is no voter registration requirement for any voter in the State with respect to an election for Federal office.

(2) A State in which under law that is in effect continuously on and after August 1, 1994, or that was enacted on or prior to August 1, 1994, and by its terms is to come into effect upon the enactment of this Act [enacted May 20, 1993], so long as that law remains in effect, all voters in the State may register to vote at the polling place at the time of voting in a general election for Federal office.

42 U.S.C. § 1973gg-3. Simultaneous application for voter registration and application for motor vehicle driver's license

(a) **In general.**

(1) Each State motor vehicle driver's license application (including any renewal application) submitted to the appropriate State motor vehicle authority under State law shall serve as an application for voter registration with respect to elections for Federal office unless the applicant fails to sign the voter registration application.

(2) An application for voter registration submitted under paragraph (1) shall be considered as updating any previous voter registration by the applicant.

(b) **Limitation on use of information.** No information relating to the failure of an applicant for a State motor vehicle driver's license to sign a voter registration application may be used for any purpose other than voter registration.

(c) **Forms and procedures.**

(1) Each State shall include a voter registration application form for elections for Federal office as part of an application for a State motor vehicle driver's license.

(2) The voter registration application portion of an application for a State motor vehicle driver's license—

(A) may not require any information that duplicates information required in the driver's license portion of the form (other than a second signature or other information necessary under subparagraph (C));

(B) may require only the minimum amount of information necessary to—

(i) prevent duplicate voter registrations; and

(ii) enable State election officials to assess the eligibility of the applicant and to administer voter registration and other parts of the election process;

(C) shall include a statement that—

(i) states each eligibility requirement (including citizenship);

(ii) contains an attestation that the applicant meets each such requirement; and

(iii) requires the signature of the applicant, under penalty of perjury;

(D) shall include, in print that is identical to that used in the attestation portion of the application—

(i) the information required in section 8(a)(5)(A) and (B) [42 USCS § 1973gg-6(a)(5)(A), (B)];

(ii) a statement that, if an applicant declines to register to vote, the fact that the applicant has declined to register will remain confidential and will be used only for voter registration purposes; and

(iii) a statement that if an applicant does register to vote, the office at which the applicant submits a voter registration application will remain confidential and will be used only for voter registration purposes; and

(E) shall be made available (as submitted by the applicant, or in machine readable or other format) to the appropriate State election official as provided by State law.

(d) **Change of address.** Any change of address form submitted in accordance with State law for purposes of a State motor vehicle driver's license shall serve as notification of change of address for voter registration with respect to elections for Federal office for the registrant involved unless the registrant states on the form that the change of address is not for voter registration purposes.

(e) **Transmittal deadline.**

(1) Subject to paragraph (2), a completed voter registration portion of an application for a State motor vehicle driver's license accepted at a State motor vehicle authority shall be transmitted to the appropriate State election official not later than 10 days after the acceptance.

(2) If a registration application is accepted within 5 days before the last day for registration to vote in an election, the application shall be transmitted to the appropriate State election official not later than 5 days after the date of acceptance.

§ 1973gg-4. Mail registration

(a) **Form.**

(1) Each State shall accept and use the mail voter registration application form prescribed by the Federal Election Commission

pursuant to section 9(a)(2) [*42 USCS § 1973gg-7(a)(2)*] for the registration of voters in elections for Federal office.

   (2) In addition to accepting and using the form described in paragraph (1), a State may develop and use a mail voter registration form that meets all of the criteria stated in section 9(b) [*42 USCS § 1973gg-7(b)*] for the registration of voters in elections for Federal office.

   (3) A form described in paragraph (1) or (2) shall be accepted and used for notification of a registrant's change of address.

(b) **Availability of forms.** The chief State election official of a State shall make the forms described in subsection (a) available for distribution through governmental and private entities, with particular emphasis on making them available for organized voter registration programs.

(c) **First-time voters.**

   (1) Subject to paragraph (2), a State may by law require a person to vote in person if—

     (A) the person was registered to vote in a jurisdiction by mail; and

     (B) the person has not previously voted in that jurisdiction.

   (2) Paragraph (1) does not apply in the case of a person—

     (A) who is entitled to vote by absentee ballot under the Uniformed and Overseas Citizens Absentee Voting Act (*42 U.S.C. 1973ff-1 et seq.*);

     (B) who is provided the right to vote otherwise than in person under section 3(b)(2)(B)(ii) of the Voting Accessibility for the Elderly and Handicapped Act (*42 U.S.C. 1973ee-1*(b)(2)(B)(ii)); or

     (C) who is entitled to vote otherwise than in person under any other Federal law.

(d) **Undelivered notices.** If a notice of the disposition of a mail voter registration application under section 8(a)(2) [*42 USCS § 1973gg-6(a)(2)*] is sent by nonforwardable mail and is returned undelivered, the registrar may proceed in accordance with section 8(d) [*42 USCS § 1973gg-6(d)*].

42 U.S.C. § 1973gg-5. Voter registration agencies

(a) **Designation.**

   (1) Each State shall designate agencies for the registration of voters in elections for Federal office.

   (2) Each State shall designate as voter registration agencies—

     (A) all offices in the State that provide public assistance; and

     (B) all offices in the State that provide State-funded programs primarily engaged in providing services to persons with disabilities.

(3) (A) In addition to voter registration agencies designated under paragraph (2), each State shall designate other offices within the State as voter registration agencies.

  (B) Voter registration agencies designated under subparagraph (A) may include—

  (i) State or local government offices such as public libraries, public schools, offices of city and county clerks (including marriage license bureaus), fishing and hunting license bureaus, government revenue offices, unemployment compensation offices, and offices not described in paragraph (2)(B) that provide services to persons with disabilities; and

  (ii) Federal and nongovernmental offices, with the agreement of such offices.

(4) (A) At each voter registration agency, the following services shall be made available:

  (i) Distribution of mail voter registration application forms in accordance with paragraph (6).

  (ii) Assistance to applicants in completing voter registration application forms, unless the applicant refuses such assistance.

  (iii) Acceptance of completed voter registration application forms for transmittal to the appropriate State election official.

  (B) If a voter registration agency designated under paragraph (2)(B) provides services to a person with a disability at the person's home, the agency shall provide the services described in subparagraph (A) at the person's home.

(5) A person who provides service described in paragraph (4) shall not—

  (A) seek to influence an applicant's political preference or party registration;

  (B) display any such political preference or party allegiance;

  (C) make any statement to an applicant or take any action the purpose or effect of which is to discourage the applicant from registering to vote; or

  (D) make any statement to an applicant or take any action the purpose or effect of which is to lead the applicant to believe that a decision to register or not to register has any bearing on the availability of services or benefits.

(6) A voter registration agency that is an office that provides service or assistance in addition to conducting voter registration shall—

(A) distribute with each application for such service or assistance, and with each recertification, renewal, or change of address form relating to such service or assistance—

(i) the mail voter registration application form described in section 9(a)(2) [42 USCS § 1973gg-7(a)(2)], including a statement that—

(I) specifies each eligibility requirement (including citizenship);

(II) contains an attestation that the applicant meets each such requirement; and

(III) requires the signature of the applicant, under penalty of perjury; or

(ii) the office's own form if it is equivalent to the form described in section 9(a)(2) [42 USCS § 1973gg-7(a)(2)], unless the applicant, in writing, declines to register to vote;

(B) provide a form that includes—

(i) the question, "If you are not registered to vote where you live now, would you like to apply to register to vote here today?";

(ii) if the agency provides public assistance, the statement, "Applying to register or declining to register to vote will not affect the amount of assistance that you will be provided by this agency.";

(iii) boxes for the applicant to check to indicate whether the applicant would like to register or declines to register to vote (failure to check either box being deemed to constitute a declination to register for purposes of subparagraph (C)), together with the statement (in close proximity to the boxes and in prominent type), "IF YOU DO NOT CHECK EITHER BOX, YOU WILL BE CONSIDERED TO HAVE DECIDED NOT TO REGISTER TO VOTE AT THIS TIME";

(iv) the statement, "If you would like help in filling out the voter registration application form, we will help you. The decision whether to seek or accept help is yours. You may fill out the application form in private."; and

       (v) the statement "If you believe that someone has interfered with your right to register or to decline to register to vote, your right to privacy in deciding whether to register or in applying to register to vote, or your right to choose your own political party or other political preference, you may file a complaint with _____," the blank being filled by the name, address, and telephone number of the appropriate official to whom such a complaint should be addressed; and

    (C) provide to each applicant who does not decline to register to vote the same degree of assistance with regard to the completion of the registration application form as is provided by the office with regard to the completion of its own forms, unless the applicant refuses such assistance.

  (7) No information relating to a declination to register to vote in connection with an application made at an office described in paragraph (6) may be used for any purpose other than voter registration.

(b) **Federal Government and private sector cooperation.** All departments, agencies, and other entitles of the executive branch of the Federal Government shall, to the greatest extent practicable, cooperate with the States in carrying out subsection (a), and all nongovernmental entities are encouraged to do so.

(c) **Armed Forces recruitment offices.**

  (1) Each State and the Secretary of Defense shall jointly develop and implement procedures for persons to apply to register to vote at recruitment offices of the Armed Forces of the United States.

  (2) A recruitment office of the Armed Forces of the United States shall be considered to be a voter registration agency designated under subsection (a)(2) for all purposes of this Act.

(d) **Transmittal deadline.**

  (1) Subject to paragraph (2), a completed registration application accepted at a voter registration agency shall be transmitted to the appropriate State election official not later than 10 days after the date of acceptance.

  (2) If a registration application is accepted within 5 days before the last day for registration to vote in an election, the application shall be transmitted to the appropriate State election official not later than 5 days after the date of acceptance.

42 U.S.C. § 1973gg-6. Requirements with respect to administration of voter registration

(a) **In general.** In the administration of voter registration for elections for Federal office, each State shall—

    (1) insure that any eligible applicant is registered to vote in an election—

        (A) in the case of registration with a motor vehicle application under section 5 [42 USCS § 1973gg-3], if the valid voter registration form of the applicant is submitted to the appropriate State motor vehicle authority not later than the lesser of 30 days, or the period provided by State law, before the date of the election;

        (B) in the case of registration by mail under section 6 [42 USCS § 1973gg-4], if the valid voter registration form of the applicant is postmarked not later than the lesser of 30 days, or the period provided by State law, before the date of the election;

        (C) in the case of registration at a voter registration agency, if the valid voter registration form of the applicant is accepted at the voter registration agency not later than the lesser of 30 days, or the period provided by State law, before the date of the election; and

        (D) in any other case, if the valid voter registration form of the applicant is received by the appropriate State election official not later than the lesser of 30 days, or the period provided by State law, before the date of the election;

    (2) require the appropriate State election official to send notice to applicant of the disposition of the application;

    (3) provide that the name of a registrant may not be removed from the official list of eligible voters except—

        (A) at the request of the registrant;

        (B) as provided by State law, by reason of criminal conviction or mental incapacity; or

        (C) as provided under paragraph (4);

    (4) conduct a general program that makes a reasonable effort to remove the names of ineligible voters from the official lists of eligible voters by reason of—

        (A) the death of the registrant; or

        (B) a change in the residence of the registrant, in accordance with subsections (b), (c), and (d);

    (5) inform applicants under sections 5, 6, and 7 [42 USCS § § 1973gg-3, 1973gg-4, 1973gg-5] of—

(A) voter eligibility requirements; and

(B) penalties provided by law for submission of a false voter registration application; and

(6) ensure that the identity of the voter registration agency through which any particular voter is registered is not disclosed to the public.

(b) **Confirmation of voter registration.** Any State program or activity to protect the integrity of the electoral process by ensuring the maintenance of an accurate and current voter registration roll for elections for Federal office—

(1) shall be uniform, nondiscriminatory, and in compliance with the Voting Rights Act of 1965 (*42 U.S.C. 1973* et seq.); and

(2) shall not result in the removal of the name of any person from the official list of voters registered to vote in an election for Federal office by reason of the person's failure to vote.

(c) **Voter removal programs.**

(1) A State may meet the requirement of subsection (a)(4) by establishing a program under which—

(A) change-of-address information supplied by the Postal Service through its licensees is used to identify registrants whose addresses may have changed; and

(B) if it appears from information provided by the Postal Service that—

(i) a registrant has moved to a different residence address in the same registrar's jurisdiction in which the registrant is currently registered, the registrar changes the registration records to show the new address and sends the registrant a notice of the change by forwardable mail and a postage prepaid pre-addressed return form by which the registrant may verify or correct the address information; or

(ii) the registrant has moved to a different residence address not in the same registrar's jurisdiction, the registrar uses the notice procedure described in subsection (d)(2) to confirm the change of address.

(2) (A) A State shall complete, not later than 90 days prior to the date of a primary or general election for Federal office, any program the purpose of which is to systematically remove the names of ineligible voters from the official lists of eligible voters.

(B) Subparagraph (A) shall not be construed to preclude—

     (i) the removal of names from official lists of voters on a basis described in paragraph (3)(A) or (B) or (4)(A) of subsection (a); or

     (ii) correction of registration records pursuant to this Act.

(d) **Removal of names from voting rolls.**

   (1) A State shall not remove the name of a registrant from the official list of eligible voters in elections for Federal office on the ground that the registrant has changed residence unless the registrant—

     (A) confirms in writing that the registrant has changed residence to a place outside the registrar's jurisdiction in which the registrant is registered; or

     (B) (i) has failed to respond to a notice described in paragraph (2); and

         (ii) has not voted or appeared to vote (and, if necessary, correct the registrar's record of the registrant's address) in an election during the period beginning on the date of the notice and ending on the day after the date of the second general election for Federal office that occurs after the date of the notice.

   (2) A notice is described in this paragraph if it is a postage prepaid and pre-addressed return card, sent by forwardable mail, on which the registrant may state his or her current address, together with a notice to the following effect:

     (A) If the registrant did not change his or her residence, or changed residence but remained in the registrar's jurisdiction, the registrant should return the card not later than the time provided for mail registration under subsection (a)(1)(B). If the card is not returned, affirmation or confirmation of the registrant's address may be required before the registrant is permitted to vote in a Federal election during the period beginning on the date of the notice and ending on the day after the date of the second general election for Federal office that occurs after the date of the notice, and if the registrant does not vote in an election during that period the registrant's name will be removed from the list of eligible voters.

     (B) If the registrant has changed residence to a place outside the registrar's jurisdiction in which the registrant is registered, information concerning how the registrant can continue to be eligible to vote.

(3) A voting registrar shall correct an official list of eligible voters in elections for Federal office in accordance with change of residence information obtained in conformance with this subsection.

(e) **Procedure for voting following failure to return card.**

    (1) A registrant who has moved from an address in the area covered by a polling place to an address in the same area shall, notwithstanding failure to notify the registrar of the change of address prior to the date of an election, be permitted to vote at that polling place upon oral or written affirmation by the registrant of change of address before an election official at that polling place.

    (2) (A) A registrant who has moved from an address in the area covered by one polling place to an address in an area covered by a second polling place within the same registrar's jurisdiction and the same congressional district and who has failed to notify the registrar of the change address prior to the date of an election, at the option of the registrant—

        (i) shall be permitted to correct the voting records and vote at the registrant's former polling place, upon oral or written affirmation by the registrant of the new address before an election official at that polling place; or

        (ii) (I) shall be permitted to correct the voting records and vote at a central location within the same registrar's jurisdiction designated by the registrar where a list of eligible voters is maintained, upon written affirmation by the registrant of the new address on a standard form provided by the registrar at the central location; or

        (II) shall be permitted to correct the voting records for purposes of voting in future elections at the appropriate polling place for the current address and, if permitted by State law, shall be permitted to vote in the present election, upon confirmation by the registrant of the new address by such means as are required by law.

    (B) If State law permits the registrant to vote in the current election upon oral or written affirmation by the registrant of the new address at a polling place described in subparagraph (A)(i) or (A)(ii)(II), voting at the other locations described in subparagraph (A) need not be provided as options.

    (3) If the registration records indicate that a registrant has moved from an address in the area covered by a polling place, the registrant shall upon oral or written affirmation by the registrant before an election official at that polling place that the registrant continues to reside at the address previously made known to the registrar, be permitted to vote at that polling place.

(f) **Change of voting address within a jurisdiction.** In the case of a change of address, for voting purposes, of a registrant to another address within the same registrar's jurisdiction, the registrar shall correct the voting registration list accordingly, and the registrant's name may not be removed from the official list of eligible voters by reason of such a change of address except as provided in subsection (d).

(g) **Conviction in Federal court.**

    (1) On the conviction of a person of a felony in a district court of the United States, the United States attorney shall give written notice of the conviction to the chief State election official designated under section 10 of the State of the person's residence.

    (2) A notice given pursuant to paragraph (1) shall include—

        (A) the name of the offender;

        (B) the offender's age and residence address;

        (C) the date of entry of the judgment;

        (D) a description of the offenses of which the offender was convicted; and

        (E) the sentence imposed by the court.

    (3) On request of the chief State election official of a State or other State official with responsibility for determining the effect that a conviction may have on an offender's qualification to vote, the United States attorney shall provide such additional information as the United States may have concerning the offender and the offense of which offender was convicted.

    (4) If a conviction of which notice was given pursuant to paragraph (1) is overturned, the United States attorney shall give the official to whom the notice was given written notice of the vacation of the judgment.

    (5) The chief State election official shall notify the voter registration officials of the local jurisdiction in which an offender resides of the information received under this subsection.

(h) [Omitted]

(i) **Public disclosure of voter registration activities.**

(1) Each State shall maintain for at least 2 years and shall make available for public inspection and, where available, photocopying at a reasonable cost, all records concerning the implementation of programs and activities conducted for the purpose of ensuring the accuracy and currency of official lists of eligible voters, except to the extent that such records relate to a declination to register to vote or to the identity of a voter registration agency through which any particular voter is registered.

(2) The records maintained pursuant to paragraph (1) shall include lists of the names and addresses of all persons to whom notices described in subsection (d)(2) are sent, and information concerning whether or not each such person has responded to the notice as of the date that inspection of the records is made.

(j) **"Registrar's jurisdiction" defined.** For the purposes of this section, the term "registrar's jurisdiction" means—

(1) an incorporated city, town, borough, or other form of municipality;

(2) if voter registration is maintained by a county, parish, or other unit of government that governs a larger geographic area than a municipality, the geographic area governed by that unit of government; or

(3) if voter registration is maintained on a consolidated basis for more than one municipality or other unit of government by an office that performs all of the functions of a voting registrar, the geographic area of the consolidated municipalities or other geographic units.

U.S.C. § 1973gg-7. Federal coordination and regulations

(a) **In general.** The Federal Election Commission—

(1) in consultation with the chief election officers of the States, shall prescribe such regulations as are necessary to carry out paragraphs (2) and (3);

(2) in consultation with the chief election officers of the States, shall develop a mail voter registration application form for elections for Federal office;

(3) not later than June 30 of each odd-numbered year, shall submit to the Congress a report assessing the impact of this Act on the administration of elections for Federal office during the preceding 2-year period and including recommendations or improvements in Federal and State procedures, forms, and other matters affected by this Act; and

(4) shall provide information to the States with respect to the responsibilities of the States under this Act.

(b) **Contents of mail voter registration form.** The mail voter registration form developed under subsection (a)(2)—

(1) may require only such identifying information (including the signature of the applicant) and other information (including data relating to previous registration by the applicant), as is necessary to enable the appropriate State election official to assess the eligibility of the applicant and to administer voter registration and other parts of the election process;

(2) shall include a statement that—

(A) specifies each eligibility requirement (including citizenship);

(B) contains an attestation that the applicant meets each such requirement; and

(C) requires the signature of the applicant, under penalty of perjury;

(3) may not include any requirement for notarization or other formal authentication; and

(4) shall include, in print that is identical to that used in the attestation portion of the application—

(i) the information required in section 8(a)(5)(A) and (B) [42 USCS § 1973gg-6(a)(5)(A), (B)];

(ii) a statement that, if an applicant declines to register to vote, the fact that the applicant has declined to register will remain confidential and will be used only for voter registration purposes; and

(iii) a statement that if an applicant does register to vote, the office at which the applicant submits a voter registration application will remain confidential and will be used only for voter registration purposes.

§ 1973gg-8. Designation of chief State election official

Each State shall designate a State officer or employee as the chief State election official to be responsible for coordination of State responsibilities under this Act.

§ 1973gg-9. Civil enforcement and private right of action

(a) **Attorney General.** The Attorney General may bring a civil action in an appropriate district court for such declaratory or injunctive relief as is necessary to carry out this Act.

(b) **Private right of action.**

   (1) A person who is aggrieved by a violation of this Act may provide written notice of the violation to the chief election official of the State involved.

   (2) If the violation is not corrected within 90 days after receipt of a notice under paragraph (1), or within 20 days after receipt of the notice if the violation occurred within 120 days before the date of an election for Federal office, the aggrieved person may bring a civil action in an appropriate district court for declaratory or injunctive relief with respect to the violation.

   (3) If the violation occurred within 30 days before the date of an election for Federal office, the aggrieved person need not provide notice to the chief election official of the State under paragraph (1) before bringing a civil action under paragraph (2).

(c) **Attorney's fees.** In a civil action under this section the court may allow the prevailing party (other than the United States) reasonable attorney fees, including litigation expenses, and costs.

(d) **Relation to other laws.**

   (1) The rights and remedies established by this section are in addition to all other rights and remedies provided by law, and neither the rights and remedies established by this section nor any other provision of this Act shall supersede, restrict, or limit the application of the Voting Rights Act of 1965 (42 *U.S.C. 1973* et seq.).

   (2) Nothing in this Act authorizes or requires conduct that is prohibited by the Voting Rights Act of 1965 (42 *U.S.C. 1973* et seq.).

42 U.S.C. § 1973gg-10. Criminal penalties

A person, including an election official, who in any election for Federal office—

   (1) knowingly and willfully intimidates, threatens, or coerces, or attempts to intimidate, threaten, or coerce, any person for—

      (A) registering to vote, or voting, or attempting to register or vote;

      (B) urging or aiding any person to register to vote, to vote, or to attempt to register or vote; or

      (C) exercising any right under this Act; or

   (2) knowingly and willfully deprives, defrauds, or attempts to deprive or defraud the residents of a State of a fair and impartially conducted election process, by—

(A) the procurement or submission of voter registration applications that are known by the person to be materially false, fictitious, or fraudulent under the laws of the State in which the election is held; or

(B) the procurement, casting, or tabulation of ballots that are known by the person to be materially false, fictitious or fraudulent under the laws of the State in which the election is held, shall be fined in accordance with title 18, United States Code (which fines shall be paid into the general fund of the Treasury, miscellaneous receipts (pursuant to section 3302 of title 31, United States Code), notwithstanding any other law), or imprisoned not more than 5 years, or both.

Civil Rights Act

42 U.S.C. § 1983. Civil action for deprivation of rights

Every person who, under color of any statute, ordinance, regulation, custom, or usage, of any State or Territory or the District of Columbia, subjects, or causes to be subjected, any citizen of the United States or other person within the jurisdiction thereof to the deprivation of any rights, privileges, or immunities secured by the Constitution and laws, shall be liable to the party injured in an action at law, suit in equity, or other proper proceeding for redress, except that in any action brought against a judicial officer for an act or omission taken in such officer's judicial capacity, injunctive relief shall not be granted unless a declaratory decree was violated or declaratory relief was unavailable. For the purposes of this section, any Act of Congress applicable exclusively to the District of Columbia shall be considered to be a statute of the District of Columbia.

Crimes against One's Civil Rights

42 U.S.C. § 1988. Proceedings in vindication of civil rights

(a) **Applicability of statutory and common law.** The jurisdiction in civil and criminal matters conferred on the district and circuit courts [district courts] by the provisions of this Title, and of Title "CIVIL RIGHTS," and of Title "CRIMES," for the protection of all persons in the United States in their civil rights, and for their vindication, shall be exercised and enforced in conformity with the laws of the United States, so far as such laws are suitable to carry the same into effect; but in all cases where they are not adapted to the object, or are deficient in the provisions necessary to furnish suitable remedies and punish offenses against law, the common law, as modified and changed by the constitution and statutes of the State wherein the court having jurisdiction of such civil or criminal cause is held, so far as the same is not inconsistent with the Constitution and laws of the United States, shall be extended to and govern the said courts in the trial and disposition of the cause, and, if it is of a criminal nature, in the infliction of punishment on the party found guilty.

(b) **Attorney's fees.** In any action or proceeding to enforce a provision of sections 1977, 1977A, 1978, 1979, 1980, and 1981 of the Revised Statutes [*42 USCS § § 1981*-1983, 1985, 1986], title IX of Public Law 92-318 [*20 USCS § § 1681* et seq.], the Religious Freedom Restoration Act of 1993, the Religious Land Use and Institutionalized Persons Act of 2000, title VI of the Civil Rights Act of 1964 [*42 USCS § § 2000d* et seq.], or section 40302 of the Violence Against Women Act of 1994, the court, in its discretion, may allow the prevailing party, other than the United States, a reasonable attorney's fee as part of the costs, except that in any action brought against a judicial officer for an act or omission taken in such officer's judicial capacity such officer shall not be held liable for any costs, including attorney's fees, unless such action was clearly in excess of such officer's jurisdiction.

(c) **Expert fees.** In awarding an attorney's fee under subsection (b) in any action or proceeding to enforce a provision of sections 1977 or 1977A of the Revised Statutes [*42 USCS § § 1981* or 1981a], the court, in its discretion, may include expert fees as part of the attorney's fee.

Americans with Disabilities Act (ADA)

42 U.S.C. § 12133

The remedies, procedures, and rights set forth in section 505 of the Rehabilitation Act of 1973 (*29 U.S.C. 794a*) shall be the remedies, procedures, and rights this title provides to any person alleging discrimination on the basis of disability in violation of section 202 [*42 USCS § 12132*].

42 U.S.C. § 12134

(a) **In general.** Not later than 1 year after the date of enactment of this Act [enacted July 26, 1990], the Attorney General shall promulgate regulations in an accessible format that implement this subtitle. Such regulations shall not include any matter within the scope of the authority of the Secretary of Transportation under section 223, 229, or 244 [*42 USCS § 12143, 12149,* or 12164].

(b) **Relationship to other regulations.** Except for "program accessibility, existing facilities," and "communications," regulations under subsection (a) shall be consistent with this Act and with the coordination regulations under part 41 of title 28, Code of Federal Regulations (as promulgated by the Department of Health, Education, and Welfare on January 13, 1978), applicable to recipients of Federal financial assistance under section 504 of the Rehabilitation Act of 1973 (*29 U.S.C. 794*). With respect to "program accessibility, existing facilities," and "communications," such regulations shall be consistent with regulations and analysis as in part 39 of title 28 of the Code of Federal Regulations, applicable to federally conducted activities under such section 504.

(c) **Standards.** Regulations under subsection (a) shall include standards applicable to facilities and vehicles covered by this subtitle, other than facilities, stations, rail passenger cars, and vehicles covered by subtitle B. Such standards shall be consistent with the minimum guidelines and requirements issued by the Architectural and Transportation Barriers Compliance Board in accordance with section 504(a) of this Act [*42 USCS § 12204*(a)].

Section 7 of the Privacy Act of 1974 (uncodified)

Disclosure of Social Security number P.L. 93-579, § 7, 88 Stat. 1909

(a) (1) It shall be unlawful for any Federal, State or local government agency to deny to any individual any right, benefit, or privilege provided by law because of such individual's refusal to disclose his social security account number.

   (2) the provisions of paragraph (1) of this subsection shall not apply with respect to—

   (A) any disclosure which is required by Federal statute, or

   (B) the disclosure of a social security number to any Federal, State, or local agency maintaining a system of records in existence and operating before January 1, 1975, if such disclosure was required under statute or regulation adopted prior to such date to verify the identity of an individual.

(b) Any Federal, State, or local government agency which requests an individual to disclose his social security account number shall inform that individual whether that disclosure is mandatory or voluntary, by what statutory or other authority such number is solicited, and what uses will be made of it.

Appendix C. Code of Federal Regulations

28 CFR 35.130

(a) No qualified individual with a disability shall, on the basis of disability, be excluded from participation in or be denied the benefits of the services, programs, or activities of a public entity, or be subjected to discrimination by any public entity.

(b) (1) A public entity, in providing any aid, benefit, or service, may not, directly or through contractual, licensing, or other arrangements, on the basis of disability—

    (i) Deny a qualified individual with a disability the opportunity to participate in or benefit from the aid, benefit, or service;

    (ii) Afford a qualified individual with a disability an opportunity to participate in or benefit from the aid, benefit, or service that is not equal to that afforded others;

    (iii) Provide a qualified individual with a disability with an aid, benefit, or service that is not as effective in affording equal opportunity to obtain the same result, to gain the same benefit, or to reach the same level of achievement as that provided to others;

    (iv) Provide different or separate aids, benefits, or services to individuals with disabilities or to any class of individuals with disabilities than is provided to others unless such action is necessary to provide qualified individuals with disabilities with aids, benefits, or services that are as effective as those provided to others;

    (v) Aid or perpetuate discrimination against a qualified individual with a disability by providing significant assistance to an agency, organization, or person that discriminates on the basis of disability in providing any aid, benefit, or service to beneficiaries of the public entity's program;

    (vi) Deny a qualified individual with a disability the opportunity to participate as a member of planning or advisory boards;

    (vii) Otherwise limit a qualified individual with a disability in the enjoyment of any right, privilege, advantage, or opportunity enjoyed by others receiving the aid, benefit, or service.

(2) A public entity may not deny a qualified individual with a disability the opportunity to participate in services, programs, or activities that are not separate or different, despite the existence of permissibly separate or different programs or activities.

(3) A public entity may not, directly or through contractual or other arrangements, utilize criteria or methods of administration:

    (i) That have the effect of subjecting qualified individuals with disabilities to discrimination on the basis of disability;

(ii) That have the purpose or effect of defeating or substantially impairing accomplishment of the objectives of the public entity's program with respect to individuals with disabilities; or

(iii) That perpetuate the discrimination of another public entity if both public entities are subject to common administrative control or are agencies of the same State.

(4) A public entity may not, in determining the site or location of a facility, make selections —

(i) That have the effect of excluding individuals with disabilities from, denying them the benefits of, or otherwise subjecting them to discrimination; or

(ii) That have the purpose or effect of defeating or substantially impairing the accomplishment of the objectives of the service, program, or activity with respect to individuals with disabilities.

(5) A public entity, in the selection of procurement contractors, may not use criteria that subject qualified individuals with disabilities to discrimination on the basis of disability.

(6) A public entity may not administer a licensing or certification program in a manner that subjects qualified individuals with disabilities to discrimination on the basis of disability, nor may a public entity establish requirements for the programs or activities of licensees or certified entities that subject qualified individuals with disabilities to discrimination on the basis of disability. The programs or activities of entities that are licensed or certified by a public entity are not, themselves, covered by this part.

(7) A public entity shall make reasonable modifications in policies, practices, or procedures when the modifications are necessary to avoid discrimination on the basis of disability, unless the public entity can demonstrate that making the modifications would fundamentally alter the nature of the service, program, or activity.

(8) A public entity shall not impose or apply eligibility criteria that screen out or tend to screen out an individual with a disability or any class of individuals with disabilities from fully and equally enjoying any service, program, or activity, unless such criteria can be shown to be necessary for the provision of the service, program, or activity being offered.

(c) Nothing in this part prohibits a public entity from providing benefits, services, or advantages to individuals with disabilities, or to a particular class of individuals with disabilities beyond those required by this part.

(d) A public entity shall administer services, programs, and activities in the most integrated setting appropriate to the needs of qualified individuals with disabilities.

(e) (1) Nothing in this part shall be construed to require an individual with a disability to accept an accommodation, aid, service, opportunity, or benefit provided under the ADA or this part which such individual chooses not to accept.

(2) Nothing in the Act or this part authorizes the representative or guardian of an individual with a disability to decline food, water, medical treatment, or medical services for that individual.

(f) A public entity may not place a surcharge on a particular individual with a disability or any group of individuals with disabilities to cover the costs of measures, such as the provision of auxiliary aids or program accessibility, that are required to provide that individual or group with the nondiscriminatory treatment required by the Act or this part.

(g) A public entity shall not exclude or otherwise deny equal services, programs, or activities to an individual or entity because of the known disability of an individual with whom the individual or entity is known to have a relationship or association.

Notes

1. 2 U.S.C. §§1, 7.
2. *Bush* v. *Palm Beach County Canvassing Board*, 121 S. Ct. 471 (2000) (per curiam), and, *Bush* v. *Gore*, 121 S.Ct. 525, 533 (2000) (Rehnquist, C. J., concurring), suggest that this general rule may have one significant exception. As a matter of federal constitutional law, state law might sometimes trump state constitutional law. See *Bush* v. *Palm Beach County Canvassing Bd.*, 121 S.Ct. at 475 (remanding case to Florida Supreme Court because it was not clear to what extent "the Florida Supreme Court saw the Florida Constitution as circumscribing the legislature's authority under Art. II, § 1, cl. 2."); *Bush* v. *Gore*, 121 S.Ct. at 534 (Rehnquist, C. J., concurring) ("[T]here are a few exceptional cases in which the [federal] Constitution imposes a duty or confers a power on a particular branch of a State's government.").
3. 118 U.S. 356, 369-370 (1886) (emphasis added).
4. See, for example, *Harper* v. *Virginia Bd. of Elections*, 383 U.S. 663 (1966).
5. See, for example, *Nixon* v. *Herndon*, 273 U.S. 536 (1927).
6. See *City of Mobile* v. *Bolden*, 446 U.S. 55 (1980).

7. See *Western & S. Life Ins. Co. v. State Bd. of Equalization*, 451 U.S. 648, 667-68(1981).

8. 471 U.S. 222 (1985).

9. *Richardson v. Ramirez*, 418 U.S. 24 (1974).

10. 377 U.S. 533 (1964).

11. Id. at 578.

12. See *Kirkpatrick v. Preisler*, 394 U.S. 526 (1969) (no deviation from population equality among congressional districts may be considered de minimis, and all variances must be justified); *Karcher v. Daggett*, 462 U.S. 725 (1983) (where it can be demonstrated that challenged plan has higher population deviation than competing plan, deviations from equality must be shown to satisfy "some legitimate state objective"); *Wesberry v. Sanders,* 376 U.S. 1 (1964) (congressional districts must be as equal in population as practicable).

13. See *Mahan v. Howell*, 410 U.S. 315 (1973) (approving 16.4 percent total deviation in order to preserve political subdivision); *Gaffney v. Cummings*, 412 U.S. 755 (1973) (deviations of up to 7.8 percent in state legislative plan acceptable as result of effort to achieve "political fairness"); *White v. Regester*, 412 U.S. 755 (1973) (state house plan valid despite 9.9 percent total deviation).

14. 42 U.S.C. § 1973aa-1.

15. 405 U.S. 330 (1972). See also *Burg v. Caniffe*, 315 F. Supp. 380 (D. Mass. 1970), aff'd 405 U.S. 1034 (1972) (Massachusetts one-year residency requirement invalid); *Andrews v. Cody*, 327 F. Supp. 793 (D. N.C. 1971), aff'd 405 U.S. 1034 (1972) (North Carolina one-year residency requirement invalid); *Hadnott v. Amos*, 320 F. Supp. 107 (D. Ala. 1970), aff'd 401 U.S. 968 (1971) and also aff'd 405 U.S. 1035 (1972) (Alabama one-year state, 6-month county, and 3-month precinct residency requirement invalid).

16. See, e.g., *Burg v. Caniffe*, 315 F. Supp. at 380, *aff'd* 405 U.S. at 1034 (1972) (six-month Massachusetts town residency upheld), *Smith v. Climer,* 341 F. Supp. 123 (D. Ark. 1972) (Arkansas 30-day precinct residency requirement upheld).

17. 121 S.Ct. 525.

18. Id. at 530.

19. Id. (citing *Harper*, 383 U.S. at 665, and *Reynolds*, 377 U.S. at 555).

20. Id. at 531.

21. Id.

22. Id.

23. Id. at 532.

24. Id.

25. Id.

26. Id.

27. Id. (italics added).

28. Id.

29. Id. at 545 (Souter, J., dissenting).
30. *Greidinger v. Davis*, 988 F.2d 1344, 1352-55 (4th Cir. 1993).
31. Id. at 1354 n. 11.
32. 357 U.S. 449 (1958).
33. *Smith v. Allwright*, 321 U.S. 649 (1944). See also *Terry v. Adams*, 345 U.S 461 (1953) (private, all-white association whose unofficial endorsement was controlling in Democratic primary was subject to constitutional limitations because association played an "integral role" in the politics of county).
34. 479 U.S. 208 (1986).
35. Id. at 224.
36. *Storer v. Brown*, 415 U.S. 724, 730 (1974).
37. *Timmons v. Twin Cities Area New Party*, 520 U.S. 351, 358-59 (1997).
38. *Tashjian*, 479 U.S. 208.
39. *San Francisco County Cent. Democratic Comm. v. Eu*, 826 F.2d 814 (1987).
40. *California Democratic Party v. Jones*, 530 U.S. 567 (2000).
41. 384 U.S. 214 (1966).
42. Id. at 220 (italics added).
43. 838 F.2d 380 (9th Cir. 1988).
44. Id. at 385.
45. Id. at 387.
46. Id. at 385.
47. *CBS Inc. v. Smith*, 681 F. Supp. 794 (S.D. Fla. 1988) (150 foot no-polling zone); *NBC v. Cleland*, 697 F. Supp. 1204 (N.D. Ga. 1988) (250 foot zone); *NBC v. Colburg*, 699 F. Supp. 241 (D. Mont. 1988) (200 foot zone).
48. *Cleland*, 697 F. Supp. at 1215.
49. *Pell v. Pecunier*, 417 U.S. 817 (1974); *Saxbe v. Washington Post Co.*, 417 U.S. 843 (1974).
50. U.S. Const. Art. I, § 3. cl. 1.
51. See *Harper*, 383 U.S. 663.
52. 121 S. Ct. 1038 (2001) (quoting *Smiley v. Holm*, 285 U.S. 355, 366 (1932)).
53. *Roudebush v. Hartke*, 405 U.S. 15, 24-25 (1972) (authority to regulate recount of elections); *United States v. Gradwell*, 243 U.S. 476, 483 (1917) (full authority over federal election process from registration to certification of results).
54. In re *Coy*, 127 U.S. 731, 752 (1888) (authority to regulate conduct at any election coinciding with federal contest); Ex parte *Clarke*, 100 U.S. 399, 404 (1879) (authority to punish state election officers for violation of state duties vis-à-vis congressional elections).
55. U.S. Const. Art. I, §2, cl. 1 (House of Representatives); U.S. Const. Amend. XVII, § 1 (Senate).
56. *Foster v. Love*, 522 U.S. 67, 69 (1997) (internal quotation marks and citations omitted).
57. Id. at 72 n.2 (quoting *Smiley v. Holm*, 285 U.S. at 366).

58. Ex parte *Siebold*, 100 U.S. 371, 383-84 (1880).
59. 121 S.Ct. at 1037-38 (internal quotations and citations omitted).
60. See, for example, *ACORN* v. *Miller*, 129 F.3d 833 (6th Cir. 1997); *ACORN* v. *Edgar*, 56 F.3d 791 (7th Cir. 1995); *Voting Rights Coalition* v. *Wilson*, 60 F.3d 1411 (9th Cir. 1995).
61. *United States* v. *McCranie*, 169 F.3d 723, 727 (11th Cir. 1999).
62. See 42 U.S.C. § 1971(b).
63. 290 U.S. 534 (1934).
64. Id. at 545 (internal citation omitted); accord, *ACORN* v. *Miller*, 129 F.3d at 836 n.1 ("While Article I section 4 mentions only the election of Senators and Representatives, Congress has been granted authority to regulate presidential elections").
65. The one exception might be the selection of the District of Columbia's three electors. Even here, however, current federal criminal law dealing with election fraud applies to elections conducted in part to select "any candidate for the office of . . . Delegate from the District of Columbia." 42 U.S.C. § 1973i.
66. See, for example, *Harper*, 383 U.S. 663.
67. See *Katzenbach* v. *Morgan*, 384 U.S. 641 (1966). The Fifteenth Amendment, which targets racial discrimination in voting, contains a similar enforcement clause, to which the Supreme Court has given a similarly expansive reading. See *South Carolina* v. *Katzenbach*, 383 U.S. 301 (1966). So do the 13th, 19th, 23rd, 24th, and 26th Amendments.
68. See 42 U.S.C. § 1973l(e); 42 U.S.C. § 1988.
69. 521 U.S. 507 (1997).
70. 42 U.S.C. § 2000bb-1.
71. *City of Boerne*, 521 U.S. at 517.
72. Id. at 518, 520 (quoting *Fitzpatrick* v. *Bitzer*, 427 U.S. 445, 455 (1976)).
73. See, for example, *Board of Trustees* v. *Garrett*, 121 S.Ct. 955 (2001); *Kimel* v. *Florida Board of Regents*, 528 U.S. 62 (2000); *College Savings Bank* v. *Florida Prepaid Postsecondary Educ. Expense Bd.*, 527 U.S. 627 (1999).
74. *United States* v. *Morrison*, 529 U.S. 598 (2000).
75. 121 S.Ct. 955 (2001).
76. As the majority put it: "Our consideration is limited to the present circumstances, for the problem of equal protection in election processes generally presents many complexities." 121 S.Ct. at 532. The two dissenting justices made clear that *Bush v. Gore* would not extend so far: "It is true that the Equal Protection Clause does not forbid the use of a variety of voting mechanisms within a jurisdiction, even though different mechanisms will have different levels of effectiveness in recording voters' intentions; local variety can be justified by concerns about cost, the potential value of innovation, and so on." Id. at 545 (Souter, J., dissenting).
77. *United States* v. *Butler*, 297 U.S. 1, 66 (1936).
78. Id. at 65.

79. Its future robustness is somewhat less certain. Will a Supreme Court that has restricted Congress's powers under the Commerce Clause and the Fourteenth Amendment leave the sweeping scope of the Spending Clause untouched? This is currently an issue of substantial discussion among constitutional lawyers and the subject of much scholarly commentary. See, for example, Lynn A. Baker, *Conditional Federal Spending After Lopez*, 95 Colum. L. Rev. 1911 (1995).

80. 483 U.S. 203 (1987).

81. Id. at 207; see also *New York v. United States*, 505 U.S. 144, 166 (1992) (applying the same test and finding Congress's use of the Spending Clause to create incentives for states to deal with low-level radioactive wastes was appropriate).

82. *Heart of Atlanta Motel v. United States*, 379 U.S. 241 (1964), and *Katzenbach v. McClung*, 379 U.S. 294 (1964).

83. See *Seminole Tribe v. Florida*, 517 U.S. 44 (1996).

84. See generally Pamela S. Karlan, *The Irony of Immunity: The Eleventh Amendment, Irreparable Injury, and Section 1983*, 53 Stan. L. Rev. ___ (forthcoming 2001).

85. *United States v. Morrison*, 120 S.Ct. 1740 (2000); *United States v. Lopez*, 514 U.S. 549 (1995).

86. U.S. Const., amend. XIV, § 2.

87. 2 U.S.C. § 2a(a).

88. *United States Department of Commerce v. Montana*, 503 U.S. 442 (1992).

89. Id. at 464.

90. 2 U.S.C. § 2b.

91. Id. §§ 1,7.

92. 3 U.S.C. § 1.

93. 2 U.S.C. § 8.

94. 3 U.S.C. § 2.

95. U.S. Const., Art. II, § 1; see also 3 U.S.C. § 3.

96. Id.

97. *McPherson v. Blacker*, 146 U.S. 1 (1892). Congress can, of course, override state rules pursuant to its authority under the enforcement clauses of various constitutional amendments, particularly section 5 of the Fourteenth Amendment.

98. 3 U.S.C. § 5.

99. Id.; see *Bush v. Palm Beach County Canvassing Bd.*, 121 S. Ct. 471, 474 (2000).

100. U.S. Const., Amend. XII.

101. Id.

102. Id.

103. 42 U.S.C. § 1971 et seq.

104. See, for example, *Oregon v. Mitchell*, 400 U.S. 112, 132-34 (1970).

105. 383 U.S. 301, 309 (1966).

106. *Morgan*, 384 U.S. 641.
107. *City of Boerne*, 521 U.S. 507 (1997). See also, for example, *Board of Trustees v. Garrett*, 121 S. Ct. 955, 967 (2001).
108. 42 U.S.C. § 1973c.
109. Id. § 1973.
110. See, for example, *Hunt v. Cromartie*, 121 S. Ct. 1452 (2001); *Miller v. Johnson*, 515 U.S. 900 (1995); *Shaw v. Reno*, 509 U.S. 630 (1993).
111. *Bolden*, 446 U.S. at 61.
112. See, for example, *Davis v. Bandemer*, 478 U.S. 109 (1986); *Whitcomb v. Chavis*, 403 U.S. 124 (1974); *White v. Regester*, 412 U.S. 755 (1973).
113. *Abrams v. Johnson*, 521 U.S. 74, 90-91 (1997); *Bolden*, 446 U.S. at 80.
114. *Thornburg v. Gingles*, 478 U.S. 30, 35 (1986).
115. § 1973b.
116. Id.
117. Id. See S. Rep. No. 97-417, 97th Cong., 2d Sess. (May 1982).
118. *Gingles*, 478 U.S. at 36-37 (1986) (quoting S. Rep. No.97-417, at 28-29 (1982)).
119. Id. at 37 (quoting S. Rep. No. 97-417, at 29 (1982)).
120. See, for example, *Miller v. Johnson*, 515 U.S. 900, 906-07 (1995); *Shaw*, at 635.
121. *Shaw v. Reno*, 509 U.S. 630 (1993).
122. *Hunt v. Cromartie*, 121 S.Ct. 1452 (2001).
123. See *Roberts v. Wamser*, 679 F. Supp. 1513 (E.D. Mo. 1987), rev'd on other grounds, 883 F.2d 617 (8th Cir. 1989); *United States v. Post*, 297 F. Supp. 46 (W.D. La. 1969).
124. See *Hernandez v. Woodard*, 714 F. Supp. 963 (N.D. Ill. 1989).
125. Compare *Wesley v. Collins*, 791 F.2d 1255 (6th Cir. 1986) (rejecting section 2 challenge to felon disenfranchisement law), with *Farrakhan v. Locke*, 987 F. Supp. 1304 (E.D. Wash. 1997) (denying motion to dismiss section 2 claim by disenfranchised felons), and *Baker v. Pataki*, 85 F.3d 919 (2d Cir. 1996) (*en banc* panel evenly divided on whether disenfranchised felons could assert VRA claim).
126. 42 U.S.C. § 1973b(b).
127. Id. § 1973b(a).
128. The list now comprises the states of Alabama, Alaska, Arizona, Georgia, Louisiana, Mississippi, South Carolina, Texas, and Virginia; some counties within California, Florida, New York, North Carolina, and South Dakota; and some townships within Michigan and New Hampshire. 51 C.F.R. App. (2000).
129. 42 U.S.C. § 1973c.
130. Id.
131. Id.
132. See text and tables available at www.usdoj.gov/crt/voting/sec_5/about.htm.

133. *Allen* v. *State Bd. of Elections*, 393 U.S. 544 (1969).
134. Id. at 555.
135. *Young* v. *Fordice*, 520 U.S. 273, 283 (1997); *Perkins* v. *Matthews*, 400 U.S. 379, 387-88 (1971).
136. *Allen*, 393 U.S. 544, 566-67.
137. *Beer* v. *United States*, 425 U.S. 130 (1976).
138. *Reno* v. *Bossier Parish Sch. Bd.*, 528 U.S. 320 (2000).
139. 42 U.S.C. §§ 1973(a), 1973b(f)(2).
140. Id. § 1973(b).
141. Id. § 1973b(f)(3).
142. Id. §§ 1973aa-1a, 1973b(f)(4).
143. The current jurisdictions covered under the minority language provisions are counties in Alaska, Arizona, California, Colorado, Connecticut, Florida, Hawaii, Idaho, Illinois, Iowa, Louisiana, Massachusetts, Michigan, Mississippi, Nevada, New Jersey, New Mexico, New York, North Carolina, North Dakota, Oklahoma, Oregon, Pennsylvania, Rhode Island, South Dakota, Texas, Utah, and Wisconsin. 55 C.F.R. App. (2000).
144. 42 U.S.C. § 1973b(f)(4).
145. 28 C.F.R. § 55.2(b) (2000).
146. Pub. L. 103-31, Sec. 2, 107, Stat. 77.
147. 285 U.S. 355 (1932).
148. Id. at 366.
149. *United States* v. *Classic*, 313 U.S. 299 (1941).
150. 42 U.S.C. § 1973gg-3(a)(1).
151. Id. § 1973gg-3(c).
152. Id. § 1973gg-5(a)(2)-(3).
153. Id. § 1973gg-5(a)(4)(B).
154. Id. § 1973gg-6(a)(4).
155. Id. § 1973gg-6(h).
156. Id. § 1973gg-6(c)-(d).
157. Id. § 1973gg-6(e). Although the title of this subsection limits the fail-safe voting requirements to those registrants who have failed to return the form the registrar has sent to confirm their addresses and the Senate and House reports suggest a similar limitation, the words below the title do not include this limitation, and the Federal Election Commission since 1994 has interpreted these provisions as applying to all registrants. Federal Election Commission, *Implementing the National Voter Registration Act of 1993: Requirements, Issues, Approaches, and Examples* 6-1,-2 (1994). No reported court cases address this ambiguity and states and localities appear to have followed the FEC's interpretation.
158. Id. §1973gg-9(a).
159. Id. §1973gg-9(b).
160. Id. §1973gg-9(c).

161. Id. §405(c)(2)(C)(i).
162. "Elections: Issues Affecting Military and Overseas Absentee Voters," Statement of David M. Walker, Comptroller General of the United States for the Subcommittee on Military Personnel, Committee on Armed Forces, House of Representatives, May 9, 2001, p.1.
163. 42 U.S.C. § 1973ff-3.
164. Id.
165. Id. § 1973ff-1(1).
166. Id. § 1973ff-6(5)(B)-(C).
167. Id. § 1973ff-1(2).
168. Id. § 1973ff-1(3).
169. Id. § 1973ff-2(e)-(f).
170. Id. § 1973ff-2(b)(2)-(3).
171. Id. § 1973ff-2(b)(1).
172. Id. § 1973ff-2(c)(1)-(2).
173. Id.
174. Id. § 1973ff-2(c)(3).
175. *Dipietrae* v. *City of Philadelphia*, 666 A.2d 1132 (1995), aff'd 673 A.2d 905, 543 Pa. 591 (1996).
176. 42 U.S.C. § 1973ee-4(a)(italics added).
177. Id. § 1973ee-6(1) (emphasis added).
178. Id. § 1973ee-4(a) and (c). Although 42 U.S.C. section 1983 normally allows suits for both damages and injunctive relief against government officials and local (but not state) governments that deprive a citizen of any right secured by either the Constitution or federal law, there is one important limitation to the availability of section 1983 in cases based on the violation of federal statutes (as opposed to deprivations of constitutional rights). Congress can foreclose a remedy under section 1983 "expressly, by forbidding recourse to § 1983 in the statute itself, or impliedly, by creating a comprehensive enforcement scheme that is incompatible with individual enforcement under § 1983." *Blessing* v. *Freestone*, 520 U.S. 329, 341 (1997). In *Middlesex County Sewerage Auth.* v. *National Sea Clammers Ass'n*, 453 U.S. 1, 13 (1981), for example, the Court held that the "unusually elaborate enforcement provisions" of two environmental statutes—which required prior notice to federal and state authorities and authorized only prospective relief—foreclosed damages suits under section 1983. Applying *Sea Clammers*, the Fourth Circuit held that the Americans with Disabilities Act likewise provided a comprehensive remedial scheme and thus did not permit use of section 1983. *Zombro* v. *Baltimore City Police Dep't*, 868 F.2d 1364 (4th Cir. 1989). It is not entirely clear whether the detailed exhaustion requirement and remedial scheme of the VAEH would also be held to preclude section 1983 actions, which permit damages and attorneys' fees.
179. 28 C.F.R. § 35.130.

180. 42 U.S.C. § 12134(a).

181. Id. § 12133 (providing remedies available under 29 U.S.C. § 794a [Rehabilitation Act], which include private actions for damages and attorneys fees).

182. 121 S.Ct. 955 (2001).

183. *New York v. County of Delaware*, 82 F. Supp.2d 12 (N.D.N.Y. 2000) (preliminary injunction); *New York v. County of Delaware*, 2000 U.S. Dist. Lexis 12595 (N.D.N.Y. Aug. 16, 2000).

184. *Lightbourn v. County of El Paso*, 904 F.Supp. 1429, 1433 (W.D.Tex. 1995), rev'd on other grounds, 118 F.3d 421 (5th Cir. 1997), and vacated 127 F.3d 33 (5th Cir. 1997).

185. *Lightbourn v. Garza*, 118 F.3d 421 (5th Cir. 1997).

186. Tex. Elec. Code § 122.0111; see also 1 Tex. Admin. Code § 81.57; Tex. Elec. Code § 43.034.

187. *Nelson v. Miller*, 170 F.3d 641 (6th Cir. 1999).

188. *Lightbourn v. County of El Paso*, 118 F.3d 421 (5th Cir. 1997).

189. 418 U.S. 24 (1974).

190. U.S. Const., Amend. XIV, Sec. 2 (emphasis added).

191. *Frequently Asked Questions about Election Day and Voting Procedures* at www.fec.gov/pages/faqvdayprocedures.htm (June 19, 2001).

192. See *Gingles*, 478 U.S. at 36-37 (1986) (quoting S. Rep. No. 97-417, at 28-29 (1982)).

193. *United States v. Gradwell*, 243 U.S. 476, 485 (1917).

194. Compare *Hendon v. North Carolina State Bd. of Elec.*, 710 F.2d 177, 181 (4th Cir. 1983) ("A state may employ diverse methods of voting, and the methods by which a voter casts his vote may vary throughout the state.") with *Bush v. Gore*, 121 S. Ct. 525, 530-31 (2000) (holding that lack of rules resulting in "unequal evaluation of ballots. . . . is not a process with sufficient guarantees of equal treatment"), and *NAACP v. Harris*, No.01-Civ-120-Gold (S.D. Fla.) (class-action complaint alleging Fourteenth Amendment equal protection and VRA section 2 claims arising from non-uniform election practices and machinery).

195. U.S. Const. Art. I, § 4, cl. 1.

196. See *Foster v. Love*, 522 U.S. 67, 69 (1997) ("[I]t is well settled that the Elections Clause grants Congress the power to override state regulations by establishing uniform rules for federal elections, binding on the States. The regulations made by Congress are paramount to those made by the State legislature; and if they conflict therewith, the latter, so far as the conflict extends, ceases to be operative.") (internal quotation marks and citations omitted).

197. *Cook v. Gralike*, 121 S. Ct. 1029, 1038 (2001) (describing the term "manner" as encompassing "matters like notices, registration, supervision of voting, protection of voters, prevention of fraud and corrupt practices, counting of votes, duties of inspectors and canvassers, and making and publication of election returns") (quoting *Smiley v. Holm*, 285 U.S. 355, 366 (1932)).

198. U.S. Const., Art. 1, § 8, cl. 1.
199. See, for example, *South Dakota* v. *Dole*, 483 U.S. 203 (1987).
200. See *Roberts*, 679 F. Supp. 1513 (holding that refusal to manually review cast ballots rejected by punch card tabulation equipment which resulted in rejection of large numbers of ballots cast by black voters violated section 2), rev'd on other grounds, 883 F.2d 617 (8th Cir. 1989); *United States* v. *Post*, 297 F. Supp. 46 (W.D. La. 1969) (holding that changing voting machine such that pulling lever for political party's candidates did not cast vote for one of that party's candidates, contrary to previous instructions, violated section 2).
201. 384 U.S. 214.

What Counts as a Vote?

MELISSA CLINE, THAD HALL,
KURT A. HOHENSTEIN, AARON LONGO,
MICHAEL A. MUGMON, DAVID F. OLSKY,
DANIEL R. ORTIZ, AND LEONARD M. SHAMBON

As the confusion last year in Florida revealed, states and localities employ a variety of sometimes inconsistent standards to determine what counts as a vote. Does a chad have to be completely detached; detached at all but one, two, or three corners; or merely dimpled? What if a voter circles the chad's position instead? What if a voter punches a chad for a particular candidate and also writes in that candidate's name in the separate write-in portion of the ballot? Punch card systems pose all these questions, and optiscan and paper ballots pose still more.

We have surveyed all fifty states and the District of Columbia to analyze the prevalence of various approaches to counting. Our research indicates that states now employ three different schemes. The most common is a general intent-of-the-voter standard. Well over half the states employ it in one form or another. The Colorado scheme is typical. Colorado Revised Statute § 1-7-309 states that "[v]otes . . . shall not be counted if . . . for any reason it is impossible to determine the elector's choice of candidate or vote concerning the ballot issue" and the Colorado Supreme Court has acted consistently: "a ballot cast by a qualified elector should be rejected only if the elector's intent cannot be ascertained with reasonable certainty."[1]

The next most common approach is an objective standard. Nearly 20 percent of states employ it with all or some of their voting technologies. The Hawaii scheme is illustrative. For both paper and optiscan ballots, it gives a detailed series of graphic examples of acceptable and unacceptable marks. A voter must (1) draw two lines that intersect somewhere within the choice-box on a paper ballot, (2) make any mark within the choice-dot on an optiscan ballot, and (3) punch a chad out completely in a punch card, to make a vote count.[2]

The least common approach is a hybrid standard. Only a few states employ it. The Texas scheme illustrates how it works. Its punch card provision reads as follows:

---

1. *Moran v. Carlstrom*, 775 P.2d 1176, 1180 (Colo. 1989).
2. See Haw. Admin. R. § 2-51-80; also at § 2-51-85.1, and at § 2-51-83(e).

(d) Subject to Subsection (e), in any manual count conducted under
this code, a vote on a ballot on which a voter indicates a vote by
punching a hole in the ballot may not be counted unless:
(1) at least two corners of the chad are detached;
(2) light is visible through the hole;
(3) an indentation on the chad from the stylus or other object is
present and indicates a clearly ascertainable intent of the
voter to vote; or
(4) the chad reflects by other means a clearly ascertainable intent
of the voter to vote.
(e) Subsection (d) does not supersede any clearly ascertainable intent
of the voter.[3]

We characterize this scheme as hybrid because it combines aspects of
both the intent-of-the-voter and objective approaches. Although the intent
of the voter clearly trumps in the end, Texas does try to constrain the discretion of the person counting punch card votes by giving some objective
guidelines.

Some cautions are in order. First, although for every state we have both
contacted elections officials and researched the code, administrative materials, and court cases, we cannot claim to have a solid idea of how the
counting process works in practice. In some cases, when we asked officials
in the Office of the Secretary of State how particular things were done, we
were told that no one had ever previously asked the question. Since it seems
improbable that the simple issues we raised had never occurred in practice,
we concluded that there is often some gap between the top election office
and the field. Election officials somewhere in the state were surely making
these decisions but largely on their own.

Second, the gap worked in other directions as well. Even when the top
elections officials knew how a particular issue should be handled, there was
often no guarantee that fieldworkers would know. In some states, fieldworkers do receive detailed instruction on how to count ballots, but we
have no reason to believe that that is the case everywhere. In some other
states, top elections officials told us that fieldworkers were given a copy of
the appropriate state statutes, but in our reading those same statutes gave
no real guidance at all.

Third, the relevant legal materials were often incomplete or unclear. The
law in a few states, for example, clearly indicates a particular approach but

---

3. Tex. Elec. Code Ann. § 127.130(d)-(e)(West Supp. 2001).

describes it purely in terms of a technology—for example, paper ballots—that we have reason to believe the state no longer employs widely, if at all. In a few other states, the legal sources are silent or contradictory on critical counting matters, and election officials were unable to furnish any authoritative guidance.

In short, our survey is best approached as a general guide to the prevalence of particular approaches rather than as an authoritative statement of how each state approaches ballot counting. In a few cases, in fact, we had so little confidence in our understanding of how the state counted votes that we declined to categorize counting procedures with respect to some or all technologies.

Table 1   State Approaches to Counting Ballots

| State | Standard | | |
	General intent	Objective	Hybrid
Alabama	■		
Alaska	■ (nonpaper ballots)	■ (paper ballots)	
Arizona	■		
Arkansas			
California		■	
Colorado	■		
Connecticut	■ (absentee ballots)	■ (paper ballots)	
Delaware	■		
District of Columbia	■		
Florida		■	
Georgia		■	
Hawaii		■	
Idaho	■		
Illinois	■		
Indiana			■
Iowa	■		
Kansas	■		
Kentucky	■		
Louisiana			■
Maine	■		
Maryland	■		
Massachusetts	■		
Michigan		■	
Minnesota	■		
Mississippi	■		
Missouri			■
Montana			■
Nebraska	■		
Nevada		■ (punch card and optiscan)	
New Hampshire	■		
New Jersey			■
New Mexico	■ (absentee ballots)		

(Continued)

Table 1   State Approaches to Counting Ballots (*Continued*)

| | Standard | | |
State	General intent	Objective	Hybrid
New York			■
North Carolina	■ (other)		■ (punch card)
North Dakota	■		
Ohio	■		
Oklahoma		■	
Oregon	■		
Pennsylvania	■		
Rhode Island	■		
South Carolina	■		
South Dakota	■		
Tennessee	■		
Texas	■ (other)		■ (punch card)
Utah	■		
Vermont	■		
Virginia	■		
Washington	■		
West Virginia	■		
Wisconsin	(other)		■ (paper ballots and write-ins)
Wyoming	■		

RECOUNTS AND CONTESTS

ROBERT F. BAUER AND JASON C. RYLANDER

We have set out some general observations, with specific examples, of the various approaches states have taken to the construction of recounts and contests. In any state, of course, the statutes may speak clearly to some issues and less so to others. Issues not covered by statute are addressed by rule, decided by the time-honored discretion of local officials, or entrusted to the courts.

Since time did not permit a comprehensive review of all the sources of authority for the conduct of recounts or contests, our focus has been the statutes. The state speaks first by statute. If the statute is incomplete or vague on material points, this presents serious problems for the efficiency of the process and undermines public confidence in the result—even if a court or elections official ultimately decides the issue. If nothing else, the presidential recount controversy makes that point.

A survey or summary necessarily overlooks or minimizes significant issues or even differences in state approaches. The Federal Election Commission's National Clearinghouse for Election Administration, in its 1990 summary of state recount and contest statutes, stated then that these laws were "enormously complex," varying by type of elections, criteria, and process. The discussion below isolates and summarizes basic issues of common concern that likely will be found in most state codes, including

- who may, and in what manner, initiate a recount or contest
- grounds for seeking either recounts or contests
- timelines established for actions by the parties or state, including for the resolution of the contest
- nature of the relief that may be requested—whether for partial counts, counting some ballots and not others, or allowing recounts in part but not all of the electoral jurisdictions (for example, some precincts but not all)
- provisions for bearing costs
- legal standards, if any, for deciding issues such as voter intent (to be covered in a separate chapter)
- rights of appeal
- remedies

Following a general overview on these points, the discussion turns to selected states with approaches sufficiently distinct, or illustrative of a certain approach, that their codes merit additional comment.

Review of Election Results

Election results are commonly subject to two different types of review: recounts and contests. Although their character can vary from state to state, recounts are typically administrative proceedings (often subject to judicial review) in which the votes are recounted—either mechanically or by hand—to determine whom they were cast for. Contests, on the other hand, are more exceptional judicial proceedings in which votes can be excluded as improper. A recount is only one possible remedy in a contest. Recounts precede contests when both are available.

Application to Federal Elections

Many states clearly include federal elections within the class of elections subject to recounts or contests. Others are less clear, and some provide for contests and not recounts, or vice versa. Some of this ambiguity about the availability of contests may reflect the awareness of states that the House and Senate are empowered under the Constitution to judge the returns of their members, and perhaps the belief that any "contest" properly lies with those bodies.

Initiation of Recounts and Contests

States provide for a range of procedures for initiating a recount or contest. By and large, the largest numbers of states initiate recounts on petition or request of the candidate. A number of others provide for "automatic" or mandatory recounts in the event of a "tie," where the margin is close (typically 0.5 percent or less), for all elections or for federal elections in particular.

In some states, voters may initiate a recount. In certain of these states, including states the size of California and Florida, a single voter may request a recount, whereas in others a larger number is required to initiate the action.

Provisions conferring on political parties the authority to seek recounts are rare and may also be limited in scope. For example, in Indiana, a party may seek the recount but only if a candidates does not.

With regard to contests, once again the largest number of states confers on candidates the right to seek a contest. Voters may also initiate contests, and in a handful of states, a political party. In one state, Oregon, a county clerk may also do so.

Time for Requesting Initiation

The time frames for initiating an action vary widely across the states and run either from the day of the election, the day the canvass is completed, or the day the result is officially certified. The canvass, which can vary from state to state, is a postelection process that usually begins with the initial counting of ballots and ends with the official report of the election results by the appropriate elections official. A review of tables 2 and 3 tells the tale.

Table 2 Time Frames for Recounts

When recounts are required	States
On election night	Oklahoma
Within 2 days of canvass	Michigan, West Virginia, Wyoming
Within 3 days of election	New Hampshire
Within 3 days of canvass	Alaska (for gov./lt. gov.), Maryland, Nevada, New Hampshire, North Dakota, Oklahoma, Washington, Wisconsin (within third day following the last meeting of the board of canvassers)
Within 5 days of official canvass/certification	Alaska (except gov./lt. gov.), California (a second voter may request a new recount within 24 hours of the completion of an initial recount), Florida, Georgia, Maine, Montana, Ohio, Pennsylvania, Texas (5 days after election or 2 days after canvass)
Within 6 days of canvass	New Mexico
Within 7 days after election	Indiana (by candidates—7; by party chairmen—10), Missouri, Rhode Island
Within 7 days of canvass	Utah
Within 10 days of election	Massachusetts, South Dakota, Vermont
Within 10 days of certification	Virginia
On or before 2nd Saturday following election	New Jersey
Within 15 days of election	Connecticut (within 14 days if initiated by state)
Within 20 days of canvass	Idaho
Within 5 days after the 29th day following state election	California
Within 35 days of election	Oregon (supplemental demand permitted until 50th day)

Table 3 Time Frames for Contests

When elections may be contested	*States*
Within 5 days after canvass	Georgia, Kansas, South Carolina
Within 7 days after canvass	Minnesota
Within 9 days after election	Louisiana
Within 10 days of state review or certification	Alaska, Delaware (for presidential electors), Florida (or within 5 days of certification following a protest), Iowa, Tennessee, Washington
Within 13 days of election	Texas
Within 5 days of recount, 14 days of election	Nevada, North Dakota
Within 15 days of election	Kentucky, Wyoming, Ohio, and Vermont (or within 10 days of recount)
Within 20 days of election	Hawaii, Mississippi (local offices), Pennsylvania
Within 15 days of official proclamation	Illinois
Within 20 days of certification	Arkansas (except within 15 days for election to state House of Representatives), Delaware (and within 60 days before first day of court term)
Within 30 days of election	Massachusetts, Mississippi (state offices), New Jersey, Virginia
Within 30 days of certification	Missouri, New Mexico
Within 40 days of election	Nebraska, Oregon, Utah

Note: Table focuses on general elections, with the caveat that time frames for primary contests could be shorter.

Scope of Relief (Partial versus Complete Recount of Ballots)

It is generally the case that where a state statute speaks to the question at all, candidates are expressly entitled to select for recount some but not all of the geographic voting units within a jurisdiction. California, Georgia, Idaho, Indiana, and Massachusetts are just a few of the states that permit the candidate or initiator to designate individual precincts or counties for recount.

Many statutes are silent, though practice in this area suggests that candidates are encouraged to ask for the most limited geographic recount compatible with the grievance they have experienced or the relief they hope to obtain. Mandatory recounts, triggered by a close election, generally extend to all ballots for the election subject to recount.

Contest provisions are also not particularly detailed on the point, but it is fair to say that candidates or others initiating a contest would be looking to identify particular problems—specific "irregularities," as many statutes refer to them—and it would be common that the relief sought would be tailored to those problems. So by its nature, a contest is selective.

The grounds for seeking a recount in various state codes may be classified as shown in table 4. The grounds for contests are as shown in table 5.

Financial Liability for Recounts and Contests

The question of who pays for recounts also varies widely by state and by type of recount (see table 6). Typically, when states have mandatory recount provisions, the state or locality will pick up the tab. States in which candidates or individuals may request a recount may charge nominal filing fees, demand payment of the entire cost of the recount, or request posting of a bond for the possibility that the outcome does not change. Costs may also vary depending on the extent of the recount and the margin of votes cast.

Most contest statutes contemplate filing with a state court, and fees are typically handled by the courts in a manner consistent with allocation of costs and legal fees in civil procedure. Some states, however, do require payment of a bond by the initiator to cover contests in the event the outcome does not change.

Rights of Appeal

The process for appealing recount and contest decisions also varies widely (see table 7). Generally, if a state lacks a separate contest procedure, a peti-

Table 4 State Grounds for Recount

Reason for recount	*States*
Belief of mistake or error	Alaska, California, Georgia, Indiana, Massachusetts, Michigan, New Jersey, New Mexico, North Carolina, Oklahoma, Pennsylvania, South Dakota, Texas, Wyoming
Misconduct or fraud affecting outcome	California, Idaho, Michigan, Oklahoma, Pennsylvania, Wyoming
Mechanical failure	Indian, Oklahoma, Texas
Close election	Alaska, Arizona, Colorado, Georgia, Missouri, North Carolina, North Dakota, Ohio, South Dakota, Texas, Utah, Vermont, Virginia, Wyoming

Table 5 State Grounds for Contests

Reasons for contest	States
Misconduct, fraud, or corruption on part of election official	Alaska, Arkansas, Arizona, California, Colorado, Connecticut, Delaware, Florida, Georgia, Hawaii, Illinois, Iowa, Kansas, Louisiana, Minnesota, Nebraska, Nevada, New Jersey, Oklahoma, Oregon, Texas, Utah, Vermont, Virginia, Washington, Wyoming
Ineligibility of candidate	Alaska, Arkansas, Arizona, California, Colorado, Delaware, Florida, Georgia, Iowa, Kansas, Minnesota, Nebraska, Nevada, New Jersey, North Dakota, Oregon, Utah, Virginia, Washington, Wyoming
Erroneous count sufficient to change the result of election	Arizona, California, Colorado, Connecticut, Georgia, Hawaii, Illinois, Iowa, Kansas, Kentucky, Louisiana, Minnesota, Nebraska, Nevada, New Jersey, North Carolina, North Dakota, Oregon, Texas, Utah, Vermont, Virginia, Washington, Wyoming
Illegal votes	Alabama, Arizona, Arkansas, California, Colorado, Connecticut, Delaware, Florida, Georgia, Illinois, Iowa, Kansas, Minnesota, Nebraska, Nevada, New Jersey, North Carolina, North Dakota, Oregon, Texas, Utah, Washington, Wyoming
Rejection of legal votes	Alabama, Colorado, Iowa, Kansas, Minnesota, Nebraska, New Jersey, North Dakota, Oregon, Utah, Wyoming
Bribery, intimidation, or malconduct designed to prevent a fair election	Alaska, Arkansas, Arizona, California, Delaware, Florida, Iowa, Kansas, Kentucky, Louisiana, Minnesota, Nebraska, Nevada, New Jersey, Oregon, Texas, Utah, Washington, Wyoming
Candidate's prior felony conviction	Iowa, Nebraska, New Jersey, Washington
For any other reason casting outcome in doubt	Colorado, Florida, Georgia, Hawaii, Iowa, Kansas, Louisiana, Minnesota, Missouri, Nebraska, Nevada, New Jersey, Vermont, Virginia

tioner can appeal the final recount determination to state court. In the interest of expedition, recount decisions generally cannot be appealed when a separate contest proceeding exists. Contests conducted in court are generally appealable to the next highest court.

Variations: Specific States

We offer a series of comments on specific states, less to establish a typology of approaches than to illustrate more concretely the differences among them. We do not believe that a model can be found in any one state, in the

Table 6 Establishing Who Pays

Entity paying	*States*
Recounts	
Paid by state/locality	Alaska, Arizona, Colorado, Idaho, and Virginia (if close); Massachusetts, Missouri, Montana, Nebraska, North Dakota, Ohio, and Washington (if automatic); North Carolina and Oregon (if requested by government); Rhode Island, South Dakota, Utah, Vermont
Paid by campaign/candidate	Arkansas, Nevada, Idaho ($100/precinct); Maine and New Hampshire (fee varies by margin); Nebraska (if not automatic); New Mexico ($50/precinct); Virginia (if margin > 0.5% and no change in result); Wisconsin (no fee if close; $5/precinct); Wyoming (max. $500 if no change)
Paid by initiator (if not candidate)	Alaska (deposit req. unless close); California (costs daily); Colorado (total estimate); Indiana ($100 minimum); Michigan ($10/precinct); Montana and New Jersey (costs vary); Ohio (max $10/precinct if not automatic); Oklahoma (costs vary); Oregon ($15/precinct); Texas (costs vary)
Bond or deposit required	Maryland and Montana (if margin > 0.25%); New Mexico (in lieu of advance); North Dakota (if not automatic); Pennsylvania (deposit or bond); Washington (deposit of $.05/ballot)
Contests	
Paid by initiator	California (daily advance); Colorado (postjudgment liability); Georgia (contestant and defendant postjudgment liability); Illinois ($15,000 fee–potential liability up to $75,000); Tennessee and Wyoming (if result is confirmed)
Bond required from initiator in event outcome does not change	Arizona, Connecticut, Delaware, Iowa, Kansas, Minnesota, Missouri, Nebraska, Ohio, Oklahoma, Pennsylvania, Utah

sense of an ideal type, but a model might be constructed from the different parts of several states' codes to reflect the best practices currently in place.

One additional note of caution, rooted in the experience of practitioners. Recount and contest statutes, particularly the former, typically work as well as the good faith and competence with which they are administered—and no more. Washington State, for example, was widely lauded last year for a United States Senate recount conducted for the most part free of complaints about fairness or impartiality. The Washington Code discussed below is constructed adequately in most respects. But more important to the successful outcome was (1) an administrative structure and staff that

Table 7 Appeals of Recounts and Contests

Appeals	States
Recounts	
To courts	Alaska, Colorado (for local elections/ballot measures), Idaho (within 24 hours of recount), Maine (if disputed ballots sufficient to affect result, secretary of state shall forward ballots to Supreme Judicial Court for determination), Maryland, New Mexico, South Dakota, Wisconsin
To legislature	Alaska
To secretary of state	Colorado (for state elections)
Citizen-suit enforcement of election procedures	Maryland (court may declare election void or order other relief)
Contests	
Higher courts	Arkansas, California, Connecticut, Georgia, Illinois, Kansas, Louisiana, Minnesota, New Jersey, New Mexico, North Carolina, North Dakota, Ohio, Oregon, Pennsylvania, Tennessee, Texas, Utah, Washington, Missouri, Nebraska (except from legislative hearing)

commanded respect and (2) an expectation within the state that the candidates and parties would not, without reason, fail to exhibit that same respect in their own legal and public responses to the recount.

Alaska

Alaska allows for recounts initiated by candidates or by ten voters, and it mandates recounts where the margin of victory is 0.5 percent or twenty votes or less. One of its unusual features is a provision allowing formal participation by "organized groups," as well as by candidates and political parties. Also of interest is the provision that requires the state to pay for the recount not only when the result changes (which is typical), but also if the applicant's vote increases by 4 percent or more, even if the outcome does not change. Timelines for the conduct of the recount are tight: the recount must be completed within ten days, and an appeal to the courts, if any, must occur within five days thereafter. A court hearing an appeal must review all of the ballots in the election, not only a disputed subset.

California

Detailed provisions for the conduct of recounts in California include some of interest, particularly as they affect the right of voters seeking recounts to specify how they should be conducted. Any voter may ask for a recount, and the statute is clear that this right applies to federal offices and to the election of slates of presidential electors. For statewide elections, the secretary of state may also ask for a recount but only within five days of the twenty-ninth day after the election.

For a statewide race, the initiator may seek a recount of all counties and may specify the order in which they will be counted. Where punch cards or computer systems are used, the initiator may specify either a manual or machine recount and may also request a recount of all ballots "whether voted or not." Ballots may be challenged for "incompleteness, ambiguity or other defects."

Florida

Attention has been paid to the recently enacted reforms in Florida, which include new requirements for the approval of electronic or electromechanical machines. The state also amended its recount procedures, providing that counties must direct machine recounts where the margin of victory is 0.5 percent or less and requiring that they be completed by the second day after the election. If the machine recount shows a difference of 0.25 percent or less, then a manual recount of undervotes and overvotes is required "in the entire geographic jurisdiction of such office. . . ." Where the difference lies between 0.25 percent and 0.5 percent, the candidate is "entitled" to a manual recount if timely requested (by 5:00 p.m. of the second day after the election).

Florida also made changes to its counting rules, requiring that a vote be counted where there is a "clear indication . . . that the voter has made a definite choice." The Department of State is charged with implementing this mandate with further rules, but it is enjoined from resorting to vague formulations, such as "catch-all provisions" that state, tautologically, that a vote is "any other mark or indication clearly indicating that the voter has made a definite choice." The department may also not promulgate a rule relying exclusively on the question of whether the voter "properly" marked the ballot.

Florida also made changes to its contest provisions, deleting certain open-ended language on the grounds for contests and the authority of the courts in disposing of them. The law had previously allowed for contestants to allege "[a]ny other cause or allegation" that the certified outcome was wrong, and this language was deleted in the recently enacted reform. Also courts considering a contest could "fashion such orders" as necessary to investigate each allegation, to "prevent or correct any alleged wrong," or to "provide any relief appropriate."

Michigan

Michigan offers considerable detail in the construction of its recount provisions. Of some interest are provisions intended to provide for "speedy and efficient means for the preservation of evidence of the intention of voters" in United States Senate and House elections. Recounts are automatic in statewide elections when the margin of victory is 2,000 votes or less. In all other instances, a recount may be ordered on the petition of a candidate, but only upon pleading fraud or mistake within forty-eight hours of an election. In addition to detailed pleading requirements, the code provides clear timetables for notices to candidates and for hearings. The State Board of Canvassers, the administrative body that manages recounts, has broad investigative powers, including subpoena power, "in all matters relating" to the recount as well as the power to make rules and regulations. The statute reflects an overall policy favoring uniformity, as well as fairness and impartiality, in the recount process.

New Hampshire

New Hampshire offers an example of an anomaly on one important issue. Its contest provisions do not appear to apply to federal elections. As noted, this may be a function of state deference to the constitutional process under which a "contest" may be brought directly to the U.S. House or Senate. In any event, the state provides at the same time for a specific process for the "resolution of ties" for U.S. Senate and House races.

Washington State

Washington State provides clearly in its recount process for federal candidates, who may file for recounts with the secretary of state. The state has structured a two-tiered "mandatory" process. One applies where the margin of victory is less than 0.5 percent. The other, when the margin is still less—under 0.25 percent and fewer than 150 votes—calls for a full manual recount. Candidates, however, may agree on alternatives to the manual process, if it is appropriate to the balloting system used and also involves the use of a vote tallying system. The code also contains a provision allowing for no more than two recounts of the vote in any county, reflecting a statutory policy favoring "closure to the recount process."

Contests in Washington are available upon petition by registered voters who must plead by affidavit "particular causes." Grounds include official misconduct, bribes paid to voters or election officials, and illegal votes, and the asserted irregularity must be material. An illegal vote does not include a vote by an "improperly registered" voter who was not challenged in the first instance as authorized by law.

Concluding Comments

This survey is intended to provide only an overview of variations in state codes, with attention to basic issues and some of the more significant differences in approach. Many codes are remarkably similar in a number of respects—for example, the circumstances in which a mandatory recount is provided (where the margin is 0.5 percent or less) or the grounds for a contest. The differences reside in factors such as

- detail or comprehensiveness on process, pleading requirements, and the like
- clarity and internal consistency
- reasonableness of time frames, balancing the need for "closure" against the imperatives of accuracy and fairness
- discretion afforded election officials and reviewing courts, and related coherence of the case law construing that discretion.

It is also true that to understand the state legal structures for recounts and contests in their entirety, attention must also be paid to administrative rules and judicial decisions, which this analysis has not focused on. One important and related question facing a legislature in considering its code is a basic one of responsibility—how much may the code reasonably prescribe and where does the discretion of the courts and election administrators lie? This is a fundamental question with broad implications for democratic practice and for public acceptance of the outcome.

CONGRESSIONAL AUTHORITY TO REGULATE WHEN VOTES CAN BE COUNTED

Memorandum

To: National Commission on Federal Election Reform
From: Daniel Ortiz, Coordinator, Task Force on Legal and Constitutional Issues
Re: Congressional Authority to Regulate When Presidential Votes Can Be Counted
Date: June 28, 2001

Can Congress prevent the states from counting presidential votes before a certain time?

Yes, Congress can regulate the time when the states can count presidential votes. Although Congress very likely has the power to regulate the time of counting presidential votes directly, it certainly can regulate the timing indirectly through its power to regulate the time of counting congressional ballots and its power to attach conditions to any federal election spending.

Until last year, it was clear that Congress had very broad power to regulate presidential elections directly. In *Burroughs* v. *United States*, for example, the Supreme Court rejected the view that Article I, section 2's explicit grant of power to Congress to "determine the Time of chusing the Elector[s] and the Day on which they shall give their Votes" excluded other powers not mentioned. 290 U.S. 534, 544 (1934) ("So narrow a view of the powers of Congress in respect of the matter is without warrant."). In particular, the Supreme Court held, Congress could regulate the process of selecting presidential electors in order to prevent violence, fraud, and corruption:

> While presidential electors are not officers or agents of the federal government . . . , they exercise federal functions under, and discharge duties in virtue of authority conferred by, the Constitution of the United States. The President is vested with the executive power of the nation. The importance of his election and the vital character of its relationship to and effect upon the welfare and safety of the whole people cannot be too strongly stated. To say that Congress is without power to pass appropriate legislation to safeguard such an election from the improper use of money to influence the result is to deny to the nation in a vital particular the power of self pro-

tection. Congress, undoubtedly, possesses that power, as it possesses every other power essential to preserve the departments and institutions of the general government from impairment or destruction, whether threatened by force or by corruption.

Id. at 545; *accord Ex parte Yarbrough*, 110 U.S. 651, 657-58 (1884) ("That a government whose essential character is republican, whose executive head and legislative body are both elective . . . has no power by appropriate laws to secure this election from the influence of violence, of corruption, and of fraud, is a proposition so startling as to arrest attention and demand the gravest consideration."). Thus, it was settled law that Congress could legislate somewhat beyond setting the time of choosing electors and the day on which the Electoral College would vote. Under this broad view, Congress would almost certainly have the power to prevent the states from counting presidential votes before a certain time, particularly if its aim was to protect the integrity of the electoral process in western states.

Last year, however, in *Bush* v. *Palm Beach County Canvassing Board*, 121 S.Ct. 471 (2000) (per curiam) (*Bush I*), and *Bush* v. *Gore*, 121 S.Ct. 525 (2000) (per curiam) (*Bush II*), the Court suggested that Congress's power might not be so broad. In *Bush I*, the Florida Supreme Court had ordered Florida's Secretary of State to accept the results of recounts that she believed too late under Florida law. In reaching its conclusion that the Florida statutes required the Secretary to accept these recount results, the Florida Supreme Court "relied in part upon the right to vote set forth in the Declaration of Rights of the Florida Constitution. . . ." *Bush I*, 121 S.Ct. at 473. The United States Supreme Court found this reliance extremely troubling. Believing that Article II, section 1 might not allow the state constitution to circumscribe the legislative power in this way, it unanimously remanded the case back to the Florida Supreme Court for a clarification of the basis of its decision. It avoided deciding this issue until it was sure the Florida Supreme Court's ruling presented it.

When the case returned as *Bush II*, seven individual justices decided the issue. Four justices explicitly decided that a state constitution *could* limit a state legislature's power to select presidential electors, 121 S.Ct. at 539 (Stevens, J., dissenting) (Ginsburg and Breyer, JJ., joining) ("[Article II, section 1] does not create state legislatures out of whole cloth, but rather takes them as they come—as creatures born of, and constrained by, their state constitutions."); id. at 549 (Ginsburg, J., dissenting) (Stevens, Souter, and Breyer, JJ., joining) ("a State may organize itself as it sees fit"); id. at

552 (Breyer, J., dissenting) (Stevens, Ginsburg, and Souter, JJ., joining) ("[N]either the text of Article II itself nor the only case . . . that interprets Article II . . . leads to the conclusion that Article II grants unlimited power to the legislature, devoid of any state constitutional limitations, to select the manner of appointing electors."); three justices explicitly indicated a state constitution *could not* limit this power, id. at 534 (Rehnquist, C.J., concurring) (Scalia and Thomas, JJ., joining) ("Art. II, § 1, cl. 2 . . . conveys the broadest powers of determination and leaves it to the legislature exclusively to define the method of appointment.") (internal quotation marks and citations omitted); while two justices were silent on the issue. In short, the litigation over the presidential election created doubt where none existed before. The extent to which a state legislature's power over the selection of presidential electors can be controlled is now somewhat unsettled. Although *Bush I* and *Bush II* specifically raised the issue only of whether a state constitution could circumscribe this power, their outcome raises even more doubt about Congress's authority to circumscribe it. If, as at least three justices believe, a state constitution—the law that defines the state's fundamental political organization—cannot circumscribe a state legislature's power to appoint electors, then *a fortiori* the United States Congress should not be able to.

Even under this narrow view, however, Article II, section 1 likely gives Congress the power to set the time when presidential votes should be counted. The section expressly grants Congress two powers: the power to determine (i) the time of "choosing" electors and (ii) the day the electors should cast their votes. Although there is no judicial precedent even remotely on point and no helpful legislative history, the commonsense ("plain") meaning of "choosing" strongly argues in favor of Congress having this power. In ordinary speech, we clearly use "choosing" to refer to the casting of votes but we just as clearly use it sometimes to include their counting as well. In fact, we often go further to use the term to include not only the casting and counting of ballots, but also the announcement of the results. We do not, for example, say that the Academy of Motion Picture Arts and Sciences has chosen its Academy Award winners when just the voting is complete or even when the accountants have counted the ballots, but only later when the results are publicly announced. In politics, moreover, the winners are not chosen until any post-election contests are over. Thus, any prior phase of the election that bears on the ultimate choice should be considered part of the "choosing" as well. For these reasons, Congress's express power to determine the time of choosing of electors should encompass setting the time when presidential ballots can be counted.

Even if Congress cannot directly regulate the timing of counting presidential ballots, however, it can certainly regulate their counting indirectly by regulating the time of counting congressional ballots in the same election. Under the Elections Clause, Congress has plenary power to regulate the "times, places, and manner" of congressional elections. In its most recent decision discussing this clause, the Supreme Court stated that "in our commonsense view [the] term ['Manner of holding Elections'] encompasses matters like 'notices, registration, supervision of voting, protection of voters, prevention of fraud and corrupt practices, counting of votes, duties of inspectors and canvassers, and making and publication of election returns.'" *Cook v. Gralike*, 121 S. Ct. 1029, 1038 (2001)(quoting *Smiley v. Holm*, 285 U.S. 355, 366 (1932)). The term certainly sweeps broadly enough to encompass the time of counting of votes for a congressional election. And since presidential elections are held at the same time as congressional elections, barring the states from counting or handling congressional ballots or machinery until a certain time would effectively stop them from counting presidential ballots as well—at least with respect to most existing voting technologies.

Congress could also condition the receipt of any federal funds related to elections upon state agreement not to count presidential votes until a certain time. In *South Dakota v. Dole*, the Supreme Court identified three key limitations on the scope of the spending power: (i) the exercise of the spending power must be in pursuit of "the general welfare"; (ii) the congressional regulation must be unambiguous so that states understand the choice they are making in agreeing to receive the funds; and (iii) the conditions on the federal funds must be related to the purposes of the federal spending. 483 U.S. 203, 207 (1987). A congressional grant of funds for the states to improve their voting technologies, poll worker training, or voter education would certainly be in pursuit of the general welfare. And Congress could easily make unambiguous the condition that presidential votes not be counted before a certain time. That would be a simple matter of legislative drafting. Such a condition would also be related to the purposes of the federal spending. Both aim to improve the election process. In sum, the spending power certainly allows Congress to lay down this condition for the states to receive federal election funds.

Nothing, of course, requires the states to accept the federal bargain. They can, if they want, simply walk away from the offer. And, for those that do, Congress's condition has no bite. They can continue to count presidential votes whenever they want. The effectiveness of the spending power, then, depends not so much on Congress's constitutional authority as on the attractiveness of the overall bargain it proposes.

Although Congress clearly has the power to set the time of counting presidential votes—either directly or indirectly—one small issue remains. Would Congress's exercise of this authority in order to prevent media from forecasting results in some states before polls had closed in others violate the First Amendment? The answer is no. Although the First Amendment grants great protection to the press once it has acquired information, it gives the press little right against the government to provide it with information it does not make available generally. *Pell* v. *Pecunier*, 417 U.S. 817 (1974); *Saxbe* v. *Washington Post Co.*, 417 U.S. 843 (1974). In particular, no case has ever held that the First Amendment requires the government to structure activities other than trials in such a way as to generate information for the press. Without such a right, there is no First Amendment claim here.

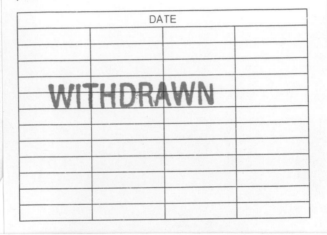